SEEKING GOD IN STORY

Seeking God in Story

John Navone, S.J.

THE LITURGICAL PRESS
Collegeville, Minnesota

Cover design by Donald A. Molloy

Cover art: *Christ the Pantocrator.* Greek ikon by Elias Moskos, 1653. Ikonenmuseum, Recklinghausen.

Seeking God in Story is a revised and expanded edition of the author's *The Jesus Story: Our Life as Story in Christ* published in 1979 by The Liturgical Press.

Acknowledgements. The author's previously published work is included here with the permission of the copyright owners: *Commonweal* (June 16, 1978) 358-62. Selections from chapters 1, 2, 3, and 4 from *Towards a Theology of Story* (Slough, England: St. Paul Publications, 1977). *Scottish Journal of Theology* 29 (July-August 1976) 4, 311-33. *Irish Theological Quarterly* XLIII (July 1976) 3, 171-85; LII (1986) 3, 212-30. *New Blackfriars* 55 (November 1974) 654, 511-16. *Sciences Religieuse / Studies in Religion* 5/2 (Autumn-Fall 1975-76) 152-76. *Theology* LXXX (September 1977) 677, 348-53. *Cross and Crown* (December 1977) 29, 346-49. *Doctrine and Life* 25 (December 1975) 12, 859-68; 30 (1980) 346-52. *Spiritual Life* 22 (Summer 1976) 2, 115-24. *Review for Religious* 34 (January 1975) 1, 132-39; 38 (1979) 668-73; 39 (1980) 558-67; 40 (1981) 436-50; 41 (1982) 5, 738-43; 42 (1983) 11, 192-96; *The Furrow* 11, 698-708.

Library of Congress Cataloging-in-Publication Data

Navone, John J.
    Seeking God in story / by John Navone.
        p.   cm.
    Rev. and expanded ed. of: Jesus story. 1979.
    Includes bibliographical references.
    ISBN 0-8146-1919-3
    1. Storytelling—Religious aspects—Christianity. 2. Jesus
Christ—Person and offices. I. Navone, John J. Jesus story.
II. Title.
BT83.78.N38   1979
230—dc20   90-48697
                                                                      CIP

CONTENTS

PREFACE

In his commentary on the Metaphysics of Aristotle, St. Thomas Aquinas remarked that the philosopher as much as the poet must be *philomythes,* a lover of stories.[1] This is because philosophy, like poetry, has its origins in a natural wonder about ourselves and the world in which we live. Aquinas points out that the first people to explore the basic truths of our existence did so by means of stories, and they may be called "theologizing poets." Academic theology that strays too far from its roots in poetry and story-telling becomes desiccated, rootless, and, ultimately, sterile. If academic theologians ought to be good story-tellers, the same is even more true of catechists and all who seek, like Paul, to hand on what they themselves have received. Bernard Lonergan wrote of the pure, disinterested desire to know, the spirit of inquiry that characterizes the very young, who tire adults with their ceaseless questioning. The answers to such questioning are nearly always cast in the form of stories. Young children have an insatiable desire for stories, as anyone who has presided over a child's bedtime knows.

The need to listen to stories is not confined to the very young. The liturgy, the official worship of the Church, is by and large a matter of telling and listening to stories. The Gospel readings tell us not only stories about Jesus but also the stories that Jesus himself told. The Hebrew Scriptures, the Old Testament, is largely made up of the stories which were told to Jesus in his childhood and which he later drew upon when fashioning new stories of his own. The Eucharist tells us over and over again, in word and gesture and action, the story of the last day of Jesus' life, a day that started with a supper and ended with his death upon the cross. The yearly cycle of fasts and feasts tells over and over again the story—myth—of the creation of the world

[1]*In XII Metaphys. Aristot.* I, 3, 55.

xii SEEKING GOD IN STORY

and its redemption by the very Son of God. The worshiper, as much as the theologian and the child, must be *philomythes,* a lover of myths and stories.

At the start of his manual for novices in theology, St. Thomas remarks that the theologian does not employ metaphor, imagery, and symbol for its own sake, for fun, as we might say, but "out of necessity and because it is useful."[2] Metaphor, imagery, and symbolism are the very stuff of story-making. For many years, Father Navone has been investigating the role of story-telling in Scripture, in theology, and in the formation of spiritually mature Christians. His life's work has not been done for its own sake, out of fun, but, as Aquinas would say, *propter necessitatem et utilitatem.* He has been constructing a Method in Theology, conducting an investigation into who we do theology and what would be the conditions of this fruitfulness. In *Tellers of the Word,* he and I tried to set out in a systematic way some of the riches of this approach to understanding and communicating the faith we have received from the apostles.

This present volume takes up the same theme. It is Father Navone's special task and talent to be able to help us think about our theology and storytelling.

Thomas Cooper
Towcester, England
20 May 1990

---

[2]*Summa Theologiae,* Ia, 1, 9.

INTRODUCTION

The use of story, and especially autobiography, as a tool and as subject matter in the teaching of religion has swept the United States. An account of this use appeared in *Horizons* 1, No. 1, and covered much of what needs to be said about the methodology of such courses. The approach seems to be a natural outgrowth and structuring of the interest in religious experience, with an emphasis on the whole of life, the actions people perform, the values and self-understanding that they bring to or find in their everyday lives. Religion is understood here as a wide functional term of delineating the behavior shaped by one's most serious values or philosophy of life. The religious drive is a master sentiment, giving comprehensive ultimate shape to all our experiencing, whereas the poetic drive would be a further concrete specification of this same basic dynamism. The biblical stories of God, for example, are literary and poetic accounts of the stories that particular lives told.

Michael Novak's *Ascent of the Mountain, Flight of the Dove* was among the first extended treatments of the presuppositions underlying the use of autobiography for the study of religion. John S. Dunne has also pioneered the methodology of using autobiography for the examination of religious questions in his book *A Search for God in Time and Memory*. James McClendon's essay, "Biography as Theology" in *Cross Currents* 21, offers a paradigm of this method, in which he examines the images and metaphors that express the self-understanding of persons whose identity is from the beginning aligned with religion. Stanley Hauerwas' article "Story and Theology" in *Religion and Life* 45 explains the indispensability of story for our understanding of God and the self. John F. Haught, in his book *Religion and Self-Acceptance,* affirms that our world is still able to be reached as our world only through some story. Primal narrative consciousness has not been abrogated by theory: "Story-telling, through which men express their feelings and concerns and in which they symbolize what they consider to be ultimately fulfilling and the ways in which to achieve 'salvation,' is as ineradicable and prototypical a gesture as are playing and laughing."

My interest in the theology of story began with my doctoral dissertation, which treated of the principles that historians employ for the interpretation of historical experience: *History and Faith in the Thought of Dr. Alan Richardson* (London: SCM Press, 1966). My second book, *Personal Witness: A Biblical Spirituality* (New York: Sheed and Ward, 1967), extended this interest to biblical interpretations of personal and historical experience. *Themes of St. Luke* (Rome: Gregorian University Press, 1970), my third book, studied the thematization of such experience in the context of one Gospel.

My fourth book, *Everyman's Odyssey: Seven Plays Seen as Modern Myths About Man's Quest for Personal Integrity* (Rome: Gregorian University Press for Seattle University, 1974), recognizes the implicitly religious character of every life story, affirming that in the innermost depth of every person there is alive a fundamentally religious sense with its standards of true and false, good and evil; that every person is pre-programmed to a sense of wonder and awe before the mystery of his existence and meaning within the universe. Every life story inevitably bears witness to that reality which underlies human awareness and, nevertheless, transcends human definition. A life story is not only religious, but also dramatic; for action is the response of every life story to the Mystery that encompasses it.

A Theology of Failure (New York: Paulist Press, 1974), my fifth book, focused on the tragic dimension of every life story in its inevitable confrontation with suffering, pain, and death.

Communicating Christ (Slough, U.K.: St. Paul Publications, 1976), my sixth book, attempts to explain what makes a life story Christian. This collection of seventeen previously published articles contained much that should have appeared in my seventh book, *Towards a Theology of Story* (St. Paul Publications, 1977).

This present work rectifies this situation by incorporating certain key articles from *Communicating Christ*. Among them is "The Gospel Truth as Re-Enactment," which both David Tracy and John Shea — two leading contributors to the theology of story — especially liked. In fact, Tracy's notion of the classic, which is treated in my last chapter, implicitly corroborates the thesis of my article. Playwright ("The Rainmaker"), novelist, and philosopher N. Richard Nash similarly found my article "The Dream and Myth of Paradise" very meaningful. His evaluation as a professional storyteller, concerned about the deeper meaning of human life stories, was conducive to my inclusion of this article in the present work.

My introduction to *Towards a Theology of Story* gives special attention to the travel story as an expression of religious experience. It examines the narrative quality of all religious experience, whether in the story that one's life tells or in that which is related by others. The governing entelechy in a biblical writer's and his public's experiencing, in the form of the literary work itself, is the religious drive, given definite poetic (literary) expression. There is a dynamic continuity in the story that Christ's life tells with that of the biblical storyteller and the Christian community: all share the intentionality of the story that Christ's life tells. The dynamic continuity takes on the character of a travel story. There is the journey of the Age of Jesus and the journey of the Age of the Church. The outer journey in both ages bespeaks an inner journey with ever broadening horizons and increasing self-transcendence in response to transcendent grace and demand. The Christian community throughout the course of history, with the Risen Christ as its ultimate horizon, embraces the travel story of its Lord's self-transcendence as its own hope and promise.

Everyone's (and society's) travel story centers on moments of decision within the story as a whole. The present moment of decision is the moment of crisis between the past remembered and the future anticipated. Memory and anticipation constitute the dramatic tension of everyone's travel story; both are qualified by the quality of our consciousness. Although the past cannot be undone, it can be radically reinterpreted in the light of new experiences. The Old Testament is reinterpreted in the light of the Risen Christ.

This book is part of an expanding theological discourse on the narrative quality of religious experience. It is, more precisely, an introduction to a theology of story, taking "story" in its most generic sense to include that of individuals, communities, and nations, the stories that their lives tell as well as those which re-present (interpret) their lives. It includes the myths and models men live by in the one integral process of human experiencing.

Everyone's (and society's) story is lived within the context of manifold stories. The quality of his story depends on his attentiveness to and understanding of others' stories. The Gospel truth of the Christ story is the ultimate possibility for every life story. It has become a part of the world story; it is the part which the New Testament compares to the salt which gives the whole its flavor.

The life story of Jesus Christ and his Church is paradigmatic for the Christian's lived-understanding of our God—self—neighbor relationship. Theology is a systematic articulation of this story, of the Christian myth: the truth by which a Christian believes that he must live, the story that is normative for judging the true meaning and value of every human life story. Christian faith is the acceptance of the summons to live by the truth of Jesus Christ's life story as the way to becoming our true selves. Christian life, therefore, is a question of maturation and growth into our ultimate personal identity as constituted by our fidelity to the grace and demand of God for authenticity. Faith in the Risen Christ involves the summons to authentic existence with and in him, a summons to the consummation and fufillment of our life stories as a community in search of its true stories in the same way that his loving responsiveness to the Father led to the consummation and fulfillment of his life story. Seeking to know and to do the Father's will, in the Spirit of Jesus Christ, is the way to find our true life stories. We do not create them *ex nihilo;* God alone creates out of nothingness. Rather, we receive our true story, our authentic identity, from the God — the Storyteller — who wills or intends it for us. Our reception or finding of our true story — what we ultimately become in accordance with the grace and demand of God — is by no means a purely passive event; rather, it demands our full collaboration and effort. The cross is the mystery that reveals to Christian faith the glory of the divine love in the Risen Christ as the Father's free gift. Jesus enters into his glory through his loving obedience to God in voluntarily giving his life for others. The cross is the mystery of the divine love giving itself to be known and loved that we might be empowered to discover and accept our true life story. Our Father's love, symbolized by the life, death, and resurrection of Jesus Christ, is a summons to that life that culminates in the resurrection, in the ultimate gift of his story for us. It is the experience of this love that enables the Christian community to grasp the true meaning of Jesus Christ's and its own life story, even though in a glass darkly. The faith community's foundational experience of God's love in Jesus Christ's and its own life story is the interpretation that interprets the interpreter: the identity, meaning, and mission of the interpreting faith community. Its foundational experience inspires its prayerful confidence in the Father's efficacious and loving intention for the consummation of its true story in the resurrection of the just, i.e., in what is both our ultimate freedom from sin and death and our ultimate freedom for love and life.

PART I
Story and Conversion

1

CONVERSION EXPRESSED IN DIALOGUE AND STORY

Christian conversion is expressed in the dialogue and story of the New Testament. The meaning of the event and process of Christian conversion seeks and finds its appropriate outward expression in both the oral and written tradition of the Church. The inner transformation of human consciousness at every level (imagining, understanding, reasoning, judging, desiring, deciding, acting) that God effects through the gift of his love in Jesus Christ and his Holy Spirit grounds the life of the Christian community, which takes the form of spoken utterance before it is set down in writing. Even when the New Testament authors did come to write, we can overhear the living voices, speaking and praising.

DIALOGUE

The dialogue[1] of the New Testament expresses the interpersonal communication that God effects through the gift of his love that transforms human consciousness in the event and process of Christian conversion. Dialogue, address and response, question and answer, certainly represent the fundamental relationship between the God who speaks his word of love and all who are transformed by accepting it. God's word implies a hearer: his speech means speech to an "other." His address anticipates a reply: his self-expression calls for an interpersonal encounter. Dialogue expresses conversion as the personal transformation that is effected by a God who speaks, calls, initiates agreements or covenants, invites to mutual converse and understanding. It is he who says, "Come now, let us reason together" (Is. 1:18), or "Son of man, stand upon your feet, and I will speak with you" (Ez. 2:1). The Bible is full of searching dialogue between God and human persons, between his messengers and human listeners. Dialogue, the form of prayer itself, expresses the interpersonal communications that the conversion-event inaugurates and that the conversion-process develops. It implies the conviction of faith that the God who speaks his word of love to us for dialogue has created us not merely to be, but to be loved. The voice from heaven, which addresses Jesus as "the beloved" (e.g., Mk. 1:1), expresses the radical conviction of Christian conversion that God's unfailing word is that of his love for his Beloved Son, the Incarnate Word, and of his love for all human beings. The heavenly Lover identifies the beloved, affirming and constituting the meaning and goodness of his life for all who are willing to hear that same voice in their own lives. The word of God's love initiates, grounds, and brings to an eternal fulfillment the dialogue that is religious conversion. When this same word is heard in Jesus Christ and his Church, the dialogue is that of Christian conversion.

In the Gospels we hear Jesus questioning or being questioned. Vivid colloquy in direct discourse often occurs in the parables of Jesus. In the parable of the talents (Mt. 25), for example, each of the three servants reports in direct discourse to the master as to his disposition of the entrusted funds, and to each the master replies. Implicit dialogue also occurs where a fateful naming or calling goes forth from God himself or from Christ, as when Jesus is identified as the Beloved Son at his baptism, or when Jesus himself addresses Peter as the Rock, or when he addresses Jerusalem in lament for its refusal to respond.

The recurrent pattern of conversation between Jesus and his antagonists or his disciples pervades the Gospels. The word of God creates and sustains the saving tension of challenge and reply in the life story of Jesus Christ. The challenge and reply of the faithful, when brought to trial, is reflected in passages where the confession of Christ by the Spirit is set against the summons to deny him. Each represents the dialogue of the Christian and the world, with the implication that Christian conversion is precarious and requires the unfailing courage of a steadfast love that is the gift of the Father of Jesus Christ in the Holy Spirit. As Jesus confessed his Father by his life (as in Jn. 5:41; 8:50), so the disciples will have to give witness to the Lord (Mk. 13:9; Jn. 15:27). As long as Jesus was living with them, they feared nothing. He was their paraclete, always there to defend them and to get them out of difficulties (Jn. 17:12). After he departs the Spirit will take his place as their paraclete (Jn. 14:16; 16:7).

Distinct from Jesus, the Spirit will not speak in its own name, but always of Jesus, from whom it is inseparable and whom it will "glorify" (Jn. 16:13-14). The gift of the Spirit grounds the dialogue of interpersonal love among divine and human persons in the event and process of Christian conversion. The Spirit will recall to the disciples the works and words of the Lord and will give them an understanding of them (Jn. 14:26). It will give them the courage to confront the world in the name of Jesus, to discover the meaning of Jesus' death, and to give testimony to the divine love that has been revealed and communicated in this event (Jn. 16:8-11).

Christian interiority is expressed in the divine and human dialogue of reciprocal love that is consequent upon the acceptance of the Spirit given to us. This interior dialogue finds its outward expression in the evangelists' presentation of Jesus' conversation scenes. The Risen Christ is presented as the revealer of divine wisdom and love to certain favored men and women: his disclosures are often made in the form of dialogue or conversation. All the conversation and dialogue of Jesus represent for Christians the ever-present grace and challenge of their Risen Lord, who speaks his word of love for the transformation of all who will hear it, uniting them with himself and with each other by drawing them into his filial relationship under the lordship of his Father's love.

Dialogue (conversation) in the Gospels is transformational more than informational: it is directed to the heart no less than to the mind. It is profoundly a matter of personal involvement with the triune God's word of love for all, for "anyone who loves God must also love his brother" (1 Jn. 4:21).

Authentic communication with others: "We can be sure that we love God's children if we love God himself and do what he has commanded us" (1 Jn. 5:2). The quality of our dialogue or conversation with the brother that we can see discloses our relationship to the God whom we cannot see: "a man who does not love the brother that he can see cannot love God, whom he has never seen" (1 Jn. 4:20). God speaks his word of love to us in human persons. We reject that word in their lives when we reject it in our own. Only they who recognize that word of love as the origin and ground and destiny of their own lives will recognize and welcome it in others.

The quality of our interpersonal relations with divine and human persons is all of a piece. The pure of heart see God in relation to all others, and all others in relation to God: they love God in his creatures and his creatures in God. God speaks his word of love to them in all that he creates and sustains and destines for his Beloved Son. As the Word of God, Jesus Christ gives birth to Christian faith, hope, and love: the transforming dynamic of the dialogue among divine and human persons at the heart of Christian conversion.

Dialogue in the Gospels leads us to encounter the Good News that Jesus Christ is for all humankind (Mk. 1:1). Through and in him, God himself invites all human persons to colloquy in the living encounter of heart and heart, voice and voice. Dialogue, as a dramatic form of the Gospel itself, is an outward expression of Christian sharing in the interpersonal life of Jesus Christ with his Father and Spirit. In our interpersonal life with Jesus we hear the Word of God's love for us and for all who partake with us in the universal story. Our mutual love in Jesus Christ and his Spirit expresses our reception and acceptance of the interpersonal love and life of Jesus Christ with his Father and their Spirit. Christian conversion means our sharing in Jesus Christ's dialogue of love with all divine and human persons. Being-in-Love, the Blessed Trinity, is Being-in-Dialogue; it is the Supreme Goodness of interpersonal life that Christians affirm to be revealed in Jesus Christ, the Word of God, as the meaning and purpose of the universal story. The "I" that is Jesus Christ is the Being-In-Love whose interpersonal existence is that of addressing every "You," both divine and human, with the love that is the supreme Goodness at the heart of the universal story.

STORY

God is revealed through human stories.[2] God is a particular agent that is known and revealed in his story. Inasmuch as God is the giver of all human life-stories, they are manifestations of his grace and are measured by the demands of his intention. Human life-stories are implicitly coauthored with God and neighbor. The transcendent Spirit of God is, and is known, where it acts in the self-transcending faith and hope and love through which it transforms our lives. The gift of God's love through the Spirit of Jesus grounds the story of Christian conversion. The telling and the hearing of the Gospel story are the work of the same Spirit working in both the teller and the hearer. Christian conversion is the gift of God that enables us to hear the story of Jesus and his Church: it enables us to recognize that story as *our* story and to tell it. In appropriating that story we appropriate our own life story. Our distinctive ways of telling the story of Jesus correspond to the divers ways in which God can tell us that we are loved and trusted. The names of Jesus connote the ways that God's gift of his love transform our lives and constitute the life story of the Church. The story of Jesus being in agony in the garden discloses the inescapable tension in the life of Christian conversion. His suffering is disclosed to us not as the sign that something is wrong but as the sign that he is on the right path. The Gospel presents the way of the cross as *Good* News, as the growing pains that attend the process of self-transcendence, as the birth-pangs that herald the new creation. We must not attempt to tell anyone of the meaning of suffering, as illuminated by the cross of Jesus Christ, until we have, for ourselves, appropriated the meaning by experiencing what it is to live out the self-transcending and costly love of the way of the cross.

That every person who has ever lived has lived out a story of storytelling and storylistening posits a comprehensive universe with a permanent meaning at the heart of things. The life story of Jesus Christ discloses that meaning to faith: it is the primordial sacrament of God's gift of his love, experienced by the Christian as underlying and informing all human life-stories. The life story of the crucified and risen Jesus is recognized in Christian conversion as the icon and parable of God, the key to the Christian interpretation of every human story's ultimate meaning and value. An understanding of Jesus Christ's life story as a story growing out of the web of interpersonal relations that made up his community is essential for an understanding of our own life stories as Christians and for an understanding of the way in which our own life stories are incorporated into his universal life story.

Since the personal is interpersonal, we cannot grasp the significance of Jesus Christ apart from his relationships with the persons — both divine and human — who enter his life, *from* whom he receives his life and *for* whom he gives his life. The life of Jesus Christ, like all interpersonal existence, is rooted in the giving and receiving of love, in knowing and being known, in reciprocal intercommunication between persons. The interpersonal life of Jesus Christ — his relationships to God and to his fellow humans, to divine and to human persons — is the prime analogate for the Christian community's experience and understanding and judgment of its own interpersonal relationships with divine and human persons, and of the relationship between the universal story and the Triune God. We express our interpersonal life in the form of story. The Gospel writers express God's transformation of our interpersonal life in Jesus Christ — Christian conversion as event and process — in narrative form. They tell the Jesus story, the story of the Christian community's participation in his interpersonal life and love, the story of God's loving us so much that he sent his only Son to die and rise for us and breathe upon us his Holy Spirit.

Ultimate reality is disclosed in the life story of Jesus as the interpersonal life of Being-in-Love without limits. To be or not to be, for persons, is to be-in-love or not to be-in-love, to be interpersonally related or not to be related. For Christians, that boundless, limitless Being-in-Love is incarnate in the life and story of Jesus Christ, an existing person whose interpersonal love-life embraces and integrates all persons, human and divine. Human persons are free to accept or to reject the interpersonal love-life that he reveals and communicates as the integration of all persons, human and divine, in one life of interpersonal love and friendship, the eschatological fulfillment of which is the communion of saints in the kingdom of God, the locus of our true selves, the culmination of the event and process of Christian conversion. Christian conversion expresses the Good News that we belong to his life story.

Christian conversion is to be in love as Jesus Christ is in love: to accept Being-in-Love, God himself who is love, and the interpersonal life that is being given us in the universal story. Being-in-Love, the Triune God, is the Supreme Goodness of interpersonal life that Christians affirm to be revealed in Jesus Christ as the meaning and purpose of the universal story. The cross represents the total self-investment of Being-in-Love for the achievement of this purpose. God is Love, investing his interpersonal life in the universal story. The "I" that is Jesus Christ is the Being-in-Love whose interpersonal existence is that of addressing every "You," both human and divine, with the love that is the Supreme Goodness at the heart of the universal story.

Jesus tells his disciples that belonging to the interpersonal love-life of God (Lk. 10:20) is a deeper motive for their rejoicing than whatever power they possess over evil: ". . . rather rejoice that your names are written in heaven." Luk envisions Jesus as *the* person whose interpersonal love-life embraces both the world of his Father in heaven and that of his disciples on earth. This is the ultimate basis of all Christian rejoicing in the event and process of conversion. This foundational experience communicates our assurance of our ultimate interpersonal fulfillment. In our interpersonal life with Jesus we hear the Word of God's love for us and for all who partake with us in the universal story. The dialogue and story of the New Testament express the gift and demand of this life. The very meaning of Christian conversion comes to expression in dialogue and story, the primal modes of interpersonal communication and life. It is through the life story of Jesus and his Church that Christians hear God speaking his saving and purposeful word of love for all human persons. And through this hearing Christians are enabled to return that word of love to God and to all others in the saving dialogue of Christian conversion; for no one speaks it who has not heard it at the depth of his own life story. *Nemo dat quod non habet.*

2

CONVERSION AND CONFLICT

The New Testament is an external expression of the internal reality of Christian conversion. It brings to expression the mystery of God as a history of transforming love in Jesus Christ and in his community of faith: "No one has ever seen God; it is the only Son, who is nearest to the Father's heart, who has made him known" (Jn. 1:18).

The "conflict stories" of the New Testament imply that God's word of love will encounter human resistance.[1] The adversaries of Jesus give expression to the various forms that human resistance takes to the grace and demand of God for our truest and fullest life in his love. His adversaries represent the mind-sets and heart-sets that oppose the event and the process of Christian conversion — the personal and social transformation that results from the surrender of oneself to the love that is God.

The Synoptic Gospels contain a number of episodes prior to the passion narrative in which there is a verbal exchange between Jesus and his contemporaries on some crucial issue, exchanges in which Jesus and the other parties are adversaries.

In these episodes the crucial issue generally arises because of some action of Jesus, or of his disciples, that is unacceptable to the other parties. Sometimes they arise because Jesus (or someone else) asks a question that provokes conflict.[2]

There are three parts to the formal structure of these "conflict stories": (1) an introductory narrative; (2) the opponent's question or attack; and (3) Jesus' reply — the so-called "dominical saying."

These stories are always preceded by some narrative. This narrative functions not only as a transitional link with what has preceded, but it also establishes the setting in such a way that the reader is prepared for the inevitable conflict. Thus the narrative stages a polarity or tension, with speaking and acting persons as the poles of the tension.

Except in Mk. 3:1-5, the conflict stories begin with a question or accusation that is usually directed toward Jesus or his disciples. In two instances, however, the questions begin from Jesus himself (Mt. 22:41-46 and Lk. 14:1-6). At times the silence of Jesus' opponent (as in Mk. 3:2) can have the significance of a statement in the ensuing dialogue of question and answer.

All materials of the conflict story are organized to stress Jesus' reply — the dominical saying — which brings the dialogue to a close. This pronouncement of Jesus has some bearing on an aspect of Christian belief or conduct. It implies the need of understanding, and it explains both the grace and the demand of God's word of love in Jesus Christ that calls for human transformation in the process of Christian conversion.

These conflict stories were formulated at various stages in the process of formation of the Gospels, and in diverse circumstances.[3] Some were shaped within the living context of the early Church's apologetical concerns in response to Jewish criticism. Others were shaped in the context of the catechetical concerns of the Church in its response to the need of teaching converts and regulating the life of the believing community.

Central to all conflict stories, however, is their focus on the person of Jesus, on his words, attitudes, and actions. Christian conversion always has as its object the interpersonal life of Jesus Christ: his relationships to God and his relationships to fellow-humans — his relationships to divine and human persons. This interpersonal life of Christ is the prime analogate for the Christian community's experience, understanding, and judgment of its own interpersonal relationships with divine and human persons.

The object of Christian conversion, then, is not just a set of truths or an ethical code. It is participation in the interpersonal life of Jesus Christ, as this is itself rooted in receiving and giving the Father's love, in knowing and being known.

The Gospels' conflict stories imply the difficulty with which the mystery of God becomes a history of love in the actual life stories of Jesus and of his followers. These stories imply that Christian conversion, both as event and as process of maturation, must have a dimension of conflict at both the intra- and interpersonal levels. "Not my will but thine be done" itself tells of a conflict relationship with the self that is always to be transcended in the individual's response to the grace and demand of the self-giving love that is God.

God's coming into our lives creates the transforming tension between his grace and its demand for an ever-greater selflessness, which brings about a lasting communion with God's own self, and thereby with one another, among his followers. Jesus Christ's way of the cross represents the costly love of divine and of human self-giving and self-investment.

Christian conversion, then, is the new life that derives from our accepting for ourselves God's own life of boundless love for all. The cross expresses the suffering that the acceptance of boundless love must entail — even for the sinless Son of God. It makes manifest that our acceptance of this love will inevitably place us in a conflictual relationship with others:

> If the world hates you,
> remember that it hated me before you.
> If you belonged to the world,
> the world would love you as its own;
> but because you do not belong to the world,
> because my choice withdrew you from the world,
> therefore the world hates you.
> Remember the words I said to you:
> A servant is not greater than his master.
> If they persecuted me,
> they will persecute you too . . . (Jn. 15:18-20).

If the conflict stories of the Gospels are an expression of the interpersonal life of Jesus Christ, of his receiving and giving his Father's love for the transformation of all, they imply also that Christian conversion, our participation in his life, must inevitably entail conflict at both the intra- and interpersonal levels. At both levels it must entail an ever deeper penetration into the mystery of that love which itself embraces our lives and constitutes the term towards which our whole beings strive.

The God whose word of love is addressed to us in the conflict stories gives us the ability to make that word our own by the process of Christian conversion.[4] Not only do we hear Jesus' story, but we tell the same story in our own lives, making his struggle to overcome the unlove of the human heart our own.

The Church tells these conflict stories of its Lord as an expression of the life that derives from his love. His struggle reveals the way that God's kingdom comes to us. Consequently, we might well question our tendency to believe that conflict at the intra- and interpersonal levels of Christian life is always an indication that something is wrong. Rather it would seem we might be more concerned about the authenticity of a Christian commitment that did *not* encounter resistance at both these levels.

The way of the cross is the way of inexhaustible and unquenchable love. It enables us to live in the tension and conflict that this love demands if we are to attain to the fullness of life in the kingdom of God.

These conflict stories must not be read outside the context of the Good News. This is what fills the heart with joy and enables self-sacrifice to be wholehearted. Even though these stories imply the demand of a God who challenges everything that is in us, they are expressions at the same time of the great Good News that God is Love and has given us his life and love in Jesus Christ and in his Spirit.

Even though these stories imply all the conflict, tension, suffering, and renunciation that is inherent in living as Christians, they, too, belong to the Good News, because what is primary in them and in it is the joy taken in the goodness of the life and love that God has given us: "Jesus . . . who, for the joy that was set before him, endured the cross, despising the shame . . ." (Heb. 12:2).⁵

The conflict-dimension of Christian conversion and its way of the cross is founded on the joy that is taken in the Supreme Good, in the boundless Love that we know and proclaim to be the Father of Jesus Christ.

Through the gift of the Spirit, we are enabled to rejoice in this Love and its challenges. In this context we know that where there is love, there is also struggle. The crucified and risen One reveals that Love is not indifferent to human unlove, but struggles to overcome it in the conflictual activity of Love's self-giving.

3

FOUR GOSPELS: FOUR STAGES
OF CHRISTIAN CONVERSION

Carlo Martini, S.J., rector of the Gregorian University [Cardinal of Milan, since 1983], gave several public lectures at the Gregorian in January 1979 in which he outlined his working hypothesis that the four Gospels serve the Church as a pedagogical resource — as "four manuals" — for articulating the meaning of Christian conversion. The gift of God's love in Jesus Christ is dynamically evidenced among the faithful in four stages of Christian maturation, corresponding to the four Gospels or "manuals" of the Church, that both derive from the lived experience of these four stages and aim at leading us to the goal of each progressive stage.

The process of Christian conversion and maturation is grounded on the grace and challenge of God's love in Jesus Christ. The New Testament imperatives to watch and pray always remind us that this is a precarious process in which we risk falling into temptation. Hearts grow cold. The New Testament tells of those who have fallen in love with God in Christ and who have later fallen out of love. There is no moment when Christians, as individuals and as a community, may comfortably assume there is no longer any need to watch and pray lest they fall into temptation.

Where there is God's love there is the dynamic of growth, or stages of maturation and development; consequently, it will be worthwhile to survey some of the points that Carlo Martini makes regarding the four Gospels as manuals which the Church employed and continues to employ for the cultivation of the gift of God's love in Jesus Christ and his community of faith. The four "manuals" witness the Church's conviction that Christian authenticity is a matter of ongoing growth in response to the love of God. They imply our Christian responsibility and possibility with respect to becoming what the Creator's love, as revealed in the crucified and risen Jesus, intends that we become.

The Church historically employed its four Gospels as manuals for both the initiation of baptismal candidates into the foundational experience of God's love for us in Jesus Christ and for their postbaptismal maturation in the cultivation of this experience. The four Gospels correspond to four distinctive phases in Christian conversion and maturation.[1]

Mark, the Gospel of the catechumen, leads the baptismal candidate — usually a religious person of the Graeco-Roman world — from religious conversion to Christian conversion, to a break with former images of God, to accept the new image and to enjoy the new experience of God and his love for us in obedience to the demands of the crucified and risen Jesus. The catechumen must learn a new way of living with Mystery: Jesus Christ's way. The first chapters of Mark, replete with miracle stories, identify the divine power with Jesus; however, beginning with the eighth chapter, in which Peter acknowledges the messiahship of Jesus and Jesus responds with the prediction of the passion, the divine power is understood in a radically new way. Catechumens must abandon the popularly accepted stereotypes of divine power and human success, the image of a god made to the measure of their self-interest and suited to their personal ease or comfort. Catechumens cannot have a risen Lord without a suffering Messiah; they cannot have a lived experience of God's love for us in Jesus Christ without walking his road of suffering self-transcendence.[2] The catechumen's new image of God in Jesus Christ is that of a God who demands our self-transcendence through our filial execution of his will. The death of Jesus, far from being incompatible with the divine power, is the very revelation of its true meaning: the reciprocal love of God and humans that is manifested in self-transcending love's filial obedience to the grace and demand of God's foundational love for us. Mark depicts for the catechumen a Jesus who is faithful, though encircled by evil and the threat of death, and this Jesus is meant to become the way of his commitment to the grace and demand of the divine power that is God's love for us.

Matthew, the Gospel of the catechist, is based on the assumption that an authentic commitment to the gift of God's love in Jesus Christ was possible only within the context of membership in his community. The catechumen's decision regarding Jesus necessarily involved a decision regarding his Church. Matthew provides the catechist with a manual for helping the newly baptized to mature in their foundational experience of God's love within the community of those who have submitted to his rule in Jesus. Matthew's five discourses specify what the acceptance of Christ and of his demands means for an authentic experience of his love within the community. The wealth of precepts and rules for conduct for Christian living that characterize Matthew provide the catechist with norms for instructing the newly baptized on the meaning of an authentic communion with Jesus present in the midst of his Church. Our love of God in Jesus Christ is authenticated and deepened by the self-transcendence of fellowship and service. The catechist has a standard for determining the degree of participation in this messianic community: to have brought forth fruits of the kingdom (21:43), to have done the will of God (5:16; 7:21), to have attained to the higher righteousness (5:20) and shaped one's life course to enter the kingdom by the narrow gate (7:13), with good works that glorify our heavenly Father (5:16). Adherence to Jesus Christ is gauged by fidelity to the exigency of his demands for fraternal love within the Christian community.

Those whose lives are governed by the love and mercy of God in Jesus Christ are urged, by inner compulsion, to communicate that love to others within the community (or Church). The catechist is equipped with guidelines for fostering the development of such love: true greatness in the kingdom (18:1-4), scandal (18:5-10), the lost sheep (18:12-14), brotherly care and correction, authority in the Church (18:15-18), association in prayer (18:19f), and forgiving offenses (18:21-35). The love of the Christian community evidences the fulfillment of the Emmanuel promise (1:23) and the promise to be "with us always" (28:20); for Jesus is with his followers, present in his missionaries (10:40), in all received in his name (18:5), and in the assembly (18:20). The catechist must help the newly baptized to cultivate that love which sees and experiences the risen Lord in one's brothers, in the poor, in the needy, in the weak.

Luke-Acts serves as a two-volume manual for meeting the needs of the third phase of Christian maturation. Luke, the Gospel of the witness, is meant to be read together with Acts as a single work. Luke-Acts was written for Christians who, already adhering to Jesus Christ and his community, are seeking to grasp their meaning for the world. Their foundational experience of God's love in Jesus Christ and his community is met with both acceptance and rejection by outsiders. Persecution has made the Christian community keenly aware of its impact upon the world; it has also created the need for the community to defend and explain itself. To explain oneself to others, one must first be able to understand oneself: one must be able to tell one's own story. The author of Luke-Acts, therefore, explains the roots of the Christian community in the Jewish world and relates the salvation promised to Israel to the entire world. The plan of Luke-Acts is dictated by the commission of the risen Christ to his disciples: "You shall be my witnesses in Jerusalem and in all Judaea and Samaria and to the ends of the earth" (Acts 1:8). Luke-Acts serves as a manual to meet the need for dialogue with Jewish, Hellenistic, and Roman worlds, to explain the relationship between salvation history and world history. Inasmuch as a theology mediates between a cultural matrix and the significance and role of a religion in that matrix, Luke-Acts serves as a manual to foster a mature theological reflection on the complexity of the Church's relationship to the world. The author envisions this complexity in a nuanced, existential way. Committed Christians cannot flee historical complexity; they cannot pretend that complexity is an illusion to be conquered by turning away from it. Christian maturation demands the courage and intelligence to confront the social, political, cultural, and religious complexities of the times. Luke-Acts represents the mature Christian's response to the challenge of the world: to the questions, crises, and culture of the times.

John, the Gospel of the presbyter (of the mature and wise), represents the culmination of the foundational experience of God's love in Jesus Christ and his community, of an all-embracing, universal love, to be preached to all nations. John serves as the Church's manual for ascertaining the attainment of full development. It assumes the achievements of the three previous phases of Christian maturation in fidelity to the grace and demand of the foundational experience. It represents the simplicity of vision of one who has mastered the complexity of the three Synoptic manuals and their corresponding horizons. This Gospel is not marked by a multiplicity of commands, orders, parables, precepts, and rites. The long discourses on themes characteristic of Christian piety are not pieced together out of separate sayings, as are the discourses in the Synoptics. This Gospel locates the unifying principle underlying the complexity of the previous phases of development in the gift of the Father's love that we receive in the Son and the Holy Spirit. Christian faith consists in the reception of this gift. Whoever possesses it begins to love as Christ has loved us. Consequently, love is the only law. John synthesizes the entire Christian experience in terms of the gift of God's love in Jesus Christ and his Spirit. The Church's confessions of faith, Eucharist, fellowship, Gospels, prayers, precepts, proclamation, rites, service, and witness are called into existence and sustained by the gift of this love that alone constitutes their true meaning and value. Fidelity to the grace and demand of God's love, the foundational principle of both the Church and the world, is the key to Christian authenticity and engagement with the world. John, the manual of Christian wisdom, promotes an integrated vision of the entire Christian experience in both its internal (Church) and external (world) relationships.

The experience of God's love grounds religious conversion. The experience of God's love in Jesus Christ and his Church, in both its internal and external relationships, grounds Christian conversion and maturation.[3] The four Gospels serve Christians in every age as manuals for authenticating and renewing their fidelity to the grace and demand of the Church's foundational experience.[4]

Progress, decline, and renewal are categories for reflection on Christian authenticity in individual subjects and, in their togetherness in community, service, and witness, the history of salvation that is rooted in the experience of God's love for humankind.[5] Our Christian living may be authentic or unauthentic or some blend of the two. The Gospels as manuals help us to determine the degrees of our saying ''Yes'' or ''No'' to the gift of God's love in Jesus Christ and its engagement with the world through the Church. They raise the question of our lived understanding of the divine power in Jesus Christ and his Church, and its relationship to the world. They define what God's gift of love should mean for anyone who would follow Jesus Christ in his community, in the concrete particularities, actualities, and potentialities of the contemporary world.[6] They demand that the interior journey of the soul to the Father be linked with the exterior coming of his kingdom in all its historical dimensions. Our fidelity to the ''first and greatest'' commandment is gauged by the quality of our engagement with others both within and without the community of Christian faith.

The New Testament writings help us to discern what authentic love does and what it does not do: ''Love is always patient and kind; it is never jealous; love is never boastful or conceited; it is never rude or selfish; it does not take offence, and is not resentful. Love takes no pleasure in other people's sins but delights in the truth; it is always ready to excuse, to trust, to hope, and to endure whatever comes'' (1 Cor. 13:4-7).

The entire New Testament serves as a manual to attain that lived knowledge of God that is based on the order of Jesus Christ's love for the things presented to him within the historical particularities of his life and death.[7] This is the love that, surviving and transcending death itself, culminates in the resurrection; every other love might be called a form of ''tomb love,'' a love that ultimately fails the lover, betraying the ultimate promise and possibility available to all humankind in the gift of God's love in Jesus Christ and his community. ''Tomb love'' is a metaphor for that selfishness, or disordered love, of one who remains buried in oneself, rejecting the authenticity that is available in self-transcendence and openness to the true and the good without limits or qualifications or conditions or reservations.

The story that the gift of God's love tells the world in Jesus Christ and his community is the theme of the entire New Testament. The Gospels, together with all the New Testament writings, serve as a catalyst for cultivating the foundational experience of Christian faith (the experience of God's love in Jesus Christ and his community) by activating our imaginations for discovering the concrete ways that the grace and demand of this experience are to be embodied in our lives. The New Testament, for William F. Thompson, falls within the ambit of an imaginative hermeneutics in which the text serves as a catalyst for our own imaginative capacities.[8] It is not arbitrary, however, so long as it builds upon two other hermeneutical methods and adequately accounts for their findings: the first aims at delineating the author's original intention or the various historical contexts underlying each text; the second analyzes the text as something qualitatively distinct from either its author's original intentions or its original historical contexts. Besides the analyses of what is either implied by the text itself (intention of the author) or ideally present in the text (the meaning of the text is an ideal one, "distanced" from the implied author and contexts), there is the meaning that we ourselves give to the text. The method here, according to Thompson, is neither psychological (penetrating the intention of the author) nor semantical, but imaginative. The first two methods are more past-oriented: what does the past "imply" or "say?" This method is more future-oriented: the text is treated as a catalyst for developing and partially confirming present self-understanding.[9] In this respect, the sense of a text is not entirely *behind* the text (its historical origins) but also in front of it (the world it opens up). The New Testament text originated as an expression of the dynamic interrelating of Christian faith (hope and love) and imagination to the world; it retains its primordial sense, as the orientation of God's love in Jesus Christ and his Church, when it continues to activate the imagination of Christian faith in concrete ways that authentically embody the same orientation of God's love for the world.[10] The love that Jesus Christ revealed in word and deed had to be imagined, at least in some way, before it could be done. The Father's will could be done only on the condition that it was truly imagined. The New Testament continues to respond to the Father's love in Jesus Christ and his community when it serves as a catalyst for the imagination of Christians seeking to do his will within the historical particularities of their unfolding life stories.[11]

Jesus realized how important it is for us to imagine God as he truly is; for our way of imagining God is all of a piece with the way that we imagine ourselves, our neighbor, and our world.[12] His many parables attempt to correct our false ways of thinking and feeling about God, ourselves, others, and the world, for such ways distort and frustrate our lives. For Christian faith, Jesus Christ is the parable of God enabling us to imagine our true possibilities for a fully lived-experience of the grace and demand of God's love in a lifelong self-transcendence culminating in the resurrection. Jesus' way of the cross, the dying and rising of self-transcending love, images the true meaning of the grace and demand of the Father's love for a life that culminates in the resurrection. He enables faith to live according to the promise of a love that he imaged as "power made perfect in weakness" (2 Cor. 12:9). He creates a radically new image and experience of the divine power that the Christian community proclaims in the mystery of one who "was crucified in weakness, but lives by the power of God" (2 Cor. 13:4). The true meaning of the divine power as the gift and demand of God's love is, for Christian faith, imaged in the words, deeds, and destiny of Jesus. This meaning, perceived by Christian faith, specifies religious conversion as Christian and renders community possible. It requires the mediation of a process of tradition that originates with Jesus' contemporaries; at an early stage it is committed to writing. The New Testament presents a linguistic expression of the meaning that is the gift and demand of God's love in Jesus. Subsequent Christian tradition accepts this expression as in some sense normative.

The Christian community preached the good news of God's love for us in its crucified and risen Lord. The acceptance of this good news, or gospel, entailed a conversion *(metanoia),* thematized under the rubric of becoming a follower of Jesus. Christian preaching proclaimed such conversion and discipleship as normative for both the authentic fulfillment of human life and for deliverance from our incapacity to break with our own evil ways. The call to follow Jesus is an invitation to accept the grace and demand of God's love for us the way that Jesus accepted it as the integrating center of his life. The New Testament thematizes the meaning of Christian conversion, the demand of the unrestricted love that the Christian has received and accepted as the integrating center of his life. The New Testament teaches us to identify the ultimate source and term of that love as the Father of Jesus Christ; it points to Jesus as the revelation of the Father who completes his mission by sending the Spirit of their love for us. The New Testament symbolizes the realm in interpersonal terms. Authentic human fulfillment and redemption through the gift of God's love for us in Jesus Christ and his Spirit is interpreted in interpersonal terms. In this context, sin is understood as some form of impersonalism (the failure to be attentive, grateful, responsible, compassionate, merciful, faithful, reliable, etc.).

The Christian community expresses in many ways its foundational experience of the mystery of God's love in Jesus, the mystery of an unrestricted love to which every person is constitutively oriented or summoned for the attainment of authentic fulfillment. The Church's fellowship, prayer, precepts, preaching, proclamation, service, and witness originated as expressions of this experience and offer continuing evidence of its present demand and summons for our authentic fulfillment (conversion, self-transcendence). The writings of the New Testament express the same experience and its demands for our religious conversion and development. The New Testament expresses the kerygmatic motive of the Christian community that generated the effort to convince us of the meaning Christian faith found in Jesus and to persuade us to live out the values inherent in that meaning. This task, according to William P. Loewe, was that of bringing to full expression and linguistically articulating the meaning incarnate in Jesus:

For this task the imagination provided a principal instrument. Endeavoring to express and communicated Jesus' identity in all its forcefulness, those who contributed to the formative tradition of the New Testament constructed dramatic narratives. Guided by their interest in conversion and redemption, they enriched and reshaped their memories of Jesus' words and deeds with appropriate images drawn from the Hellenistic world and above all from the Old Testament. The one who died on the cross became the prophet who was to come, the Messiah, the Suffering Servant, the Lord, the Son of God. Each image placed at the service of Christian faith a wealth of symbolic power evoking the meaning incarnate in Jesus.[13]

The biblical witness thematizes the meaning of its central, controlling image of the New Testament — that of the crucified and risen Jesus — by locating it in the dramatic context where Jesus' words and deeds, death and destiny, fulfill the intention of a loving God for his creation. Jesus courageously faces opposition with an unconditional affirmation of his Father's true meaning and goodness. He confronts evil with a love rooted in that of God. His death is the fate of the innocent one. The New Testament affirms that Jesus' voluntary acceptance of his suffering and death is not in vain; rather, in accepting death as the culmination of the resistance of evil to his words and deeds of loving fidelity to the grace and demand of his Father's love, Jesus went on to further life. He becomes a source of the same life for those who accept his orientation of fidelity to the grace and demand of the same Father's love for them. Accepting Jesus' words and deeds involves our following Jesus through death to resurrection in self-sacrificing love for others, a love that manifests the authentic meaning of the "divine power" that Christian faith affirms in the mystery of the cross and resurrection.

The mystery of God's love for us in Jesus Christ generates the faith, hope, and love at the heart of Christian conversion.[14] Such conversion means faith in the reality of God's love for us revealed in Jesus Christ. Although the wisdom of the world deems the self-sacrificing life and death of Jesus foolishness, the converted subject finds in the cross and resurrection both the strength to reject that wisdom and the firm hope that his self-sacrifice will not prove futile. The authenticity of our response to Jesus' injunction to love God above all else finds its verification in the decisions and actions by which we follow Jesus in costly self-transcending love for the neighbor both within and without the Christian community. Christian conversion unfolds as our self-transcending love adheres to the demands of God's love in Jesus (Mark), in the Church (Matthew), and in the world (Luke-Acts). The process of Christian conversion and development is distorted or stifled by the failure to respond to the demand of God's gift of love for continuing self-transcendence. It demands more than the individual's acceptance of Jesus in baptism and the feeling that "I'm saved"; it demands more than Church membership and fellowship.

The four Gospels serve as a norm for following Jesus within his community. They indicate the four consecutive phases that are essential to the fulfillment of the Christian conversion and maturation process. The lived achievement of one phase is called forth to the achievement of the next. Failure to respond to the summons for further self-transcendence jeopardizes present achievements. The basic temptation to self-sufficiency, to making oneself the ultimate guarantor of one's own well-being and security, threatens to short-circuit the authentic development of the conversion and maturation process.[15] Membership within the Christian community, in terms of a gratifying role within that community, may be used as a solution to the problems of life. Another form of covert self-seeking is a legalism in which the concern with rectitude is the expression of the urge to self-justification rather than of self-transcendence. There is a search for "religious experience" that tends to make God an instrument for the fulfillment of one's wishes. With the Gnostic deviation, religious knowledge is understood and sought as a personal possession that enables one to be master of one's own destiny, to take control of one's eschatological fulfillment. Because Christianity is not a mere worldliness, but a holy worldliness, it is distorted if it is reduced to a mere social gospel. Fanatic, apocalyptic mysticisms, formalism, illuminism, quietism, and sectarianism are among the many aberrations that frustrate the Christian conversion and maturation process, when the love of God is not strictly associated with self-transcendence.

The New Testament's Trinitarian imagery symbolizes the realm of transcendent love in terms of three persons who are not closed inwards, each upon himself, but opened outwards towards one another. The perfection of human personhood occurs in the actual love of authentic friendship, in the dynamics of self-giving and reciprocal love. John (13:34f) affirms that the realm of God's transcendent love in Jesus Christ has a meaning that is most effectively communicated in the reciprocal and self-transcending love of the disciples.

The New Testament appeals for conversion and maturation on a level prior to that on which doctrinal systems and organized institutions arise.[16] It supplies in its symbolic narratives of Jesus' meaning a basis upon which Christians may and in fact do make common judgments and decisions. Religious community arises only when religiously transformed subjectivity begins to mediate itself through meaning. The mediation of Christian conversion and maturation through meaning provides the context for the Christian community's use of the New Testament in the service of a Love that summons us to be one, holy (authentic), catholic (whole), and apostolic (outgoing witnesses.).

4

BIPOLARITIES IN CONVERSION

Conversion, whether religious or Christian, is characterized by *bipolarities*. There is the experience of a Love beyond words and our "stories of God" that attempt to express it. There is the manifestation and proclamation of eternal love in the Word of this Love made flesh. There is the bipolarity of manifestation and proclamation at the heart of our experience and understanding of the sacred. There is the bipolarity that we experience as the gap between the reality of our conversion as event and process and the ideal that it intends. Within our experience of the Church there is the bipolarity of the external forms that serve to communicate its inner life of the Spirit of Jesus Christ and his Father. The bipolarity of the one and the many underlies the Christian community's confession of the Triune God, of the Absolute as Interpersonal Love. The mystical tradition of the Church bears witness to the bipolarity of light and darkness in our experience of God's gift of his love, in the relationship between the divine and the human that is grounded in the activity of communicating the incommunicable. In the Christian understanding of this relationship, there is the bipolarity of being drawn to the Father by the Son. The superstructure of belief and the infrastructure of faith, the bipolarities of word and spirit or form and content or means and end, characterize the Christian project of life according to the Gospel truth.

Bernard Lonergan tells us that conversion, the transformation of the subject and his or her world, is prior to its expression. Religious conversion is the reality of personal transformation, whether its subject has any notion of what it is or whether it has occurred, that spontaneously produces effects. It occurs when the subject becomes a being-in-love-with-God, when the supreme value is God, and other values are God's expression of his love in the world. Conversion to what is transcendent in lovableness, when that is unknown, is an orientation to transcendent mystery.[1] Lonergan explains the specificity of Christian conversion in terms of the mission of the Son and the gift of his Spirit: "Without the visible mission of the Word, the gift of the Spirit is a being-in-love without proper object; it remains simply an orientation to mystery that awaits its interpretation. Without the invisible mission of the Spirit, the Word enters into his own, but his own receive him not."[2]

God's gift of his love flooding our hearts, according to Lonergan, constitutes the dynamic state of being in love, the foundational event and process of religious conversion that is prior to and distinct from its expression. Only God can give that gift; it is not the result of human reasoning; rather, it is the cause that leads us to seek the knowledge of God.

RELIGIOUS CONVERSION: THE EXPERIENCE OF A LOVE BEYOND WORDS

Religious conversion makes one what one is. It is a basic consciousness that is operative at every level of one's being, that overflows into one's imagining, understanding, judging, deciding, and acting. It is at the root of the understanding that people have of themselves, their situation, their role of the human condition. The converted have a basic consciousness that is quite different from that of the unconverted. The difference is implied in a passage where Lonergan links transcendent value with other values:

> As other apprehensions of value, so, too, faith has a relative as well as an absolute aspect. It places all other values in the light and the shadow of transcendent value. In the shadow, for transcendent value is supreme and incomparable. In the light, for transcendent value links itself to all other values to transform, magnify, glorify them. Without faith the originating value is man and the terminal value is the good man brings about. But in the light of faith, originating value is divine light and love, while terminal value is the whole universe. So the human good becomes absorbed in an all-encompassing good.[3]

The experience of God's love in religious conversion creates a basic consciousness that relativizes all things as gifts from the All. In terms of this, the limit of human expectation ceases to be the grave, and human concern reaches beyond the ultimate limits of man's world to God himself. If the world, and one's own existence, are accepted in gratitude as unmerited gifts of an incomprehensible Love, this is not passivity. For if the world is good, it deserves to be improved. Commitment takes nothing for granted, and least of all the gifts of God. Rather, it manifests the depths of human appreciation and gratitude with regard to the originating value of every finite good: God.

In the first moment of religious conversion, and in our ordinary faith experience, our most fundamental understanding (basic consciousness) is at once preconceptual, prelinguistic, and supraconceptual. It is not expressed in words, though it shapes our lives and guides our thinking and judging and deciding. The deepest truths of our faith rest not so much on particular texts of Scripture as on a global view, a "sense" of rightness, that we cannot easily articulate, but we *can* recognize faulty formulations. In both the most tragic and most joyous moments of life we experience our inability to say anything appropriate; yet, in each, there is an understanding by which we react appropriately but silently. Lacking the word of rational discourse, we fall back on gesture or metaphor — where far more is meant and understood than is uttered.[4]

The first moment in religious conversion and experience is interior, intensely personal and intimate; however, it is not so private as to be solitary.

Jesus made his community of faith possible by communicating in his words and deeds of instruction the meaning of the transcendent Love which he experienced in the immediacy of his consciousness. From his own inner resources, he spoke the prophetic word of the Lord for the creation of a new people. He employed finite words to express his experience of a reality beyond them. What he experienced in himself as the realm of God's transcendent love he knew to be God's ultimate purpose in creation. His summons to conversion is an invitation to share his experience of the transcendent Love that is the integrating center of his life and destiny.

For Christian faith, the manifestation and proclamation of Eternal Love has taken place in the Word of this Love made flesh. Jesus Christ is the incarnate meaning of this Love for humankind. His life, death, and destiny mediate the meaning of his interiority, and his interiority of a mind and heart completely oriented to God, mediates the transcendent world of his Father, a world of supreme value, truth, beauty, a world of mystery, one that inspires awe and yet attracts us so powerfully as to put all other attractions in a subordinate place.

As the outward being of Jesus is transparent to his interior, so his interior can be said to be transparent to the transcendent realm of God's unrestricted and self-giving love.[5] Jesus' world of immediacy is constituted interiorly by the mystery of his Father's love. By expressing in word and deed the love that he experiences in the immediacy of his consciousness, Jesus becomes a word of meaning pointing to God. Jesus mediates the meaning of a word (the mystery of God and his love) that is already in some sense present to us, if we believe that God's gift of his love is always offered to all mankind. By the same token, Jesus also mediates an understanding of what this transcendent Love does *not* intend (mean) for mankind.

The Church carries the meaning of Jesus forward through the gift of his Holy Spirit. It carries the meaningfulness of his Father's transcendent, self-revealing, self-investing love for Jesus and for all mankind. Jesus' experience of being cherished and graced by his Father is communicated in his cherishing and gracing others. The theme of sharing God's gift of his love in Christ with others appears in Eph. 4:32: ". . . be kind to one another, tenderhearted, forgiving one another, as God in Christ forgave you."

If God's gift of love is offered to all, religious conversion can happen to many, and they can form a community to sustain one another in their self-transformation, helping one another to work out the implications and fulfill the promise of their new life.[6] The gift itself, as distinct from its manifestations, is transcultural.[7] It is given with the same gracious meaning for all mankind, even if it is apprehended in as many different manners as there are different cultures.

The life, death, and resurrection story of the incarnate Word can be seen as making the ineffable meaning and love of God for us more comprehensible. Jesus had to struggle to bring to expression through words, images, and parables, through the use of his senses and imagination, the meaning and goodness of the ineffable reality of his Father's love, that fullness of mind and heart that he himself enjoyed and knew to be God's ultimate purpose in creation. The Father's love that he receives and accepts as the integrating center of his life is the reality to which Christian faith believes every person is constitutively oriented and ultimately destined. Jesus summons everyone to this destiny and warns them of the risks involved: ". . . it is a narrow gate and a hard road that leads to life, and only a few find it" (Mt. 7:14). The rejection of God's gift of love, and the ultimate destiny it intends for all humankind, seems to be a grim possibilty in the exercise of human freedom. The misuse of human freedom, and its dire consequences, are of concern to one who always did the things that were acceptable to his loving Father.

THE MANIFESTATION AND PROCLAMATION OF GOD'S GIFT OF HIS LOVE

The *manifestation* of the sacred precedes its *proclamation*. The incarnate meaning of God's love in Jesus precedes the proclamation of that meaning.[8] The manifestation of God's gift of his love and its effects constitute the foundational experience, as distinct from its expression. Jesus accepts his life from beginning to end confidently, in patience and humility, as the gift of an incomprehensible Love whom he addresses as "Father." His acceptance is possible because of his lived conviction that such incomprehensible Love exists. His acceptance is a powerful manifestation of the sacred that initiates, inspires, preserves, and perfects the same conviction in others. It has the power of a sacrament, something that communicates the grace it signifies. Inasmuch as we cannot do what we cannot imagine, at least in some way, we need the incarnate Word of God's incomprehensible love for us in order to

imagine that love and to follow Jesus' way of fidelity to its grace and demand. Jesus empowers the "imagination" of Christian faith with a new way
of imagining ourselves, our world, and our God. He empowers a new way
of life to overcome the impotency of the human spirit to imagine and to do
what God's gift of love demands for the resurrection of the just. The crucified and risen Jesus has radically transformed the human consciousness and
imagination of believers in a way that inspires them to believe, to hope, and
to love as he did in response to God's gift of his love. What he is and does
empowers believers to go and do likewise, so that they in turn are able to
inspire others to accept God's gift of his love as Jesus did.

For Christian faith, Jesus Christ manifests the sacred Love that he
proclaims. The power of manifestation grounds the impact of his proclamation. The impact of the sacred is apprehended and felt before it is articulated in parables and "stories of God." The Christian community lives in
and by the same powerful reality that Jesus Christ manifested and proclaimed.
It manifests and proclaims the Good News that Jesus Christ is the decisive
word and true manifestation of God and humanity. The Christian community is the sacrament of the Good News of the incomprehensible Love that
encompasses every human life within the universal story. The Word of this
Love is the origin, ground, and fulfillment of that story's ultimate meaning.
Made flesh in Jesus Christ, the Word manifests and proclaims that story's
ultimate value and goodness as deriving from the Father.

Christian communities trace their origin to the person of Jesus; his incarnate meaning functions as an outer word that mediates their religious conversion, specifies it as Christian, and renders community possible. Individuals
enter the field of experience that renders religious community possible when
they begin to "fall in love in an unrestricted manner," when they "surrender to what is transcendent in lovableness."

Only when religiously transformed subjectivity begins to mediate itself
through meaning can religious community take rise: "Before it enters the
world mediated by meaning, religion is the prior word God speaks to us by
flooding our hearts with his love. That prior word pertains, not to the world
mediated by meaning, but to the world of immediacy, to the unmediated
experience of the mystery of love and awe."[10]

This mediation of conversion-through-meaning provides a key for understanding the formation of the Church and its use of the New Testament and
other means to communicate its inner word, God's gift of the Spirit of Jesus
Christ. The authenticity of Christian conversion finds its measure not so much
in words (proclamation) as in deeds (manifestation) by which we follow Jesus'
self-sacrificing love in obedience to God and in the service of the neighbor.
Jesus manifests self-giving Love in the service and salvation of others; he
proclaims that same Love in the Great Commandment. He manifests and

proclaims the grace and demand of that Love that is the ground of Christian conversion as event, process, and fulfillment.

CONVERSION: THE AIM OF MANIFESTATION AND PROCLAMATION

The process of tradition, originating with the contemporaries of Jesus, mediates the incarnate meaning of Jesus' words, deeds, and destiny. The meaning perceived in Jesus by Christian faith was committed to writing at an early stage of the process. The books of the New Testament present a verbal expression of the meaning of Jesus that subsequent Christian tradition has accepted as adequate and in some sense normative of what constitutes the event and process of Christian conversion.

Literary criticism has drawn attention to the prehistory of the New Testament documents, and form criticism has traced that prehistory back to its oral stage. Scholars recognize the importance of the preaching situation, with its intent and requirements, at the beginning of the process from which the New Testament emerged.

Early Christian preaching attempted to communicate a "gospel" or good news. Its acceptance entailed a conversion on the part of the hearers. The interest of the early Christian witness lay in religious conversion. Christian preaching thematized this dynamic under the rubric of becoming a disciple of Jesus, and proclaimed it as the authentic fulfillment of our humanity.[11] The witness to Jesus was "good news" for all humankind; the call to follow him promised authentic fulfillment and deliverance from the power that evil has to thwart that fulfillment. In this perspective, the unity of the New Testament lies in the proclamation *(kerygma)* from which it originates. Witness to Jesus formed the content of the preaching; and its intent was religious conversion. It proclaimed the importance of Jesus' life, death, and destiny for others in an effort to convince its hearers of the meaning that Christian faith found in Jesus and to persuade them to accept and live out the values inherent in that meaning. For Christians themselves, it implied the task of bringing to full expression and verbally articulating the meaning that was incarnate in Jesus.[12]

The foundational experience of God's gift of love is affirmed by Christian faith in its expression of the meaning incarnate in Jesus. *Kerygma* is the public proclamation or preaching of this meaning. *Didache* is the teaching that expresses the revelation of this incarnate meaning conceptually and logically in doctrines. *Paraenesis* is the ethical teaching that expresses the moral demands of God's gift of love, the incarnate meaning Jesus has for human conduct.[13] *Diakonia* is the ministry and service that is the task consequent upon the reception of the gift whose incarnate meaning is Jesus. *Eucharistia* is celebration of the sacramental rite in thanksgiving for the gift; it is the central act of the Christian community's worship and, implicitly, the manifestation of the unrestricted and transcendent character of God's gift of love. *Martyrion* is the witness or evidence of faith in the truth of the incarnate meaning of God's gift of love in Jesus and in one's own life. *Koinonia* is the fellowship and communion of the faithful who share this incarnate meaning in Jesus and in their own lives as a common good. *Leitourgia,* the divine worship of those who share this common good, expresses its presence and promise.

United by the same fundamental meaning of God's gift of his love incarnate in Jesus and in their own lives, individual Christians give a common expression to it in all these and other ways.

The principle of unity that is operative (the interior word) in Jesus and his followers unites them in the manifestation and proclamation of the Good News (outer word). All the external expressions of God's gift of his love and more are secondary, derivative, and subordinate. Their role is to dispose us for an interior union with God-effected grace (God's gift of his love).[14] All these external expressions (outer word) make their appeal for conversion on a level prior to that on which doctrinal systems and organized institutions arise.[15] By conveying the meaning incarnate in Jesus, they supply a basis of meaning upon which religiously converted subjects may, and in fact do, make common judgments and decisions. The New Testament, for example, is the expression of faith for the cultivation of faith. It exercises its proper function by conveying symbolically the meaning of God's gift of his love for us that is incarnate in Jesus. It makes its appeal in symbolic mode for a conversion to the same faith, hope, and love that was the response of Jesus to God.

The New Testament symbolizes the realm of God's transcendent love in Trinitarian imagery, interpreting that realm in interpersonal terms. From the New Testament, the converted subject learns to identify the ultimate source and term of the love that he has received and accepted in Christian conversion as the Father of Jesus Christ, the God of Israel who has sent his Son among humankind. The New Testament proclaims that Jesus is the incarnate Word or expression and meaning of the Father, who completes his mission of creative and redemptive love by sending the Spirit.[16]

The New Testament's Trinitarian imagery of the realm of God's love would seem to reflect the human experience of it in the two moments of religious conversion. The Father and the Son are analogously as distinct as the speaker and his word. The word is rooted in and at the service of the subject who speaks it. Ineffable Mystery makes itself effable in its incarnate Word. The incarnate meaning of Jesus proceeds from the transcendent meaning of his Father's love for humankind; it is rooted in and at the service of that love which means more than mere human words can adequately express. Our linguistic and conceptual expression of this love proceeds from our prelinguistic and supraconceptual consciousness of it and "intends" the transcendent realm of this love beyond words and concepts. Jesus is the human expression of a suprahuman Love for humankind; he is, for Christian faith, the incarnate Word or meaning of that Love for humankind.[17]

RELIGIOUS CONVERSION IN BOTH LIGHT AND DARKNESS

The two moments of religious conversions might be illuminated in terms of Christian *apophatic* and *kataphatic* mysticisms. The apophatic way of mystical life, the *via negativa,* stresses that because God is the ever-greater God, so radically different from any creature, God is best known by negation, elimination, forgetting, unknowing, without images and symbols, in darkness. The kataphatic way of mystical life, the *via affirmativa,* underscores finding God in all things. It stresses a definite similarity between God and creatures, that God *can* be reached by creatures, images, symbols, because he has manifested himself in creation and salvation history. Above all, God has expressed himself in his incarnate Word, in his real symbol, the icon of God.

Any genuine Christian mysticism, according to Harvey Egan, must contain apophatic as well as kataphatic elements.[18] Egan affirms that both traditions proffer many strengths.

The apophatic tradition underscores the fact that the human heart is satisfied by nothing other than God. It points to the God greater than our hearts, the ineffable, nameless, utter Mystery, who can be loved only because he has first loved us. Egan asserts that through dark, simple, nonconceptual, loving surrender, this mysticism tramples our rigid concepts of God, destroys our idols, lets God be God. It offers a more Father-and-Spirit-centered spirituality to correct certain Christological imbalances:

> The radical depths of Jesus, his identity as the Son of God, as God-with-us who leads us to God-above-us and gives us God-in-us, are mystically tasted and insisted upon. Precisely because Jesus Christ is the real symbol of God in the world, and a real symbol is one with its origin and yet distinct, the apophatic tradition highlights the ''What-is-symbolized'' by the symbol. Moreover, only in the light of the divinity does the full meaning of Jesus' humanity reveal itself.[19]

The kataphatic tradition affirms that God has communicated himself in a history whose highpoint is the person of Jesus Christ. His life, death, and destiny is the ''history'' of God himself. The way to God is through the incarnate meaning of that history. The Ineffable has expressed itself in the history of Jesus Christ, disclosing to faith the ultimate meaning and significance of all life. To enter into that history, therefore, ensures the proper entry into transcendence, the experience of the Father, Son, and Holy Spirit, and not some other experience of transcendence easily confused with the God experience.[20] This tradition focuses upon God-with-us, Egan affirms, as the way to the ever-greater God and the Giver of God-in-us.[21] Its incarnational foundation is its strength.

Both traditions apprehend the same purifying, illuminating, transforming Love in complementary ways that are characteristic of Christian conversion and its expression. The apophatic apprehension of this Love as secretly animating and transforming creation is complemented by the kataphatic apprehension of this same Love in its external expressions. The same Love is experienced and affirmed in darkness and in light. The Love experienced in apophatic interiority and darkness expresses itself, incarnates itself, and unfolds itself in a visible, tangible way through all the dimensions of human life. The apophatic experience of this Love in authentically Christian living is never divorced from the kataphatic elements of the Church's sacramental, liturgical, and scriptural life. We experience the transcendental as well as the historical dimension of God's self-communication in the foundational event and process of religious conversion and its expression within the community of Christian faith.[22] By surrendering to the Mystery of God in Christ, the human subject also surrenders to the deepest dynamism of his being, his deepest meaning as a person. This loving surrender is apophatic in relation to Mystery and kataphatic in relation to Jesus Christ and his community of faith. Egan affirms that what Christ is by nature, created self-transcendence perfectly surrendering to the Father's loving Mystery, man is by grace.[23] Grace, God's gift of his love, leads faith into the Father's Mystery, the Son's Truth, and the Spirit's Love. The transparency of the Father's meaning incarnate in Jesus Christ is the kataphatic entrance into apophatic mystery.[24]

CHRISTIAN CONVERSION AS COMMUNICATING THE INCOMMUNICABLE

In his article, "Communicating the Incommunicable," Thomas Cooper casts light upon the Christian paradox of having to communicate an experience that is incommunicable, inasmuch as we cannot divide God from his mystery. We cannot separate the comprehensible from the incomprehensible, the communicable from the incommunicable:

> As Catholics, we confess with the Fourth Lateran Council that God is at once incomprehensible and inexpressible. With Clement of Alexandria we know that in Christ we come to apprehend God who remains the unknowable. We are faced here with the paradoxical nature of all Christian theology: that in Christ the immortal has taken on our mortality, the transcendent Godhead has revealed itself immanent to the world in the ikon which is Jesus Christ. With the fathers of Chalcedon we have to assert the unity of the Creator with the creature in Christ, neither confusing the natures nor dividing the person. All theology resolves itself into an

affirmation of contradictory statements united only by the experience of the mystery of their conjuction. With Nicholas of Cusa we experience God as the *coincidentia oppositorum*. . . . God remains unknown and yet we can address Him as *Abba,* Father.[25]

The experience of the self, according to Karl Rahner, is not only anterior to every other experience, but the very condition of the possibility of all other experiences; it is a unity with, though not of course identical with, the experience of God.[26] The openness of man to the transcendent, his orientation to mystery, implies for Rahner a real, though nonthematic, experience of God: it is neither expressed nor expressible in concepts or categories. It is an awareness of myself, prior to every thought, feeling or wish, that is grounded in God's gift to me of my humanity (human nature). It precedes both my learning to speak and my ability to think in concepts.[27]

If Rahner is right, it is through this prior experience that we are able to accept the incarnate meaning of Jesus Christ as our own, for we have experienced the same meaning prior to our study of the Gospels. The imagery of the Gospels gives form to the amorphous primordial experience of God's gift of himself that grounds our acceptance of his incarnate meaning in Jesus Christ.[28] The same Love is experienced in both moments. The primordial experience leads us to its incarnate meaning in the crucified and risen Jesus, God's self-revelation.

The power of the crucified and risen *Jesus* to draw men to himself (Jn. 12:32) is conditioned by the prior drawing by the *Father:* "No man can come to me unless he is drawn by the Father who sent me" (Jn. 6:44). And that prior drawing is an attentive listening and learning: "everyone who has listened to the Father and learned from him, comes to me" (Jn. 6:45).

Eric Voegelin, on the basis of this drawing, distinguishes between revelation and information. Jesus answered to Peter's confession at Caesarea Philippi: "Simon, son of Jonah, you are favored indeed! You did not learn from mortal man; it was revealed to you by my heavenly Father" (Mt. 16:17). Voegelin comments:

> The Matthean Jesus thus agrees with the Johannine (Jn. 6:44) that nobody can recognize the movement of the divine presence in the Son, unless he is prepared for such recognition by the presence of the divine Father in himself. The divine Sonship is not revealed through information tendered by Jesus, but through a man's response to the full presence in Jesus of the same Unknown God by whose presence he is inchoatively moved in his own existence. . . . In order to draw the distinction between revelation and information, as well as to avoid the derailment from one to the other, the episode closes with the charge of Jesus to the disciples "to tell no one that he is the Christ" (Mt. 16:20).[29]

THE SUPERSTRUCTURE (BELIEF) AND INFRASTRUCTURE (FAITH) OF LOVE

Voegelin's distinction finds a counterpart in William Johnston's distinction between a superstructure which he calls belief and an infrastructure which he calls faith.[30] The superstructure is the outer word, the outer revelation, the word spoken in history and conditioned by culture. The infrastructure, Johnston explains, is the interior word, the word spoken to the heart, the inner revelation.[31] In the Gospel narrative Jesus encounters men of faith who do not know clearly the object of their faith (e.g. Jn. 9:36). Such is the inner word uttered by the Holy Spirit who floods our hearts with his love.

This inner gift, according to Johnston, is at first formless: it is prior to any outer cultural formulation and often lives in the hearts of the most un-suspecting people who could never formulate it in words. The inner gift or light of faith leads to the outer revelation and is nourished by it: the inner prompting of the Spirit leads us to the Word so that we cry out, "Jesus is Lord" (Rm. 10:9) with the realization that the God who speaks to the heart also speaks through history.[32] The inner gift and light of faith leads one to the outer word of Scripture and sacrament and community, where it is nourished by the exterior revelation; here it develops and grows through an ongoing self-surrender to the grace and demand of God as apprehended in the historical particularities of our individual and corporate life stories.

Our knowledge and love are never perfect in this life; our authenticity is never fully achieved. Conflicts, struggles, imperfections, and failure are part of the experience of being in love with God. Fidelity to the gift of God's unrestricted love is the life-project of faith, as formulated in the Hebrew-Christian tradition. The Gospel recalls Deuteronomy's imperative: "You shall love the Lord your God with all your heart, and with all your soul, and with all your strength, and with all your mind; and your neighbor as yourself" (Lk. 10:27).

The meaning of the Gospel narrative is not, primarily, informational or cognitive. The prime function of its meaning is constitutive, as Lonergan uses the term. *Constitutive* meaning is the meaning that modifies the one who means, making us who we are, as the constitution of a state is the basis of its existence.[33] What is "meant"? The term of this transforming meaning is the subject in his conscious existence and relationship to other subjects before God. The Gospel constitutes a community in its relationship to itself, to all others, and to God. The Gospel intends our conversion as both event and process.

The Church employs its Gospels as means for communicating and cultivating its foundational experience of God's love in Jesus Christ and in his Spirit given to us. A gospel is not an end in itself; it is meant to be used for fostering that gift of God's love which is the life of the Church. A gospel is written to serve the purpose of the grace and demand of God's transcendent love in Jesus Christ and his Church; it articulates and objectifies the meaning and value and demands of this love for us, both as individuals and as a community. It symbolizes the call of a transcendent love empowering and summoning individuals to transcend themselves by accepting its grace and demand for life within the Christian community. Similarly, it symbolizes God's transcendent love summoning the Christian community to transcend itself in communicating its foundational experience to the world through its distinctive service of the world. All true theology is a reflection on the role of conversion in the lives of individuals and of society.

Carlo Martini's working hypothesis about the four gospels functioning as four manuals that correspond to the needs of four distinct moments in Christian formation can be applied to the realm of God's self-investing love. Thus, Mark serves as the Christian community's manual introducing the catechumen to the mystery of God's self-investing love in Jesus Christ. Matthew functions as the catechist's manual for helping the newly baptized to live according to the exigencies of this self-investing love within the Church. Luke-Acts is the manual for learning how to bear witness to the meaning and value of this love for the world. John is employed as the manual for the grand synthesis of the mature Christian who has lived out the demands of this self-investing love in following Jesus and his Church in the service of the world and now asks what is at the heart of his Christian experience. The self-investing dynamic of God's love is understood to be the origin and ground and destiny of the Jesus story, the Church story, and the world story.

Not to have grasped this is to have missed the point of the dynamic which constitutes the ultimate meaning of the fourfold Gospel. Communion with God implies a participation in the dynamic of his self-investing love on a level prior to that on which doctrinal systems and organized institutions arise. The Gospels can be effective only in proportion as we receive them as new information about someone we already know. They presuppose a prior love of God, a love which God, through his Spirit, has poured into our hearts. The Gospels symbolize the realm of God's unrestricted love to which human kind is constitutively oriented by presenting Jesus as God's self-revelation, or Word. They summon us to follow Jesus in his fundamental "self-others-world-Mystery" relationship for the authentic fulfillment of our humanity. The authenticity of our response to Jesus' injunction to love God above all else finds its measure in the deeds by which we follow his way to human authenticity through self-investing love for the neighbor. The Gospels are meant to illuminate our careful and intelligent reflection upon that prior gift of God's love and its demands for human authenticity.

5

WRITING A GOSPEL

Writing a gospel is one way of learning to *use* a gospel for discovering the quality of our relationship to the transcendent love of God in Jesus Christ, in his Church, and in his world. Jesus symbolizes the meaning and value of this love, what it does and what it does not. The way we tell his story implies the way *we* comprehend the purpose of God's love in ourselves, others, and the world. The storyteller is in his storytelling. The gospel writer tells us about himself in telling us his story of Jesus.

At the beginning of a course I teach on the spirituality of the Gospels, I have had my students write a gospel in order to come to some experiential understanding of what it means to be the author of a gospel. For an appropriate psychological state, they were to imagine that all the New Testaments throughout the world had been destroyed and that theirs would be the one and only written link with the original four Gospels. They were to write their own synoptic gospel, using only the words of the four actual Gospels. The title of the gospel would be "The Gospel According to (Student's Name)." Not more than two thousand words were allowed for telling the Good News. Each gospel was to have an architectonic unity, at least one parable, one miracle, one saying of Jesus. About one-fourth or one-fifth of the gospel had to treat of the passion and death of Jesus.

When the gospels had been written, they were exchanged. Each student wrote a commentary on the gospel that was given to him aimed at discerning (1) the portrait of Jesus and (2) the portrait of the author. What is the meaning and value of Jesus for the writer of this gospel? At what levels of consciousness does Jesus speak to the author? What does the author expect of Jesus? At what level of personal need does Jesus encounter the author? What is the author's particular interest in Jesus? What is his particular feeling toward Jesus?

General questions for a critical reading of these gospels — to help discern the portrait of Jesus and of the author — are the following.

1. Make a list of all the verbs that describe the agency of Jesus. What Jesus does in the gospel implies what he does for the author of the gospel. The author implies that Jesus will do this also for the reader of his gospel.
2. What does Jesus say in this gospel? This is what the author hears Jesus saying and, therefore, implicitly expects his reader to hear the same Jesus addressing him with the same words.
3. Is the risen Christ active in this gospel? Does the gospel end with Jesus' resurrection from the dead?
4. How does the author see Jesus' basic self-others-world-God relationships? Is Jesus regarded as more solitary than social? As more receptive than active? As more suffering than joyful? As more among women than among men? As more among friends than among adversaries? As more a speaker than a doer? As more often rebuking than encouraging? As more often criticizing than approving? As more demanding than accepting? As more comprehensibly human than mysteriously divine? As more courageously confronting difficult situations than being welcomed by admiring followers?

The original Evangelists do not exclude one or the other of these elements in creating their balanced portrait of Jesus as both their crucified and risen Lord, illuminating the mystery that defines every human life. On the one hand, Jesus symbolizes the grace of God's love accepting persons wherever they are; on the other hand, he symbolizes the summons of the gracious love to transcend what we are in becoming sons of God.

Some students wrote a gospel in which the third person prevails, creating the perspective of a detached spectator. Their avoidance of the second person suggests the absence of a personal relationship with the crucified and risen Jesus. It suggests that they do not hear him speaking to them today. Luke's Gospel, in contrast, underscores the ever-present grace and demand of God's love: "Today this scripture has been fulfilled even as you listen" (4:21); "Today I must stay at your home" (19:5); "Today salvation has come to this house" (19:9); "Today you shall be with me in Paradise" (23:43). Luke's use of the second person, his use of such words as "today" and "now," implies that the transcendent realm of God's love, symbolized by the entire story of Jesus, is ever-present and summoning us. Its reality and goodness actually touch Luke's existence as an individual within the community of Christian faith, inspiring him to write a gospel about it for others. His Gospel thematizes the immediacy of an understanding beyond words, his religious conversion, the love that he has received and accepted as the integrating center of his life.

The exercise of writing a gospel helps the writer to discover those areas of life that are most affected by the meaning and value of God's love in Jesus Christ. The writer should treasure whatever dimension of the Good News that especially moves or interests him. This is its special value for him. This is the particular sector of his consciousness where the mystery of God's love finds its point of entry into his life; consequently, it must be cultivated with care so as to become fruitful. Its fruitfulness will vary with the cultivation it receives. The radicalism of the New Testament message is an ideal toward which growth will always be slow and often uncertain. Inasmuch as our action must always be within the limits of possibility, a rigorism that would challenge us beyond our powers is counterproductive. Discouragement is the temptation of temptations. One persons' effective freedom is limited to such a way that he cannot achieve what many others find feasible. The focus of the Gospel-summons is on the use, rather than measure, of our effective freedom. It challenges us to stretch the limits of our freedom, but not to the breaking-point. It manifests a readiness to meet us wherever we happen to be and to lead us on from there. As William V. Dych notes:

> "What must *I* do to gain eternal life," Jesus is asked in the Gospel story. What *I* must do might be quite different from what somebody else must do, and I am the one who has to discover it in the particular configuration of concrete circumstances which make up my life and existence. There is no antecedent blueprint in a book somewhere simply to be copied or imitated. In fact, when "living by the book" makes me miss the very concrete realities right there before my eyes, then "the letter kills," as St. Paul says.[1]

The most severe threats of the Gospel are for those who do not want to be led at all, those committed to the illusion of self-sufficiency:

> But alas for you who are rich: you are having your consolation now.
> Alas for you who have your fill now: you shall go hungry.
> Alas for you who laugh now: you shall mourn and weep.
> Alas for you when the world speaks well of you! This was
> the way their ancestors treated the false prophets (Lk. 6:24-26).

The Gospels are rich in pedagogical resources for cultivating the gift of God's love at the many different levels where we had become conscious of its presence and summons. No situation of human life is too extreme to be included within the scope of its redemptive purpose. It implicitly invites everyone to write his own gospel within the effective limits of our freedom for responding to the gift of God's love in our basic self-others-world-God relationships. It invites us to witness to its reality and goodness.

The exercise of writing a gospel, using only the words of the four Evangelists, has the advantage of not taxing the creative resources of individuals. The Gospels provide a basic *lingua franca* that we may employ to describe our relationship to the mystery that defines our lives. The use of this *lingua franca* respects the privacy of the writer, who might not wish to publicize the events of his interior life; at the same time, it permits the individuality of the writer's perspective to emerge in the selection of material. The writer does not have to invent a religious language or set of religious symbols. The number of words is arbitrary; however, the fewer permitted, the more radical the selectivity and the clearer the manifestation of the writer's perspective.

Students writing a gospel are generally unaware of how self-revealing their gospels are. The experience of becoming a synoptic writer of a gospel creates a context for a meaningful discussion of the process that brought the first four Gospels into existence, and of the relation of this process to the religious conversion that occurs in the immediacy of the subject's consciousness, in a supraconceptual, existential experience beyond words. Only when religiously transformed subjectivity begins to mediate itself through meaning, myth, narrative, stories of God and the like can religious community take rise. This mediation of conversion through the objectification of its meaning provides the context for the Church's use of the New Testament.

Writing our own parables is an exercise related to that of becoming contemporary synoptic gospel writers. In this exercise, however, students were not expected to use the texts of the New Testament. They were to compose a story, based on their own personal experience, to communicate one dimension of their lived understanding of what it means to receive and share the gift of God's love. Creating our own parables is doing what Jesus did; in some respects, it can express a greater fidelity to the Gospel truth than the merely mechanical repetition of Jesus' parables.

John Drury relates that the poet Edwin Muir in his autobiography saw his own life as a narrative on the two levels of individual difference and shared mystery, calling them story and fable.[2] Story refers to a man's biography, where fact is linked to fact: birth and parents, changes of address, marriage and jobs. It marks him off from other people. It is his alone. But the fable is always impinging on it. This is a chain of images and archetypes which we do not entirely understand and which only become clear in dreams, visions, and myths: the country of innocence, the fall, the journey, and transfiguration. Thus story tells us that when the poet was a boy, the Muir family moved from a good farm on the Orkneys to a bad one, and then to Glasgow. But what is happening in the realm of fable is a fall from innocence into experience and alienation. It is in the realm of fable that we have our deepest connections with one another. In biography we are distinct. It must be to the fable that his wife Willa refers when she says that "he never ceased to believe that his experience resembled the experience of everyone else living on earth."[3]

The quality of our experience ultimately determines the shape of our autobiographies, biographies, histories, novels, parables, stories of God, theologies. We express in these manifold ways what can be found within our conscious experience on successive, related, but qualitatively different, levels: the *empirical,* on which level we sense, perceive, imagine, feel, speak, move; the *intellectual* level on which we inquire, come to understand, express what we have understood, work out the implications and presuppositions of our expressions; the *rational* level, on which we reflect, marshal the evidence, judge the truth or falsity, certainty or probability, of a statement; the *responsible* level, on which we are concerned with ourselves, our own operations, our goals, and so deliberate about possible courses of action, evaluate them, decide and carry out our decisions.[4] Our manifold ways of storytelling, of philosophizing and of theologizing, are indices of what is going on at the four levels of our consciousness and intentionality; they are objectifications of our conscious intending of the true and the real, of the good and the worthwhile, as unique individuals with a unique history. As such, they are objectifications that are not deduced from abstract laws about human nature in general; rather, they derive from the concrete life stories of individuals in search of true meaning and value. The authenticity of our lives grounds the authenticity of the manifold ways in which we objectify our search.

6

THE BEATITUDE OF GOD
TRANSFORMING HUMAN STORY

Imagination and motivation are closely linked. The way we imagine ourselves, others, the world, and God conditions the way we feel about ourselves, others, the world, and God. Jesus told many parables to educate our
imaginations, our feelings, and our thinking about ourselves, others, the
world, and God; for there is no decision-making, action, and life story whose
shape is not conditioned by a particular way of imagining, feeling, and thinking about ourselves and our interrelationships. The content that we give our
basic images of truth, love, happiness, success, and failure should be defined
(in terms of our commitment to Christ) by the content that his entire life
story gave to them. "Love" in the statement, "God is love," is not an abstraction; its content has been sharply defined in all the particularities of the
life story of Jesus Christ. The experience of Jesus Christ's life, death, and
resurrection story has given Christian faith its definitive way of thinking and
feeling about love, truth, happiness, goodness, success, and failure. Jesus'
way of imagining God was radiated at every level of his being, permeating
his thoughts, desires, interests, ideals, feelings, decisions, and actions. His
life story is the historical articulation of what Christian faith means by God-
in-relation-to-man and man-in-relation-to-God. This unique relationship, affirmed to exist in Jesus Christ, is normative for our thinking and feeling about
God. Only in Jesus Christ does it become clear what truth, goodness, happiness, and life, for which humankind strives, really are. In his life story the
question about human and divine truth, goodness, happiness, and life, is
definitively answered.

Everything that Jesus is and does images God for Christian faith. His parables provide many images of God, whose content ultimately derives from

his own life as the parable of God. His cross is the image of God as life-giving; it defines the meaning of "love" in faith's affirmation that "God is love." Authentic love, then, is life-giving in the way that the cross has made this clear to Christian faith. Our understanding of human and divine love is correlative. The story that Jesus' life tells, together with his many stories (parables) about God, is meant to give a definite content to our basic images of God, ourselves, others, the world, life, love, truth, happiness, etc. St. Ignatius of Loyola, for example, in his *Spiritual Exercises,* is powerfully affected by the image of a life-giving God when he envisions the creator as graciously serving his creatures as a humble slave. God is graciously present in all his creatures that we might have life more fully. Our experience of being "graced" enables us to affirm that God is gracious; our experience of the cross enables us to affirm that God is life-giving love, unqualified and unconditional love.

Our Image of God

The Gospel truth of the story that Jesus' life tells educates our belief about the God we know exists. Everyone implicitly believes in some god or other: reality cannot be interpreted and evaluated without an implicit belief in some ultimate principle of interpretation that gives its meaning to the manifold of human experience. Aquinas taught that the existence of God is not the object of faith: we know that God exists, however differently we interpret and imagine him, his world, ourselves, and salvation. For Aquinas, we believe in Jesus Christ and what his Church teaches about God and the way to him. Christian revelation deals with what we *believe* about the God we *know* exists. It concerns what we think about him, how we are affected by our way of imagining and experiencing him. Do we see him as the businessman that the elder son in the parable of the prodigal saw when he was unable to understand how his father could celebrate the return of a son who had squandered so much of his goods? Is he the God of *quid pro quo* relationships, the bookkeeper who values us according to some mystical profit system? Jesus does not think so; in fact, his parable of the prodigal son (Lk. 15) not only compares God's love to the unconditional love of a father, but also implies that the elder son's false image of his father and his unconditional love made it impossible for him to understand how his brother could be forgiven. The elder son's complaint that no celebration had ever been held in his honour, after years of faithful service, implied his own bad self-image, one based on his inability to understand a father's love. He sees himself as a hired man.

Jesus realized how important it is for us to imagine God as he truly is; for our way of imagining God is all of a piece with the way we imagine ourselves, our neighbour, and our world. His many parables represent many attempts to correct our false ways of thinking and feeling about God, ourselves, others, and the world. The way we grasp the complexity of life conditions the way we relate ourselves to the things of life; it involves the meaning and the value that we attach to the complexity of life as a whole and to the things of life in particular.

As the parable of God, Jesus Christ enabled faith to imagine its true possibilities. Our vision of the world may not give sufficient attention to our objective possibilities for growth and development, with the result that we spend a lifetime in a relatively closed but safe universe without approximating geniune selfhood. The inability to imagine such possibilities characterizes the routine work and conventional values unquestioningly accepted by the spiritually obtuse. Jesus has enabled faith to imagine that life which really counts as one of life-giving love's dying and rising for and with others in the power of the creator's life-giving Spirit of love, the Spirit that the Church confidently cries out for in its prayer *Veni Creator Spiritus*. Life-giving love creates new lives by dying and rising for others. Christ does not keep his risen life to himself.

We cannot do what we can in no way imagine. The story that Jesus Christ's life-death-resurrection has told, however, empowers a new way of imagining ourselves, our world, and our God, and therefore a new way of life. He has overcome the impotency of the human spirit to imagine and do what the creative Spirit of life-giving love demands for the resurrection of the just in faith's orientation to a new life in the kingdom of God. Human hearts have been graced with the Spirit of life-giving love, truly empowering them to experience, imagine, believe in, and live according to the love that survives death itself. Jesus Christ has radically transformed the human consciousness and imagination of believers.[1] On the assumption that every person is an incipient story in search of his true story, Jesus Christ has empowered faith to imagine the way to our true life story as one of dying and rising for others in the life-giving Spirit of his love.

OUR TRUE STORY

John's theology of the pre-existent Word implies that our true story is in the storyteller; his theology of the Word made flesh implies that the storyteller is in his true story. The Church is the community of persons helping one another to find their true story in Jesus Christ, the way to our true life story in the resurrection of the just. The lifelong orientation to our true story implies that the just are even now rising in the daily experience of self-transcending, life-giving love, creatively imaging in their lives the coming of the kingdom. Faith can "see" what God is doing in their lives. Such lives make God's doings understandable, truly credible, and imaginable; they make it possible for us to go and do likewise. That is most important for the coming of the kingdom of God; for we cannot do what we can in no way imagine. To receive what God is giving and to give that in turn to others is the storylistening that empowers our lives to tell the story of the good news that we have learned in Jesus Christ.

Christ's teaching of the beatitudes describes the way to our true story, to the kingdom of God where our true story has its origin and destination. His beatitudes bespeak the harmony of divine and human wills that Jesus Christ experiences and reveals in his story of life-giving love. The truth of the beatitudes, like that of the way to our true story, is not at all apparent; in fact, it seems to contradict everything that we commonly associate with human happiness and the good life. Jesus' radically different way of imagining human happiness recalls Isaiah's words: "My thoughts are not your thoughts" (Isa. 55:8). God's ways are not to be judged by man's ways; his happiness (beatitude) must not be imagined according to our norms of the good life. The cross, the symbol of life-giving love, is not what anyone could humanly imagine as the way to true happiness in the kingdom of God; however, Jesus Christ has empowered faith to imagine the life-giving love of the cross as our true way to the happiness of God himself.

TRUE HAPPINESS

The happiness of life-giving love is not precluded by poverty, hunger, and mourning; on the contrary, it spontaneously relates itself to the poor, the suffering, the persecuted. It is the happiness of the spontaneously life-giving to the life-needing that Jesus himself experienced in both seeking and doing his Father's will in the concrete particularities of every day. It is the happiness of the Father whose life-giving will (= love) is being done in the accomplishment of Jesus Christ's true story. The Father, the storyteller, is in his Son, his true story. And the truth of his story is heard in the darkness of human poverty, misery, and suffering. The beatitudes reflect faith's way of seeing God in the darkness of the human condition.[2] Life-giving love is experienced by faith as an omnipresence that empowers us to rejoice with those who rejoice and to weep with those who weep.

The God of Christian faith is not the detached observer of Mount Olympus; rather, he is the fullness of life participating in the fullness of human life in both its light and darkness, joy and sorrow, pleasure and pain, strength and weakness.[3] The joy of life-giving love, in the fifteenth chapter of Luke's Gospel, is that of a shepherd finding his lost sheep, of a housewife finding her lost coin, of a father finding his lost son. The beatitude, the joy, the happiness of life-giving love is never absent from our darkest moments, when such finding generally takes place; it is not dependent upon human prestige, human success, human power, human wealth, and excellence.

Only after the death and resurrection of Jesus Christ would the disciples be able to understand the meaning of the beatitudes. Only after their experience of Christ's life-giving Spirit of love (Pentecost) would they be able to imagine truly and joyfully the beatitude of God that Christ himself had experienced and communicated to them. Now they understood the scriptural provisions concerning the Messiah's suffering as the true way to humankind's ultimate possibilities for happiness. The beatitudes are implicitly an articulation of the way of the cross as the only true way for experiencing the joy of life-giving love and for affirming that "God is love," that he has given us his Spirit of love through the gift of his beloved Son.

Freely giving what he freely receives, Jesus Christ communicates his Father's meaning for us as the Word of God and his Father's happiness to us as the beatitude of God. His lifelong fidelity to the grace and demand of his Father's will discloses to faith the gift of the true meaning and happiness that his Father intends for every life story. "Not my will, but thine," Jesus prays in struggling to discern within the particularities of daily life the truth to be done for the realization of his true story. God is the giver of life stories; he intends that they should be truly good life stories. The life story of Jesus Christ reveals to faith both what God means by a truly good life story and a truly happy ending. As the Word of God, he is the storyteller's truly good life story for us; as the beatitude of God, he is the storyteller's joy in his telling it for us.

The beatitudes express the felt presence and dynamism of life-giving love in the hearts of those with whom it is pleased: "Glory to God in the highest and on earth peace among men with whom he is pleased" (Lk. 2:14). Christian faith implicitly associates the joy of the beatitudes with the birth of Jesus, with the glory of God, and with the peace that God has brought us in Christ. Jesus' way of the cross tells us that the crucified is beatified through his perfect receptivity to the life-giving love of his Father that he, in turn, communicates to "the poor, the captives, the blind, the oppressed" (Lk. 4:18) . . . "the hungry, the mourners, the persecuted" (Lk. 6:20-22) . . . "the blind, the lame, the lepers, the deaf, the dead, the poor" (Lk. 7:22; 14:21). Beatitude, in this context, is the gift of God rather than the creation of man; and only he who is free enough to lay down his life for others in the spirit of life-giving love finds it. By embracing the fate of the grain of wheat, Jesus Christ communicates the beatitude of his Father: ". . . unless a grain of wheat falls into the earth and dies, it remains alone; but if it dies, it bears much fruit" (Jn. 12:24).

Christian faith is summoned to the beatitude of God through the continual exodus (Departure) of stepping outside itself in living for others. Jesus' cross and resurrection are a restatement of the exodus-idea of the Old Testament. By voluntarily laying down his life for others, Jesus discloses the way to the beatitude of God, the beatitude of life-giving love in its very activity of giving life. Our openness to the beatitude of God can be understood in terms of the Christian exodus-principle: we must no longer live for ourselves, but for others; we must leave ourselves in the spirit of life-giving love to enjoy the beatitude of life-giving love in his giving life to others. The beatitudes are, therefore, no abstract norms to be followed in order to please God; rather, they describe the impact of God's own life in human recipients, that life in which God actually takes pleasure. They bespeak the happiness of life-giving love (God) in Christ and among men.

7

CONVERSION AND BEAUTY

Concreteness communicates in a way that abstractions cannot. The Word is made flesh in Palestine to tell us something about God that no philosophical and theological theorizing can, or ever could, communicate. In fact, the Bible finds the concreteness of stories an indispensable means for telling us the truth about ourselves and God. The excellence of God attracts us in the particulars of the biblical stories. To say who someone is, whether that someone be ourselves or another, eludes precise speech. Hannah Arendt has pointed out that "the moment we want to say *who* somebody is, our very vocabulary leads us astray into saying *what* he is; we get entangled in a description of qualities he necessarily shares with others like him; we begin to describe a type or a 'character' in the old meaning of the word, with the result that his uniqueness escapes us."[1] But she suggests that we can surmount this problem with a story. "*Who* somebody is or was we can know only by knowing the story of which he is himself the hero — his biography, in other words; everything else we know of him, including the work he may have left behind, tells us only *what* he is or was."[2] A story can and does function like a proper name and vice versa.[3] They are indispensable for communicating the irreducible particular, that which cannot be other than it is and thus cannot be accounted for by any other. The concreteness of stories is required for the communication of those matters that we can only describe analogically.[4]

We are drawn to the Father by the dramatic action of the story which Christ's life tells and which the Evangelists retell. This is the indispensable story through which Christians have learned to speak of God. The Church is the community that has been formed by embracing this life story as its own. It exists for the communication of this life story, for the communication of the life that the dramatic action of Christ's life reveals. Action has the dramatic quality of telling a story even when it is that of the Risen Christ within his Church and its history and within his saints and their histories. Who God is, in the Christian context, is communicated in the life story of the Church and its members, a story composed of stories sharing the same intentionality within diversity. As an agent who must be known like other agents, God is known through his story. However, as Stanley Hauerwas remarks, we do not know God's story as told from his point of view; rather, we must learn of God through others' stories of this relationship with him.[5] God is not a concept, a universal, a common noun, but a proper name.

BEAUTY OF GOD MADE FLESH

If Christ is called the "Word" of God made flesh to express our understanding of the meaning of the story that his life tells, he may be called the "Beauty" of God made flesh to express the powerful attraction that the meaning of his story exerts upon us. Our mind-set is the context of the "Word of God"; our heart-set is the context of the "Beauty of God." The unauthentic Christian is a divided person. Although he recognizes the true meaning of the dramatic action of God in the story that Christ's life tells, he is not sufficiently attracted to it that it fully becomes a part of his own life. The unauthentic Christian knows the meaning of Christ, but does not experience the powerful impact of its excellence. Two persons may see (understand) the same painting; however, only one of them may be enraptured by it. Two persons may hear the same music; however, only one may resonate with it. The parable of the sower, found in the three Synoptic Gospels, implies that not all those who recognize the meaning of Christ respond to his beauty. The meaning of the Christ story achieves its appropriate impact only when it is cherished; otherwise, it remains an empty meaning, an unfulfilled meaning, in the recipient. The meaning of the dramatic action of God in Christ is, in one sense, "missed" when it is not lived, enjoyed, and concretely productive. In this case, the Word that God intends to be made flesh is resisted and remains purely an abstract word, unlike the paradigmatic Word that is Christ.

Beauty and happiness are related. Happiness is activity; it is to act to the fullest of one's capacities. The impact of such excellence is that of beauty. The dramatic action of the Christ story, culminating in the resurrection, manifests the fullest of human capacities in the splendor of the Risen Christ and his activities. The personal splendor of God is communicated in the Risen Christ and his Church. We learn that we are Christians through the dramatic action of God in the Christ story that we embrace as our own in the context of his Church, the guarantor of its authenticity.

Plato, systematizing what he found implied in the ordinary Greek use of the word for beauty, held that the beauty of anything is that in which it compels us to admire and desire it: the beautiful is the proper object of love. His theory of beauty is linked also with his theory of moral behavior. Beauty is that for the sake of which we act when action is at its highest excellence. Applying his principle to the self-understanding of Christians, we may say that the dynamic activity of the risen Christ is human action at its highest excellence and that our awareness of it is based on our experience of the moral and spiritual beauty (excellence) of those whose lives are consciously motivated by it. The impact of such persons as individuals and as a community maintains the Christian community in existence by powerfully attracting generation after generation to the ultimate reality of their conscious lives: the Risen Christ. (Mother Teresa's ideal of "something beautiful for God" expresses both the beauty of the motive and of the effects of noble action. It recalls Aristotle's affirmation that noble actions are done for beauty's sake.)

BEAUTY INSPIRES SEARCH FOR TRUTH

Plato linked his theory of beauty with that of knowledge: beauty is that which attracts and lures us for the quest of truth. The great variety of goodness embodied in Christian lives bespeaks the truth of the Risen Christ that inspires them. Persons are simply different; consequently, there will be different excellences among committed Christians that contribute to the powerful attractiveness of the Church's witness to the active presence of the Risen Christ in its midst. The progressive growth of Christians into the fuller reality of God's action in Christ is necessitated both by the new contingencies we face as individuals and by the Risen Christ and his Church, the object of our loyalties. The progressive growth of Christians both as individuals and as a community implies the prolonged and deepening impact of the Risen Christ upon human development. The Christian witness of every generation augments the evidence of what God has done in Christ. The angularity of Christian vision is enhanced by the distinctiveness and number of new witnesses, each with his or her own starting place, unique possibilities, experiences, feelings, perceptions, and tendencies.

Authentic Christians are persons who have found Christ to be beautiful; for beauty is the attractiveness of persons, of their lives. Authentic Christians recognize and embrace the excellence of God in Christ. *Beautiful* expresses their admiration, appreciation and affection for the person of Christ whose excellence they recognize. Christ implies that he is the Beauty of God made flesh when he affirmed that "No one can come to me unless he is drawn by the Father who sent me" (Jn. 6:44). To be drawn or attracted to Christ is to experience him as beautiful; however, not everyone experiences him in this way, except those to whom the Father has given this experience. To see

Jesus is to see the Father; they are united in one another in reciprocal immanence (Jn. 10:38; 14:10). To respond to the excellence of Jesus is to enjoy
the beauty God made manifest in its unique concreteness, particularity,
historicity, and existential fullness.

Beautiful expresses the quality of a personal relationship: the impact of
a particular excellence upon a person. It indicates the quality of our affinities and affectivity, of our values and attitudes in relation to particular persons, places, and things. It reveals our personal relationship to the existential
reality of the irreducible particular, that which cannot be other than it is and
thus cannot be accounted for by any other. The grammar of existing persons is not that of indefinite nouns, but rather of proper names.

The experience of beauty is expressed with the grammar of proper names.
Abstract concepts and ideologies are not its proper object; for such experience
and critical understanding are grounded in the particular, the existing, the
definite. An intelligent appreciation of beauty concerns embodied meanings
and values in the fullness of their particularity and existential impact; it concerns the relatedness and uniqueness that mark the excellence and impact
of an existing reality.

Our actions possess the dramatic quality of telling our life story. If we
define ourselves by our actions, we also define ourselves by the beauty that
has motivated them. The drama that is our life story emerges in response
to particular manifestations and embodiments of an excellence that has attracted and motivated our most significant actions and decisions. Through
the experience of beauty we become aware of our response-ability, of our
love-ability, of our life-ability within the possibilities of our particular environment. What we find beautiful reveals the quality of our unique personhood; it uncovers our hidden interests and invites us to pursue them for new
relationships with our life-context. What we find beautiful is that dimension
of reality which speaks to us, addresses us with its special meaning for us
and reveals our personal affinity for its excellence; it captures our attention
and often challenges us to the decisions that most shape our life story. Beauty,
therefore, is a dramatic quality of every person's life story, through which
we discover our unique meaning not only in remembrance of the past and
attention to the present but also in expectation of the future. There are elements throughout the temporal span of our consciousness that especially attract and interest us; these elements alone have the power to shape our lives,
for we never achieve anything with what fails to attract us. If our lives are,
in many respects, no greater than our thoughts, perhaps our achievements
are no greater than the envisioned excellence that has motivated them.

The primitive Church's reference to the Risen Christ as "the Lord of glory"
(1 Cor. 2:8) expresses its profoundly transforming experience and appreciation of the beauty of his person revealed by the dramatic action of God at

the conclusion of his life story. For Christians, Christ is not only the Word (true meaning) of God, but also the Beauty (attractive power) of God made flesh. His concrete, historical, personal distinctiveness differentiates Christian from non-Christian religious experience. The Christian's experience of God is qualified by the Christ consciousness and the Jewish religious heritage that it interprets. The unique excellence of Jesus of Nazareth is proclaimed by the Church in word and sacrament as the ultimate truth of human existence. His singular history represents this truth with factual finality.

LIFE STORY A VISION OF REALITY

As a personal response to the mystery of existence, a life story is a metaphor for a particular vision of reality. The angularity of its vision is rooted in its concreteness. The art of living, somewhat like that of photography, achieves its excellence through an angularity and concreteness of vision that is not experienced apart from our moods and concerns. The personal and social stories that combine to form a particular life story give these moods and concerns their specificity, their coloring.

The life story is a quest for specificity. Visions, hopes, and dreams must be concretized to be fully enjoyed. The story that the dramatic action of our life tells is a process that takes on a certain coloring (tonality). It is marked by the amorphous feelings with which we reach out to embrace some totality, or vision, that is given a specific shape and direction in our attempts to experience and communicate fully what is of utmost significance and concern to ourselves.

We need other persons to become persons. Inasmuch as other persons are known to us through the dramatic action of their life stories, we need such stories for the creation of our own, which, in so many respects, discloses our awareness of many "worlds." Through the narrative mode of our experience and the grammar of proper names, we disclose our personal worlds to one another and orchestrate the many elements that constitute our own story. This mode of experience enables us to share in common the meaning of persons, places, and events. Fidelity to the particularities of our historical context and its challenges endows our life story with an existential relevance for other life stories, even though they may be emerging in diverse historical contexts. Our fidelity to existential particulars tends to endow our story with a universal, transcultural value and communicability, recalling that of the "stories of God" that have come down to us from the Jewish and Christian tradition. Such stories convey a sense of reality and somehow satisfy our desire for meaning.

Because we act out our lives according to stories (models, metaphors, and myths), we may understand who we are through the stories we have embraced as our own. They are so central to our existence that without them life is experienced as empty.[6] The story of our lives is structured by the stories in which we understand our personal meaning to emerge.[7] Whatever personal excellence we achieve is largely a question of the quality of the personal stories we have embraced as our own. Particular life stories have the power to attract and to transform others; they display a personal excellence with extraordinary impact; they awaken us to new possibilities for our own life story.

The stories we most value are those that suggest a better way of being in the world, a new way of dealing with the world by transforming it through self-transformation. The life stories of particular persons have the healing effect of exposing false and self-destructive attitudes; they have the enlightening effect of displaying models of wisdom and ingenuity. Those life stories are especially valued that help us to fulfill what Maxwell Anderson has called "the dream of the race." "The dream of the race is that it may make itself better and wiser than it is . . ."[8] Such stories orientate us to life's real possibilities through their powerful appeal to our minds, our imaginations, and hearts; they may also reorientate our most basic moods, feelings, reactions, and actions.[9]

Our lives are shaped more by models, metaphors, stories, and myths than by abstract sets of rules and principles. We try to become like certain types of persons whose way of life appeals to us. Our actions tend to be imitative of individuals rather than guided by rules. They are imitative of those individuals whose excellence and attainments please and inspire them; consequently, they participate in the same intentionality and orientation.

The unique story that the actions of Christ's life have told is, for Christian faith, the normative story for every human being. The actions of his life display for Christian faith who God is. They tell us that through Christ and his Church we may share in the same story in our personal and communal experiences, at different cultural and historical moments, within our various horizons. There is always more to the Christ story than we can possibly say. There is always more to start with than we can fully take into account. There is always more to end with than we can imagine. It is the story of the infinite possibilities of God's self-gift for everyone in Christ. Beauty tells the story of these possibilities, of "the power to become children of God" (Jn. 1:12), through the attractive power of Christ's life in the Church and its members. It draws us to the Father in Christ; it draws us to Christ and his Church in individual Christians. The Father is revealed in the beauty of the Christ story and Christ and his Father are revealed in both the individual and corporate lives of all those who participate in its beauty. This is the beauty of God himself, which can be experienced and recognized only through the medium of others. Their life stories tell us who he is and that he is beautiful.[10]

PART II

Vision and Norm in Story

8

MYTH AND THE GOSPEL MESSAGE

1. MYTH AND ENLIGHTENMENT

That the theologian must meet men where they are is implied in the
Gospel's affirmation that God has come into the midst of human life and
meets men in their world. The Good News that God does not dwell apart
must be communicated. The Good News of the Incarnation must itself be
incarnated in the contemporary world's language, as opposed to the dimly
understood and half-forgotten language and concepts of former times; it
must be related to the questions, crises and culture of our times, which are
not identical with those of the primitive Church.

The heart of the problem of communicating the Good News is often that
men do not recognize where they really are. Ludwig Wittgenstein affirms
that "the aspects of things that are most important for us are hidden
because of their simplicity and familiarity. (One is unable to notice something—because it is always before one's eyes.) The real foundations of his
enquiry do not strike a man at all. Unless *that* fact has at some time struck
him. And this means: we fail to be struck by what, once seen, is most
striking and powerful."[1] Hence the theologian, in order to demonstrate the
relevance of the Christian message, must first discover what has struck man
and then relate his message to this.

The literary imagination is particularly important as an expression of
what is experienced as important by man. Russell Kirk suggests that
mythical expression in literature is intended to wake us from inattention to
important human truths and values.[2] As such, literature[3] is one form of the

contemporary world's challenge to any theologian who takes seriously his task of vindicating the claims of faith and of showing that there is a knowledge of God and of man having its own reasonableness, such as entitles it to a place in the spectrum of the thought of intelligent, educated people. Like the Old Testament Joseph he must interpret the dreams of the times. He is challenged to bridge the gap between the assertions of faith and the dreams, feelings and convictions of his times. He is challenged to make sense of his claim to have had an experience of God and to relate this experience to that of the contemporary world communicated through the use of myth.

The relationship between theology and fiction has not always been a comfortable one; in fact, religious attacks on the novel were frequent in the first quarter of the nineteenth century. The leading Anglican periodical, *Christian Observer,* declared in 1803 that "the majority of authors live by diverting men's thoughts from themselves; and subjects of eternal importance are either overlooked as strange and unserviceable or approached with repugnance, examined without interest, and dismissed with infidel impatience." Today, the relationship between theologian and contemporary culture has improved. Novels and plays are no longer held to be the fiefdom of the unholy trinity of the world, the flesh and the devil; rather, their myths may be recognized as the dreams of the times which the theologian must interpret and judge. He must, therefore, understand their language; otherwise, his interpretation may be false and his response unintelligible for a generation with whom he is out of touch.

2. *LITERATURE'S ANGULAR VIEWS OF REALITY*

Literature expresses what has been sensed by others. It permits a re-examination of what has been lived by isolating elements of a complex, by holding them in stasis, and by concentrating on what for the moment is essential. It captures the encompassing resonance of personal life, a particular attunement of the self in relation to the world, the pervasive tone of a man's existence; hence, it rescues the theologian from sterile intellectualism and moralism by reminding him that man is an affectional as well as a rational and volitional being, and that any journey to God must be travelled through a welter of personal affectivity.

Literature, then, calls his attention to the experience itself from which believing arises. It reveals how contemporary man finds himself in a world of powers which converge upon him, enlarging and diminishing him, arousing and modulating his affections, provoking fear and giving birth to joy. It tells the theologian how his contemporaries are being moved and disturbed by the surrounding world. Along with all the communications media it expands the theologian's participation in the experience of others.

It exposes him to and vicariously involves him in human suffering and the weight of fellow-feeling, in an era when men live together on a new scale of inclusiveness and intensity.

The changing times are marked in literature by a distinctive way of perceiving, imagining and feeling. In different ages there are different ways of talking and feeling about growth, morality, guilt and freedom. Differing images may suggest an atomic individual or communality; metaphors may suggest that the basic energy of life is a search for peaceful interrelatedness or a drive to bring life under the domination of autonomous wills. Individual persons, epochs and cultures have their distinctive angular vision of reality and affective response to it; whatever enters into their awareness is received according to the history of each, illuminating the structures of the past and the expectations for the future. Although what is experienced from one standpoint is not the whole of reality, it is an important part of the whole.

The imaginative world of literature is charged with expectancy. It suggests to the theologian the kind of world his contemporaries would like to see; the kind of world that they hate, fear and deplore. Its words, symbols, patterns of thought or action may arouse his approval or rejection. Its angular vision of reality will reveal possibly as much perception as oversight. This imaginative world inevitably expresses contemporary concerns. Are these concerns to be contrasted to mere intellection, to apathy, to lack of fervor, to lack of moral drive, to peace and restfulness, to cynicism, to determination to endure without trying to change the world? To what vices and misrepresentations are concerned persons prone? These are some questions with which the world of creative thought challenges the theologian.

The dominant theme of frustration, for example, takes many forms that should engage the theologian in his efforts to explain the meaning of Christ's victory over sin. In the plays of O'Neill, through the best of Anderson, Sidney Howard and his contemporaries, the underlying log jam, so to speak, the unresolvable paradox, is that, try as he will, the individual is doomed to frustration when once he gains a consciousness of his own identity. The image is that of the individual scratching away at a wall beyond which stands society. Sometimes he pounds at the wall, sometimes he tries to scale it or even blow it up, but at the end the wall is always there, and the man himself is dead or doomed to defeat in his attempt to live the human life. Christ's profound experience of non-culpable failure has a meaning which must be communicated to the theologian's contemporaries in a language that they will understand. Before the theologian speaks on this subject, he would do well to listen to the language of failure employed by the playwrights and authors who have succeeded in articulating the experience of it.[4]

3. MYTH AND THE MYSTERY OF MAN

In examining the dreams of the times it is important that the theologian determine what is of genuine value and what is specious, because the wrong dream may destroy a man and a society. Sometimes the dream is associated with sin and madness when a man, tragically deluded and mistaken about the meaning of his life, destroys himself in his attempt to force reality to conform to the shape of his illusions. There is a profound pathos in a man's (or society's) faithful response to a destructive illusion, to the wrong dream; even this, however, is perhaps better than no dream at all. In any case, literature reveals much about man and the quality of his dreams. The theologian is called to judge how man and his society can be transformed for the better or for worse by them. He will judge contemporary myths in the light of the Christian myth that stretches from creation to re-creation (Genesis to Revelation), of the redemption myth that stretches from Exodus to Revelation; for he believes that there is no kind of experience which cannot be brought to judgment by this myth.[5] Myth, in this case, implies truth, not falsehood; not primitive, naive misunderstanding but an insight more profound than scientific description and logical analysis can ever achieve. The language of myth in this sense is consciously inadequate, being simply the nearest we can come to a formulation of what we see very darkly.

The myths which the theologian must interpret and judge are a tissue of symbolism clothing a mystery. They reflect everyman's odyssey through time in which he searches for answers to the mystery of his existence. They express an awareness of the tensions and paradoxes that are constitutive of man's being as one who knows in himself freedom, finitude, guilt, hope and the imminence of death. They wrestle with the mystery of man's own being and try to find answers to its apparent contradictions. They deal with problems arising out of the very structure of human existence, with the self-questioning that underlies everyman's quest for that personal integrity that would be the fulfillment of his dream.

There are mythic qualities in any world-view because the ultimate mystery of human living is never completely accessible to discursive reason.[6] There are cultural, psychological and spiritual realities which underlie myth. Myth is recognized as a symbolic expression of truths about man's own life and thought. Parallels have been noted between myths and dreams, in which myths have been seen as projections of, or objectifications of, man's inner strivings and desires. Myths express man's self-understanding or his groping towards an identity.

4. MYTH AND TRANSCENDENT HOPES OF MAN

Scientific research assures us that myth is not merely a story told but a reality lived; it is not an idle tale, but an active force in human living. It not only represents a vital meaning for a people, but gives a cultural and social coherence to a people whose unity would disintegrate with the loss of a common mythological heritage. Myth expresses the experience of that which is most sacred and pre-eminently real in the human life-story of individuals and societies. It attempts to express man's position in a mysterious universe, his efforts to gain that self-understanding which is inherent in his very mode of existence.

The theology of hope also implies that attention must be paid to the contemporary myths of creative artists, and affirms that men live by their dreams and hopes, defining themselves and their societies by their expectations. Hope is the force and power behind the dreams that influence their lives, whether at the personal or at the social and political level. There is hope in the possibility of realizing the dream, in the power of the dream, when realized, to transform and fulfill men's lives. Creative works give concrete expression to hope and are ultimately judged by that hope. If they fail to satisfy that hope, or if hope stretches beyond them, they are rejected by it. The theater, literature and films are among the means that man has created for communicating his dreams. Expressing man's experience of the world around him and of the world within him, they are a form of enacted myth, embracing the many-sidedness of man, revealing the simultaneous disparity and coherence of that which is and of that which ought to be. However implicitly, these works communicate the experience of what their creators believe to be most real in the world. They may even lead us to experience a type of personal completion through a higher vision of reality. They may invite us to experience a new way of living, of becoming a new man with a new horizon.

The failure to achieve the dream will be rooted in some flaw that can be found in everyone; however, the flaw need not be fatal. There is always the possibility of healing; otherwise, there would be no drama, no myth. The healing of the flaw may be seen in purely human terms or in terms of divine assistance. It is the possibility of such healing which grounds the hope pervading the odyssey to whatever one is seeking. The attitudes and images, the symbols and metaphors of the myth, disclose the character of the individual's (and society's) hopes, the quality of his dreams.

Literature embodies myths of everyone's odyssey in quest of personal integrity through the fulfillment of a dream. These myths spell out different ways in which man seeks wholeness, personhood and dignity; they imply, by the same token, different ways in which man seeks to avoid meaninglessness, hopelessness and disintegration. The myths tell us that man defines himself by whatever he is seeking, whether the goal be simply insight of a human kind or some transcendent ideal such as peace. They remind us that whatever the self is seeking, it cannot help taking certain attitudes and forming certain judgments that imply a dream, a world-view, a concept of and a search for wholeness. Such attitudes are theological in the broadest sense of the word, inasmuch as they imply that there is more to ourselves and to our myths than meets the eye. They imply this whether or not there is any explicit awareness of the need for suprahuman aid in the achievement of personal integrity. They embody a certain dream of human happiness according to which men are judged as fortunate or unfortunate, admirable or contemptible, reasonable or absurd, human or less than human.

The theologian's attention to these myths of his time is based on the conviction that in the innermost depth of every human being there is alive a sort of natural religion with its standards of true and false, good and evil; that man is preprogrammed to a sense of wonder and awe before the mystery of his existence within the universe; that, in Tertullian's phrase, the soul is naturally Christian. He recognizes that significant drama and literature often imply this basic openness to the transcendent when a man's dreams are seen to surpass his personal resources and those of his society for their attainment, yet dream he must.[7] In fact, his dreams (and those of his society) may become more real for him than any other reality of his historical condition, bearing witness to that reality which underlies human awareness and, nevertheless, transcends human definition. Ultimately, one's own dream will find expression.

The theologian may well recognize in these myths diverse models of a kind of personal and social salvation, or integrity, diverse ways of passing from darkness into light, from oppression to freedom, from frustration to peace, from conflict to reconciliation. The multiplicity of salvation models not only bespeaks the complexity of the human spirit but also the character of the individual person's angular vision. No individual person, epoch or culture will adequately grasp and exhaustively comprehend all the implications of personal and social salvation, or integrity, or fulfillment.

The images, symbols and metaphors of these models are, then, a means used to construct myths which subsequently become objects of comparison, just as for Wittgenstein the language games are set up as "objects of comparison which are meant to throw light on the facts of our language by way not only of similarities but also of dissimilarities."[8] Amos Wilder comments on this phenomenon by indicating different levels of language.[9] He suggests, for example, that:

> In ordinary language, then, the Christian believes that the health and fulfillment of human society are linked with some aboriginal pattern of atonement at the heart of things; in dogmatic terms, that the world is redeemed by the death of Christ; and in mythological terms, that on the cross Christ overcame the principalities and powers of evil.

5. CONTEMPORARY MYTH AND COMMUNICATION OF THE CHRIST-EVENT

Even the theologian struggles to grasp more satisfactorily just what is meant by the salvation which has been imparted to mankind by the Christ-event. "Almost twenty centuries have elapsed since the Christ-event took place and yet no completely satisfying over-all explanation of that fact has been proposed," according to Joseph Mitros.[10] Contemporary cultural developments have opened up new vistas concerning the origin of man and his physical, psychic and moral state, concerning the problem of evil and liberation from it. In the light of these achievements the new data must be evaluated, the old ones revised and all of them integrated before more satisfying answers can be found. Although there is no doubt among Christians about the reality of the Christ-event and experience of it in their lives, the theologian's challenge is that of giving as adequate an explanation of it as possible.

Such an explanation will mediate between the biblical revelation and secular culture, between the Christian's experience of the Risen Christ and the secular world's experience of suffering and fulfillment. If the theologian accepts the challenge, he will have to immerse himself in the cultural forms of the times and to become attuned to the feelings which they communicate. He will follow the example of Paul at Athens when he spoke of the cult of the unknown God and when he cited the verses of a pagan poet, and found in those things belonging to contemporary culture of the people points of contact through which he might demonstrate the relevance of Christ's message. He will follow the example of the Fathers of the Church who drew on the resources of their secular culture environment for the articulation and communication of Christian truth. He will detect in the myths of his contemporary culture both expressions of that suffering which faith is meant to heal and articulations of that dream which faith is meant to realize.[11] Through an awareness and an understanding of contemporary culture's myth, of its models of salvation, and by an understanding of the Church's traditional teaching, the theologian will be able to address the world that lies outside the doors of the Church in a language that it will understand.

The theologian must be aware of himself as part of a pluralistic society. Hence, he will have to conduct his apologetic on several fronts and must learn to communicate his faith in various ways, suited to the needs of different people. "What we have to learn," according to Dr. Ramsey, "is that there is no single inward track to mystery, and no single outward road from the infinite."[12] Within the limits laid down by the Gospel itself, the theologian must be prepared to become "all things to all men" (1 Cor. 9:22), recognizing the legitimate diversity of explanation which enables the Christ-event to be discovered and treasured.[13] There are a number of languages available for articulating the Christian experience, and these are not all mutually exclusive. The language of the creative arts is one such language which should facilitate the theologian's task of communicating the mystery of Christ.

9

THE SEARCH FOR THE SELF

A great deal of psychoanalytic literature is concerned with the many causes and manifestations of the failure to achieve some sort of integration of the self because of radical breaks in the temporal growth of the individual. A trauma, for example, is a shock experience creating a disruption in the normal continuity and structure of the self. On the other hand, every man encloses within himself certain antinomies, a war of instincts. There lies deep in human nature the dividedness from which tragedy springs. There is a diversity of conflicting claims and urgencies that divide man; there are conflicting values with authentic claims that create severe tension. There is a pulling apart within the self, a disturbance, though not a pathological one, of integration. The self experiences a profound disharmony through the conflict of different incentives, different needs and desires.

1. INTERNAL DISCORDS AND UNDERSTANDING

Theodosius Dobzhansky (in "Evolutionism and Man's Hope," *Sewanee Review* [1960], 282, 284) relates man's discords to the development of self-awareness:

Man became, and he still remains, a creature rent by internal contradictions. He is a paradoxical being, capable of unspeakable egotism and cruelty, but also of love, abnegation, and self-sacrifice. . . . But man is also ashamed of his defeats and suffers from his depravity. He is able to construct in his imagination worlds different from the actual one, and can visualize himself in these imaginary worlds. . . . Man's biological success becomes a reality despite the tragic discords within him.

The internal discords of the self are not only the occasion of self-awareness or self-knowledge; they are the material of self-knowing. Division is a summons to understanding; it is the inconsistent and contradictory that demand comprehension. Human nature, according to Erik H. Erikson *(Young Man Luther,* New York: Norton, 1958, p. 16), can best be studied in the state of conflict; and human conflict comes to the detailed attention of interested recorders under special circumstances. One such circumstance is the clinical encounter in which the sufferers, for the sake of securing help, have no other choice than to become case histories; and another special circumstance is history, where extraordinary beings, by their own maneuvers and through the prodding of the charismatic hunger of mankind, become (auto)biographies.

The psychiatrist Kazimierz Dabrowski has developed a theory of mental growth through positive disintegration. To reach a high level of dynamic integration of the cognitive, moral, social, aesthetic and other mental functions in accordance with one's own authentic ideal of personality, one must undergo a disintegration of a more primitive integration which previously had been achieved.[1] The positive disintegration of the lower-level, primitive integration characterized by biological determinism, automatism, rigidity, stereotype and a lack or low degree of consciousness, is effected through the psychic dynamism of growing insight into oneself and understanding of oneself and others, and a conscious and deliberate choice based on multi-level, multi-sided, highly integrating insights.

Without such disintegration personal growth through self-transcendence is impeded, and a state of satiety pervades consciousness. Gabriel Marcel, the French existentialist philosopher, warned that when a man is perfectly satisfied he is like an apple which is perfectly ripe: there is only one step left, and that is to rot. For Marcel, the spirit of personal satiety brings good things to a bad end. Chesterton recognized that completeness and comfort are almost the definitions of insanity: "There is but an inch of difference between the cushioned chamber and the padded cell." The lunatic is the man who lives in a small world and thinks that it is the whole world: he lives in a tenth of the truth and thinks it is the whole truth. The more completely sated we are, the more certain we may be that we are slowly and quietly going mad, for the real world is not satisfying. The real world is full of bracing bewilderments and brutal surprises. The thoroughly satisfied man is no longer in contact with the real world; he has separated himself from his context, from the elements, the oppositions and the problems with which he must deal if he is to live. Isolation from one's context, indifference to it, are a form of death.

Boredom characterizes stagnation of both the individual and society. There is much wrong with a society which breeds people so bored, so lonely and so unloved as to be continually turning toward sensual stimulation (obscenity is one of these stimulants) in hope of release. In Bernanos' *Diary of a Country Priest,* the cure writes of his bored parish: "My parish is bored stiff; no other word for it. Like so many others! We can see them being eaten up by boredom, and we can't do anything about it." In what Vance Packard has described as America's "fun culture," so many well-to-do suburbanites drift from one vague disappointment to the next, never thinking of themselves but always of their diversions, entirely unaware that they are neither giving nor receiving anything of authentic value.

The effects of boredom, drift and purposelessness can be disastrous on a national scale. Many feel no part of the city where they work and are disinterested in the monotonous district where they live. They are moored to nothing and make no decisions. They say neither yes nor no when their martinis are replenished, and it is a short step from this kind of acceptance to acceptance of crime in the cities, thievery in the government, knavery in labor unions, unconscionable business practices, mindlessness in the public schools, and the disappearance of anything that could remotely be called the national will. Such are the penalties of that moral failure that is drift, boredom, satiety, stagnation. Seeing the problem on a universal level, George Bernard Shaw stated that "the tragedy of the modern world is that nothing ever happens and dullness kills us." Boredom, resulting from a lack of purpose and motivation, gives us no reason for choosing and doing one thing rather than another.

2. BECOMING AN AUTHENTIC SELF

Human needs are manifested as inner tensions, and determining the ways in which the self strives to fulfill them requires choice. Tension is resolved when a need is satisfied through the appropriate choice. There are alternatives underlying man's dividedness, and man must select one or the other. Often our reluctance to make serious decisions and choices is less a fear of suffering than a secret dread of irreversible results that permit few illusions or certainties about what will follow. We share with Hamlet the human tendency to indefinite postponement, to drift; we might, with Heyst in Joseph Conrad's *Victory,* choose drift. Conrad shows that even that fails. Heyst elects something that is not there to elect: security by withdrawal and passivity. In Heyst, we see a man who chooses to ignore the demands of his context and becomes irrelevant through a decision that itself is a form of death.

If internal conflicts require choice, choice demands strength and awareness. The inability to make choices signifies a weakness that cannot produce a man of stature. The lack of such strength makes men pathetic rather than tragic. On the other hand, strength is meaningless if a man is not aware of the alternatives. If choice is to be fully free and human, there inevitably comes into play all that one knows, one's visions of ends to be sought and of what may be done, one's responsiveness to imperatives and awareness of impulses; the inspection of alternatives and of one's talents and hardiness; the willingness to detect self-flattery and self-deception.

An awareness of the dividedness of the self implies some concept of its wholeness. Literature depicts man as a center of active, dynamic forces capable, or incapable, of controlling, synthesizing, and organizing the heterogeneous elements of experience into a functional unity, structure, and identity called a person or character. The self is shown not only as a repository of perceptions and memories, but also and predominantly as a center of active, self-regulative functions that serve to convey to the reader that fact of the self's unity.

The self attains authenticity by its fidelity to its basic dynamic orientation and drive for the significant, the true, the worthwhile, the beautiful, and the divine. It develops by fidelity to its natural exigencies and dynamic structure.

3. BECOMING THE CHRIST-SELF

To the extent that the human self fails to become the authentic, understanding, rational, responsible, and loving self that it is summoned to be, it succumbs to the hollow anti-self that is the false self, the caricature of the true self. Sin and madness, ignorance and disharmony, characterize the anti-self. It is in this context that Bernard Tyrrell, S.J., in his book, *Christotherapy: Healing through Enlightenment,* remarks that when there is a failure to obey the natural exigencies of the spirit, there is added a rejection of the light of Christ, and the anti-Christ-self appears: everything in man opposed to the Christ. Finally, if there is a final and lasting rejection of the exigencies of the self and the Christ-self, then the zero-self, the Hell-self, is born, only to die forever since its birth is eternal death itself.

There are various dimensions of transformation into the Christ-self, and each mode of participation in it is rich in meaning. Tyrrell explains that Christ is not only the Word made flesh but also incarnate value; hence, to participate in the Christ-self is to be morally converted, to be ruled not by desire and fear, by mere personal satisfaction, but by the authentic values revealed in Christ. Moral transformation into the Christ-self involves dying to all that is unauthentic and uncompromising commitment to the truly good and worthwhile as unveiled in the event of Jesus Christ. Paul refers to the realization of the perfect Christ-self when he writes that "the knowledge that I have now is imperfect; but then I shall know as fully as I am known" (1 Cor. 13:12). The individual must choose the self he wishes to become; and, to as many as freely receive Him and open themselves to His transforming power, Christ gives "power to become children of God" (Jn. 1:12) and to be transformed into His glorious image.

The Christian's life in Christ has always been understood in terms of growth, transformation, and development. The Parable of the Talents condemns the notion of a person's spiritual stagnation; the servant who buried his one talent in order to save it fails to meet with Jesus' approval. Such personal stagnation, largely motivated by an obsession with personal security and a failure to trust in God, reminds us that the man who tries to save his soul shall lose it. Authentic living in Christ means ongoing transformation and growth in Christ; there is no standstill.

Teilhard de Chardin appreciated the dynamic growth which characterizes authentic Christian life when he sought to develop a new understanding of Christian anthropology. Christ, he affirmed, is not only the figure in which the Incarnation becomes historical event but also the eschatological goal of anthropogenesis (beginning of man), in which the genesis of the universe "converges." This "greater Christ" is the focal point not only of the individual but also of the collective salvation of the "living stones" of the faithful being fit together into His body. In the New Testament Letter of Paul to the Ephesians, the goal of the development of Christendom is already described with the words: "until we all attain to the unity of the faith and of the knowledge of the Son of God, to mature manhood, to the measure of the stature of the fullness of Christ" (Eph. 4:13).

Man is not a complete being, placed in a finished world like a methodically provided-for tenant in a prefabricated, newly built residence ready for occupancy. Redemption cannot be understood statically, as if salvation were only a restitution and restoration of the lost divine image, a patching up of fragments through ecclesiastical remedies. The New Testament summons both the individual and mankind to growth in Christ: "Beloved . . . it does not yet appear what we shall be, but we know that when he appears we shall be like him, for we shall see him as he is" (1 Jn. 3:2). Christ promises His disciples a future term to their glorious transformation in Him: "Then the righteous will shine like the sun in the kingdom of their Father" (Mt. 13:43). Such growth implies that a prior stage of human thought, desire, and attitude is left behind. Life and growth in Christ imply a death for what preceded the new creation.

4. CHRIST-FIGURES IN LITERATURE

Edwin M. Moseley, in his book *Pseudonyms of Christ in the Modern Novel* (Pittsburgh: University of Pittsburgh Press, 1962), notes the recurrence of the Christ archetype in a series of novels quite dissimilar on the surface. The first three novels in Moseley's study express orthodox religious attitudes and tend to treat the Christ figure traditionally and respectfully: Conrad's *Lord Jim* (1900), Dostoyevsky's *Crime and Punishment* (1866), and Turgenev's *Fathers and Sons* (1861). The first novel presents Christ as tragic hero; the second presents Christ as death-in-life and life-in-death; the third presents Christ as the archetypal son. The authors of these novels are aware of the "scientific" rejection of religion in their time and they are concerned with criticizing the new scientism. These novels, according to Moseley, take a last stand on behalf of the essential values of any religion.

The next three books reflect the new naturalism, psychological and sociological, following the First World War: Lawrence's *Sons and Lovers* (1913), Remarque's *All Quiet on the Western Front* (1929), and Fitzgerald's *The Great Gatsby* (1925). These novels reflect a nostalgia for a traditional religious pattern or the irony of its absence. Lawrence presents Christ as artist and lover; Remarque gives us Christ as doomed youth; Fitzgerald offers us Christ as the missing Orient.

The next group of novels are socially-conscious works. Faulkner's *Light in August* (1932) implies Christ as social scapegoat; Forster's *A Passage to India* (1924) offers us Christ as one avatar; Steinbeck's *The Grapes of Wrath* (1939) suggests Christ as the brother of man. Christ as Marxist variant appears in Silone's *Bread and Wine* (1936), in Malraux's *Man's Fate* (1933), and in Koestler's *Darkness at Noon* (1941). Solutions for social problems run the gamut from the individualism of Forster to the socialism of Steinbeck, to the synthesis of these in Silone. In themselves these novels form a history of social attitudes from the 1920's to the 1940's and remind us of the primary concern with solving material problems in the 1930's. The Christ of the social novels is more concerned with the here than with the hereafter.

Finally, Moseley considers Christ as the existentialist anti-Christ in Camus' *The Stranger* (1942) and as the old champion in Hemingway's *The Old Man and the Sea* (1953).

The Christ-figures represent heroes in current mythology, a belief in ultimate and original good, the discovery of a transcendental oneness in diversity, the possibility of the exemplary life, and a reverence for an authentically human life. Moseley compares them to Jung's "mythological types," "archetypes." He is dealing with the peculiarly Western version of the savior-archetype in the figure of Christ, and with topical variations as the men-and-the-moments change. They reflect the heroic quality of a courageous and intelligent confrontation with the problems of their times.

5. CHRIST-FIGURES AND THE HEROES

These Christ-figures recall the godlike figures among the Greek heroes which Carl Jung (in *Man and His Symbols,* New York: Dell, 1973, p. 101) affirms to be symbolic representations of the whole psyche, the larger and more comprehensive identity that supplies the strength that the personal ego lacks. Jung believes that the essential role of the heroic myth is the development of the individual's ego-consciousness—his awareness of his own strengths and weaknesses—in a manner that will equip him for the arduous tasks with which life confronts him. The complete hero myth in which the whole cycle from birth to death is described presents the image of the hero which evolves in a manner that reflects each stage of the evolution of the human personality. The hero's death is linked with the achievement of personal maturity. Similarly, the New Testament's criterion for authentic participation in Christ's life (the Christ-self) is implicitly linked to his death: "We know that we have passed from death unto life because we love the brethren." Christ's death enables that fellowship that brings release from egoism into the perfect Christ-self in whom God initiates and completes all the individual's thoughts and deeds. Through Christ's death man is enabled to participate in the paradigmatic experience of God as the Risen Christ as affirmed and guaranteed by the faith of His Church. The Christian believes that such a participation in the perfect Christ-self of the Risen Lord represents the ultimate possibility and gift of personal maturity.

The fulfillment of human striving and aspirations in the perfect Christ-self is implied in the Christ-figures and their embodiment of human ideals. Lord Raglan's study, *The Hero, A Study of Tradition, Myth, and Drama* (New York: Oxford University, 1937), argues that the lives of traditional heroes, as told in stories, legends, tales, drama, epics, sagas, and other forms of art, can be reduced to a pattern composed of twenty-two elements. He took typical incidents in the lives of symbolic heroes, tabulated these typical incidents, and discovered a pattern. The value of studying the symbolic patterns of dramatic forms in this manner has been well established by Joseph Fontenrose's *Python: A Study of Delphic Myth and Its Origins* (Berkeley: University of California, 1959). Like Raglan, he concluded that the fantasies of myth are in themselves but a disguise for "the fundamental truths of the human spirit." The Christ-figures of literature illuminate dimensions of the perfect Christ-self and express the longing of the human spirit for an ideal self-image.

6. THE CHRISTIAN VISION OF LIFE

The Christian believes that the transformation of his self-image involves a continuous process of maturation which, if it is to reach its perfection in the perfect Christ-self, is first and last the gracious work of God. The process of maturation in Christ presupposes our free response to God's transforming, healing, and enlightening initiative which would endow us with the self-image which was also in Christ. The divine graciousness aids us in confronting sin, sickness, suffering, and death; it aids us in the process of self-transcendence, in overcoming the gap between the self that we are and the perfect Christ-self that we are summoned to become. In this respect Jung notes (in *Man and His Symbols,* p. 147-8) that one of the commonest dream symbols for release through transcendence is the theme of the lonely journey or pilgrimage which somehow seems to be a spiritual pilgrimage on which the initiate becomes acquainted with the nature of death. But this is not death as a last judgment or other initiatory trial of strength: it is a journey of release, renunciation, and atonement, presided over and fostered by some spirit of compassion corresponding to the merciful love of God in Christ.

The Christian envisions his life as a journey which is Spirit-inspired, love-filled, and God-centered, in its best. The symbol of the journey appropriately implies the ongoing transformation of mind and heart in the course of human development. It implies the process of overcoming the old illustory desires of the self about which the author of the Ephesians (4:22-4) has written:

> You must give up your old way of life; you must put aside your old self, which gets corrupted by following illusory desires. Your mind must be renewed by a spiritual revolution so that you can put on the new self that has been created in God's way, in the goodness and holiness of truth.

The journey is a Christian symbol of this self-transcendence, away from the self that seeks to confirm itself as primary reality and thereby creates so much of our mental, emotional, and physical suffering in its idolatrous attempts which of their very nature radically conflict with primary reality.

Modern literature's metaphors express the inner life of the author, this life which mirrors the spiritual life of the times. Many dominant metaphors depict a state of non-growth, stagnation, spiritual entrapment, determinism, automatism and all those other qualities of the unexamined, unscrutinized life where ignorance, obtuseness, silliness, and irresponsibility sustain illusions and false desires. The *prison* image, for example, is a pervading fantasy in Western literature. Inspired by a theme from Dante's *Inferno,* Eliot brings the metaphor of the prison into the twentieth century when in *The Waste Land* the protagonist of that poem watches the crowd of people flowing over London Bridge and says: "I had not thought death had undone so many." Eliot suggests the similarity between crowds of people moving in a city and convicts moving in a prison yard: "Sighs, short and infrequent, were exhaled. And each man fixed his eyes before his feet." The representation of the world as a vast purgatorial prison has persevered far more than two thousand years, and it is revealing that one of the most celebrated of modern poems should revive the idea that life in this world is a death, a death from which one may be delivered only through the mystery of spiritual rebirth, the highest actualization of human consciousness which exercises a profound transformative effect on the moral, intellectual, social, aesthetic, and other levels of consciousness. In the last section of *The Waste Land* Eliot uses the metaphor again in a somewhat more modern interpretation, expressing loneliness and isolation in the modern world through the image of the prison: "each in his prison. Thinking of the key" — of the key of sympathy which will open the door and release us from the bondage of our selfishness.

There are also prison metaphors in W.H. Auden's poem *In Memory of W.B. Yeats*. "And each in the cell of himself is almost convinced of his freedom." Franz Kafka[2] writes in his "Notes from the Year 1920": "He feels imprisoned on this earth, he feels constricted; the melancholy, the impotence, the sickness, the feverish fancies of the captive afflict him; no comfort can comfort him, since it is merely comfort, gentle head-splitting comfort glazing the brutal fact of imprisonment. But if he is asked what he actually wants he cannot reply, for — that is one of his strongest proofs — he has no conception of freedom." The spiritual state described corresponds to the traditional concept of the "slavery of sin," when man makes man his own god, himself the ultimate source of his own well-being and beatitude. "Whether he will or no," according to Augustine, "a man is necessarily a slave to the things by means of which he seeks to be happy. He follows them whithersoever they lead, and fears anyone who seems to have the power to rob him of them."[3]

The prison metaphor appears in Jean-Paul Sartre's *No Exit,* where the imprisoned self describes its repugnance to others: "Hell is—other people!" The metaphor of "no exit" expresses a feeling of the self's incarceration, the feeling of being doomed to live with other people and to suffer from the wounds they inflict upon us. The metaphor expresses the despair of those who feel there is "no way out" of a world in which the self feels miserably confined to itself by others who inhibit its enjoyment of the freedom for self-expression. Walls, prisons, guards, keys, the trial, the conviction, the sentence, the shutting of the door, the confinement, and the escape—all the images of imprisonment occur frequently in literature, describing intense feelings and thoughts about freedom. The Christian believes that the freedom which really counts is a gift, the work of the Incarnation which enables him to escape from enslavement to self. The Incarnation is the ultimate accommodation of the divine to the human need for freedom, for a freedom which centers on and delights in the positive and is nourished by the true, the good and worthwhile, the beautiful and the divine.

Basic to Christian thought is the idea that man needs salvation from himself, from his self-centeredness; he cannot, by himself, save himself. Sin is primarily — "originally" — self-deification, the attempt to warp all life, and all that lives, into one's own orbit. It is the reduction of all things to one's own dominion, the exaltation of the self above all else. It is the manner in which man is enslaved to himself, to his own ultimacy. There is no escape from the prison of the self unless man fosters and encourages his natural openness to the true, the real, the worthwhile, and to God's gracious gift of himself to man when this gift is offered. Christians believe that the way out of the prison of self involves a multifaceted process of transformation, of constant self-transcendence, of conversion on the intellectual, moral, religious and psychological levels; that it is ultimately the graced transformation whereby the Christian becomes a "new man" in Christ and comes to share "the divine nature" (2 Peter 1:4) through the gift of a new mind and a new heart in Christ.

The transition from the prison-condition of the human spirit to that of freedom is implicitly described by the author of Ephesians (4:22-24): "You must give up your old way of life; you must put aside your old self, which gets corrupted by following illusory desires. Your mind must be renewed by a spiritual revolution so that you can put on the new self that has been created in God's way, in the goodness and holiness of truth."

7. HISTORY AND SELF-JOURNEY

Historicity underlies the link between the journey as a symbol of transcendence and our maturation in the perfect Christ-self. God Himself accepted historical limitation by incarnation in Jesus Christ. Although Jesus continued to be God, he accepted limitation by life and by history. The two volumes of St. Luke depict his life and that of his Church as a journey: the Gospel of Luke is structured in terms of Jesus' journey from Nazareth to Jerusalem, the city of peace, where he accomplishes his Father's will; the Acts of the Apostles is structured in terms of the disciples' journey from Jerusalem to Rome, to the ends of the earth, the universal city, capital of most of the known world. The work of the perfect Christ-self, historically accomplished in Jerusalem, is extended throughout history and the world, so that at every time and in every place the Messianic peace which Christ achieved between God and man and among men in Jerusalem may be shared. For those who are putting on Christ, there is a way in which their historical setting becomes Jerusalem, the Jerusalem of Christ's peace with God and man, the *locus* of salvation; and there is a way in which the life, death, and resurrection of Christ is contemporary with their time. Mircea Eliade (in *Myths, Dreams and Mysteries,* New York: Harper and Row, 1960, p. 31) asserts that "through the mystery of the Passion or of the Resurrection, the Christian dispels profane time and is integrated into time primordial and holy." For Eliade the Christological *illud tempus* of these events will not be done away with at the end of history; in fact, it is contemporary with the Christian's pilgrimage through history as the special quality of his time as experienced by his Christ-self.

The literary reconstruction of one's life, according to Hans Meyerhof (in *Time in Literature,* Berkeley: University of California, 1968, p. 26), invariably involves both a subjective pattern of significant associations and an objective structure of verifiable biographical and historical events. Both dimensions are present, not only in biographical and autobiographical forms of literature, but in any literary portrait of the self. There is no way of constructing a man's life except through reconstructing his past in terms of significant associations supervening upon the objective, historical data, or through showing the inseparable intermixture of the two dimensions. What may be called a "literary reconstruction" of man has always used, in addition to the objective historical data, the pattern of significant associations in the stream of consciousness and in memory as the most important clue to the structure of the personality or the identity of the self.

Man may not have a nature, but he certainly has a history, as Dilthey said. Time, the historical aspect of human existence, has become the focal point for an "existentialist" analysis of man. Time, as experienced by the self, as contrasted with its recording by the natural scientist, is charged with "significance" for the self because the question, what *am* I, makes sense in terms of what I have *become,* that is, in terms of the objective historical facts together with the pattern of significant associations constituting the story or the identity of the self.

There are different times and "turning-points" in the story of the self's becoming which can be detected by our use of metaphor. Weller Embler, in his book *Metaphor and Meaning* (DeLand, Florida: Everett Edwards, 1966, p. v), affirms that a whole philosophy of life is often implicit in the metaphors of creative writers, the philosophy of an entire generation, indeed, of an entire civilization. The way we choose to talk about experience tells us more about ourselves, about our beliefs, feelings, hopes, fears, intentions than about the objective "facts" of our historical moment. And the way we feel about ourselves, our self-image, is of considerable importance. Our metaphors tell us about ourselves and our world, about the self and its reaction to its historical, existential context; for every self lives within a context, a surrounding that provides both strengths and struggles for vital organisms and for conscious life. Our metaphors reveal how the self interprets its context and the problematic raised by it: the elements, the oppositions and the problems with which the self must deal if it is to live and mature. Our metaphors may indicate a flight from the problems of our context, our feeling of isolation from our context, or our feeling of hopelessness in coming to grips with it. Just as these metaphors change from generation to generation, they also change within an individual's life. St. Paul, for example, after his conversion, begins to describe his reaction to the external world in terms of Christ; his metaphors reveal the change that has taken place within him.

Paul's language indicates his really new self-image, his personal transformation and new self-understanding in terms of a participation in the Christ-self: "The life I now live in this body I live in faith; faith in the Son of God who loved me and sacrificed himself for my sake" (Gal. 2:20).

Paul's internal transformation makes him a kind of metaphor for Christ, a Christ-figure. Paul recognizes his new self-image, and the fact that it is the gift of God's gracious election:

> We know that by turning everything to their good, God cooperates with all those who love him, with all those that he has called according to his purpose. They are the ones he chose specially long ago and intended to become true images of his Son, so that his Son might be the eldest of many brothers (Rom. 8:28-9).

10

THE DREAM AND MYTH OF PARADISE

Although we may be said to define ourselves by our expectations, hopes and dreams, there is generally a discrepancy between them and in our present condition. There is often a conflict between the story our life tells and the life-story that we attempt to make our own. This conflict has its roots in that existential gap or moral impotence to achieve our ideals; it bespeaks our need to seek a liberation which we cannot attain on our own. Our painful awareness of this existential gap conditions our receptivity to the Father's compassionate self-communication in Christ. He is the basis of the Christian hope which is the radical refusal to put limits on the possible. The liberating experience of his love enables our self-ideal to become the reality of our life story. Our hearts, to paraphrase St. Augustine, were made for this self-ideal, and they will not rest until they achieve it in Christ, the archetypal man, the ultimate meaning and value of man.

The communication of Christ originates in the Father's compassionate love for the hoping, aspiring and dreaming creature that is man. Jesus is criticized for communicating with sinners (e.g., Lk. 5:29-32; 7:34-50; 15:1-3). His critics fail to understand that it is only the sinners for whom Jesus has any authentic meaning. Sinners recognize that Jesus is the ultimate source of human righteousness, and that he is the Father's gift; the self-righteous, on the contrary, either do not experience that existential gap between their self-ideal and their present condition, or, if they do, believe that they can close the gap with their own resources. The former recognize that their self-ideal is in another as gift; the latter believe that it does not involve self-transcendence in accepting Christ.

The existential gap between human ideals and the human reality is the relevant context for communicating Christ. Many solutions are offered for closing that gap; however, Christian faith affirms that Christ alone, the Father's gift, is the answer. Paradise lost, the origin of the gap, becomes Paradise regained in Christ: "I tell you that this day you shall be in paradise with me" (Lk. 23:43). Man quests as a pilgrim for his ideal self, in a quest symbolized by the dream and myth of paradise in one of its many forms; for the Christian, the way of the Cross is the Father's designated way to that paradise which is to be with him in Christ.

1. THE MYTH AND THE DREAM OF PARADISE

Tertullian coined the phrase *"anima naturaliter christiana,"* affirming that in the innermost depth of every human being there is alive a sort of natural religion with standards of true and false, good and evil. He recognized that man is preprogrammed to a sense of wonder and awe before the mystery of his existence and meaning within the universe; that his spirit is dynamically oriented to the meaningful, the true, the real, the good, the beautiful and the divine.

The archetype of paradise has, in one form or another, expressed the aspirations of both individuals and societies for a kind of self-transcendence.[1] Paradise signified a royal park for the ancient Persians. In the Greek translation of the Hebrew Scripture it designated the garden of Eden, the original, blissful abode of man on earth; in later Jewish writings it became the name of a heavenly realm, understood as the archetype of the earthly Eden, where the righteous enjoy rest and fulfillment in the glorious presence of God. Some belief in paradise as either an original or a final state is probably to be found in all religions.[2]

There are religious implications in the relation between dream and myth and the archetype of paradise, on the level both of individuals and societies, and of the mythic re-enactment of this relation in drama.[3] This chapter attempts to analyze elements on the first level, then to apply this analysis to Tennessee Williams' plays *The Glass Menagerie* and *A Streetcar Named Desire*.

Dream, in this study, implies both a way of thinking and a way of desiring; implies a vision, or world view, of the self and of society, of how they attain true meaning and value; and it implies the hopes and aspirations of both the self and society for fulfillment through realization of the vision.[4]

The dream may be true or false, clear or unclear, beneficial or destructive.[5] The dream is true and beneficial to the extent that it corresponds to the genuine exigencies of the human spirit for what is meaningful, good and worthwhile. It brings peace to the individual and to society to the extent that it embodies a correct understanding of living in accordance with these exigencies. On the other hand the dream may be associated with madness when a man (or society), tragically deluded and mistaken about the meaning of his life, destroys himself in his attempt to force reality to conform to the shape of his illusions. There is a profound pathos in a man's faithful response to a destructive illusion, to the wrong dream.[6]

Men (and societies) live and define themselves by the quality of their dreams, by the quality of their vision and hope.[7] Hope is the force and power behind the vision that shapes their lives. There is hope in the possibility of realizing the vision and in the power of the vision, when realized, to transform and fulfill men's lives. The quality of the vision gives concrete expression to a man's hope and is ultimately judged by that hope. If the vision fails to satisfy that hope, if hope stretches beyond it, then the vision is rejected by the very hope that first brought it into being. It is recognized as an empty illusion, a false dream.

The dream of every man (and society) works itself out in a multi-levelled and multidimensional tissue of symbolism that becomes his life story or myth.[8] The visionary landscape of the human psyche ultimately takes on the form of a story, a personal history; hence it is in the basic sense of the Greek word *myth*—a story, a tale, the plot of a play—that the lives of men (and societies) are ultimately comprehensible.[9] The dream becomes a story, history, myth; it becomes the historical self-definition of the dreamer. The myth as a life story is the unique embodiment of personal vision and values in terms of the specific symbols of a particular time and place.[10]

There are mythic qualities in the expression of any world view because the ultimate mystery of human living is never completely accessible to discursive reasoning.[11] Mythological language bears witness to that reality which underlies human awareness and yet transcends human definition. Mythological language is a symbolic, approximate expression of a truth which man cannot perceive sharply and completely but can only glimpse vaguely and therefore cannot adequately or accurately express. Mythological language is consciously inadequate because it is the closest that man can come to the articulation of a mystery, of those realities — known unknowns—that transcend his full comprehension.

Paradise is among the archetypal symbols repeatedly found in myths, religions, dreams, fantasies and literature.[12] It is a primordial image of a fundamental aspect of human experience. Paradise belongs to a constellation of archetypal symbols concerned with the perennial idea of human pilgrimage that arises out of the very structure of human existence, with the self-questioning that underlies everyman's quest for that personal (and social) integrity that would be the fulfillment of his dreams.[13] Paradise (garden) is the archetypal symbol both at the beginning and at the end of the pilgrim's path through the wilderness (desert); it is at the beginning and the end of the human enterprise.[14]

As a questing animal man can formulate and pursue ideals that are different in kind from the goals of animal instinct, even though the relations between the ideal and the instinctual are intricate and confused. The self-transcending spirit of man is always asking further questions and never perfectly satisfied with its achievements; the object of its quest is always just beyond its grasp and comprehension. Out of this process of self-transcendence arise certain archetypal symbols and myths: paradise (garden), wilderness (desert), pilgrim, path (way).

There are three existential moods that generally characterize the archetypal symbols of the pilgrimage experience. The moods of innocence, of alienation and of aspiration are symbolized respectively by the garden (paradise), the wilderness (desert) and the path (pilgrim).

In terms of the Judaeo-Christian mythos we look backward with nostalgia to the garden of Eden and forward with hope to the garden-like splendor of paradise. Innocence resides at both the beginning and the end of the archetypal cycle: there is pristine innocence, then loss or corruption of it, then redemptive reaffirmation that renews and fulfills whatever was essential in the original innocence lost.

The wilderness (desert, wasteland) is the central image of alienation from God, from neighbor and from self.[15] Man is "bewildered" in an alien environment where the civilization that normally orders and controls his life is absent. Such an environment produces a state of mind in which man feels lost, stripped of guidance, perplexed, and at the mercy of alien, mysterious and malign forces. Wilderness is the environment of the non-human and even the anti-human where man is an alien presence. It is a region where a person is likely to get into a disordered, confused, or 'wild' condition. The semihuman wild man, for example, was the most important imaginary denizen of the wilderness of medieval Europe; he symbolized what happened to the isolated and alienated man, living outside the human community.

Among most early cultures paradise was man's greatest good; wilderness, its antipode, was his greatest evil. In one condition the environment ministered to his every desire ('Eden' is the Hebrew word for 'delight'). Human happiness, security and development all seemed dependent on rising out of the dangerous wilderness condition.

The wilderness, in the Old Testament, is a cursed land which becomes the condition of sinful man in his alienation from God. As a punishment for their sin Adam and Eve are driven from Eden into the wilderness, a cursed land full of thorns and thistles. The identification of the wilderness with God's curse led to the belief that it was a kind of hell populated by malign spirits, by all those menacing forces which upset, oppress and play havoc with the human spirit. Among them were the howling dragon or *tan*, the winged female monster of the night called *Lilith* and the familiar man-goat *seirim.* Presiding over all was *Azazel,* the arch-devil of the wilderness.

Wilderness, for Christians, has long been a powerful symbol applied either to the moral chaos of the unregenerate or to the godly man's conception of life on earth as a pilgrim in an alien land struggling against temptations endangering his spiritual life. Jesus says that he is the Way (Path) by being the Truth and the Life (Jn. 14:4-6), a source of revelation and regeneration, enabling reconciliation with God and thereby the restoration of that human beatitude that had been enjoyed in paradise.

The pilgrim differs from the wanderer in that the one has assurance of direction, the other not. The assurance of direction corresponds to the theological virtue of hope, the spirit with which the pilgrim confronts the wilderness condition, that compound of the natural inclination to "hope of the wrong things," the temptations of the material world and the illusions of the spiritual world. Other symbols of this third existential phase, besides the path (way) and the pilgrim, are the stair or ladder, the bird or winged soul, unveiling, change of heart (*metanoia*), and cleansing whether by water or by fire.

Man's dreams, both as vision, ideal, world view, and as hopes and aspirations, inevitably embody themselves in images. In themselves such images are the path to whatever the self is seeking: to insight of a human kind, to some transcendent emotional ideal such as peace, to beauty, or to God. Whatever the self is seeking, it cannot help taking certain attitudes, forming certain judgments, and this is an immediate and spontaneous way, towards the images it experiences. These attitudes are theological in a broad sense of the word, inasmuch as they imply that there is more in ourselves and in our images, myths and dreams than meets the eye. These attitudes permeate the images, myths and dreams so that they are always mutually forming, creating, sometimes even distorting each other.

Drama is one of the many means that man has created for communicating his pilgrimage experience, his particular path through the wilderness condition of the human race, his nostalgia for the spiritual and physical plenitude of a far distant but not forgotten time—"in the beginning"—his dreams, aspirations and hopes to attain a final state of bliss and abundant life, at peace with himself, his neighbor, his God.

Drama is a form of enacted myth, telling a story of a particular pilgrimage experience, of a man's self-understanding or groping towards an identity, of his experience of what is most sacred and pre-eminently real, of his wrestling with the mystery of his own being within the problematic of a concrete historical context, of his attempts to discriminate between true and false meanings and values, and to live accordingly. Drama represents the story of the way in which a man seeks wholeness, personhood and dignity; it implies, by the same token, the way in which a man seeks to avoid meaninglessness, hopelessness and disintegration.

Drama tells a story which renders a verdict on the pilgrim and the quality of his pilgrimage. The verdict indicates whether the protagonist of the story was a pilgrim or a wanderer, whether his odyssey was a genuine pilgrimage or a directionless wandering, whether the odyssey's direction was right or misguided. It may show that the cacophony of the wilderness condition produced deafness to, or distraction from, the Logos which imparts the criterion of worthy choice in thought and action alike, or that the pilgrim succeeded in discerning true meanings and values and living accordingly.

Myths, as dramatic and narrative embodiments of man's pilgrimage experience, may be grouped into three major categories. The first category attempts to explain the origins of the pilgrimage condition, the second to represent the critical life-and-death struggle of the pilgrim, the third to describe the state of affairs at the end of the pilgrimage experience. The three categories of myth focus respectively on three aspects of time which transcend any particular time: a past, primeval time, a critical present time, a future end-time.

Beginnings are the theme of creation and origin myths. Cosmogonies tell how the world began; theogonies relate the origin of the gods; anthropogonies narrate the origin of man. Myths of the original state describe the conditions which obtained after the world came to be. The paradise of the primeval age, the Garden of Eden or the Garden of God, is such a myth.

Myths of crisis, struggle and transformation relate how suffering, evil, death and sin originated and changed the idyllic, primeval state of bliss into the present situation of conflict. They tell of seduction, of the fall and of the flood. They tell of man's struggles with the powers of nature, of inner conflicts of man with himself, of the problem of death. As a counterpart to the myths of crisis and transformation there are savior myths in which a savior-god struggles with the powers of evil and eventually conquers them.

Eschatological myths of the end-time relate the destruction of the universe by catastrophes at the end of time and its renewal with the dead rising to life. They deal with the restoration or 'salvation' of the universe which is achieved by a savior-god or king or hero. They tell of the return to a paradise in the eschatological age, of man's future and endless peace and perfect happiness, of the restoration of the condition lost in primeval time. It is a state of union with the divine, of ultimate and perfect reconciliation with God.

The Glass Menagerie and *A Streetcar Named Desire* can be interpreted as enacted myths of the human pilgrimage condition.[16] The archetypal symbols and moods of the pilgrimage condition, as well as characteristic elements of the three major categories of myths, pervade both dramas. In both there are archetypal images of paradise: Blue Mountain and Belle Reve.

Blue Mountain, in *The Glass Menagerie,* is the home of Amanda

Wingfield's youth. It is the idealized world of her past — long ago and far away — symbolizing youth, beauty, gentility, honor and a cultural tradition. It represents everything that Amanda sees vanishing from the world around her. Blue, for Tennessee Williams, is the color of nostalgic memory, and Blue Mountain therefore represents all the beautiful memories, ideals and values to which Amanda clings. It is, like her daughter Laura's glass menagerie, a world which Amanda recalls in order to derive strength to endure the hardships of the present. Amanda's aspirations are based on the hope that something of that Blue Mountain world remains for herself and her children.

Blue Mountain recalls the archetypal sacred mountain where heaven and earth meet, the cosmic mountain, the highest point of the earth, the point at which the creation began at the center of the cosmos, the primordial paradise where man and God had free and happy association and in which man enjoyed abundant life. After the fall there was a rupture between heaven and earth (the cosmic mountain) which brought paradisiac beatitude to an end.

Belle Reve (Beautiful Dream), a plantation in Mississippi, had been the home of Blanche DuBois. Belle Reve, a symbol of the southern aristocracy, had provided her with security, status and a grand tradition of elegance, refinement and culture. The ideals symbolized by Belle Reve demand that Blanche be superior, special, a lady in the grand tradition. Although Blanche has undergone the devastating consequences of the ''fall'' in her failure to live according to these ideals, she is haunted by them. Her pilgrimage condition is sustained by her desperate hope of finding a gentleman who will marry her, protect her, maintain her honor, and thus enable her to become the lady that Belle Reve had destined her to be.

Blue Mountain and Belle Reve symbolize an idealized, paradisiac, past time that is identified with the experience of self-esteem, security and self-acceptance. It is recalled as *the* good time, paradigmatic of happiness and goodness, to be cherished as the measure of every subsequent time.

Blue Mountain and Belle Reve are images of hope and aspirations as well as images of a past golden age. As archetypal symbols of the pilgrim's hope, possibly the most basic of all religious impulses, they are projections of an inward wishing and desiring. They are paradisiac images expressing the hope that is essential for mental and spiritual wholeness and that can be identified with the capacity for fantasy.[17] In the pilgrimage experience fantasy is the absolutely necessary and indispensable source of what can become a more stable and pervasive sense of self-transcendence, for it is a moment of opening up new ranges of energies and symbols which not only lead to religious reality but also can be significant psychologically. In fantasy lies the beginning of religion; its absence from the psychic life of the person is the most fundamental meaning of mental illness.

The longing for everything that Blue Mountain and Belle Reve represent corresponds to the firm hope that the crisis of the present can be resolved and that its meanness can be transcended. Both are paradisiac images of hope which symbolize that higher vision of human possibilities experienced during a period of intense suffering; they imply, despite the evidence of the present, that happiness is the ultimate human possibility.

Both Blue Mountain and Belle Reve are images of that hope which is derived from the past, from the recollection of a better time. It is to such places that Amanda Wingfield and Blanche DuBois retreat in memory to recapture the experience of that time when their lives had purpose, love, hope and beauty. Both places symbolize the possibilities in life for beauty, purity and love; they suggest that these possibilities ultimately reside in and issue from the imagination which transforms the everyday experience of occurrences into events, which has the power to fill the void in lives which are incomplete and to ease the pain of their longing. Both Blue Mountain and Belle Reve are that permanent vision of a higher reality without which the attainment of that missing part of reality is unlikely; both images of hope impel the quest for self-completion and reflect the power of fantasy to shape and sustain human pilgrimage experience.

Blue Mountain and Belle Reve share the quality of dreams. They reveal the dreamer's self-image, his expectations from the future, his imagined solutions to pressing problems, his thoughts, desires, impulses, memories, concerns and mood. They reflect the dreamer's view of the nature and meaning of life, the quality of relationships and the degree of relatedness, the dreamer's subjectivity and personality structure. Blue Mountain and Belle Reve reveal the aspirations and hopes of two deeply troubled women attempting to renew and reconstruct their lives in terms of their most positive past experiences. It is the very positive way of remembering the past that inspires and sustains the hope of these women; they have chosen to remember what they deemed was most worthy of remembrance. They are implicitly convinced that the promise of the future cannot be less than the best of the past.

There are elements in *Glass Menagerie* and *Streetcar* that correspond to myths of crisis and struggle which focus on the problematic of the present time between the cherished primeval time and the end-time.[18] In fact, Amanda and Blanche draw upon the paradigmatic experiences of Blue Mountain and Belle Reve in order to confront their life-crises in the unresolved time of transition, the time of the pilgrimage experience, of alienation from a cherished ideal and of hope for its recovery. Both dramas focus on the present context of the human struggle which furnishes man with the elements, the oppositions and the problems with which he must deal if he is to live. Like crisis myths both dramas relate how things came to be what they are, how one state of affairs became another; both concern the conflict between the forces of life and death, of good and evil; both concern the hope, provided by the strengths of man's context, of overcoming the death-pull of those evils which threaten to impede the attainment of true meaning and value; both look to a person through whose agency a deliverance from threatening evils may be achieved. Amanda looks to Jim O'Connor and Blanche looks to Mitch with the hope that a 'savior-god' has finally come to deliver them from the meanness and life-diminishing evils of their present context. Both look to a "savior-god" for the realization of the hopes and aspirations symbolized by the paradisiac archetypes of Blue Mountain and Belle Reve.

The crisis is reflected by the clash between the symbols of the idealized past and the life-diminishing present, between a pastoral paradise and an urban jungle. Blue Mountain and Belle Reve, like Eden, are paradises in an idyllic pastoral setting, close to nature, recalling a time when their former inhabitants were in harmony with nature, and especially in harmony with their own personal natures. The former, idyllic time of pastoral delight contrasts with the dreadful, critical time of urban tawdriness. Amanda and Blanche have been driven by misfortune, the equivalent of original sin, to the urban jungles of St. Louis and New Orleans respectively. In each case the "fall" is linked with a tragic marriage. Amanda's husband abandoned his family; Blanche's young husband committed suicide. Matrimonial bliss is associated with a paradisiac pastoral setting and time. The pastoral past contrasts with the meanness, complication and spiritual poverty of the present urban crisis setting. The city is a metaphor for the bewildering, maddening, terrifying and apparently insoluble complexity of life; it contrasts with the bliss and simplicity of an uncomplicated time. The contrast in symbols reflects the hope, pervading the pilgrimage experience, of simplifying one's life by mastering the bewildering complexity of one's present, critical context. Blue Mountain and Belle Reve are visions of a simpler time which must be remembered in order that that time may be resumed in some new way. We find in the past whatever we seek for the future. If what we seek is trivial, the past we discover will be trivial. If what we seek is noble, reflecting true meaning and value, what we find will be authentically human.

The idealized past of Blue Mountain and Belle Reve is a kind of screen upon which Amanda and Blanche respectively project their vision of the future; it expresses their judgment of the past in terms of paradise images of hope rooted in their earliest recollections. The recollections of youth precondition their apperceptions and expectations as adults. From their earliest days Amanda and Blanche have regarded certain places and persons as particularly important and memorable; these have become the historical matrix from which both have formed their vision of reality. Later, when times are out of joint, Amanda and Blanche are especially disposed to recall the past to discover why it did not usher in a better state of affairs.

Blue Mountain and Belle Reve symbolize the way man organizes his past around the direction of his future. A condition for sanity is the capacity to organize the past in the direction of the intentional thrust towards the future, a thrust which is not added to man but which constitutes him the unique being that he is. The intentional thrust towards the future is at the heart of the archetypal symbols of the pilgrimage experience. Blue Mountain and Belle Reve express the hopes, aspirations and ideals that stir Amanda and Blanche into action; they create their style of life, the form of their response to the challenge of the future. There is a sense in which Blue Mountain and Belle Reve possess them and determine what they are. They are inseparable from their dream. They are what they will to remember, and their memories make their future.

Inasmuch as our dreams, visions and hopes in some way transcend time, they share the quality of myth: they concern a time that is not restricted to particular time, a time that is relevant to the entire pilgrimage condition of mankind.[19]

The paradisiac archetypal images of hope in *The Glass Menagerie* and *Streetcar* are oriented to an ultimate time that is the final goal and condition of the pilgrimage experience. In this respect both dramas share the concern of eschatological myths with the future, final and permanent time that is to be reached at the end of the temporal process. There is an ineluctable and final time that is ushered in by a chain of catastrophic and apocalyptic events in the eschatological myth that is reflected in the apparent permanence of time and condition which the tragic women of *The Glass Menagerie* and *Streetcar* reach after having been abandoned by their respective gentlemen callers.

If these women were not idealistic, sensitive persons aspiring to something more than that with which most people are content, there would be no tragedy in their life stories. There is no tragedy without a dream. Ultimately these women understand that their dreams transcend both their own personal resources and those of their society for their attainment. They understand, in terms of their paradisiac archetypal images of their pilgrimage condition, what should be, in contrast to what is. (In fact, for Blanche what should be ultimately is more real than what is, and she is led off to an asylum.) They painfully experience the inner conflict between their dream and their personal limitations; yet dream they must, for the future is promising on condition that they remember a past of promises. The dream, whether Blue Mountain or Belle Reve, transcends the resources of the dreamer for its fulfillment; it is, in fact, an experience of the transcendent. Like all myth, being essentially vague and imaginative, these plays do not render a definite judgment about the personal character of the transcendent; nevertheless, they possess the religious character of myth which is described by Schubert Ogden as "that manner of representation in which the unworldly and divine appears as worldly and human—in which the transcendent appears as immanent."[20] If Plato called upon myths in the service of human discourse about divine things and the mystery of human existence, it seems that Williams calls upon his *Glass Menagerie* and *Streetcar* with their paradisiac archetypal symbols of the human pilgrimage condition for much the same purpose.[21]

There is no dream without wish, no Blue Mountain or Belle Reve without human longing, and no dream-telling, myth-making, *Glass Menagerie* or *Streetcar,* without owning up to one's wish. There is a dream of paradise at the very center of everyman which works its way out in that tissue of symbols that is myth, expressing through images of limitation the reality of every individual's life story, personal drama, or myth.

11

RE-PRESENTING THE GOSPEL TRUTH

Communicating Christ is a question of making the truth of Christ, the Gospel truth, present to all men at all times. It is a question of making present the Father's true meaning and saving purpose both as individuals and as his community in the Church of Christ; for the Gospel truth is the truth of God in Christ for man's salvation. The Gospel truth is a personal truth, a truth about a personal God, communicated in the person of Christ, and addressed to all persons through persons. Just as God and Christ wholly communicate themselves in the Gospel truth, those who effectively communicate Christ in their lives do so with a love that engages their whole heart, whole mind and whole soul. The Gospel truth affirms that to know and to see Christ is to know and to see the Father (Jn. 14:7-9); consequently, it implies that it is effectively communicated only when to know and to see us is to know and to see Christ. Through baptism Christians are committed to being known and seen in this way; they are committed to a living and personal communication of the Gospel truth of God in Christ. Through baptism they participate in the gift of Christ's openness to God and in God's openness to Christ; they participate in the friendship of Christ for his Father and in the Father's friendship for his Son.

Each new generation presents the Gospel truth within the limits of its graced human resources; and each individual within each generation has his unique contribution to make for communicating the same truth. Like variations on a theme, they do not exhaust its true value; for the same Gospel truth that was in Christ has an ongoing impact upon the historical development of the Church, of individuals, societies and generations. Its mission continues until the end of time; each new generation offers a new framework of historical reference within which the Gospel truth, cherished by previous generations, continues to emerge until its ultimate emergence in the last judgment at the end of the historical continuum; until then, the historical evidence of the Gospel truth's impact is always somewhat partial and incomplete.

Theological development is based on the premise that the full historical meaning of Christ, of the Gospel truth, of the resurrection event, of the Christian movement, will not be fully revealed until it can be affirmed in a final assessment, a last judgment, of all the historical evidence bearing witness to their historical impact. Although the implications of the Gospel truth for world history have been partially ascertained, they cannot be fully ascertained before their having been fully realized at the conclusion of the entire historical process. In this context, it may be said that there is more historical evidence confirming the credibility of the Gospel truth, of the resurrection account, today than there was at the time of the apostles.

In different ways both Hegel and Pannenberg have recognized that the complete understanding of the significance of any persons, event, or movement presupposes a knowledge of their relationship to everything else in the universe, from the beginning to the end of time. Because every existent in the continuum of history is actually related to every other existent, its meaning is only partially ascertainable until its full context of relationships emerges at the end of history. Hence, Pannenberg affirms that God's historical revelation of himself—the Gospel truth—will reach completion only at the completion of that historical process through which it is taking place. The fullness of human history will be marked by the fullness of all the human lives through and in which the Gospel truth has found expression. Only then will the Christ story have been fully told.

The world of the fine arts provides paradigms for explaining the role of the imagination in the development of new theologies and the communication of the Christ-event. Although there is but one definite script for a play or an opera, plays and operas admit of widely diverse representations because the script and its characters are imagined differently. For example: Amanda Wingfield, the mother in *The Glass Menagerie,* has been represented as a rather high-strung woman in one production, and as a serene and gracious lady in another. The script had remained the same in both productions; however, the spirit of Amanda Wingfield had changed because the directors of these productions had not imagined her in the same way. The written script is static, definite, one; the enacted representations, on the other hand, allow for the dynamics of change, diversity and imagination.

1. MEANING AND VALUE THROUGH IMAGES

Meanings and values are grasped in images. Our insights into true meaning and authentic value occur with respect to some schematic image of concrete expression that serves as a proportionate and appropriate substrate.
The power of the imagination to represent or to create this substrate is
required for our grasp of true meaning and authentic value. Through the
imagination, images, words and symbols are made present to us; and it is
through these that we grasp what is represented or signified, whether this be
present and actual, or absent, past, future, merely possible, ideal, normative, or fantastic.[2] Through the imagination we are in contact with our
immediate surroundings, with the world revealed through the memories of
other men, with the cultural heritage of the community, with the thought of
scholars, scientists, writers. Through the development of reflexive techniques a culture may safeguard the authentic meaning and value expressed
by the images, words and symbols; through these techniques it may determine the adequacy of the particular images, words and symbols employed
for the expression of the authentic meaning and value in question.

The literary paradigm suggested by the Roman Church's reaction to the
Reformers' representation of Jesus, the Bible and the Church is that of
Tennessee Williams' rejection of the East Berlin theatre production of his
play *A Streetcar Named Desire*. Williams protested that the play had been
entirely distorted and falsified; the director had missed the point of the play
and its spirit by interpreting Blanche DuBois as a symbol of the corrupt
middle class and Stanley Kowalski as a symbol of the proletariate engaged
in class warfare. The Marxist director had not used his imagination intelligently; despite his possession of the script, he failed to represent it. In fact,
Williams attempted to have the production stopped because he claimed that
his play had been falsified, misrepresented and violated to such an extent
that the director had no right to claim that this was the play of Tennessee
Williams.

Although, as Edward Bozzo affirms,[3] "one's own imagined Jesus" is
significant in a spiritual (not academic) quest, there is a tension between the
historical Jesus and the Jesus of the imagination. The imagined Jesus may
be one that serves personal prejudices. Each person exists within his own
social and cultural tradition and is called upon to make the intention of
Jesus relevant to his own context. The only relevant claim to the term
Christian is the claim to share the continuity of purpose and intention of
Jesus' life. This intention is to be discerned in Christian living—in actions
more than in words, and manifests the historic continuity of Christ. In
order to emulate the intentionality of Jesus, sound and systematic interpretation is necessary. There will be a variety of typifications to suit the
varied current needs. Each sector of the current spectrum will have to

construct its own typification if the message of Jesus is to be meaningful today.

The film version of Anouilh's *Becket* does violence to history and the person Becket by making him the representative of Saxon resistance to the Normans when Becket was not a Saxon nationalist and when there existed no such racial strife in that historical period.[4] Similarly the tendency to imagine Jesus as a Jewish insurgent and political revolutionary is the work of the imagination unchecked by responsible historical and theological research.[5] Knowledge of the historical Jesus is important to help provide faith with its necessary content and to contribute to one's own faith-image of Jesus; it checks false or inappropriate faith-images, or aspects of faith-images.

New churches and religious sects are formed when God, Jesus and the Church (usually the primitive Church described in the New Testament), are imagined, represented and interpreted in radically different and conflicting ways.[6] Although the members of all these churches may claim to be Christian and to derive their existence from the revelation in the Bible, these radical differences among and within denominations suggest that polytheism may be a genuine problem in the Christian world.

The ambivalence of images, words and symbols offers certain advantages for theologizing on the meaning of the biblical revelation, inasmuch as no image, word or symbol completely defines the significance of God, Jesus and his Church. Theologizing evinces a trait of the creative mind that psychologists have called a tolerance for ambiguity.[7] This implies a recognition that the images, words and symbols for God and the Christ-event never exhaustively represent these realities; they are not rigidities which entrap or immobilize further speculation about them. God alone has an adequate idea of what God is. Human images, words and symbols offer analogies suggesting what God is; hence, an analogous knowledge of God is all that is possible for the human mind. Its character is always approximative.

Representations of the *dramatis personae* of a play have this same approximative quality that derives from the analogous character of human language.[8] A written text cannot fully represent a person. The complete person that the playwright had in mind and fully imagined is represented by the complete person of the actor who, through the medium of the text and with the aid of a director, attempts to interpret, imagine and represent as fully as possible what the playwright had in mind. Now the written text never fully succeeds in communicating the persons *(dramatis personae)* intended, and so a perfect or identical representation of the character which the author has in mind would presuppose that the subsequent directors of a play had exactly the same imagination as the author with his particular reservoir of images and symbols. Hence, although the different productions of a play or opera may be faithful to the spirit of the creative mind from which the works originated, each representation is approximate and highlights a particular facet of the truth.

2. BIBLICAL REVELATION AND THE IMAGES OF TRADITION

Jesus himself taught in parables. He employed illustrative stories answering to a question or pointing a moral or lesson. The parables and allegories of Jesus reveal the different ways in which Jesus imagines his Father and himself. The primitive Church adapted parables by creating a new setting in the narrative for the utterance of the parable; it adapted parables to its own homiletic needs. The Church's imagining of God and Jesus in different ways derives from the fact that Jesus himself did this. Jesus and the primitive Church communicate the ultimate truth and the ultimate value that is God by imagining it in various ways. The unique experience of this truth and value is represented through the intelligent use of the creative imagination and its resources.

Although the writers of the New Testament believed in the same Jesus, they imagined him diversely. Dr. Vincent Taylor's study[9] enumerates some fifty-five names and epithets applied to Jesus in the New Testament. Some of these are the following: Rabbi, Teacher, Master, The Prophet, The Christ, The Son of Joseph, Our Savior, The Lord, The King, He That Cometh, The Holy One, The Righteous One, The Judge, The Lion of the Tribe of Judah, The Root and Offspring of David, The Servant, The Only-Begotten Son, The Bridegroom, The Shepherd, The Author or Pioneer, The Stone, The Head of the Body, The True Vine, The Lamb, The Paraclete, The Expiation, The Mediator, The High Priest, The Radiance of the Divine Glory, The Light of the World, The Bread of Life, The Door of the Sheep, The Resurrection and The Life, The Way and the Truth and the Life, The First-born, The Last Adam, Alpha and Omega, The Beloved, The Word, The Amen, The Image of God. Each of these titles reflects diverse dimensions of the impact of the Risen Christ on the lives of those within the community of the Church formed by that impact. The titles correspond to the different ways in which the once-and-for-all Christ-event is imagined by those who have experienced it in their own lives and that of the community. The titles imply the quality of the change this event has effected in men's lives.

There was no single formulation of the doctrine of the Christ-event in the patristic period.[10] The theological minds of the time formulated this doctrine according to different models.[11] The creative imagination provided models from secular culture for the elaboration of new theologies. The exemplarist tradition tended to explain the event in terms of moral rebirth and redirection. The Western liturgical tradition expressed the doctrine of the redemption of Christ as a saving and atoning victim offering his own manhood to the Father. For the West, *cultus* is interpreted chiefly as transaction, sacrificial oblation and atoning death. The Eastern liturgical tradition imagined the event both in terms of mystical transfiguration and of a rescue and a healing. Christ the Victor rescues mankind from evil by conquering it; Christ the Illuminator heals mankind by bringing it from darkness to light. Hence the particular perspectives of individual Fathers mediated the truth of the Christ-event according to the mythic patterns of thought and discourse of their culture. The same experience of the Risen Christ may be further communicated and complemented by expression in the mythic categories of contemporary culture.

Although the founders of religious orders and the founders of new Christian churches adhered to the same Jesus and the same Bible, they imagined them in different ways. The ways in which the former imagined them were compatible with that of the Roman Catholic and aided that church in its mission. The implications of the ways in which the latter imagined them were incompatible, at least in the thinking of that time, with continued membership in the Roman Church. In terms of the analogy of the script for a play or opera, the Roman Church made it clear that it did not recognize the reformers' representation of the script as authentic; in fact, the way the reformers interpreted Jesus and the Bible implied an undisciplined, wild imagination that failed to communicate their true character.[12]

3. THE GOSPEL TRUTH FOR RE-ENACTMENT

In terms of the paradigm of the play, Jesus is the *dramatis persona* of the New Testament, meant for re-enactment in the lives of men. The salvation, enlightenment and healing of mankind are achieved through our re-enactment and representation of his true meaning and value by putting on his mind and heart, sharing his consciousness and intention towards the Father and mankind. The Christian is committed to the prayerful and healing process of understanding and re-enacting the ultimate truth and value of God in Christ, under the direction of the Risen Christ and his gift of the Holy Spirit. Jesus, as incarnate Word, represents God and, as the new Adam, he represents mankind in its ultimate and final perfection before God. As a divine person, Jesus is God the communicator, the eternal Word, the perfect representation and communicative self-expression of God the Father. He historically communicates by his physical presence, by speaking, by gestures, by his style of life and above all by his death and resurrection. Through his life, death and resurrection, Jesus historically enacted the ultimate truth and the ultimate value of God. He designated disciples and apostles to receive and to represent his own (and the Father's) decisively final and enduring communication to men. The Christian community, then, by successive approximations, must attempt to acquire a deeper understanding of the central mystery of Jesus' lived experience related in the New Testament; Christ *is* the New Testament message, the Gospel Truth. The witness of the New Testament writers to this truth is characteristically varied. No one witness can say everything, even though each presents the whole truth in a different and distinctive way.

4. THE NEW TESTAMENT AS CHRIST'S COMMAND TO RE-ENACT

The central message of Jesus is the call for the re-enactment of the life that he had received from his Father. Jesus historically invited men to re-enact the life that he himself enacted: "Be merciful as your heavenly Father is merciful" (Lk. 6:36), and "Be perfect, therefore, as your heavenly Father is perfect" (Mt. 5:48).[13] The heavenly Father is always merciful (perfect) but the Christian *becomes* merciful (perfect).

Even the Old Testament taught that the people of God were to re-enact (represent to the world) the character and qualities of their God: "You shall be holy, because I, Yahweh, your God, am holy" (Lev. 19:2). If holiness is the way of being which is proper to the God of Israel, then his people, bound to him in covenant fidelity, must re-enact that holiness in their own lives and represent it to the world. The holiness of God's people derives from their community with him. Because God is with his people, they are empowered to re-enact, represent and communicate his holiness. Israel must live according to the spirit of God and re-enact the way he acts: "Yahweh does justice for the fatherless and the widow, he loves the foreigner, giving him food and clothing. Love the foreigner, therefore, for you were foreigners in Egypt" (Deut. 10:18ff).

The New Testament maintains a continuity with the Old in its doctrine on the law of holiness and its relation to resemblance, imitation and re-enactment: "As he who called you is holy, be yourselves holy in all your conduct; since it is written you shall be holy, for I am holy" (1 Pet. 1:15). Paul comments, "Put on then, as God's chosen ones, holy and beloved, the sentiments of compassion, kindness, lowliness, meekness and patience, forbearance; as the Lord has forgiven you, so you must also forgive" (Col. 3:12f); "Be good and full of compassion for one another, forgiving one another as God has forgiven you in Christ. Be imitators of God, as beloved children of God" (Eph. 4:32-5:1). Thus Christians reveal that they are authentic children of their heavenly Father, for they have been generated by and live by (represent or re-enact) his spirit.

Jesus' teaching made it clear that he was enacting his Father's spirit. His parable of the lost sheep (Lk. 15:47) is addressed to the Scribes and Pharisees who disapprove of Jesus' friendship with publicans and sinners.

The parable emphasizes the joy of the shepherd in rediscovering his lost sheep; it represents the loving affection God has for sinners, his desire to pardon and re-establish them among his children. The parable reveals the sentiments of God and explains the conduct of Jesus, in whom the divine loving-kindness and compassion for sinners are re-enacted.

Jesus explains his Father's actions in terms of parables: he is like the man who sows the mustard seed, like the woman who puts a piece of leaven in the bread. In every case, Jesus refers to his Father's way of acting and summons his hearers to re-enact the way of his Father. Because his heavenly Father is what he is, his true children will, as a matter of course, be like him.

5. COMMUNICATION THROUGH RE-ENACTMENT

For Jesus to function paradigmatically today, an individual must assess the tradition(s) stemming from Jesus. As an agent, each Christian bears the burden of a tradition transmitting what Jesus did to human history by his life, death and resurrection.[14]

The New Testament authors bear witness to the fact that the Word was made flesh to establish perfect personal communication with men; that this communication occurred at a definite time and place; that it is nevertheless an ongoing reality, because the incarnate Lord is still living and operative among those he chose to be his people for a progressively more perfect communication of God to men in the continuum of a lived personal experience of his true meaning and value. In the eschatological perspective of the resurrection-parousia, the fully loved personal communication between God and man becomes existentially more and more realized in terms of lived experience, in which one becomes more richly that which he always is and is to be as this acting (and re-enacting) man in contact with other men. For example, the titles bestowed on Jesus in Acts 2:36 are in reference to this man as now to be recognized by what he has personally communicated to his disciples, the Spirit which makes them a prophetic community. The titles are in terms of effected personal relationships; nothing is added to the person of Jesus. As God is hallowed by what his people become, so Jesus is constituted divine Messiah by the manifestation of his people. Jesus' being Lord is historically revealed by his communication of God to men in the community of the Church charged with the Spirit.

The Church, the community of men in Christ, historically and distinctively (in each generation and epoch) makes this divine self-communication present to the world. It communicates the unique personal experience of God in Christ Jesus, so that it becomes normative of ours and we represent the Gospel truth for others. Ultimately, the Gospel speaks to us through persons; for only persons really speak and understand.

6. RE-ENACTMENT UNDER THE DIRECTION OF THE RISEN CHRIST

The witness of the New Testament writers to God's self-communication in Jesus Christ is characteristically varied. No one witness can say everything, even though each presents the whole truth in a different and distinctive way. Correspondingly a variety of interpretations is possible. Christians believe that the Risen Christ and his Holy Spirit are actively present in the Church and in the hearts and minds of the faithful, assisting them to grasp the meaning and value of the written biblical revelation. The Risen Christ and his Holy Spirit direct the hearts and minds of the faithful, in a role analogous to that of the director of a play, in the prayerful process of representing the Christ-meaning and the Christ-value to the world. The authenticity of such Christian witness is commensurate with the receptivity of Christians to the grace of the Risen Christ and his gift of the Holy Spirit. Only those who receive the Risen Christ have the power to communicate him. Ultimately, the written biblical revelation exists as a kind of text that enables the faithful to represent Christ and his Spirit to the world.

7. RE-ENACTMENT THROUGH COMMUNITY OF INTENTION

The Christian community generally agrees that the influence of Jesus on life and action is what counts.[15] Christianity is constituted by the personal continuity of Jesus' action, by the sharing of his interiority, his intention with others. The knowledge of Jesus passes from historical to historic knowledge when Jesus becomes significant to a contemporary in his own conduct; his intentionality of mind and heart pattern the aspirations and intentions of this man. To recognize Jesus as the paradigm of one's life requires that one participate in some degree in the Spirit which has been made manifest in Jesus. An authentic Christian is a person who shares and continues in his own life the intention and activity of Christ. His life is in historic continuity with that of Jesus and acts upon his social context for its transformation. The emphasis must be put on the life that Jesus transmits rather than on his ideas as such; for the wisdom of Jesus is communicated in his activities as a lived-wisdom. The Word is incarnated; wisdom is lived and communicated in an historical, social context, even though it may be rejected by it. Human action is properly intelligent and reasonable action; this rational dimension of action is intention. Hence, to discover whether individuals or institutions are Christian we must know whether they share the historic continuity of purpose and intention uniquely expressed in the life of Jesus and first defined by him in his teaching. His teaching is important primarily because it defines a purpose, not because it defines a set of ideas about the world or the way men ought to live. Hence the only relevant claim implied in the term Christian is that of sharing in the continuity of purpose and intention of Jesus' life: in acting deliberately, consciously and effectively for the realization in life of his ends.

8. WAYS OF RE-ENACTMENT

Jesus historically re-enacted the reality of God in a rich variety of ways, suggesting the ways in which the Church may re-enact this same reality.

The written or spoken word has always been a primary way of representing and communicating the ultimate meaning and value of God.[16] The spoken word, the oral tradition, especially characterized the communication of the Good News in the first generation of the Christian era. The content of faith was called the Gospel or Good News, or *kerygma,* which referred to the way in which it was conveyed (by the proclamation of official heralds). The New Testament depicts the Church as founded by Christ, the Word of God; and, after Christ, on men of the word, on prophets and apostles. The prophet speaks in the name of God and the apostle is sent forth to bear witness to the Word of God. Christ is the Word of God in all that he is, says and does; similarly, the prophets and apostles communicate (represent and re-enact) the unique expression of God in Christ by all that they are, say and do. The Word made flesh, in Christian revelation, marks the distinctive way in which God represents himself to man and man becomes acceptable to God. Christ as the Word made flesh is effectively communicated to the extent that his mind and heart are made flesh in the lives of prophets, apostles and ordinary men of faith.

There is a form of wordless giving and wordless receiving that is especially effective in representing the healing and enlightening power of God. The Good Samaritan goes about his compassion wordlessly; Mary sits quietly at Christ's feet listening to him speak (Lk. 10:39). The wordless initiative of the Samaritan on behalf of his neighbor and the quiet receptivity of Mary to the word of God in Jesus communicate the true meaning and true value of that world in which God reigns, in which he acts and is re-enacted. The story of Simon the Pharisee and the sinful woman (Lk. 7:36-50) is one in which Jesus interprets the word-character of human actions:

> I came to your house: you provided no water for my feet; but this woman has made my feet wet with her tears and wiped them with her hair. You gave me no kiss; but she has been kissing my feet ever since I came in. You did not anoint my head with oil; but she has anointed my feet with myrrh (Lk. 7:44ff).

Man's deeds have a word-character, as Gerhard Ebeling has noted, from which it can be learned whether he has understood something of the situation in which he finds himself, or whether he completely misunderstands it.[17] It can become plain from a man's deeds—more clearly and more convincingly than by words—what is in the man. An ordinary deed can be extraordinarily eloquent and significant in the dramatics of divine and human communication. It can awaken hope and open up a whole world. For the Emmaus disciples the Lord's wordless deed in the breaking of bread communicated the resurrectional joy of Christ. Christ communicates not only by formal teaching (doctrine) but also by dramatic action. Individuals communicate the Gospel, or fail to communicate it, by doing what they do and by being what they are, by their entire style of life as well as by spoken or written words.

Knowledge of the Word of God requires choosing and loving. In John the heart of the conversion process is a love that fructifies in knowledge and a knowledge that leads to ever deeper love. Knowledge of the Word of God is a loving knowing: "Everyone who loves is begotten by God and knows God. Anyone who fails to love can never have known God, because God is love" (1 Jn. 4:7f). For John, to love God is to know the Word of God, for the love and knowledge of God grow together.

Repentance is a key element in understanding how God in Christ is effectively represented, re-enacted and communicated.[18] It involves a rejection of false values, attitudes, habits and a personal commitment in love and fidelity to God in Christ. It is the work of God, who alone blots out our transgressions and gives us a new mind and heart full of righteousness, love and truth. Belief in Christ as the Word made flesh and in his unique saving deeds involves the process of self-transformation into his image through a new love and knowledge that becomes the source of all our thoughts, desires and deeds. Paul expresses the key moment in religious conversion: "The love of God has been poured forth into our hearts by the Holy Spirit which has been given to us" (Rom. 5:5). Only through the gift of God's love and knowledge can the Word of God be authentically re-enacted, represented and communicated. Hence, Paul prays for the Ephesians (3:17-18) that:

> Christ may live in your hearts through faith, and then planted in love and built on love, you will with all the saints have the power to grasp the breadth and the length, the height and the depth; until knowing the love of Christ, which is beyond all knowledge, you are filled with the utter fullness of God.

The love and knowledge of God is a divine gift which does not eliminate the distinctivess of those who receive it; hence, each individual who receives this gift represents a version of it that is a particular re-enactment of it. At the same time, there is an interpenetration of unity and multiplicity, of sameness and difference, within the community of those who have freely received the power to become the sons of God.[19] There is also distinctness and unity among the persons of the Triune God. The Three Persons are not closed inwards, each upon himself, but opened outwards towards one another. They are three distinct ways of being God: the Father as divinity wholly communicating; the Son as divinity wholly communicated and wholly communicating; the Holy Spirit as wholly communicated. They exist and communicate in a rational order: the Father simply giving; the Son receiving and giving; the Holy Spirit simply receiving.

9. COMMUNITY IMAGE OF GOD

The interpersonal union of friendship is the best possible image for the God of the Christian faith.[20] Christ would make us friends, his friends and friends of the Father (Jn. 15:13-15; 16:26-27). This friendship is to be seen (like any image of our relationship with God) in terms of the distinctive way in which the Three Persons constitute the godhead. There is also a historical distinctiveness in the way that the Word made flesh possesses his divinity after the immediate communication of the Word's personal being to human nature. Finally there is a historical distinctiveness in the way that we become the brothers and friends of Christ, sharers in the divine nature and participants in the dynamic inner life of the Triune God. To this end the Father "sent his Son, born of a woman" to redeem us and "to enable us to be adopted as sons" (Gal. 4:5). Moreover, the Father has sent "the Spirit of his Son into our hearts: the Spirit that cries, 'Abba, Father' " (Gal. 4:6). God's love is poured forth into our hearts by the Spirit (Rom. 5:5), and through the power of the Spirit, Christ's Spirit and our own through God's gift, we are enabled to call the Father "Abba" each in his own language and with his own personal distinctiveness of temperament, imagination, intellect and culture. Through the power of the Word made flesh we are enabled to become children of the Father, brothers of Christ and possessors of the Spirit of the Father and the Son; through this power we make the Father the vital center of our consciousness just as the Father was and forever is the center of the consciousness of Jesus the Christ. In this way, an authentic Christian consciousness pervades the entire being of individuals and their communities, their historical and existential particularities, and enables them authentically to represent, to re-enact and to communicate the life of Christ Jesus.

10. RE-PRESENTATION: THE INEFFABLE BECOMING EFFABLE

If we see the historical life-death-resurrection of the Word made flesh as the making the ineffable more and more effable, we may have a clue to the way in which the distinctiveness of Christian witness, whether in individuals or in communities, shares in this same process.[21] The ineffable element is the movement of the Spirit beyond the possibilities of human expression. The effable element is the possibility of expression through human means, through words, images and the use of the senses and imagination.

If the basic reality affirmed in both Testaments is clearly that of the Transcendent entering into history, then the fundamental element, including the fundamental element in the consciousness of Jesus Christ, is the ineffable. If Jesus Christ is God, then his person or consciousness is the divine and ineffable consciousness. As truly human, the Word made flesh in the Jesus of history had to struggle, as every human being must, to make effable the ineffable person he is. Authentically human, Jesus might have struggled to find new ways to discover, express and make effable who he is.

In the experience of learning we have an analogy that helps to explain the process of making the ineffable effable. From kindergarten to college, one can recognize in oneself a certain development, an opening to further and further possibilities. Central to this development is the continual understanding of who I am. To find out who he is, man must first of all make use of his senses, his body-constitution. It is impossible for anyone to have ungrounded acts of self-understanding, to have an insight in himself without a self-image based on his relationship to other concrete selves, particular achievements, social status symbols. There must be the continually deepening recognition that I learn who I am by means of my senses, my imagination, my memories and dreams for the future, my ideas, judgments, convictions and decisions.

Just as Jesus humanly struggled to make the ineffable become more effable during his own historical lifetime, the Risen Christ, through the gift of his Holy Spirit to those who believe in him, continues to make the ineffable historically effable. The ineffable who is Jesus Christ becomes effable, expressible and communicable at the death-resurrection. The meaning of the resurrection may be spoken of as the becoming fully expressible of God, who *is* Jesus Christ.

11. ENLIGHTENMENT FROM CONTEMPORARY COMMUNICATIONS

The distinctiveness of the individuals receiving and representing the gift of the Spirit of the Son makes communication within the Christian community, and therefore the existence of that community, possible; however, it also raises problems. These problems can be illuminated by various studies in communications.

Don Fabun in *Communications: The Transfer of Meaning*[22] provides many insights into the transfer of meaning that are applicable to the Christian's (individual or communal) representation, re-enactment and communication of the divine life proclaimed in the Scriptures. The following are some basic principles of Fabun.

a. "In the beginning was the word—'And'."[23] Perhaps all stories should begin with the word "and." Fabun believes that this would remind us that no experience ever begins; there was always something that preceded it. What really began, for us, was our awareness of something going on. Perhaps all stories should end with the word "and" too. This would remind us that no story every really ends—something more will happen after.

The story of God and man in the Bible affirms that God pre-existed before man's experience of him. God's existence is not the product of human experience, of the human imagination and of human needs. The same story of God and man affirms that it is incomplete in proclaiming a Second Coming and the resurrection of the dead on the Last Day. The Christian experience of God and man in the New Testament is preceded by the Jewish experience of God and man recounted in the Old Testament. The Protestant experience was preceded by the Catholic experience. A secularized Marxist messianism takes its departure from biblical messianism.

Because no experience ever begins, Fabun concludes that it may be said that we live in the world of "etc." There is always more to start with than we can take into account. There is always more to say than we can possibly say. There is always more to end with than we can imagine.

b. "When you talk or write about something, what you are describing is those interactions that happened inside of you—not just what happened outside of you."[24] The individual is immersed in a great ocean of happenings. The interactions between the happening that is you and the happenings that are not you are the basic stuff about which we try to communicate.

All the writers of the Old and New Testament are describing their personal experience of God within the community. If all the authors had the identical experience, their expression of it would probably be identical, resulting in only one book that would categorically and definitively describe the human experience of God. Because the one, true God of both Testaments is experienced and understood in distinctively different ways, we have two Testaments and many authors within each Testament attempting to give an account of the community's relationship with its God. Although the accounts are distinctive, there are important common elements. The transcendence and immanence of God with respect to the community and its individuals is one pervasive conviction which, however distinctively affirmed, is maintained throughout.

c. "Many of our problems in communication arise because we forget to remember that individual experiences are never identical."[25] Fabun notes that we select that part of the world that we want to experience at any one time. If we choose to stay indoors instead of going out, we have already selected one field to experience—and cut ourselves off from all the rest. The particular place you are in and the direction you choose to look, decide what experiences you are going to have. Since no two people can be in exactly the same state of internal dispositions and external circumstances, their experiences are to that extent different.

Even the religious experience of those of the same Christian denomination, of the same parish, hearing the same homily, will differ in that the individuals attend to diverse aspects of the homily; or if they attend to the same aspect, they draw different conclusions or make different personal applications.

On another level, different Christian denominations are distinguished from one another by the aspect of the Christian mystery given most attention and by the aspects ignored. The denomination originates with a kind of selective attention to the biblical revelation and the experience of the Lord.

12. THE ANGULARITY OF REPRESENTATION

The Word of God is communicated by the incarnate, concrete, particular, unique. It operates differently in each of us—upon different individuals, in different rhythms, within different horizons, towards different concrete goals in different societies. This diversity, often thought to be our enemy, is actually a source of joy and enlargement. To be members of the Christian community (as well as of the world community), we do not all have to be alike but only to be aware of our own partiality and to recognize our need of each other in sharing and giving witness to the same mind and heart that was in Christ Jesus.

The Word of God becomes incarnated, represented, and communicated in personal and communal experiences, at different cultural and historical moments.[26] Experience in this case includes everything that a person is aware of.[27] Hence the Word of God conditions our experience of insight, or our experience of acting decisively, or our experience of falling in love, or our experience of solving problems, or our experience of acting with courage. The Word of God may condition our experience either as a part of our immediate awareness, without reflection, or as a part of our second awareness, our reflective experience which draws upon the richness of unreflective experience, to bring its latent elements to the surface in theologizing, in preaching and teaching.

The Word of God that enters into human awareness—explicitly or implicitly, dimly or clearly—is part of experience, and is received according to the history of the receiving organism. The reflective task of Christians is to question this experience of the Word. We must bring to light the distinctive structures of our own past, so as to see as accurately as we can the shapes we ourselves impose upon the Word of God as we represent and re-enact it in our lives. We recognize our finitude and partiality in understanding and communicating the Word of God; the vision of each of us is angular. To be faithful to our personal Christian vision is not to deny the truth in others' Christian vision, or even to minimize the conflicts between their truth and ours. It is, rather, to affirm what we know within the limits of our competence and partiality, assured that what we know contributes at least in a slight way to the sum of all the human angles whereby the Word of God is actually, effectively and authentically represented and communicated. What one authentic and dedicated Christian experiences from his standpoint is not the whole of reality, but it is an important part of the whole. If he does not give testimony to it, who will?

We are becoming increasingly aware of the limits of each cultural tradition in its understanding, representing, re-enacting, and communicating of the Word of God. The understanding of the Word of God is not exhausted and absolutized by any one tradition. The communal knowledge attained in the experience of the Word of God by Christians is the sum of the contributions made by each tradition. Each has its variants and highly personal elaborations; each contributes to a communal Christian wisdom.

The individual's authentic experience of the Word of God, with its unique shape and direction in his life, with its own encompassing horizon, is more useful to others the more self-aware we make it. By helping each other discern where our experience of the Word differs and is unique, we become clearer about this experience and more exact in understanding and in assimilating what is of value. The revealed Word of God has been and is effectively represented and communicated in personal and historical diversity. A multiplicity of individuals and cultures bear distinctive witness to the historical impact of the Word, a witness that is even stronger, more attractive, more authentic and complete by virtue of its diversity.

The Word of God operates in and is communicated through the trajectory of an individual's (or society's) imagination.[28] It is conditioned by the determinants of social class, region, place in the structure of status and power that emerge in the individual's metaphors. The individual is angular and sees only in part; as he grows, develops and changes, the path of his change is discernible. The authentic Christian witness is an ideal of many shapes and colors, depending upon the imaginative context in which it is employed; and understanding of authentic Christian witness in concrete, historical, existential cases arises out of matrices of imagining and stands upon the groundwork of particular images, which may well change as an individual grows and develops. The Word of God as operative in authentic Christian witness is experienced and understood according to particular imaginative structures, according to the rhythms of our past experience, of the lived relationships in the family that nurtured us, according to a finite cultural tradition and the native metaphors of our consciousness.[29]

The Word of God is communicated with the encompassing resonance of an individual personal life, within a particular personal attunement of the self in relation to the world, through the pervasive tone of an individual's existence. Modern communications media have greatly expanded man's participation in the experience of others. Modern man is, therefore, exposed to and vicariously involved in a greater awareness of human diversity and distinctiveness than his forebears; consequently, he is also more aware of the rich diversity of personal witness to the Word made flesh.[30] Through and in such diversity the ultimate meaning and value of the Word for mankind is made historically and existentially enlightening and healing.

Jesus prescribes that we re-enact the perfection of life that is his Father's and his own. Scripture, in this respect, is a script that is also a prescription to be re-enacted for that healing and enlightenment that is our salvation.

12

THE CHRIST STORY AS NORM

Just as Christ himself communicated the meaning of his Father and the purpose of his mission in parables, the Church employs the Christ-stories of the Gospel to communicate its Lord. Parabolic teaching makes use of analogy for the purpose of illustration. The parables of Jesus often caused his listeners to turn angrily away from him. When he told the Pharisees the story of the wicked husbandmen, they recognized themselves in the story and became angry. Jesus expressed his judgment of them in terms of a story. He also used these stories to initiate his audience into the mysteries of the transcendent, either comparing a human reaction with a divine reaction, or contrasting the volatile character of man with the eternally self-consistent character of the Creator. The human is used in these stories to mirror the divine.

The four Gospels are narrative accounts of the words and deeds of Jesus, which serve as the foundation of faith, the rule and criterion of Christian life. The four Gospels and the other twenty-three separate compositions of the New Testament were produced in the Church, for the Church, and by members of the Church. Like the books of the Old Testament, they constitute God's written word, communicated to us for our salvation. Despite the considerable variety of temperament, formation and situation among the various authors, they display a remarkable unity of theme, of outlook and of belief. The Holy Spirit impelled the human authors to write these stories as members of the Church to communicate the true meaning of Christ for the strengthening, or edification, of the Church. The apostles' teaching and instruction in the faith drew upon their memories of their association with

Christ; this testimonial material is the content of the New Testament, expressing the teaching and requirements of the Lord whom they had accepted as their Savior.

All the stories of the Bible, for Christians, are a part of the Christ-story. They all serve to communicate his true value. The Christ-story is normative for Christian conduct and belief; it recalls the Lord's instructions, discourses and sentences for those who believe his promise.

Every dimension of Christ's life and teaching has a healing value and meaning for mankind. The gospels recount the Christ-story for human feeling. They resemble the text of a play rather than a novel, inasmuch as the truths and values recounted are meant to be re-lived in the spirit of Christ and to transform the lives both of those who re-present them and those to whom (the audience) they are re-presented. Scriptures, in this respect, are like a script to be performed and a prescription for human healing and transformation. They aim at healing through performance and re-presentation. They tell the Christ-story because of its ultimate truth and value for all men and all times. They are myth, in the basic Greek sense of the word which means story,[1] and they constitute the myth or life-story which is normative for judging the meaning and value, truth and goodness, of every human life-story (myth).[2]

The Christ-self is revealed in the Christ-story, a story meant for our healing by participation in its spirit, meaning and value.[3] The Christ-story (myth) enlightens and heals us by communicating the spirit, meaning and value of Christ; it is the form of Christotherapy, the healing life-story (myth), which grounds the Christian's understanding of his Christ-self, the gift of "the power to become children of God" (Jn. 1:12). The Christ-story reveals that the Father wants to be Father to all men as he is to Jesus, and will become such if men accept union with his Son by possession of the Son's (and the Father's) Holy Spirit, through whom the gift of the Christ-self is communicated. What follows is an analysis of those elements of myth as life-story which illuminate our understanding of the Christotherapeutic meaning and value of the Christ-story.

1. ARCHETYPAL CHARACTER OF HUMAN EXPRESSION

The recurrent phases of human action and passion in their variant historic and individual forms constitute the material of mythopoesis. There are recurring patterns in human behavior based on general inherited tendencies that can be modified and varied according to particular family and individual experiences. Freud holds that the development of the individual is an abridged repetition of racial evolution ('ontogeny recapitulates phylogeny'), and that this development is modified by the individual's historical and social perspective.[4] To begin with, the memory of "psychical antiquities" is received by the individual in the form of his specific family mores which differ with varying historical cultures and particular social settings.[5]

Eden, in the Freudian drama, has but a shadowy existence, limited to the child's security, harmony, peace and unity in the mother's womb. It precedes the tensions of the divided-self. It is that state which precedes the struggle involved in humanizing and controlling the dark powers within man (anti-self, anti-Christ-self); and it can be restored on a higher, more complex level, should the struggle prove successful.

In mythopoesis the successful outcome is represented by the re-creation of an approximate Golden Age in which human happiness is achieved by converting the bad authority into the good authority of Love-Wisdom.[6] The good authority represents the authentic meanings and values that govern men's minds and hearts.

Psychoanalysis, according to Abraham Kaplan, postulates constancy, not fixity—a regularity of pattern, not recurrence of the elements composing the pattern from case to case.[7] Variability is not endless; it occurs within intelligible limits, and it is these that make for discernible regularities. Such regularities are noted in Carl Kerenyi's distinguishing between two levels of mythology.[8] There are the *archai,* or first principles, to which everything individual and particular goes back and out of which it is made. They remain ageless, inexhaustible, invincible in timeless primordinality as abstract ideas, values, themes; they are experienced only through a historic prism, in the form of a definite culture and tradition which speak in the manner of a certain people. Each historical generation is predisposed to re-enact them in its own characteristic way and to reveal the great plasticity of their expression in new contexts.

If myth attempts to present a picture of the complete man and reality through a story, mythopoesis attempts to represent this picture through a socially relevant retelling of the story. Mythopoesis recognizes that each age shapes the old myths in accordance with the needs and character of its socio-historic climate. It revitalizes the story that it retells by making it relevant to an historical time, place and atmosphere. It rescues the timeless meaning and value of a myth by historicizing it, by relating it to the needs and interests of contemporaries.[9]

The mythic pattern is like a universal archetype of meaning and value that is revitalized only when it is rehistoricized through the creative process of mythopoesis. Every age needs prophets and poets to act as priestly mediators of the archetypal, eternal verities and values, by rehistoricizing and revitalizing them with a genuinely contemporary communication of them.[10]

2. THERAPEUTIC VALUE OF CREATIVE ARTS

Freud recognizes the integrative function of art and literature. He believes that the art of the dramatist consists in decomposing his inner self into the various characters of the play, embodying his self in each of the characters and his ontogenetic self through the phylogenetic forms of the myth.[11]

While the artist at first separates himself from his audience in his imagination, he finds his way back to reality through telling his story to and sharing it with others. His art provides a path from fantasy back to reality by employing the rules operative in technique, design and structure.[12] This is a therapeutic process in that the artist masters and objectifies his emotions; it is evidence of a powerful capacity for sublimation which counteracts neurosis. As opposed to the neurotic, who would achieve his ends in imagination alone, the artist wins his ends by embodying his fantasy in particular objects, images, symbols, thereby setting limits to (defining) fantasy. The artist constructively organizes his material and thus expresses emotion in a disciplined way that is also dynamically free, creative, social and communicative. He externalizes his visionary landscape, exposing it to the critical intelligence and taste of others.

In "Dream Work" Freud finds a rough analogy between a dreamer's symbols and a writer's fantasy, and between a dreamer's associations and the writer's elaboration of his poetic or fictional creations.[13] Associations in a literary work are not free inasmuch as the work has structure, design and form; the associations are freely organized because the writer has an audience with whom he wishes to communicate.[14] In this respect the writer is both the dreamer and the one who associates to the structures the associations of his dream. By structuring the dream-work of his characters he produces a work of art, a coherent unity that is intended to say something of significance for others. The process is therapeutic in that the writer discharges psychic tensions in a controlled, meaningful, socially constructive way.[15]

Carl Jung recognizes a link between myths and dreams. The function of significant ('purposive') myths and dreams is not merely or even primarily cathartic; it is knowledge-giving. Dreams give us knowledge of ourselves. Maude Bodkin puts the matter as follows:

The difference between the two schools (of Freud and Jung) lies in Jung's belief that a synthetic or creative function does pertain to the unconscious —that within the fantasies arising in sleep or waking life there are present indications of new directions or modes of adaptation, which the reflective self, when it discerns them, may adopt and follow with some assurance that along these lines it has the backing of unconscious energies.[16]

Mythopoesis is one of the many means that man has created for the expression and communication of his dreams. It expresses his experience of the world around him and of the world within him; it embraces his many-sidedness, revealing the simultaneous disparity and coherence of that which is and of that which ought to be. However implicitly, it communicates the vision and the experience of what the writer believes to be most real in the world.

Significant mythopoesis inevitably reflects everyman's odyssey through time in which he searches for the answers to the mystery of his existence. It may invite us to experience a new way of living, or becoming a new man with new horizons, a personal completion through a higher vision of reality. Myths and dreams, the projections and objectifications of man's inner strivings and desires, characterize human life and provide the materials for mythopoesis.

Art, which Plato called a dream for awakened minds, externalizes an interior world; it brings to light what had been hidden with the artist; it realizes a world in which the inner desire and the outward circumstance coincide. The social function of the arts, therefore, seems to be closely linked with visualizing the goal of work in human life.[17] It concretely envisions the end of social effort, the world of fulfilled desires and aspirations, the free and excellent society. Art is a clue to human hopes, suggesting both their quality and content; it adumbrates the range of potentially significant actions in human life.

Through art the amorphous, indefinite and undefined become formed, determined and defined. Creativity, therefore, may be therapeutic and liberating in terms of releasing the artist from the grip of the vague, undefined mythic demons within him. By naming the demons, mythopoesis externalizes and converts them into partly known objects for critical diagnosis and exorcism.

Although psychoanalytic theory has dealt with myth and mythology, it has not clearly differentiated them from mythopoesis.[18] Mythopoesis develops from mythology; it reinterprets and readapts mythology to present concerns.[19] In keeping with the social and socializing force of art a character in mythopoesis becomes a culture's hero by assuming a sense of responsibility towards the living and creative forces of his society. Mythopoesis remembers its social sources (myths) and reshapes them to meet societal needs. It re-creates myth so that the hero's quest becomes a critique of the existing social order's meaning and values and points to a future order which integrates the authentic values of the past and present. Mythopoeic authors employ their art form to transform their society by identifying with the hero who would change the world. They do not merely explain the world to which their heroes are to adapt; they indicate the hero required for its renewal.

The hero in mythopoesis is counter to an identification and adaptation which acquiesces in and supports the *status quo.* The hero seeks to quicken the creative intelligence of society. He is engaged in the transvaluation of old values and works counter to the idealized stagnant elements of his society.[20] His efforts hold forth the promise of a new way of life in a new society. He struggles to overcome the dark, demonic and irrational power within himself in order to achieve the inner spiritual harmony and strength requisite for the achievement of his dreams, hopes and aspirations. His task cannot be accomplished without self-mastery, self-discipline and self-control.· His goal cannot be achieved by a slave to passion, to irrational desire and to blind instinct. The hero subordinates all that is within him to his overriding purpose: the achievement of a wiser and freer humanity.[21]

3. MYTHOPOESIS AS REINTERPRETATION, RETELLING LIFE-STORIES

Mythopoesis is the process of re-creating an ancient story, of reinterpreting a myth, of creating a new story from the particulars of an old one.[22] The New Testament itself is mythopoeic as a reinterpretation of the Old Testament to explain the meaning of Jesus Christ and his community.[23] The epics of the ancient Orient, although resting on a long tradition, were moulded into mythopoesis by an individual artist. The ancient story is retold because of the analogies which people find in it to their own situation; it serves as an explanation. It may serve to organize the values of a community or an epoch, providing a focus for its self-understanding, giving tone, manner and rhythm to its existence, permeating its institutions and thought, its art, science, politics, psychology, religion and folkways.

The work of mythopoesis is as ongoing as the openness of men to new meanings and true values, and their artistic ability to give them the signature and imprint of their times. Recognizing the possibility of a growth of meaning in the constituent elements of a work and, therefore, a possible development in the meaning of the work itself, Maude Bodkin writes:

> It is with the complete resources of our minds that we must appreciate, if appreciation is to be genuine. If, for instance, we have found certain elements in experience made newly explicit through the teaching of Freud, that new awareness will enter into our apprehension of *Othello,* or of *Hamlet,* though it was not present in Shakespeare's own thought, nor in the audience for whom he wrote . . . One can no more bind within the limits of the author's intention the interactions with new minds of a play or poem that lives on centuries after his death, than one can restrict within its parent's understanding the inter-relations of the child that goes forth from their bodies to live its own life in the world.[24]

Miss Bodkin refuses to allow the author's understanding of the human problem embodied in a work to tyrannize over the meaning that that same work (myth, life-story) may have for future generations. She implicitly touches upon the development of human knowledge and understanding that underlies the need for mythopoesis, the retelling and reinterpretation of traditional stories (myths) in a new social context. Mythopoesis enables the meaningful communication of true value, to whatever extent it is embodied in the original myth, to contemporaries. It is a means for healing through enlightenment, addressing itself to contemporary concerns, needs and interests.

The mythological view of the world, according to Freud, is nothing other than psychological processes projected into the outer world.[25] Our story-telling offers a map of our minds, tracing the trajectory of our imaginations in the pursuit of true value. Freud indicated that wish-fulfillment occupies a dominant place in the happy ending of the fairy-tale.[26] Utopias, like fairy-tales, indicate the quality and character of human aspirations.

Following the path-finding work of Freud, Ferenczi writes that "for any useful writings on individual psychology we have to go not to scientific literature, but to *belles-lettres.*"[27] The link between mythopoesis and psychology emerges in the growing preoccupation of writers with the depth implications of literature; likewise, psychoanalytic criticism has turned towards an examination of the arts.

The impact of psychoanalysis on literature produced styles that tend toward free association. The affinity between literature and psychoanalysis is grounded on their common concern with human motives (intentions). Both deal with them as expressed in language and gesture. Psychoanalysis is not only a science but an art. The sensitive analyst may derive his insights not only from the content of his patient's production but also from his tone, his use of metaphor and imagery. He detects the import of his patient's body-language, his gestures and physical movements. Style, in both psychoanalysis and literature, is the clue to the underlying spirit behind the multiple voices. A psychoanalytic approach to art considers the formal aspects, the dramatic sequence of how, where and to whom a character speaks.[28]

The arts express (present) the universal through the particular. The writer (story-teller, myth-maker) converts the memory of the past and the vision of the future into a present possession for his audience. He stands in collaborative relations with an entire community of fellow-writers from whom he borrows an audience to whom he speaks.[29] What he feels, thinks and wills does not remain closed within himself; it is objectified in his work, in symbols and images.[30]

Because of the variable and ambiguous character of symbols and images in their meaning, the writer's symbolic vision is open to alternate possibilities of interpretation.[31] A symbolized meaning and value are understood in different ways. A theme is always on the inside of polyhedral images. The literary imagination seeks to grasp the human condition in its concreteness, according to the measure of its very dimension, of its time phases, of all its definiteness, of comedy, tragedy and every other human facet.[32]

As ideas and patterns descend into the images or reality, they adapt themselves to every detail and difference of the concreteness into which they enter. Although the idea of several writers may be the same, their actual expression of it will differ. The act of existence is always different, as well as the possibility (the material) into which it enters. The writer's symbolic vision, therefore, finds expression in the unqualified interpenetration of sameness and difference, of unifying form (theme, idea, pattern) and differentiating materials (images, symbols, details).

4. THE TRI-DIMENSIONAL STRUCTURAL UNITY OF MYTHOPOESIS

A mythopoeic work may be studied in terms of the universal, archetypal, recurrent pattern, meaning and value that it embodies and in terms of its historical communication in a work of art which unifies the multiple cultural forms of its era, organizing its art, psychology, philosophy, religion and social currents. A structural unity is found in all mythopoesis. It consists of the analogous stages in the development of the mythopoeic heroes and it takes on the form of a drama in three acts.[33]

This pattern implies the nature of the human journey itself, whether the journey be made by the heroic or the unheroic, by the individual or by society. The "Way of the Lord," "Pilgrim's Progress," the "Odyssey," and the image-symbol of the Path and the Pilgrim who travels it, are variations of the archetypal metaphor of the journey. They suggest a profound consciousness of loss (Paradise Lost); however, they have a journey's end in view (Paradise Regained), the attainment of ultimate meaning and value with the concomitant state of peace, rest and beatitude. They express the process of personal transformation with its new fields of consciousness, new horizons (conversions), new visionary landscapes, new values and meanings.

The mythopoeic drama begins with the First Act of Edenic communal harmony, an initial state of blissfulness (Eden, Paradise, Elysium, Islands of the Blessed, the Golden Age), when man was at home, at one with his origins, with himself, nature, his fellow men and God.[34] Home is a metaphor for the state and place where one is recognized and recognizes others with mutual affection and unqualified acceptance; it is a metaphor for our relationship with the source and ground of our being. In mythopoesis this first act may be only a nostalgic memory.

The Second Act begins with the birth of the hero, who is sent out or who invites expulsion by the powers that enjoy authority over him.[35] The initial harmony has been disrupted by the emergence of the hero who sets out on his quest (path, pilgrimage, odyssey, journey) which involves a challenge to his community, a transcending of the meanings and values of the *status quo*. It is through the pivotal action of the quest that the hero becomes a creative agent of his community, enables its transformation and its attainment of a higher viewpoint for the enjoyment of a wiser and freer way of life. The hero transforms the consciousness of his community. His nature is somewhat ambiguous from the beginning; he transgresses against what his community regards as a natural, inviolable or sacred order (e.g., Jesus' cures on the Sabbath, the accusation that he is possessed of a devil); he commits a crime against the standards of society, which leads to his fall (home-leaving or expulsion) and his journey.[36]

A central experience of all the great myths (life-stories) is the journey. In the myths of Krishna, Zoroaster, Osiris, Baldur, Adonis, Bacchus, Hercules, Mercury and Odysseus, it takes the form of a descent into Hell; in the myths of Aeneas and Dante and many other mythic heroes it involves a symbolic entry into the "dark night of the soul." The journey, in pre-Renaissance mythopoesis, has a definite goal, and we know (even if the hero does not) that the wanderer will be brought home at last. The hero's homecoming assures a great and singular benefit for his community.[37] In modern myths, the journey takes on a less definite character, the homecoming is tenuous (as in *Don Quixote, Faust, Moby Dick*). Homecoming, in traditional myths, effects a new harmony and a renewed society in peace, wisdom and friendship; the mythopoeic journey released creativity and development through openness, questing and questioning for true value.

Transfiguration (transformation through self-transcendence) demands that the pilgrim-hero undergo the rites of passage and overcome the powers of the chthonic realm (anti-self, anti-Christ-self) through his ongoing fidelity to the enlightening inspiration of his creative vision, the Logos or Wisdom-Word, the necessary condition for order, reason and harmony in human desiring, aspiration and activity. The mythopoeic hero moves in a synergic rhythm between the dark pits and the sun-lit heights (e.g., from the crucifixion to the resurrection).[38]

In Act Three there is a renewal, a rebirth or homecoming achieved by the hero's questioning of his deviation. The pilgrim-hero's self-questioning holds the promise of his victory over the chthonic, dark forces (e.g., Jesus' temptation in the desert) and his ultimate glorification. Through his existential diagnosis and discernment he reaffirms the authentic values in the very tradition he has apparently violated (e.g., Jesus and his Jewish tradition) and thereby fulfills the higher interests of his community, becoming a culture or community hero (e.g., Jesus, founder of the New Israel).

Homecoming, in one respect, is the reintegration of the pilgrim-hero with his community; however, his return is not to the earlier starting-point because his heroic quest has complemented and fulfilled his individual personhood and his achievement is assimilated by the community that it has reshaped (e.g., the Risen Christ, glorified by the Father, creates the New Israel of the Church participating in his consciousness of the Father and his healing concern for the world through the gift of the Christ-self).

The pilgrim-hero acts for others. By transforming their consciousness he becomes the agent of personal and social development and fulfillment. The revitalized community venerates him for his personal sacrifice. The pilgrim-hero's lived fidelity to true value through his free decisions and responsible activity transforms (enlightens and heals) his community by inspiring it to embrace the same ultimate meaning and value that have pervaded his life-story. (The glorified Lord glorifies others; the divinized humanity of Jesus heals and divinizes others.)

Homecoming is the term of healing and enlightenment for both the pilgrim-hero and his community.[39] Both achieve self-transcendence through a deeper self-understanding that is the result of the journey's humiliations and triumphs. Homecoming is also a process of enlightenment (journey) that transforms the mind and heart, freeing the mind from error and ignorance and the heart from false desires and values. In this respect, it is a liberating exodus that gradually frees the mind and heart from all that is illusory, ignorant and deceptive, emptying them of all the pseudo-know-ledge and concerns that trivialize human existence. The journey is an exodus from erroneous assumptions, misdirected orientations, unrealistic, illogical, negative, self-defeating thoughts and desires. Exodus (mind-fasting, existential diagnosis) precedes entry into the Promised Land (homecoming as term).

Homecoming (rebirth, renewal, destiny) represents a term of the conscious quest for growth in understanding the nature of the self. Mytho-poesis (life-stories) reveals the many paths individuals follow in their search for authentic self-knowledge, ultimate value and meaning. Homecoming is the healing and enlightenment that characterize the correct understanding of and living in accordance with the self's exigency for true meaning and value.

5. DIVINE MYTHOPOESIS

In the Christian *mythos,* the Christ-story, homecoming is understood in terms of the *Logos,* of the Father's gift of his Son's enlightenment with regard to ultimate meaning and value. John Macquarrie's paraphrase of the Prologue to St. John's Gospel states the case for Christian homecoming, destiny and rebirth in and through Christ:

Fundamental to everything is meaning. Meaning is closely connected with what men call 'God,' and, indeed, meaning and God are the same. To say that God was in the beginning is to say that there was meaning in the beginning. All things were made meaningful, and there was nothing that was made meaningless. Life was the drive towards meaning, and life emerged into the light of humanity, the bearer of meaning. And meaning shines out through the threat of absurdity, for absurdity has not destroyed it. Every man has a share in the true meaning of things. This follows from the fact that this meaning has been embodied in the world from the beginning and has given the world its shape. Yet the world has not recognized the meaning. Even man, the bearer of meaning, has rejected it. But those who have received it and believed in it have been enabled to become the children of God. And this has happened not in the natural course of evolution or through human striving, but through an act of God. For the meaning has been incarnated in a human existent, in whom was grace and truth; and we have seen in him the final meaning or glory towards which everything moves—the glory of man and the glory of God (Jn. 1:1-5, 9-14).[40]

The Bible itself, according to Geoffrey Preston, can be regarded as a whole book whose terms are the Pentateuch and Revelation contained in the overall Christian myth of the movement from creation to re-creation (Genesis to Revelation), or within the myth that stretches from Exodus to Revelation, the myth of redemption, which is situated by and also situates the creation/re-creation myth.[41]

All the individual books of the Bible with all their parts are misread if they are not read as held in tension by the myth; if they are studied as though they had not finally been included in the Book, they are misread. Preston argues that they have their final Christian significance, their enlightening revelatory function for us, only within the Book, only as set in the context of the myth that is polarized by Genesis-Exodus and Revelation.

This Book has been given to us by the instinct to tell a story, the impulse to recite, to rehearse, to re-present (or to have pointed out) some orientation and coherence in the flux of living. The story answers the human yearning for a more comprehensible world. Within the story, the narrated myth of the Bible, there can be set any number of those elements which go to make up the totality of man's life in the world: laws, love songs, anxious questions, traditional wisdom, brief *ad hoc* letters, the literary impact of a particular man's life. All these add to the richness of the myth, but are in turn criticized by it in its totality and (perhaps) answered in their own terms within some other smaller section of the total myth. Each constitutive element retains its peculiar function within the myth and its potentiality for including the whole of lived and imaginable reality. Fundamentally,

Preston believes that the Christian wants to say that anything which cannot in principle be included within this myth that runs from Genesis-Exodus to Revelation and is centered on the event of Jesus is meaningless.[42] In Johannine terms, it is sharing in the light of ultimate reality, definitely manifested in Christ.

Jesus himself can be understood as maker, fictor and poet, although he wrote nothing. He spoke with the authority of a creative artist who knew how to take hold of the deepest aspirations of his people, how to play on the resonances of their history and put them into contact with the new situation and challenge of the present.

Listening to Jesus meant being immediately called into question. He spoke in parables, uttering and bringing to light things kept secret since the world was made. This is analogous to the function of poetry. Clement of Alexandria called Christ the real Orpheus, the new Song which by its singing turns beasts into men and re-creates the universe through the power of the word.

Jesus as poet reveals the power of the first creation as an iconic power by using the language of the people to great effect in telling the story of the kingdom of heaven, that dramatic ultimate reality which comes to expression as a story into which people are invited to enter (through the gift of the Christ-self). The road to the kingdom is by way of the imagination, by way of parables for those who have ears to hear, by way of stories which are like a poem with an in-meaning that is its own guarantee.[43]

Jesus is the divine mythopoesis, the Second Adam, the reinterpretation of the story of mankind divinely intended for the homecoming, rebirth and re-integration through the Father's gift of the Christ-self, the power to become the sons of God. Through participation in his consciousness, Christ has not left his followers orphans (i.e., those who do not know who their parents are); rather, he has communicated the healing and enlightening experience of his Father's love for us.

The divine mythopoesis, the Gospel-truth of the Word made flesh, perennially re-historicizes the ultimate truth and value of God in the ongoing today of salvation wherever the Good News is proclaimed and the Lord's death and resurrection are commemorated, communicating healing, and enlightening in both word and deed.

As the divine, once-and-for-all mythopoesis, the Christ-event explains the Origin-Quest-Destiny story of man with an account that allows for the inclusion of all that is human and answers all that was lacking in every other myth about the Origin-Quest-Destiny experience of man. It stands in every age as the corrective mythopoesis with regard to all the other myths about mankind; it represents an ongoing critique of the *status quo,* of conformity to the powers and principalities of this world, summoning the individual and the collectivity to self-transcendence and transformation through the gift of that consciousness which is in Christ (the Christ-self) and to an unqualified commitment to the ultimate truth and value revealed in the Gospel truth of the Christ-story, which renders the timeless meaning of the *Logos* (Love-Wisdom) timely for men of every generation.

13

STORIES OF GOD AS VISION IN THE DARKNESS

1. DARKNESS, TERROR AND DREAD

There are no stories of God apart from the darkness, terror and dread that are part and parcel of human life.[1] There is a darkness in which the innocent are butchered, in which human bodies are consumed by worms, in which the prolonged torture of terminal cancer eventually benumbs the human spirit into a comatose vegetative state, in which sadism and mental cruelty flourish, in which the victims of plane accidents plummet through the void to their deaths. The natural human repugnance for and horror of death tells us that there is something undeniably frightening about preparing to meet our God. Terror and theophany in death are anticipated in the many horrific ways in which we become conscious of the end, of the ultimate, of the inevitable. The divine presence violently erupts into our consciousness in ways that we had not programmed; in fact, in ways that we had structured so much of our lives for avoiding.[2]

The link between terror and theophany, with meeting our God in death as paradigm, reveals our instinctive preference for a life without God. The Genesis story indicts Adam and Eve for their desire to be gods, for their illusory ideal of an absolute self-sufficiency with its implication that God should be superflous for the achievement of human happiness.

We view as progress our increased capacity for coping with reality at its many levels. A genuinely human existence would seem to be one with which we can cope. When we experience terrifying phenomena, we sense the presence of that with which we cannot cope and before which we are reduced to helplessness. We generally dread encountering such phenomena

114

which make us painfully aware of our finitude, contingency or radical transience. Such experiences have the apocalyptic quality of disclosing the
limits of the fundamental and familiar structures of our existence, of our
ordinary ways of coping with the aggregate of all the external conditions
and influences affecting our lives. We have not sought these experiences;
rather, they seem to have caught up with us, as if we had been pursued by
them from the moment of our birth.

If death is the darkest of human prospects, there is a way in which God
seems to dwell in the dark areas of human experience which are a foretaste
of death itself. A theology of darkness, terror and dread might examine the
divine therapeutic value of these elements in the awesome theophanies
recounted in the Judeo-Christian stories about God. It might reflect upon
their relationship to our experience of God, asking whether there is any
authentic understanding of God apart from them.[3] It might ask whether
there can be an authentically Christian experience, understanding and consciousness of God apart from the darkness which the existentialists and
atheists experience and whether we compromise the Christian message by
ignoring the horrific elements which seem to be a prerequisite for understanding it.

The experience of darkness would seem to be a most common psychological and spiritual locus for Judeo-Christian theophanies, the experience of
God. To the apostles facing persecution, Jesus says not to fear those who
kill the body (Mt. 10:26-31). Even the darkness that is death is within the
confines of his Father's power and through our openness to that power we
can accept the darkness with the security of his sons. The death and resurrection of Christ reveals that the darkness is habitable; the transcendent
power of God inhabits it for our healing and enlightenment.[4] The Risen
Christ tells us that we can be led through the darkness to a perfection that
surpasses human schemes and structures, to the center of the universe
beyond the self.[5]

Ironically, the hidden life of Christ is the non-revealing, comfortable part
of his life. The authentically revealing moment in which his public life
culminates is Calvary when, as Matthew reports, "from the sixth hour
there was darkness over all the land until the ninth hour," and Jesus
experienced the horror of his Father's apparent desertion (Mt. 27:45-6). The
violence of his death, the savagery of his executioners, the darkness over all
the land and the earthquake combine to form the horrific moment in which
Christian faith comes into existence: "Meanwhile the centurion, together
with the others guarding Jesus, had seen the earthquake and all that was
taking place, and they were terrified and said, 'in truth this was the Son of
God' " (27:54).

Faith is born in the apocalyptic experience of terror, violence, cosmic
upheaval, breakdown and death.[6] The Christian understanding of God is

born when darkness covers the earth. It is not derived from the experience of pleasure, success, charm, reason, politics. Rather, when all human values have been apocalyptically shattered and apparently denigrated, the ultimate and paradigmatic Christian limit-experience of Calvary illuminates human consciousness with the true meaning of God. Calvary's terror, horror, violence and darkness become the starting point and context for Christian faith, the experience of a light seen only in the darkness.

The Christian God is not found on Mount Olympus in luminosity, beatitude, satiety and splendor; rather, he is discovered on Mount Calvary in violence, rejection, earthquake, terror, dread and death. Christian wisdom begins in the darkness that covered the land from the sixth to the ninth hour.

Darkness, terror and dread seem to be indispensable elements of the divine therapy for human healing and enlightenment.[7] They serve to liberate us, despite ourselves, from destructive illusions about God and ourselves. They instill a saving fear of the Lord that includes a reverential piety and love of God (Deut. 6:1-5).

If the fear of the Lord is the "beginning of wisdom (Job 28:28; Prov. 1:7), perhaps the experience of darkness may serve as a Wisdom Therapy which overwhelms us with the realization that God is mystery and cannot be encapsulated by human definitions but always remains beyond the ken of our leading luminaries in the darkness of his transcendent mystery. The darkness of God tells us that he is not a self-induced illusion for the achievement of a man-made peace of mind. The experience of darkness liberates us from futile attempts to reduce God to human dimensions, to a useful tool to be employed for our favorite public enterprises and private consolations.

Darkness provides us with a therapeutic limit-experience, illuminating the meagerness of human resources for experiencing, understanding and communicating the divine. It reminds us that God alone has an adequate idea of who God is and that even our most successful efforts at understanding him are inadequate. Where darkness induces modesty, humility, faith and trust, it leads to a communion with God as he really is; it frees us from the self-deception of worshipping gods of our own making. Only the real God saves; not the illusion. The true Israelite is the wise man who makes his home "in the shadow of Shaddai" (Ps. 91:1).

The people of Israel experienced the wonderful works of God as "fearful and terrible deeds" (Exod. 34:10; 2 Sam. 7:34). Their saving experience suggests that terror may act as a divine Shock-Therapy by forcing us to take God seriously, by instilling that state of fear and trembling which is indispensable for our salvation. Terror purifies the mind of its illusions of grandeur; it purifies the heart of its banal attachments. Through terror God demands our undivided attention and decision, revealing himself as the preoccupying Absolute.

When terror shocks us into self-recognition, into poverty of spirit that is a blessed awareness of our contingency, perishability and insecurity, it dramatically communicates the truth of the human condition. Terror expresses our realization that we cannot save ourselves, that salvation, whatever it is, must come from outside the human condition.

That dread which is associated in Deuteronomy (6:2, 5, 13) with the loving service of God and the observance of his commandments would seem to imply a divine Accountability Therapy. Such dread intimates the healthy impact of the divine power demanding an account-ability and response-ability (i.e., love, reverence, obedience) for the quality of our lives. Dread expresses our experience of the awe-inspiring divine power which transcends both our categories and expectations, induces reverence, respect and veneration, and teaches us the appropriate human posture before God.

There are different aspects of the fear of God which draw us to deeper faith. Even when the sacred is revealed under the aspect of the *tremendum,* it is ultimately meant to reassure rather than terrify; "Fear not!" (Judg. 6:23; Deut. 10:12; Lk. 1:13, 30). "The mercy of God extends from age to age to those who fear him" (Lk. 1:50; cf Ps. 103:17); on the day of judgment God "will reward those who fear his name" (Rev. 11:18). There is a fear of God in faith which is the way to salvation.

Terror, dread and darkness express the ways in which our generally sluggish human consciousness is constrained to transcend itself. They are of therapeutic value for the human spirit when they foster attention to matters of ultimate concern; when they liberate us from boredom and a preoccupation with trivia. Violence, death and destruction jolt the human consciousness into an awareness of its contingency, perishability and insecurity; they evoke terror, dread and an awareness of darkness. Do we ever really transcend ourselves without being violently shaken out of ourselves? If the terrified seek salvation, perhaps it is the terrified who will find it. Christ warns us of the authentically dangerous condition that is self-satisfaction: "Woe to you who are rich, who are having your consolation now . . ." (Lk. 6:24-25).

The experience of terror, dread and darkness often serves as a prelude to the happiness of a religious conversion, shaking us out of our comfort and contentment within familiar forms, structures, rules, roles and institutions. We are summoned to a terrifying awareness of a Reality which absolutely transcends the familiar forms of everyday life. We are catapulted to new levels of consciousness in which we may live to the fullest of our capacities. We are left structureless, formless and terrifyingly free in our finite attempts to understand and relate to the Reality of Realities.

Our activities have a dramatic quality because they tell a story. We shape ourselves by the story that our life tells. The terrifying elements in religious experience imply that the shape we give ourselves in the story that we are acting out is not entirely of our own making. The fear of the Lord impels us to that dramatic action which Christian faith believes is our ultimate happiness.

Happiness, in the Aristotelean context, has a dramatic quality because it occurs when we act well to the fullest of our capacities. Happiness, in the Christian context, has the dramatic quality of the Christ story which culminates with the Risen Christ's revealing of the fullness of our capacities for the happiness that derives from acting as he acts. Christ, the Word of God incarnate, is also the Beatitude (Happiness) of God incarnate. The dramatic action of the Christ story, culminating in the resurrection, unfolds both the meaning and the way to the ultimate happiness that is available to all mankind. Participation in the consciousness of the Risen Christ is the ultimate possibility for human happiness. Through the gift of his Holy Spirit, his consciousness pervades the thought and activities of his Church and is evidenced by the same fear of the Lord which characterized his perfect responsiveness and obedience to his Father, even unto the death of the Cross. The dramatic action of the story which Christ's life told, and continues to tell in his Church, reveals the fullness of our God-given capacities for reverencing God (hallowing his name), for hoping in him (thy kingdom come), for realizing his love and his justice here and now in our private and public lives (thy will be done on earth), for communicating his meaning (as it is in heaven), for sharing his life (daily bread), for forgiving and being forgiven and for coping with evil (lead us not into temptation).

Death, disease, suffering and chaos are an affront to human reason which flourishes in luminosity, clarity, harmony and the general order of well-being. Death sets the ultimate limit to human experience, to the illuminating efforts of the mind and to the creative impulses of the heart. Death is the kingdom of darkness, circumscribing the transitory galaxies of intellect; it is the kingdom of stillness which ultimately engulfs even the most intense and valuable human activities. Death is the limit-experience which sets limits to, defines, every human limit-experience. It is the prime analogate of human limit-experience.

The Christ-story can become our story. It can provide us with the courage to face death, to live responsibly, reverently and realistically. The dramatic action which the Christ-story motivates in our lives involves the freedom and terrifying risks of becoming more than that which is provided for by even the best of human structures. It enables us to cope with death, the inexorable demand of the Absolute for our accountability, responsibility and reverence. It enables us to accept death as Christ accepted it; to recognize death as telling us that God alone is without limits, that our pre-suppositions of human unlimitedness, of unaccountability to an Absolute defining our lives, are a fatal illusion.

Our experience of what we most dread is intimately related to our ultimate meaning, to our ultimate future as a gift of God. Fear of the Lord is one dimension of our participation in the Christ-story. It accompanies our faith, hope and love which empower us to accept our ultimate meaning and future as the gift of God. Even though we dread to face the reality of the seed dying, we do so with the blessed confidence that this is the only way to the achievement of that life and to the bearing of that fruit which really counts before God.

History also tells a story whose terrors can be interpreted in different ways, according to the kind of person the interpeter is. Eliade writes that history was regarded as theophany among the Hebrews; every new calamity was a punishment inflicted by Yahweh, angered by the orgy of sin to which the chosen people had abandoned themselves.[8] No disaster seemed absurd, no suffering was vain, for beyond the event it was always possible to perceive the will of Yahweh. In fact, these historical catastrophes were foreseen by God so that his people should not contravene its true destiny; they brought them back to the right road by forcing them to look towards the true God. Then "they cried unto the Lord, and said, 'We have sinned, because we have forsaken the Lord, and we have served Baalim and Ashtaroth: but now deliver us out of the hand of our enemies, and we will serve thee' " (1 Sam. 12:10). This return to the true God in the hour of disaster reminds Eliade of the desperate gesture of the primitive, who, to rediscover the existence of the Supreme Being, requires the extreme of peril and failure of all addresses to other divine forms (gods, ancestors, demons).[9] Through their terrifying visions, the prophets but confirmed and amplified Yahweh's ineluctable chastisement upon his people who had not kept the faith. When such prophecies were ratified by catastrophes, historical events appeared as punishments for sin. Historical calamities became situations of man in respect to God, the epiphanies of God or theophanies.

Eliade, writing of "The Terror of History," the title of his fourth chapter, states that with Marx history no longer is seen to have a transcendental significance; it is no longer anything more than the epiphany of class struggle.[10] Historicism tolerates "the terror of history"; it justifies atrocities by the simple fact that they happened that way. Eliade believes that this approach will not free us from the terror that these events inspire.[11] He believes that as the terror of history grows worse, the positions of historicism will increasingly lose in prestige.[12] An increasingly small number of men have at their disposal means sufficient to force each individual to live immediately and continuously in dread of history. The terror of history is ambivalent: for some, it is merely a fact; for others, it points to the trans-historical reality of God. For Christian faith, the Risen Christ is the center of history, and the fullest of its God-given capacities for the achievement of that perfection which is its God-given purpose. His life story has expressed and continues to express in his Church the inner reality which God has given history, the ultimate horizon for human consciousness and achievement, within which Christ is recognized as the Lord of history, even of its terrors.[13]

2. VISION

There is no story without vision, without a way of seeing the world and ourselves. There are as many ways of seeing the world as there are persons, for each has his particular angularity of vision. Even within the community of Christian vision, a distinctiveness of vision remains.

No authentically human life is possible without vision, without a particular way of seeing, imagining, and feeling about the world and ourselves. Many elements condition our vision; in the Christian context, our way of understanding revelation is one of them. There are three "mentalities" according to Avery Dulles, in the theological understanding of revelation.[14] These mentalities imply that even within the Christian community the notion of vision is analogous; there is something which the visions of individual Christians have in common and there is something which is distinctively personal to the vision of each.

The first mentality concentrates on revelation as a fact, a concrete event. It views revelation primarily as a story of the great deeds of God in salvation history from Adam, through Moses, to Christ and his Chruch. It gives rise to biblical and kerygmatic theology. It emphasizes the reading of Scripture and the preaching of the good news, the gospel (the facts that save). The second mentality is more philosophical, reflective, and analytical. It focuses on revelation as a body of truths, seeking the meaning behind the facts; it will be interested in the doctrines which emerge or can emerge from the saving events. This mentality will stress the importance of oral and written instruction. The third mentality is intuitive and mystical, grasping revelation as an ineffable personal encounter with the divine. Those who are immanentist by inclination will tend to experience God as one with themselves and the world; those who are transcendentalist by inclination will tend to experience God as the "wholly Other." Both experience the presence of God; but they will tend to experience it differently, even though the ways they experience the divine presence are not mutually exclusive.

For the first mentality, the experience of God is conveyed not so much by an analytical system of doctrines as in story. Revelation as event will focus on the story of man's experience with God, on the stories of those chosen persons through whom the God of the Judeo-Christian tradition has told his story, and especially on the story of Jesus as unique and normative for our own stories. This mentality tends to erect an ethic of example; the actions of Christ and the earliest Christians are paradigmatic for Christian life. The second mentality is abstractive in its approach to moral conduct; it tends to view morality in terms of laws and rules to cover all particular cases. The third mentality is of a mystical and intuitive bent; it embraces a charismatic ethic, looking upon right conduct as a response to the present leading of the Holy Spirit.

The factual, doctrinal, and mystical components of the Christian vision of the world are indispensable for an authentically Christian life. The story of Israel's promise culminating in Christ is more than an historical fact; it is an event pregnant with a divine meaning. Christian doctrines are never merely abstract propositional statements; they are always doctrines illuminating the meaning of the unique event of Christ, an event which occurs not merely in the world outside us, but also within ourselves. This event has an objective and a subjective pole, neither of which can be suppressed. The event must be understood and lived; its meaning must be grasped (orthodoxy) and loved (orthopraxis). Hence, the three mentalities are a question of tendencies or emphases within the Christian community; no one mentality can exclude the values of the other two without seriously distorting the lives of Christians.

The factual, doctrinal, and mystical components of Christian life reflect the distinctive elements of the Trinitarian life. The reality of the Father is truly and perfectly expressed in the Son, and truly and perfectly loved in their Holy Spirit. Christian life is rooted in the reality of God as historically experienced, understood, and adhered to by the people of God. Christian life deteriorates whenever any one of these three essential elements is ignored by (1) the failure to attend to the reality of God, (2) the failure to grasp the true meaning of God in Christ and his Church for our lives and for our world, or (3) the failure to love that reality and to live in accordance with its true meaning. Many know the "facts" and have some genuine insight into their true meaning; however, they have never really enjoyed, relished, or thoroughly experienced them. Lacking the affective component, their lives have not been in harmony with this reality and their awareness of it. There has been no experience of an unqualified approval and full acceptance of the good that is God in Christ, in his Church, in his world; therefore, they have not been affectively moved to achieve the good that is possible, the good to be done, in virtue of such an experience.

The reality and goodness of the Christian vision are communicated in the concreteness of its effects in our lives. The failure to produce evidence of such a vision in our lives implies that the vision of God in Christ is neither affectively nor effectively a part of our lives, despite our ability to articulate its meaning and to affirm its reality and value. The fact of God and our limited understanding of it within the context of the Christian tradition has not yet become a creative motivating force contributing to, and constituting the goodness of, our lives, at least to the extent that our lives do not produce sufficient evidence for such an affirmation. Prayer and good works are evidence of friendship with God, a continuing revelation of the vision of God in Christ, conditioned by the limitations of our lives within historical time. The vision of God inheres in finite minds and moves finite hearts; it is perfective of our lives and yet contains elements which transcend all merely human possibilities: presently actual and still to be completed, mysterious yet intelligible, real yet verbal, symbolic yet doctrinal, social and yet personal.

Through the gift of the Holy Spirit moving our hearts, the facts of the Christ story become internalized and the meaning of the Logos is lived.

There are as many ways of seeing the world as there are persons, for each has a particular angle of vision. Though within the community of Christian vision differences exist, the Christian vision as such is distinctive.

The distinctiveness of the Christian vision of the world is treated by William C. Marrin's article, "The Kingdom — Models and Meaning." In the vision of the Judeo-Christian tradition, God is seen as creator, transcending the world, but not remote; the world is seen as the sacrament of God's glory, but not complete; man is seen as the head of creation, as son of God, fully defined in the risen Christ; evil is seen as the refusal to trust what God is doing; salvation is seen as God's Kingdom, the future toward which creation strains.

Two religious models of vision are contrasted with the Judeo-Christian vision. The first model is that of the closed cosmos, implying a vision of God as immanent order of the world; of the world as all that exists; of man as a piece of the world; of evil as chaos, as whatever threatens world order; of salvation as fitting into the world order and enjoying what is there. This vision characterizes Marxism as a secular religion. The second religious view of reality sees salvation as escape. It envisions God as opposite of the world, as "totally Other." It envisions the world as delusion and unreality; man, as alien and trapped in the world; evil, as worldliness, as desire binding us to the world; salvation, as escape. (Marrin's models, which I apply to vision, do not attempt to force every religion into conformity with these types; rather, they help organize the complexity of data to facilitate discussion.)

Stanley Hauerwas has underscored the significance of vision, warning that a one-sided understanding of man as actor and self-creator ignores the importance of vision for human life.[16] The metaphor "vision of good" provides an important corrective to the dominant image of "man the maker." This does not deny the importance of action for moral behavior, but actions must be based on our vision of what is most real and valuable. By making man's will the source of all value, we have turned away from the classical insight of Christian and philosopher alike that the measure of moral goodness ultimately lies outside ourselves.[17] Such an emphasis tends to make Christian ethics Pelagian and implies that the God of history does little more than confirm the irrepressible march of human creativity; it makes the aim of the Christian life right action rather than the vision of God. Human behavior, Hauerwas affirms, is primarily a question of vision.[18] When we assess other people, we do not consider just their solutions to particular problems; we feel something much more elusive which is their total vision of life, "as shown in their mode of speech or silence, their choices of words, their assessments of others, their conceptions of their own lives, what they think attractive or praiseworthy . . . in short, the configurations of their thought which show continually in their reactions and conversations."[19]

James W. McClendon, Jr., writes that a man's character is formed by the way he sees things, by his vision or subjective intentionality.[20] Although he acknowledges the role of society in conditioning that vision and in shaping character, he does not dismiss the individual's responsibility for that self that he is and its action. (The Gospel tells us that it is not what goes into a man — his environment, over which he has no absolute control — but what comes out of him — over which he does have control — that tells us what a man is. To witness obscenities is not the same as to speak obscenities.) Our vision of the world is expressed in our images, in our character, in our actions, in the stories we tell and in the way we tell them (that of Jesus, for example); it is revealed in the concreteness of the totality of elements that constitute our selves, and not by words alone, images alone, actions alone. Vision does not exist in the abstract, but in a person; hence, the totality of elements that constitute the reality of that person provide the necessary evidence for our coming to a correct understanding of what that particular person's vision of the world is. One element illuminates another: deeds, posture, mood, tone and feeling illuminate the meaning of our words and vision, and vice-versa.

Whatever our vision of the world is, it is seen only in the concrete evidence of that vision. Our vision of God, world, man, evil and salvation is evidenced by all the elements that constitute our personal reality and especially by our feelings. Not to feel compassion and to do what is within our power for a neighbor in desperate need betrays, despite our verbal protestations to the contrary, a vision of the world that is not Christian. Our feelings and actions illuminate the authentic meaning of our words and unveil the quality of our vision as a reality that is felt and acted upon and spoken of. Sin, in this respect, is the lack of coherence between our vision and the rest of ourselves, the failure to feel and act in accordance with our vision. Our awareness of the gap is also within our vision.

Everyone has some vision or other of God (ultimate reality), world, man and salvation which he attains in the concreteness of his experience and, in turn, irradiates at every level of his being. Vision permeates our thoughts, desires, interests, ideals, imagination, feelings and body language; it is our worldview, our sense of life, our basic orientation towards reality. Our vision gives rise to our character, to our style of life, to the tone of our being in the world. Vision is the way in which we grasp the complexity of life; it is the way we relate ourselves to the things of life; it involves the meaning and value that we attach to the complexity of life as a whole and to the things of life in particular.

Each person is the incarnation of a definite vision of God, world, man and salvation. Each person is a metaphor for God, world, man and salvation. Within varying degrees of truth and falsity each person embodies a kind of judgment about the God, world, man and salvation he experiences within the consciousness of his vision. Inevitably, each person communicates the effects of all that is given to him in the experience of his vision. Even the affirmation that he sees no ultimate meaning or value to a world he judges to be an absurdity communicates the reality of a personal vision. The experience of vision is fundamental to human life; it does not preclude a change in or deepening of one's vision. Our vision of God, world, man and salvation implies the way in which we envision ourselves, whether as blessed, or cursed, or both. Our vision of God in the Christ of Calvary evokes the self-awareness or our blessed deliverance, of the *felix culpa* through which we experience our being healed by the loving compassion of God in Christ.

Although each person's vision is unique, it shares common elements with the vision of certain others. Hysterical people, for example, are inclined to a Prince-Charming-will-come-and-everything-will-turn-out-all-right view of life, to nostalgic and idealized recollection of past figures and places and to a sentimental view of the present. A nostalgic or idealized vision is generally conspicuously lacking in factual detail and marked by an obliviousness to objective flaws or defects. The hysterical-romantic vision of reality has its villains as well as its heroes. Immediate global impressions of revulsion and disgust also come easily and with the same obliviousness to complicating details. This is a melodramatic view of reality which is marked by an aversion for its complexity and specificity; it is the vision of those who are sensitive to the immediately striking, vivid and colorful things in life and, by the same token, rather oblivious to neutral factual details and contradictory elements.[21]

Vision includes possibilities. Our vision of the world may not give sufficient attention to our objective possibilities for growth and development, with the result that we spend a lifetime in a relatively closed but safe universe without approximating genuine selfhood. Unawareness of such possibilities characterizes the routine work and conventional values unquestioningly accepted by the spiritually obtuse.[22] At the other extreme, we may be so overwhelmed by the vision of the immensity of our apparently endless possibilities that we become incapable of accepting our finite determinateness. The inability to choose among the multiple possibilities within the range of our vision bespeaks an illness of the spirit. Our fear of our own real possibilities may hold the seeds of our own personal stagnation and failure to achieve our true potential. Both the unreflective and the highly sensitive have their respective hazards in meeting the fundamental needs of the self and the demands of its vision of the world. The vision of the former includes too few real possibilities; the vision of the latter abounds with an apparent excess of them. Inattention dooms the one; indecision paralyzes the other.

The vision of the self moves through the real in all its temporal contours and textures. The human spirit is endowed with the potential to grasp the meaning of things in their temporal relationships. Our vision of God, world, man and salvation entails an openness to the new and the unexpected. Although the Christian has an absolute confidence that God will be true to the promises that he has made in Christ, he must be prepared for surprises in the particular ways that these promises will be fulfilled in his own life. Authentic Christian prayer implicitly expresses the maturation of a subject who does not demand the instant satisfaction of the infant but has learned how to wait and to hope in God as his vision expands within larger temporal contexts of meaning that disclose his new, God-given potentialities. The vision of a God who is faithful to his promises does not prescind from the particularities of time and space through and in which our experience of that fidelity is mediated.

Our vision of God, man, world and salvation unifies the manifold of our experiences and is mediated by them. Our vision unfolds in the particulars of our spatio-temporal experience, in the context of our maturing sensibility. It embraces what has been and is experienced; it is open and orientated to what can be and will be experienced in the concreteness of our existence. Only he who remembers the promises of God will be aware of their fulfillment. The definiteness of our expectations anticipates our experiences; so that there is a sense in which we see only what we have been prepared to see. Only the pure of heart shall see God without distortion; therefore, only the pure of heart shall enjoy the vision of God. There is a unity of vision and sensibility attained in a process of purification, revealed as our ultimate possibility in Christ, crucified and risen.

Our emotions, or feelings, often exert an unexamined influence on our vision of the world and ourselves. They may be sustained by needs as well as by values. Although we may verbalize our vision of the world and of ourselves in terms of our values, we may be largely unaware of the extent to which our vision and character are shaped by our emotional attitudes and needs. Our affective memory, the totality of our emotional attitudes, can outlive the memory of the occurrences that led to its formation.[23] Magda B. Arnold describes it as the living record of the emotional life history of each person. It is always at our disposal, playing an important part in the appraisal and interpretation of everything around us; it can be called the matrix of all experience and action; it is also our intensely personal reaction to a particular situation, based on our unique experiences and biases.[24] It is possible that we do not understand the extent to which our vision is preconditioned by our feelings.

We are related to the world through our feelings. Our vision of the world and of ourselves is a felt relationship which Lonergan helps to illuminate with his description of feeling:

> The feeling . . . relates us to an object. Such feeling gives intentional consciousness its mass, momentum, drive, power. Without these feelings our knowing and deciding would be paper thin. Because of our feelings, our desires and our fears, our hope or despair, our joys and sorrows, our enthusiasm and indignation, our esteem and contempt, our trust and distrust, our love and hatred, our tenderness and wrath, our admiration, veneration, reverence, our dread, horror, terror, we are oriented massively and dynamically in a world mediated by meaning. We have feelings about other persons, we feel for them, we feel about them. We have feelings about our respective situations, about the past, about the future, about evils to be lamented or remedied, about the good that can, might, must be accomplished.[25]

Although our vision of the world and of ourselves is always a felt vision, it is not necessarily distorted by our feelings. There is no vision without feeling, without memory, without imagination. We may infer that pure of heart mediate the vision of God without distortion. Commenting on this sixth beatitude, Maurice Nicholl asserts that to be pure of heart is to be purged in heart or cleansed by purgation: "It is about an emotional state that can be reached in which the reality of the existence of God is seen directly from the clear-sightedness of the purified emotional understanding, for we understand not only with the mind . . . When cleansed, the heart sees — that is, understands — the existence of the higher level of God, of the reality of the teaching of Christ."[26]

Christian faith is a way of seeing in the darkness: it grasps the truth, goodness and beauty of the invisible God in Jesus of Nazareth. The words addressed to Thomas (Jn. 20:29) affirm that it is the faith of those who saw Jesus and not the sensible vision itself which is the saving experience. To see Jesus is a saving vision only if it is a vision of faith. It is to know and to experience the Father (Jn. 12:44; 14:9). The New Testament believes that there is something seriously wrong in those whose physical vision of Jesus, whose experience of his words and works, did not predispose them to see the Father in him (Jn. 14:24). The saving vision of God in Jesus of Nazareth presupposes saving attitudes which predispose us to respond in a positive manner; it presupposes a readiness to grasp the full meaning of the image of

God in Christ (Rom. 8:28) and to have our lives (character) shaped by it. The New Testament presupposes our openness to the mystery of God and holds us responsible for the quality of our response to it in our personal vision of the world and of ourselves. We are judged by our vision. What we see, our sense of the world, discloses what we are. Similarly, what we fail to see discloses what we are not; consequently, the New Testament underscored the grave condition of those who failed to see God in Jesus of Nazareth.

The maturity of Christian vision involves the whole man. Its goal is symbolized not by the immortality of the soul but by the resurrection of the body as indicative of the total self that must be made whole. The fullness, or perfection, of Christian vision is manifested not only in the understanding but in the affective life and in the loving actions that are rooted in our personal adherence to Christ. Christian vision develops in Christ and to Christ. He is the perfect image of God because he possesses the perfect vision of God; and he has the power to communicate what God is. He irradiates his vision at every level of our existence. His lived vision of the meaning and purpose of man defined his character and personal history; he embodied the vision of God which he preached in word and deed. The good news of the Kingdom which he preached touched all the dimensions of human life and existence. He called men to a transcendence of all that made human life less than life and less than human. He called men to the freedom which his vision enabled him to enjoy at every level of his being: "Let not your hearts be troubled," says Jesus in his farewell discourse, "believe in God, believe also in me" (Jn. 14:1) and "Truly . . . he who believes in me will also do the works that I do; and greater works than these will he do because I go to the Father" (Jn. 14:12). His final commandment is "that you love one another as I have loved you" (Jn. 15:12). To believe in Jesus is to believe in the Father and to share their vision which, in turn, empowers us to achieve what he achieved, to have the same kind of impact that his life had on others.

Jesus Christ is a new and unique way of being in the world. He represents and communicates a unique way of thinking and feeling about God, the world, man, evil, salvation, the past and the future. He incarnates a new vision, a new sense of reality and way of relating to it, a new way of experiencing ourselves and the world. He incarnates and communicates the foundational vision of the Christian community. His foundational vision is mediated through the apostles. It is definitive and normative of Christian living. The dependent vision of individual Christians is the continuing and lived renewal of the foundational vision; it points back to the unique vision of Jesus Christ and is called to a future of maturation in the fullness of this vision.[27] The vision of the risen Lord empowers the ongoing maturation of our dependent vision within the Christian community. The foundational vision of Jesus Christ is the matrix of the specific character of our dependent vision; it gives rise to those consistencies which enable our vision to be recognized and affirmed as Christian; it is evidenced by the quality of our lives in all their specificity and definiteness.

3. STORY'S VISION OF SELF AND WORLD

We live in response to the world we perceive; if we perceive the world differently, we live differently. Our religious stories and symbols express our perception of ourselves and the world; they lead to structural living. They express a mode of awareness of a subject whose senses are functioning; consequently, they imply not only our vision of ourselves and of our world but also how we are affected by this experience.[28] We objectify this affective awareness in our religious stories and symbols, attempting to represent our primary, lived relationship with ultimate reality. Our stories and symbols reflect how we grasp ourselves and our world and how we are affected by what we grasp; they reflect the quality of our interrelatedness with reality; and they are necessarily derived from our experience. Our stories and symbols evidence our basic orientations towards the real and its potentialities; they derive from our particular experiences and images of ourselves and the world. The particular shape of our theological reflection and the particular directions that it takes are rooted in the particularity of our primal experiences. These experiences condition our possibility of trusting the real. They have to do with our capacity for experiencing the real as benign or threatening; consequently, they imply a corresponding self-image which enables us to be either open or closed, trusting or untrusting, in our lived relationship to the real.[29]

Our narrative consciousness, operative in storytelling, organizes and unifies the manifold of our experiences of the real into a comprehensible unity. This process simultaneously unifies and integrates the self into larger unities, provided that we remain open to the real as our experience broadens. Storytelling evidences personal growth in sensibility when it organizes and unifies new experiences and new images into larger unities and contexts of meaning. It discloses the potentialities of the self and the real in their dialectical relationship. Our religious stories reflect the understanding of an imagining subject in its attempt to explain the ultimate promise of the real.

PART III
God in Travel Stories

14

BIBLICAL TRAVEL STORIES OF GOD

The Bible is a book of travel stories about God and his chosen one. Abraham, Moses, Ezekiel, Jesus, Peter and Paul undertake their journeys in response to a divine call on behalf of a people. The self and God are particular agents who can be known only as we know their stories. We learn of God through others' stories of their relationship with him. The biblical travel stories imply that men come to a knowledge of God from different directions, with particular expectations; hence, we have a multiplicity of travel stories that disclose something of *who* God is and who we are. (A *Who* is known only through his story and its unique particulars). Four evangelists come to the story which Jesus' life told from four different directions, even though they affirm the same Gospel truth.

If stories are indispensable in disclosing who God is, travel stories seem to be the Bible's preferred kind of story. The Exodus story dominates the Old Testament as the Christ story dominates the New Testament. The New Testament reinterprets the Old Testament with the new travel story of a new Moses, a new Exodus and a new Israel (Matthew's Gospel). Jesus is the pre-existent Logos who is sent by the Father and returns to the Father (John's Gospel). Jesus journeys from Galilee to Jerusalem to accomplish what his disciples will communicate in their journey from Jerusalem to the ends of the earth (Rome) in the Age of the Church (Luke-Acts). Jesus journeys throughout Galilee and outside of Galilee (Mark's Gospel). Even his parables recount travel stories (e.g., the Prodigal Son).

Certain common elements characterize biblical travel stories. Our awareness of them deepens our appreciation of their implications.

1. THREE INTERSUBJECTIVE ELEMENTS IN EVERY STORY

There are three intersubjective elements in every travel story: the transcendent Spirit, the self-transcending leader, and the self-transcending community.

The Spirit of God inspires, impels, guides and empowers the journey. The two books, Luke-Acts, begin with the descent of the transcendent Spirit of God. The process of the journey is a response to the experience of the transcendent Spirit's power, light and promise, which speaks to the leader and to the community from within their deepest being. The journey is made with the consciousness of being encountered and sought out by grace and demands that overmastering reality of the transcendent Spirit. The journey expresses the response of openness and obedience to the unconditional claims of the Spirit on our lives. The Spirit's transcendence grounds our self-transcendence in the outer and inner journey experience. Our self-transcending is the created experience of the transcendent Spirit of God in our lives; self-sacrificing love (other-centeredness) expresses who the Spirit is and what it does. It is where it operates. It is called "transcendent" because the people whom it inspires, guides, and empowers become self-transcending. They look beyond themselves in the power of the Spirit.

The impact of the transcendent Spirit is recognized in the self-transcending leader, or individual. Abraham, Moses, Joshua, Jesus and Paul are powerful manifestations of the Spirit of God. Through the self-transcendence of these individuals the Spirit discloses itself to the community and transforms it by calling it to an ever more profound self-transcendence in faith, hope and self-sacrificing love. What the Spirit has done for them is also for others.

The self-transcending community or people is led by the transcendent Spirit through self-transcending leaders. The Spirit's power, immanent in their lives, impels the inner journey which the outer journey symbolizes. The journey is not made alone; its other-centeredness in self-transcendence implies a community united by a transcendent Spirit that effects their "salvation" in the achievement of their ultimate possibilities.

The life of Jesus begins with the descent of the Spirit upon Mary. His mission begins with the descent of the Spirit at his baptism. It leads him to confront Satan in the desert. Its descent marks the birth of the Church and its mission at Pentecost, bearing witness to the transcendence of the Risen Christ, achieved after a life-long self-transcendence culminating in his passion and death.

2. EVERY JOURNEY BEGINS WITH A PROBLEM, A QUESTION, A CRISIS

Every journey begins with a problem, a question, or a crisis. A crisis, a fall, an upset, or serious need demands critical attention. The present situation is unacceptable. There is a search for a solution, a way out (i.e., an ex-odus, ec-stasy, hope) that is characterized by a tension, an anxiety, a groping similar to that of a scholar researching all the data he can find which might possibly lead to an appropriate solution to his problem. The situation demands a struggle and search for a solution, for an exodus; it demands that efforts be made at every level of human existence, vertically (within the individual) and horizontally (by the entire community). Through a total and united effort the goal may be reached: the solution of the problem, the answer to the question, the relief of the particular need that constituted the point of departure for the travel story. The starting point of biblical travel stories implies that persons are called to problem-solving, question-raising and question-answering; that they are responsible for the quality of their solutions and answers. No one exists in a state of inert righteousness; rather, authentic righteousness must always be worked out in a concrete context in response to the demands of reason for a right(eous) order among persons. Righteousness bespeaks a quest, a process ("travel story" or "journey"), a dynamic with a moving horizon's ongoing demands for responsible decision and action.

3. *FAITH, HOPE AND LOVE SUSTAIN THE DYNAMICS OF THE JOURNEY*

Faith, hope and love describe a way of being-in-the-world that characterizes the self-transcending leader and people of the biblical travel stories. These attitudes are the dynamics of the journeying community's decision-making; they sustain the wholeness and connectedness of its historical existence; they inspire its striving and transforming mission with the confidence that there is a final worth and dignity in human existence. They are dimensions of that responsiveness which constitutes the journey represented in the biblical travel story. They express the dynamic openness and relatedness of the self-transcending leader and his community to the transcendent Spirit.

The community has faith in its leader. The Christian community is united by its faith in Christ. Its faith expresses its full acceptance of and commitment to him as the dynamic center of its relation to God. The community journeys with the authentic belief that God (the transcendent Spirit) is addressing and leading it through its leader. Faith implies that there is a context of meaning and value which grounds the travel story of the community in its ongoing struggle against the powers of chaos. Faith believes that there is an ultimate meaning to existence (God himself) which transcends our comprehension (as the sacred transcends the profane), despite the abundant evidence of meaninglessness in the world. Abraham, the classic symbol of faith, believes in God, the ultimate motive for his existence; he believes that God will keep his promise to him despite the fact that the very means for the fulfillment of that promise, his son Isaac, is to be sacrificed. He believes that God will keep his promises and fulfill them in his own way, not ours. His faith is compatible with his ignorance of how; his belief in God implies his unshakeable adherence to him and obedience to demands that constitute the inner journey.

The hope of reaching the promised land motivates the Exodus. There is no journey or travel story without an overriding hope of reaching its promised destination. We ask questions with the hope of arriving at a solution, a true answer. We depart only with the hope of an arrival. We act with the hope that change will be for the better just as faith is self-transcending in believing in someone beyond oneself, hope is self-transcending in anticipating a good that is attainable beyond oneself. Both look beyond one's personal resources for the successful coping with the journey project of self-transcendence: trust in the transcendent Spirit of God grounds every particular travel story of self-transcendence.

Love is responsiveness and responsibility. It bespeaks the call of the transcendent Spirit enabling the travel story; it enables the people to come to be in the Exodus event. In every travel story it brings the participants into a fuller state of being. Love overcomes the inertia prior to the journey, effecting a kind of *ex-stasis* (ecstasy), or coming out of *stasis,* to a fuller life beyond one's former self. The travel stories tell of self-transcendence in response to the power of true values drawing us out of ourselves. The transcendent Spirit of God is represented as that which empowers the response-ability of leader and community in self-sacrificing love for the common good.

Jesus is filled with the Spirit of God; he gives his life for the people, becoming their Way, Truth and Life. He is experienced as the origin and destiny (the Alpha and Omega) of human existence as well as the Way from the one to the other. God is known in Christ as Love, the compassionate and self-giving power that impels us to accept and to follow Christ in the travel story of the Christian Church's ongoing responsiveness to the concrete demand of his transcendent love.

Formalism misses the point of biblical travel stories. It grasps their plot, but not their meaning.[1] It remains at the level of the visual/aural reality without reaching a comprehension of the spiritual reality expressed by the travel stories. An inner journey accompanies the outer journey in the biblical travel stories. To read them unaware of the personal transformation re-presented would be to miss the point. Travel stories tell of a particular search for personal wholeness, of people who are modified by their experiences, of catalyst of change, of horizon-shifts in a process of raising and settling questions about oneself and one's ultimate environment. Travel stories tell us about man becoming.

4. HOME, HOMELESSNESS, AND HOMECOMING

Home, homelessness and homecoming are implied in biblical travel stories. Abraham leaves Ur, his original home, to find a new home. The Exodus of Moses starts from a place that is not an authentic home. Forty years of wandering are sustained by the hope of a promised homeland. The Exile tells of a people driven from their authentic homeland and of their painful homelessness. The Exodus journey of liberation contrasts with the Exile journey into captivity. The Return to Israel is seen as a new Exodus journey.

The New Testament extends the meaning of home and homecoming. Home refers to our origins, where our life begins. In this context, Jesus comes from the Father and returns to the Father, the source of life and mission and fulfillment.[2] On the other hand, to see Jesus is to see the Father; in this respect, Jesus is always at home in the world. Wherever he is, he is one with his Father, the origin and ground of his existence.

With regard to home as family, as flesh and blood relationships, Jesus affirms that anyone who hears the word of God and keeps it is his mother, brother and sister. Home is to be among those who abide by the Word which God speaks in Jesus. It is the shared hearing and living of God's Word which grounds the Christian community as the family of God in Christ.

Homecoming is the dynamic of hearing and keeping the Word of God: "If you make my word your *home* you will indeed be my disciples, you will learn the truth and the truth will make you free" (Jn. 8:31f). If homecoming is the dynamic of grasping the Word of God, it is also the knowing and a seeing of the Father: "I am the Way, the Truth and the Life. No one can come to the Father except through me. If you know me, you know my Father too. From this moment you know him and have seen him" (Jn. 14:6f).

Homecoming is the dynamic of going to the Father "in spirit and truth" (Jn. 4:23) and in loving trust: "Trust in God still, and trust in me. There are many rooms in my Father's house" (Jn. 14:1). We do not go home alone. There is a guide and a way: "I shall return to take you with me; so that where I am you may be too. You know the way to the place where I am going" (Jn. 14:3f). Homecoming is the dynamic of response to the truth, of responsible love: "If anyone loves me he will keep my word, and my Father will love him, and we shall come to him and make our home with him" (Jn. 14:23). Home is where the Father dwells: in truth-seeking and truth-loving persons, in truthful lives. This is where his kingdom is: where his truth and love rules our minds and hearts and governs our words and actions. Here alone, at the deepest level of our consciousness, can we know peace: "Peace I bequeath to you, my own peace I give you, a peace the world cannot give, this is my gift to you" (Jn. 14:27). Peace is the experience of home, of mutual recognition and of mutual acceptance: we recognize and accept the truth and in turn are recognized and affirmed by it as truthful persons in harmony with our origin and destiny, with the Alpha and Omega, the ultimate ground of our existence. Every biblical travel story involves the experience of a homecoming at the deepest level of our existence; i.e., the recognition and acceptance of the truth about ourselves and our ultimate environment (home).

The land promised to Moses and his people is related to the New Testament's extension of its meaning to that way of being at home in the world that is the ultimate possibility for every human being.[3] Homecoming occurs everywhere that human beings are or can be at home with Existence and its demands for personal authenticity. Because its basic demands are made on all human beings, challenging their response-ability, homecoming is a universally shared enterprise. The biblical travel stories hold the individual responsible for the quality of his response to the demands of Existence itself for a truthful, responsible, authentically human life. Homecoming is an ongoing process of personal development that occurs within the concrete range of our personal response-abilities. We come home from different directions with different feelings, moods, fantasies, impulses, talents, insights and interests. The truthfulness of our lives is enriched, rather than compromised, by these differences. The true goodness which Existence demands of us and for which it empowers us in always concrete, particular.

Christ's travel story is a paradigm of homecoming.[4] It emerges as a response to the fulfillment of his Father's will, experienced as Ultimate Reality at the center of his consciousness, present in demand and grace. Lest our travel stories become a meaningless wandering, Christ instructs us to address Ultimate Reality as Our Father and to seek deliverance from temptation and evil. The world of every human being is inhabited by others. To recognize them as brothers is to be able, at least implicitly, to recognize the demands of Existence (Being) as the will of Our Father. Homecoming is not the enterprise of atomic individuals; rather, it is the development of ourselves as beings-with-others, with the same qualities to which we all aspire. Homecoming expresses the fulfillment of Our Father's will in an enterprise of fraternal interdependence. Our Father, Ultimate Reality with its demand for truthful lives, is the underlying ground of unity which interrelates all human travel stories. As source, ground and destination, Our Father is the power for their fulfillment as purposeful journeys (as opposed to wanderings). The quality of our way of being-with-others is the key to the quality of our way of being-with-Ultimate Reality. It implies the dialectic between homelessness and homecoming, between indifference and care, between alienation and community. Every biblical travel story re-presents a way in which a better way of our being-with-others and our being-with-Ultimate Reality is achieved.

5. ASCETICISM AND RENUNCIATION

Biblical travel stories imply asceticism and renunciation. They concern people who have effected a separation from the comforting routines and familiar faces of everyday reality. The journey effects a separation which renders available in a new way the self, the world, the divine. The journey effects a separation in order to see the world in a different way through a process of development that takes us beyond the familiar world into a larger world. The travel story may be understood as a process of emancipation from the entanglements of a particular environment and its values, analogous to the process of intellectual and emotional emancipation from our childhood environment.

There is no journey, inner or outer, without asceticism. Every journey means that something must be left behind, renounced. Asceticism struggles to overcome whatever elements in our lives are an obstacle to a higher, truer life. The success of the journey depends on the ability to focus on what is essential and to overcome distractions and impediments. Asceticism implies freedom from stagnation, entrapment, imprisonment. It overcomes the disharmony and disproportion among our manifold desires in the pursuit of our highest possibilities. It is essential for the basic unity of our striving. It overcomes that repose in pleasure which threatens to bring the dynamism of our highest activities to a standstill; thus, it frees us for those experiences which point in the direction of our true happiness, in the direction that reason demands and grace enables for the achievement of such happiness.

Asceticism allows the promise of the future to emerge. It is fervently expectant, even though by itself it is powerless to lead us anywhere or to make us see anything. Asceticism implies that the travelers are able to overcome whatever elements within a particular environment might tempt them to give up their purposeful journey. The subjects of biblical travel stories must guard themselves from an all too-ready and uncritical absorption of the dominant value of their environment. Complete absorption, at any level, with a particular set of surroundings entails the loss of freedom to pursue the goal of the journey. To part is always to die a little; however, not to depart may mean that one dies altogether by stagnating in an unexamined life that never took distance from its immediate satisfactions.

6. MISSING THE WAY

The language which the biblical writers use for sin implies the evolution of our destiny as a journey.[5] To sin is to miss the way, the path, the road *(hata)* or to wander from it *(avon)*. To repent is to return *(shuv)*. Although the subjects of the travel stories may have difficulty in finding their path (or way), they must not wander aimlessly. They are set on a course which is determined by the goal that they wish to attain. They must be constantly attentive to staying on that course lest their enterprise become a wandering. The problem of fidelity to the way is a daily problem: "Let him take up his cross daily and follow me" (Lk. 9:23). If Christian life is a following of the "Way" that is Christ, his way is that of the cross which is a part of daily living. The Christian community is also called "The Way" (Acts 9:2, 18:25). Courage and discernment are required for confronting the complexity of daily life's challenges. The members of "The Way" support one another in the Spirit of God which empowers them to meet these challenges with courage and true discernment.

7. REMEMBERING THE WAY

Remembering plays an important part in biblical travel stories. No journey starts from zero. Everyone who undertakes the journey is united with his companions through a common remembered and evaluated past. The way the past has been remembered is the way that the future will be anticipated. The community which travels remembering the wonderful works of the Lord of the past, travels anticipating the wonderful works of the Lord in the future. Memories make the future. Only those who remember the promise will be aware of its future fulfillment. Biblical travel stories are about people who are faithful to their origins and to their identity. They have a future because they have understood the true value of their past. Israel lives remembering the Exodus; the New Israel lives remembering the Resurrection. Liberation and transcendence specify their orientation to the future.

8. THE CAPACITY FOR GROWTH

Biblical travel stories envision human life as indefinite growth, the product of a full engagement with temporal experience involving the whole personality.[6] The wayfarer is not to evade the challenges, the struggles, the difficulties and dangers of life, but to accept, make his way through, and grow in them. He must be willing to accept his vulnerability and to venture out, even at the risk of personal suffering, for the sake of growth. The condition of the wayfarer implies that conversion is not, as it was in the mystery religions, an immediate entrance into a safe harbor, but rather an ongoing movement whose direction has been established. Hence, the Scriptures so frequently summon us to remember the past which demonstrates God's care and will for us. The process of growth represented in biblical travel stories is one in which the past is not left behind but survives, shapes, and is absorbed into the present, providing a base for the identity alike of the individual and his society.

The travel stories assume that the essential condition of maturity is the capacity for growth. Although such growth is a movement in a direction, it knows no apparent limits in its open-endedness for both personal and social development. The refusal to grow, to cope with an open future, would effect the rejection of life as a process of maturation; it would result in a state of arrested development, remaining fixed at a given point and closed to further development. Sinfulness, in this respect, is the failure of our response-ability with regard to the demands of Existence for our personal and social development. Biblical travel stories tell us of people who are open to the future and faithful to their capacity for personal and social growth. They are narrated in order to transmit these values to the community for whom they were written. Through faith in God, wayfarers of the travel stories (and those for whom they have been written) enter an open future with confidence and grow through their experience. Every biblical travel story is an evolutionary journey of the spirit.

Freedom for growth derives from the full acceptance of creatureliness, the admission of absolute dependence on God; for the only alternative to the travel story of faith is bondage to the self, to the anxieties and the false absolutisms by which human persons are otherwise imprisoned. Faith in God is the necessary condition for the freedom to live truthful lives, to examine the dubious motives of one's own actions and the quality of the story that one's life is telling. Faith also implies the freedom to repent for what has been false in our lives, for what has impeded our authentic development, threatening to turn our personal journey into a wandering. Every biblical travel story has an inner dimension of liberation from something that would prevent us from becoming our true selves.

The sacred travel stories of Judaism and Christianity see the individual in close and organic community with others. The Pauline description of growing up in Christ, though it has obvious implications for the individual, is primarily concerned with the growth of the Christian community; it is finally the Church as one body, and ultimately all mankind, that must reach the full maturity adumbrated in every biblical travel story. The maturity of the individual is attained in loving community with others. The power of growth is a function of a pilgrim community.[7]

9. FORTITUDE

Fortitude is a basic requisite for every biblical travel story. The growth of the traveling community requires fortitude because, in the world, evil is powerful. Something must be risked whenever the obviously weak offers resistance to evil. And nobody who wishes to be a good human being, and who is unwilling to commit an injustice, can avoid this risk. Despite the presence of evil, the world, like existence itself, still remains capable of good and is directed towards it. At the same time, the good is not realized by itself, but requires for that end the effort of an individual who is willing to struggle and if necessary to sacrifice on its behalf. One cannot be consistently just without having to risk something for it. What is risked may be something less than life itself. It may be a question of immediate well-being, of daily tranquility, possessions, honor or face-saving. On the other hand, it may be a question of the acceptance of death at another's hands. What is required may be the surrender of life in which martyrdom becomes the ultimate symbol of fortitude.

The fortitude which grounds the dynamism of the travel story is not divorced from the prudence which is able to recognize the elements of life as they really are and to translate this recognition into resolution and action. Fortitude is not the recklessness of those unable to love anything or anyone; it is not the rashness of those who make a false evaluation of danger. Nor is fortitude divorced from justice. Biblical travel stories tell of those who suffer on behalf of justice (from the loss of well-being to imprisonment or bodily harm); they tell of those who are seemingly vanquished. Their criterion of fortitude consists primarily in steadfastness. The moral and spiritual steadfastness of the suffering pilgrim community is a victory of the human spirit in its lifelong quest for righteousness. (Teresa of Avila writes in her autobiography that imperfect human beings need greater fortitude to travel the path of perfection than to take martyrdom upon themselves in a brief moment). Tyranny, in one of its many forms, forces true fortitude into merciless trials. The tyranny of Egypt and the fortitude of the Hebrew people under Moses are intimately related in the Exodus event, the prototypical biblical travel story.

15

THE TRAVEL STORIES
OF RELIGIOUS EXPERIENCE

Judaism and Christianity live according to travel stories, the Exodus and the Christ story. Both confess the God of the Exodus story; however, Christianity comes into existence with its lived affirmation of the Christ story and its implicit reinterpretation of the Exodus story.

There is an outer and an inner component to the journey in the travel story. The outer journey moves through time and space; the inner journey moves deeper into the mystery of being. The outer journey is the plot; the inner journey is the meaning.[1] The outer journey is a metaphor for the inner journey of the spirit. The inner journey accompanies the outer journey when the reader grasps the meaning of the travel story. The religious formalist knows the sacred travel story of his tradition at the level of plot; however, he misses its meaning.

The Gospel of John, for example, tells the story of Christ's journey to the Father, an event which is resonant of Israel's path to life as developed in both the Mosaic and exilic Exodus accounts. The journeys between Galilee and Samaria in which Christ speaks the word of God as described in the "book of signs" are themselves signs of the journey to the Father which spans the entirety of Christ's life, culminating in his final return as risen Son and Lord. These visible journeys are signs of Christ's inner movement toward the Father; they also describe the quality of Christian religious experience as a personal vocation which is not actualized in the matter of a moment.

1. STORIES AS LIMIT-LANGUAGE OF THE SELF AND GOD

The biblical travel story is the limit-language of a faith community's limit-experience.[2] A phenomenological analysis of our common human experience and a hermeneutical analysis of the New Testament language led David Tracy to conclude that the meanings of both religious experience and religious language are helpfully characterized by the concepts limit-experience and limit-language; and that the existential meaningfulness of such language may be described as its ability to allow for the disclosure of certain possible modes-of-being-in-the-world, which *qua* religious are not trans-worldly but recognizably and authentically human.[3]

There are aspects of the Church's limit-experience which make the limit-language of the story indispensable. Although stories are not necessary for articulating everything about our limit-experience, they are indispensable for those matters which deal with the irreducible particulars of God and the self. To say who someone is, whether that someone be ourselves or another, eludes precise speech. Hannah Arendt has pointed out that "the moment we want to say who somebody is, our very vocabulary leads us astray into saying what he is; we get entangled in a description of qualities he necessarily shares with others like him: we begin to describe a type or a character in the old meaning of the word, with the result that his uniqueness escapes us."[4] She suggests that we can surmount the problem with a story. "Who somebody is or was we can know only by knowing the story of which he is himself the hero — his biography, in other words everything else we know of him, including the work he may have left behind, tells us only what he is or was."[5]

Stanley Hauerwas affirms that a story can and does function like a proper name and vice versa.[6] Its significance for the self helps us to understand why it is an essential of Jewish and Christian limit-language; for, like the self, God is a particular agent that can be known only as we know his story.[7] We cannot talk of God as if he were a universal; the grammar of God is not that of an indefinite noun, but rather of a proper name. As an agent God must be known like other agents, that is through his story and from his point of view. Inasmuch as we have no such story, we must learn of God through others' stories of their relationship with him.

The stories of the Bible imply that we learn to speak to God in terms of his action in the lives of his "chosen ones." These stories enable us to best speak of God and of our relation to him truthfully. If as agents we are irreducibly story and cannot avoid being story, then the story that is true for ourselves is the one that helps us to go on in the normative sense of enabling us to cope with the basic ontological invariable of our lives.[8]

The individual person is not merely designated by his proper name. That name has a story to it; a person's name is a symbol of the world that lives in him, shapes him, and emerges in the dynamic structure of the free actions which tell his life story. Human actions have the dramatic quality of telling a story. The story of God, told by the iife story of Jesus of Nazareth and represented in the travel story of the Gospel, is central to being a people called by God; it expresses the Christian community's sense of its own identity in its response to the only God that there is; it bears witness to a life that illuminated what an authentically human existence under the sovereignty of the living God may be.[9] The Christian community tells the Gospel story as a confession of its adherence to the God who speaks in the words, deeds and destiny of Jesus of Nazareth, the definitive limit-represen- tation of the life of God-with-humanity, re-presenting the truth of their lives as lives whose basic faith and trust is grounded in the loving action of God.[10]

The Gospel story tells us about a reality which is not experienced apart from our moods and concerns. But these are given their specific coloring primarily by the personal and social stories in which we find our lives enfolded. The amorphous feelings with which we reach out to embrace some totality are given specific shape and direction by the "narrative consciousness" which underlies the religious travel story.[11] It is especially from the narrative quality of our religious experience that we acquire our sense of the travel story's real meaning.[12] And it is in story form that our feelings of the sacred are eventually symbolized. Our narrative conscious- ness compels us communally to experience events, places and persons in the context of some story or other.[13] Stories are so central to human existence that without them life is experienced as meaningless.[14] The Christian community communally experiences the meaningfulness of its existence in the Gospel's travel story of Jesus of Nazareth.

2. EXISTENTIAL VERIFICATION AND UNIVERSAL RELEVANCE

The Christian's allegiance to the narrative symbolic mode of being-in-the- world is not abhorrent to his critical sense.[15] His need for the Christ story is coupled with his need to know. His interpretative story allows for an insightful creativity and a rigorous type of critical reflectiveness. It is found in successful recasting of the Christ story by the four evangelists to meet the diversity of problems posed by their different historical and cultural contexts. The author of Luke-Acts, for example, meets the critical demands of the Christian community's horizon-shift with regard to the conversion of the Gentiles. His two parallel volumes represent the way of the Lord as a dynamic process with distinctive phases. In parallel travel stories, the Spirit which led Jesus from Galilee to accomplish our salvation in Jerusalem, leads his apostles from Jerusalem to proclaim it to the entire world in Rome. The Age of the Church enjoys a continuity with the Age of Jesus and tells the same story of a loving, righteous Father who promises the power of a new righteousness and the new possibility of self-sacrificing love to those who will hear and abide by The Word spoken in the words, deeds and destiny of Jesus. The outer journeys of Luke-Acts symbolize an inner journey of the Christian community: the surmounting of the exclusivist insistence that only and solely in the Jewish nation may men find the meaning of their lives before a loving God. The cities at the end of each journey symbolize the horizon-shift in which the particularism of Jerusalem gives way to the universalism of Rome.[16]

The storytelling of Luke-Acts relates the Christian community to the world by conjoining its givenness, accessible to it through memory, with its possibility. But not only with its own private possibility. The storytelling of Luke-Acts discloses that the Christ story (the story that his life told of himself and God) merges with a universal story and that it is revelatory of the world's and others' possibilities as well; it implies that all our private histories are chronicles of the quest for this point of contact.[17]

The Gospel story re-presents the universalism of Jesus' limit-experience both in his addressing God as Father (*Abba*) and in his recognition of those who hear and keep the word of God as his family, his mother, brothers and sisters. Inasmuch as all persons are addressed in the depths of their beings by the word of God, they are free to become members of Jesus' family. Every human being is, actively or potentially, part of the family; hence, the experience of all others as family is the verification of our authentic limit-experience of God as our "Father," of our participation in the limit-experience of Jesus of Nazareth. The Gospel story interprets the Exodus story of Israel's being at home in the world with a universalism that does not restrict the possibilities of friendship with God and neighbor (of the family of God) to flesh-and-blood relationships based on tribe, or race, or nation, or national homeland. Rather the Gospel story tells us that God is worshiped in spirit and in truth, that the deeper meaning of Israel's promised homeland appears wherever human beings share in hearing and keeping the word of God which enables them to be at home in the entire world with the experience of all others as family and the concurrent recognition of God as Father. Israel is not repudiated; rather, its meaning is extended to the ends of the earth.

The truth of the Gospel story demands that we be true to the exigencies of the human spirit and to its authentic possibilities disclosed in Jesus. Its narrative power helps to dispel self-deception and to inspire the courage of a true self-knowledge through our acceptance and appropriation of Jesus' own encounter with God. Its truth, like that of every religious story, is properly evaluated as it intersects with concrete human lives. The truth of the Gospel story, which neither originates nor exists in abstraction from particular persons, cannot be communicated apart from particular persons. It should not, therefore, be evaluated as though it could. The truth of the

Gospel story is witnessed by saints that have been formed by its narrative power for producing truthful lives. The truthfulness of our lives is the existential verification of the claims of the Gospel story; it is the evidence that that story has been heard properly, and that it is true.[18]

The storytellers of the Gospel story express their concern for the existential verification of their story's truth. The First Letter of John, for example, tells us that "Anyone who says, 'I love God,' and hates his brother, is a liar, since a man who does not love his brother that he can see cannot love God, whom he has never seen" (1 Jn. 4:20). In the Gospel of Matthew: "Not everyone who says to me, 'Lord, Lord,' shall enter the kingdom of heaven, but he who does the will of my Father who is in heaven" (7:21). The Gospel storytellers are concerned about a lived sense of reality; hence, calling God our "Father" without the lived experience of others as our brothers is as false as calling Jesus "Lord" without the lived experience of his Father's lordship. Our grasp of the Gospel story is determined by the story that our life tells. The self-image according to which we act, the story we tell ourselves about ourselves, does not always correspond to the story that our life tells.[19] The existential verification of the Gospel story's truth unfolds in the radical singleness of our spontaneities, thoughts, words and actions. The goodness of this truth is verified only in its concreteness, for what is good, always is concrete.[20]

3. GOODNESS IN THE LIVED STORY

The storytellers' concern is for the goodness of the Gospel truth, and not for abstract definitions of authentic religious experience. They do not attempt to define the good that is the object of the Gospel story, thus running the risk of misleading its readers; rather, they employ symbol, image, myth and story to re-present and to re-experience the true goodness of God in Jesus of Nazareth, to help us to know what story we are and should be. The goodness of the Gospel truth is experienced when it brings the many elements of our lives into a fundamental integrity of consciousness, word and act. Christian authenticity leads us to inquire how adequately our actions achieve what our words say we seek in claims to have personally appropriated the Gospel story; it leads us to inquire whether we actually do what we say we do in our confession of Jesus Christ as Lord.

The dynamic structure of life according to the Gospel truth involves both the gift which God discloses in the story which Jesus' life tells and our own responsibility for our particular choices. We are responsible for the choice of the stories that we attempt to make our own; also for the human capacities we choose to make central to our actions and for the quality of their development. The Gospel story provides the context in which we can enlarge our world through the acceptance of its creative possibilities.[21] It is the context for an ongoing recasting of our life story, with trust in the present and future of an accepting God empowering us to cope with the multiple eventualities of our life.

4. STORIES FOR ACTION

The Exodus and the Christ story are the fundamental biblical travel stories which shape the Judeo-Christian community's sense of reality both in expressing what that community is trying to do (be) and what it does (is) without trying. How dominant these stories are among others in the lives of individual members of the faith community is difficult to determine; nevertheless, they reflect that community's heritage of religious experience and, like all stories that tell us about the world and how the self is situated in it, give its members a way of being in the world that is oriented towards action deriving from a basic trust in a loving God.

These stories articulate the meaning of a religious experience which involves knowing and doing. They attempt to lessen the distance between knowing and doing in such a way that the community's knowing is conceived as a species of action. They are meant to help us become a certain type of person that is actively engaged in the creation of a certain type of society. The knowers and doers of this community bring the meaning of these stories into the tangled texture of the world they are trying to shape in the spirit of justice and self-sacrificing love. They are acting out the meaning and value of these stories in a quest for the fulfillment of their promise. Their knowing is a goal-centered heuristic activity, whose concrete achievements entail a specific satisfaction.[22] The community, consequently, reveals itself in the achievements which satisfy it. Through such achievements we may discern the story that the community is acting out, the direction of its odyssey, the quality and temper of its spirit.

The travel story that the Jewish and the Christian communities are acting out determines the behavior of their respective members more than the verbally stated rules that they are following. Michael Novak has wisely observed that men seldom act according to principles and rules stated in words and logically arranged; they act, rather, according to models, metaphor, stories and myths.[23] Their action is imitative rather than rule-abiding. Prior to their intention to observe sets of rules, they are trying to become a certain type of person. To analyze adequately the religious experience and behavior of the Jewish and Christian communities, we must recognize the logical priority of the category of myth, story, symbol and ritual, with respect to the category of rules, principles, propositions and codes of behavior. It is, in fact, the acting out of the Christ story which distinguishes the Christian from the Jewish community.

The story contained in the Gospels, according to Stanley Hauerwas, is not meant to provide a world view, but rather to position the self (and the faith community) appropriately in relation to God.[24] It is best thought of not as a theory but a therapy whose primary purpose is to help us deal with the world. In this context, Hauerwas believes that theology does not create the meaningfulness of religious discourse but provides reminders of how that discourse is rightly used. Such reminders are the skills, both linguistic and moral, that help us live our lives free from self-deception. Such skills are not dependent on a system but are systematically displayed through the dominant stories that our lives require in order to be true.

The limit-language of the travel story positions the self in relation to the irreducible, ineffable mystery at the heart of all experience. We come especially close to this mystery in our coming together with others: "Life has no beginnings, middles, or ends; there are meetings, but the start of an affair belongs to the story we tell ourselves later, and there are partings, but final partings only in the story."[25]

The narrative of a life story is made, therefore, as a kind of limit-language for a limit-experience within a transcendental horizon which circumscribes it between the two "ands." Our formulation and statement of a life story (or travel story) implies our implicit awareness of the very ground of the story which transcends its limits, without which there is no story. This is where we are aware of the mystery which is not available to our comprehension within the story itself. It is a quality of the sacred that it is always beyond our comprehension, the known unknown.

5. *INTERPRETATION OF LIFE STORIES*

For Michael Novak the story of every self is both the pattern by which he lives his life and the process whereby he shapes his life through his discerning and appropriating the stories told by other lives.[26]

Life stories interpenetrate. The story of a self cannot be told without the stories of other selves. Every life story begins with the interpenetration of two life stories and is constantly being shaped by other life stories. The meaning of a particular life story emerges in a way of being-with-others that is necessarily articulated in narrative form. The "world" which emerges in the story that my life tells is inhabited by countless others who are essential to my self-understanding. They are constitutive of my life story and cannot be omitted in the attempt to give a responsible account of it. Their worlds have become parts of my world. Our communal experience of worlds is generally expressed in the context of a story. Our lives change when new people open new worlds to us that transform the quality of our consciousness. The truthfulness of their story helps us to know what story we are and should be; it qualifies our thought, word and deed.

According to Michael Novak, we come into existence and endure through the interpenetration of the stories that other lives are telling.[27] Experience of these countless stories rushes in upon us in such floods that we must break them down, select from them, abstract, shape and relate elements for the story that our own life is telling. Our story is constituted by the meaning we impose on our experience of these life stories. Imposing that meaning by every means at our disposal, we shape our lives into a manageable sequence whose meaning is necessarily expressed in a story. We endure through our ability to create a story; i.e., to impose the meaning upon our experience that enables us to give a coherent account of it. Our grasping a religious meaning in our experience entails reference to the framework of our story.

Novak affirms that what we know of the world is known only through consciousness, and we are conscious only through being in a world that is constituted for us chiefly by other persons.[28] What we know of the world is, therefore, characterized by an angularity of vision, for all known reality is known by and through human subjects who perceive, imagine, understand and act in the world in endlessly varied ways.[29] Each life story has its own tonality, tempo, directions and expectations; each has specific turning points. The life stories that have been shaped by the stories of God which people appropriated retain their distinctiveness in the process of bringing to consciousness who they are and what their lives mean. Our access to God is not direct; rather, it is mediated by the truthfulness of other life stories, by the truth that their lives tell.

The life stories of others express our experience, our way of seeing our lives, our self-image and our relations to the world of our fellow men and of nature. Life stories transmit the vital meaning of this experience; they are charged with powers of attraction or repulsion, illumination or depression, expansion or fear; they function progressively when they maximize personal and communal development in honesty, courage, freedom and the ability to value other persons for themselves; they function regressively when they foster a dark love of the absurd and the irrational rather than ethical insights and possibilities.

The problem of our becoming, of our development, of our becoming the kind of person we wish to be, is largely a question of how we interpret and evaluate the life stories that enter into our own. We each have our own starting places for the telling of our life story. Our own proper measure, experiences, feelings, perceptions and tendencies occur within a unique and shifting constellation of other life stories that form the living context of our story. The test of how well we succeed in telling our story depends upon how accurately we discern our own unique possibilities within this living context and upon how deeply instinctive and spontaneous become our efforts to keep the path of discernment clear, ferreting out our own self-deceptions, to perceive ourselves truly. Often, we sense the rightness or wrongness of a particular life story without being able to articulate why. We possess a rather connatural knowledge of its quality that is based largely on our second nature of habit, instinct and resonance. (Because we cannot exhaustively state in words everything within the horizon of our awareness, we employ symbols to express what we sense.)

Our development is interdependent with the development in other human beings of the same qualities to which we aspire for ourselves. We have no life story independently of other life stories which have laid the foundations for the very possibility of our story. Our development is a collaboration, a binding together of agents and events through the richness of our intentional activity that produces an intelligible pattern that can be expressed in narrative form. Our co-operation with other human beings is an intrinsic part of our attempt to make intelligible the muddle of things we have to do to become ourselves. In the language of narrative, we depend upon them for our characterization, motivation, description and commentary, as well as for the plot of our life story. We learn the possibilities for the action that tells our life story, not through intuition into some transcendental or abstract realm, but through reflection upon the actual, concrete story that my life is telling and upon that which is being told by the others who are constituting it.[30] We choose concrete human models as the criterion for the actions that tell our life story; we learn from the stories that their lives have told or are now telling. We learn from the turning points in their stories and from the elements that appear to have prepared the way for them. We learn how their stories are shaped by the stories of God which they have appropriated.

If whatever functions to hold our life together is our religion, there is a religious quality to the basic pattern which emerges in our response to the life stories that have constituted and are constituting our own.[31]

If religion is seen as an attempt to integrate our lives, it implies both our ultimate concern with the integrating principle which has grounded the quality of our relationships with other life stories and the risk of self-deception with regard to what should be our ultimate concern. If a communion of the saints has made the worship of the true God its ultimate concern, a communion of the foolish has been tragically mistaken in its choice, however implicit, of what to make the unconditional and unquestioned source of meaning for the story that its life tells. The integrating pattern of our lives eventually emerges, implying both the kind of person we wish to be and the kind of world we wish to inhabit. Because our lives are constituted by stories which we have embraced for our own, our personal excellence is largely a question of our ability to discern authentic excellence in the stories others have told and/or are telling; it is equally a question of our desire, willingness and decisiveness to act accordingly. The excellence of our insight and judgment comes to naught unless it leads to action which tells our life story. The true goodness of our story is in the concreteness of its existence which derives from the coherence of our thought, word and action.

The authentic Christian has chosen the Gospel story of Jesus as his basic story because he believes that this is the most truthful and worthwhile story that our lives have been empowered to tell. It corresponds to his most deeply felt need for the honesty, courage, freedom and ability to accept himself, others and God in the ongoing quest and questioning of his examined life. He believes that the Church's travel story of Jesus, the Gospel truth, discloses the true excellence of his ultimate possibilities, of his authentic destiny. The authentic Christian believes that this is available to him in the process of self-sacrificing love's daily dying and rising or conversion, deepening and developing in other-centeredness the self-transcending exodus journey of agapic love disclosed in and empowered by the story which tells of God's action in the words, deeds and destiny of Jesus. The existential verification for his story is experienced in the concrete goodness of truthful lives constituting the communion of the saints.

New Testament stories of God's love in Christ are told from different perspectives. The introduction to a story places it within a particular context with a particular image of Jesus. The kenotic image of Jesus as a man of compassion conveys one dimension of his healing meaning and value; the epiphanic image of Jesus as a miracle-worker conveys another. Just as there are a variety of ways of interpreting the point of the story and of forming an image of Jesus from them, there are a variety of ways in which the New Testament images God in its articulation of the relationship of Jesus' life with the life of God. John, for example, understands the religious significance of Jesus of Nazareth and his life as the incarnation of the life and love of God in the world, inasmuch as he images God as love (1 Jn. 4:7-8, 12). This same image of God appears in the Synoptic Gospels, where the first and greatest commandment is always that of love it is also implicit in Paul's affirmation that love is the greatest of all spiritual gifts. The New Testament stories of Jesus tell of a qualitatively new kind of life that is revealed in the story which Jesus' life told. The image of God which Jesus' life discloses is that of compassionate, self-giving love. It is an image tied to the concrete, the contingent, and the particular story of Jesus of Nazareth; therefore, it is connected with the history of the past, with the ongoing present, and with a possible future. The New Testament story of Jesus is that of the human image in which men could see the life of God himself. It invites us to believe in a Kingdom that is invisible on the basis of the signs of hopefulness in our experience of the visible. John asks how one can love God who is invisible if one does not love one's neighbor who is visible (1 Jn. 4:20). Christian faith and hope in God are grounded in the experience of having seen his image in the finiteness and concreteness of the story which Jesus' life has told and continues to tell. The authentic Christian is committed to the communication of this image in the finiteness and concreteness of his own life story; his life shares in the intentionality (mission) of Christ's life.

16

A PHENOMENOLOGY
OF TRAVEL STORIES

1. A PHENOMENOLOGY OF AT-HOMENESS

The phenomenology of at-homeness illuminates the limit-experience and the limit-language of the travel story. Theology, philosophy and science have pursued this theme in terms of the All and the One, as in Plato, Augustine, Boehme, Pascal and Whitehead. Literature abounds in concrete descriptions of the place its persons can call home. It implies a phenomenology of man as the traveller, the *Homo Viator* of Marcel or the *Journeying Self* of Natanson. Marcel intimates this link: "Perhaps a stable order can only be established on earth if man always remains acutely conscious that his condition is that of a traveller. Does not everything happen as though this ruined universe turned relentlessly upon whomever claimed that he could settle down in it to the extent of erecting a permanent dwelling for himself."[1]

In his approach to a phenomenology of at-homeness, Frank M. Buckley shows that a good part of feeling at home has to do with the satisfaction which is familiar, within a structure that one knows about ahead of time and knows reasonably well what to expect in a relatively unthreatening and comfortable manner.[2] In this context, at-homeness is an "at-easeness," which can be contrasted to dis-ease or undue experience of stress: it is a feeling of relaxation and rest in the presence of the customary, the expected and the accepting. At a deeper and more dynamic level is the feeling, "I am where I can be myself." It is the feeling that there is no need to explain our actions to anyone or to feel on guard toward the misperceptions of the other. A sense of familiarity, or security, or comfort, or at-easeness, or being oneself are common-sense meanings of at-homeness which intimate a deeper sense of dwelling at home.

There are particular qualities of life experience which, coming together, promote the feeling of at-homeness. They occur within that ever present tension between the polarities of being, found in being itself, and characterize every human being on the levels of his own distinctive capacities for awareness, feelings, reflection and intersubjectivity. Merleau-Ponty speaks of this as the fundamental ambiguity of existence which permeates our experience of being.[3]

The polarities of being create a tension in human awareness, feeling, reflection and intersubjectivity, which underlie religious experience and its expression in the travel story. The limit-language of religious experience in taking the form of a travel story implies our experience of change and its tensions in the realm of these polarities. In his approach to a phenomenology of at-homeness, Buckley describes the polarities in different ways.

The tension of nearness and remoteness characterizes the search for at-homeness.[4] Psychologically, it corresponds to the meanings of which we are deeply aware in contrast to those which are remote and buried (pre-reflective and pre-conscious). Spatio-temporally, we experience the ambivalent sequence of "Now I am here — then I will be there."[5] The experience of moving and its sequence of uprootings and its feelings of not-at-home carry with it a concurrent evocation of what it means to be at home. Changes and opportunities for a type of renewal call for a detachment and uprooting which involves a sense of loss, sadness and suffering. There is a dimension of life which exposes us to the reality of death. Every real separation is a prototype and foretaste of one's earthly end. We prefer to discountenance our real feelings (experiences) that have to do with moving, uprooting, changing, leaving, dying, and lose the actual ever cyclic intersubjective tension between nearness and distance, warmth and coldness, openness and closedness, intimacy and objectivity, in a word, the experience of at-homeness.[6] We prefer to erect a structure of defence enabling us to maintain that all is fine and to repress any contestations of feeling or spirit. The nearness of the everyday lies within the realm which, at bottom, transcends it and speaks through it. The struggle toward transcendence is a question of recognizing the realm (or home) in which the world of everyday experiences, with its movements, uprootings and changes, ultimately dwells.[7] There is no authentic at-homeness apart from this realm of Dwelling.

Buckley believes that there are equally central needs for openness and enclosure in at-homeness.[8] Openness to reality is a primary prerequisite for feeling at home — not only in a house that one knows and possesses, but in the struggle in-the-world, which is also to say, today, in the universe of spacetime as one knows it on the several levels of sense, spirit and mystery. Openness lets reality in: (to let it be, to be in touch, to let other be, to regard or re-spect the other as other, not as a projected extension of the self, and thus of the same,[9]) this is to be where one is (where the self, others and world really are).

Antithetically, it is true that an equally central component of feeling at home is that which Bachelard develops when he speaks of the house and its parts, which shows us the need for enclosure, or protection, or privacy; which are almost identified with the deepest satisfactions.[10] He speaks of somehow ultimately reaching to that "primordial phenomenological shell" (enclosure). Although the need for warmth and protection is necessary for survival itself, one man's enclosure may become the other's rejection and exposure. The tension between openness and enclosure are to be understood at the level of being itself.

At-homeness is viewed as coming-together within the polarities of being and the tensions of human experience.[11] Within the welter of objects and apparent conflict of images, associations, thoughts, aspirations and feelings, precisely here, a sense of reverence and humble wonder gives expression to the state of at-homeness.[12] There is an awareness of the presence which grounds our fundamental trust in that realm of Dwelling underlying and unifying the diverse qualities of our life experience.[13] It grounds our faith in the positive outcome of our ongoing, struggling quest for at-homeness. The experience of this presence evokes a sense of coming-together (or falling together), a coherence that partakes of creativity and constitutes the event of "home-ness," leading in a meaningful and humanly satisfying way toward the realm of Dwelling itself.[14]

Embodiment, intersubjectivity and betweenness are several major modes, according to Buckley, in which at-homeness is to be found phenomenologically.[15] The experience of intersubjectivity is seen most sharply in the reality of presence: one person being available to the other, with and for the other. Presence is that mode of relating to the other which convinces us (in the order of bodily perception and feeling) that the other is truly there and with you as another person responding in a fundamental reciprocity. This experience is radically required for authentically human existence and activity. This mode of relationship requires not only a sensory awareness of the other, but a mutual response in which the presence, meaning and value of the other is acknowledged and regarded.

Buckley reminds us that our travel story — our quest for knowledge and understanding — is older (ancestral).[16] It does not begin within the consciousness of the solitary isolated ego, but from birth (and prenatally even) onward, in actual lived experience, which is always within the context of the other (person) who interestingly enough always precedes us. This is the primordial living, an abiding and even transcendental relationship within which context all human development (travel stories) and activity (behavior), including especially sensation and perception and all forms of cognition, language, feeling, emotion and motivation, take place. This is the intersubjective base of human existence which is always a co-existence.[17]

Embodiment means that the body-subject (the person) is inextricably interwoven with the world, the body being the intermediary which links the interior to the exterior in the polarity of our being. As van Kaam puts it, "I am always in the world in and through my body: I am an embodied consciousness, an incarnated subjectivity. All my modes of existence are fundamentally modes of existence in and through my body. I am neither a disembodied self nor a mechanical organism but a living unity, a body permeated by self."[18] Since my body is my spontaneous lived presence in the world in a real, though sometimes vague and pre-reflective way, it also is my vital mode of presence to other persons in the world; it is my ever present link to the other body-subjects (persons).[19]

The fact of both this bond with others and the world, as well as the nature and major modes of this bond of betweenness (inter-ness) constitutes the foundation and possibilities of what may be thought of as an inter-subjective paradigm for psychology itself.[20] At-homeness is a coming-together based on the central significance of relations between persons and of the social nature of reality itself. Intersubjectivity or human abode is by no means to be discovered only where the experience and reality of presence is to be found, but rather needs to be understood in terms of a joyful struggle for presence within its ever shifting and alternating waves, currents and rhythms.[21]

At-homeness might be described as a feeling of both protection and lookout, of enclosure yet openness, of nearness to earth below and sky above, of coolness yet warmth, of seclusion yet availability, of solitude yet presence, of distance from all yet nearness to all, of location yet movement, of shade yet brightness, of darkness yet light, of limited air yet breath, in a world of structure yet freedom of life and thought.[22]

As a coming-together within the polarities of the human condition, at-homeness implies the movement expressed in the limit-language of the travel story, where life is seen as motion (development, growth, inquiry and discovery) in a community of shared concerns and a fundamental trust in a loving God. The travel story's quest for at-homeness implies the antipodes of movement vs. stasis, life vs. death, openness vs. self-enclosure, trust vs. fear. The faith community's travel story is its limit-language expressing its limit-experience of that coming-together of what-it-is, what-it-was and what-it-has-to-be.

If at-homeness is viewed as a coming-together in the traveller condition, it is not immune to the polarities of being in the sensation of hesitation and withdrawal from the dangers that attend all travel, all movement in and through time, that attend every moment of passing or going through, that is to say, that attend all experience. Richard R. Niebuhr notes that the English word "fear" is associated with the German *Gefahr* (danger) and *fahren* (to travel) and the Latin *experior* (to find out).[23] The sense of coming-together in the traveller condition is opposed to the sense of things having fallen apart in the hopelessness of the shipwreck condition. Niebuhr has observed the frequency with which the metaphor of shipwreck is used in entries of journals and literary works where the author's mood is one of despair and futility at having been abandoned in a chaotic and destructive welter of elements.[24]

The travel story, as the limit-language of limit-experience, implies a way of interrogating human existence and explicating its most subtle dimensions. It brings to light new understandings of the human experience in symbols, signs and images drawn from common experience. The telling of the Gospel's travel story is a response to the demand for an explanation of the event (limit-experience) which brought the Christian community into existence. Although the Gospel's storyteller has recourse to clusters of basic symbols that have always been used to express our experience of wonder, he finds that Christ is the most hopeful and meaningful interpretation of these symbols. His story must be told to unleash the illuminating power of the original experience; to communicate an entirely new appreciation of something we have always already known (as when Paul tells the Athenians that Christ is the meaning of their unknown god — Acts 17:23). And this new appreciation in turn begets an enrichment hitherto unsuspected for the human enterprise in general.

2. THEORIZING, JOURNEYING, DWELLING

The cognitive element of religious experience and its expression in the biblical travel story is implicitly illuminated by Bernd Jager's study of the deep and persistent inter-relationship between the themes of intellectual, theoretical or spiritual effort and those of travelling and exploration.[25] He notes that the very language of intellectual effort constantly refers us to the road. We are said to make progress in our science, that we advance to, or arrive at, or are on the way to new insights, that we work towards a new understanding, attempt to reach new conclusions, or hope for a break-through, all the while keeping up with the work of others, hoping not to fall behind. Our religious language also evokes the images of a road, albeit a difficult road, to be traversed as preparation for an eternal destination.

Inquiring into the earliest usages of the words "theorist" and "theory," Jager finds that the first appearance of the word *theoros* evokes the components *theo* and *eros* to read "he who regards and observes the will of God."[26] The theoretician appears as recipient of a divine message and as a faithful transmitter of that message back to the people. The foremost task of the theoretician was to question and to transmit the response. But in order to hear the voice of God he had to venture out, to risk the perils of the road and return to his point of departure. From the very beginning truth was a search, and the life of the spirit required a way (or road) for it to follow for the attainment of the truth.

Pindar speaks of a *theorion* or a place where the theorists compete in the games. They are not mere spectators but rather actual participants in the religious celebrations. They function as official participating delegates in the festivities of another city. The theorist is chosen by his people to represent them. He fulfills his religious function as a traveller. His participation in events serves his observation and his observation is the measure of his participation. The word theorist and its close derivatives never refer to participation in religious festivity in the home town. From the beginning the theorist has to journey beyond the boundaries of his own city.

Theoria implies a journey. Our word "pilgrimage" suggests a similar nexus of religious worship and travel. Herodotus, describing Solon's travels, refers to his *theoria* in terms of a "wishing to see the world," as a mission inspired by the passion for seeing and knowing.[27] The delight in the religious festival has become generalized to become a delight in seeing a new landscape, different people, curious customs and practices. Similarly, Thucydides tells how Nicias could not sway the Athenians from their resolve to sail for Sicily in part because of the strong taste for travel in many who were present. *Theoria* in this context refers to the excitement of a venture.[28] Gradually *theoria* comes to refer to the experience and knowledge one acquires while travelling. The theorist is a *sophos,* someone skilled, clever, knowledgeable about the world, a variety of people, customs, languages.

In Plato's *Laws* we find that the *theoroi* are "citizens desiring to inspect the doings (pragmata) of the outside world in a leisurely way."[29] Such a travel experience, if rightly done, would lead to a greater perfection and fuller civilization of the enterprising citizens and of the young people they might instruct upon their return. *Theoria* is thus a voyage of inquiry. A sound reason for venturing out on *theoria* was to visit men who are divinely inspired.[30] Theorizing is a voyage to a worthy sight, an inspiring spectacle to be witnessed and later to be shared with those left behind in the home town.

The first theorists were drawn towards the sacred, towards the powerful and fascinating upsurge of the real at the center or near the edge of our world; they journeyed from their homes and the world of ordinary routine preoccupations. They placed themselves outside the entanglements of the everyday world in order to see the world in a different way and to be changed thereby. They accepted an *askesis* of being separated from the comforting routines and familiar faces of everyday reality. The primordial separation and distinction accepted by the first theorists acquires the distinct form of a journey. The early theorist journeys from everyday life to the festive and awesome realm of the divine where he seeks wisdom and transformation. The departure and separation of the journey are to render available in a new way the self, the world, the divine. Turning away from the familiar, the theorist prepares to be addressed by that which is other, the emergent, the unpredictable, the awe-inspiring. In due time, however, he returns transformed by his new experience to the mainstream of ordinary life, to the familiar world of his home country and native town where his journey began.

Examining the basic attitudes and characteristics of the earliest Greek wise men and philosophers, Jager notes the close relationship between journeying and thinking.[31] The search for truth, like a journey, starts with a ridding oneself of excess baggage in a divestiture that is linked with the ideal of simplicity and clarity. The first divestiture of thought and travel is that of the comfort of being at one with one's surroundings, of sharing completely in the beliefs and ambitions of friends and neighbors. Thinking and journeying are linked with the ideal of guarding oneself from an all too ready and uncritical absorption of the dominant values of one's native surroundings.[32] They begin from everyday life and return to it. They are motivated by the ineradicable, dynamic desire to know. They are the activities of people who cannot avoid asking questions about life. The journey expresses the latent and invariant structures, the desire for imperatives, and the dynamics of the human mind itself in an ongoing openness to new vision.

Thinking and journeying imply the freedom to detach and disengage oneself from those satisfactions which would impede the restless spirit which continually prods the subject to the attainment of further vision. The desire to know, which underlies both thinking and journeying, must continually wrestle with opposing tendencies at the organic, psychic and interpersonal levels of human awareness. Thinking and journeyings involve the pursuit of vision (truth) even when it hurts. Commitment to this pursuit frees the thinker and the traveller from the entanglements which threaten to impede it. To see and to understand is both their ambition and their reward.

Nearly all the *Dialogues* of Plato open with a reference to the journey of the participants. As descendants of the ancient theorists, the participants share the theoretic yearning for new insights, for what tomorrow will bring, for what will emerge beyond the next hill. These young philosophers are in the future-oriented stage of life in which they feel the impulse to move beyond the sphere of parental and home-town influence into a larger world.

The Socratic dialogues, according to Jager, facilitate the emancipation of youth by drawing out into the open what at first was only virtual or hidden.[33] Within this conception of drawing out a new life, the beginning of the theoretic journey assumes the form of exodus rather than departure. Origins are left behind for a journey of continual transcendence, progress and expansion, without ever looking back. The theoretic journey is forever preoccupied with the beyond, activated by the dynamic, restless and irrepressible character of the basic human drive to know the truth of things. The voyage of discovery towards the light, in the Seventh Book of Plato's *Republic,* is a natural tendency that is to continue indefinitely. Man's openness to wonder is endless; his capacity for inquiry insatiable.

The first steps of the journeyer in the new direction are the hardest; for he must struggle to disentangle the innate leanings of his desire to know from more primitive orientations. The pleasures of a delightful environment may oppose change. Asceticism, on the other hand, facilitates necessary change by soliciting the dynamics and services of biological and psychic sources of excitement to bear on the passionate quest for true vision in newer and richer experience, enlarging our world and expanding our possibilities for action. Asceticism is accepted with the recognition that although to part is to die a little, not to depart may mean that one dies altogether, rotting in an unexamined life that never took distance from itself. Asceticism is an exercise in turning away from the sphere of dwelling in the direction of wisdom; it intends that our consciousness never be distracted from newer and richer experience, from more rewarding possibilities for human happiness. Asceticism is a manifestation of hope and faith in relation to the future. Faith bases itself on what is given, while hope as faith in relation to the future moves into what is to come.

Everything about the journey, Jager affirms, refers back to the sphere of dwelling.[34] It is born out of a complex interaction of nearness and distance, intimacy and strangeness, of abundance and constraint. Journeying grows out of dwelling, as dwelling is founded in journeying. The road and the hearth, journey and dwelling, mutually imply each other. Neither can maintain its structural integrity without the other. The journey, cut off from the sphere of dwelling, becomes an aimless wandering. To avoid deteriorating into mere distraction or chaos, it requires a place of origin as the background against which the figures of a new world can emerge. There would be no sense of relativity in the mind's journey forward through its irrepressible questions without the dynamic center in the self to which our forays of experience always return for insight and assent. The self that continually strives for more knowledge is the very source of the horizon over and against which relativity shows up as such. The thinker's journey into self-awareness can, therefore, lead him out of relativism at the same time that it repudiates the obsessive demand for certitude. This center of dwelling is one that continually directs him outward into the flux without making him drift aimlessly in it. The hometown, the fatherland, the neighborhood, and the parental home symbolize the dynamic, cognitional self-awareness that motivates and unifies the journey. They symbolize vision's origin in self-awareness, where the knower finds both a center of stillness within the vortex of possible world perspectives and a standpoint from which he may enter into the welter of cultural, intellectual and religious alternatives without fear of being engulfed by relativism or stymied by the obsession with certitude. This is the sphere of dwelling which maintains its vitality through the renewal made possible by the path (way) of the journey which symbolizes the differentiated demands and structures of the fully functioning human mind. The refusal of the path is the refusal of the future, a suicidal attempt to live entirely in the past. The sphere of dwelling is vital only when it is interpenetrated with journeying.[35]

Fidelity to the fullness and generosity of one's origins supports each new enterprise. The journey into self-awareness, the sphere of dwelling that also directs one outwards, requires a thoughtful remembrance of whatever supports that enterprise; for one can leave behind only what one has truly faced. Whatever has been seriously ignored will eventually reappear and complicate one's progress. The traveller attends to the ground (present) and the past because they must support his journey. Each full journey (life story), in is own manner, bears witness to the latent abundance from which we emerge and to which we must return.[36] Jager believes that Plato's prisoner of the cave cannot truly advance because he lives nowhere.[37] He emerges from a void. Unsupported by a neighborhood, a village, a parental home and therefore out of touch with the generosity of the earth, unfavored by the gods, uninstructed by benevolent elders, in the service of nobody, his journey is doomed to become a non-event, an empty abstraction. Released from his chains he will be capable of nothing except nihilistic wandering.[38]

Following the path of journey is to submit to the ordering stride, to the discipline of counting and recounting (for example, storytelling as recounting), to the intensification of memory.[39] As the outer symbol of the inner meaning, journey has the circular character of a reflection upon events which unifies them within an overall structure and binds them into coherence, so that events speak with reference to a beginning and an end, referring to preceding and succeeding events. The journey into self-awareness discloses the power of events to speak to each other and to form a whole, dependent on a place of origin.[40] The meaning of the journey grows out of that loyalty to its origins which refers the details (events) of the journey to the sphere of dwelling. The journey is structured from its origin; every step sends its echoes home.[41] A journey entirely cut off from its source would be an eternal departure. The journey of the Christian community is promising because it remembers its origins in a past of promises: "Anyone who does eat my flesh and drink my blood has eternal life, and I shall raise him up on the last day" (Jn. 6:54). The Christian community realizes that it can only complete a fruitful journey if it starts from the solid base within the fullness and generosity of the God who loved and glorified Jesus of Nazareth at its origins. The going forth of the Christian journey speaks of its having remained faithful to the limit-experience of Jesus. Within the sphere of dwelling, thought emerges in response to an observant tending of the past. The storyteller tends to the past so that the community will not perish by being cut off from its origins. His function is to see to it that the journey continues.

The quest for happiness is a continuing, ongoing process. It is characterized by certain experiences which point in the direction of happiness, which bespeak happiness, removing obstacles and uncovering the landscape of existence. The journey of the theorists unveils the landscape, discloses the past while it opens to view the distant. It involves the coming forth, in turn, of the traveller, revealing that which is of ultimate importance about the person, the past, the landscape, the gods. It discloses and brings into view what remains hidden in profane repetitive existence. The journey removes the self-evident in the past and latent in the person.[42] Journeying is an emerging into expressiveness and self-manifestation, both a seeing and a showing, the ecstatic realm of epiphany and parousia in the Gospel travel story of Christ, whose limit-language re-presents the wonder-experience of man, the world and God coming together in their fullest visibility.

The homecoming of the theorists occurs after they have experienced a fullness in the presence of a god at a distant, sacred shrine. The homeward journey links the human and the divine realm in a mutual creation by the polis, the deity and the traveller; it is a confluence of events and meanings, unifying past, present and future. The theorist re-presents the deity to the city, recollecting the major aspects of his journey; for this world is inhabited by others. His life and thought is inextricably intertwined with other citizens of the polis. His narrative interpretation of the sacred events of his journey is itself a homecoming.

17

MEDIEVAL ALLEGORY AS INWARD JOURNEY

1. THE INTERPRETATION OF DREAMS

Centuries before Christ, the inhabitants of the Near East resorted to the interpretation of dreams for resolving personal, social and even national problems. Spiritual authorities, such as priests, specialized in the interpretation of dreams. Several thousand years later, the psychologist generally replaced the priest as the authority to be consulted for the analysis of dreams. He often makes an elaborate interpretation of the individual images of the dream and relates the general significance of the dream to the life and problems of the dreamer.

The dreamer of the ancient Near East and his contemporary counterpart tend to have much in common. Both are generally faced by a serious problem that creates strong emotional tension and is felt to be beyond their volitional and conscious control. In each case the initial answer to the problem is generally provided by an enigmatic vision of a psychic authority in a place with sacred associations. Although the dreamer may be able to make some preliminary assessment of the meaning of his experience, he generally has to obtain further elucidation from an appropriate interpreter. The event, which is too complex for the dreamer to deal with, may then be presented to him either as a vision embodying appropriate symbolic images conventional to the society in question, or as a rational analysis of this symbolic imagery.

According to Paul Piehler's study *The Visionary Landscape,* most important medieval allegories also involve a dreamer who is profoundly disturbed by some spiritual crisis.[1] He has a vision (dream) of mysterious import which is interpreted by persons who are in spiritual authority and the effect of the vision and its interpretation is to resolve the crisis, generally by raising him to a higher spiritual state. These allegories were offered to their readers for spiritual participation, so that in undergoing the imaginative experience of the vision (dream) they might avail themselves of a spiritual exercise, of the same process of enlightenment, healing and transcendence as that undergone by the central figure of the allegory.[2]

In the medieval allegory the interpretation of the vision (dream) is normally entrusted to the figure of authority within the vision itself, as opposed to a professional interpreter of dreams. Such interpretation, derived from the tradition of the philosophical dialogue, often becomes sufficiently elaborate and complex to constitute the most important element of the visionary experience. It is the typical function of the dialogue to enable the poet and his readers to face and control the demonic force represented by the uninterpreted, unexamined, pure visionary or mythic experience.

2. THE PSYCHOLOGICAL PROCESS IN MYTH AND ALLEGORY

Piehler's approach to medieval allegorical visions is twofold.[3] He attempts to explain medieval allegory in terms of its most important antecedents: the ancient myths out of which developed its central imagery and the classical dialogue which contributed the basis of its intellectual structure. Piehler also seeks to interpret visionary allegory as a profound and far-reaching exploration of the human psyche, sustained and developed for over a thousand years. In this context he notes that in the last forty years not only have the psychoanalysts been accepted into the framework of society as a kind of auxiliary priesthood, but the links between psychology and literature have been strengthened by psychological scrutiny of myth and literature by such Jungians as Maude Bodkin and Erich Neumann, and of the literary man's use of the psychologist's findings on myth by such writers as Northrop Frye and W.A. Auden.

By allegorizing ancient myth the greatest poets of the Middle Ages achieved a new and higher type of mythopoeia. Every age has new and creative interpretations to make of the ancient motifs; however, medieval allegory at its best attained a balance of rational and intuitive elements, an acceptance of all levels on which the mind functions, which is the goal of those who seek psychic integration today. Piehler's concern is not with the mythical for its own sake but with the function of the mythical and intuitional elements in the human conciousness as they relate to and interact with the rational elements of our psychic life; hence, his findings may be of considerable relevance to psychotheraphy.[4]

The medieval visionary allegory frequently expresses a psychological process by which the various elements of man's spiritual life are identified in the form of personifications, analyzed in dialogue, and then either rejected or accepted for absorption into the personal life of the protagonist and, vicariously, of the reader. The allegory is a type of spiritual exercise with a serious psychotherapeutic purpose; it is a method of attaining healing through enlightenment. It attempts to communicate a sound and comprehensive view of reality that will contribute to personal renewal and transformation. It is a process for reflecting upon and experiencing the basic spiritual truths and values embodied in its healing vision.

3. ALLEGORY AS PILGRIMAGE

The medieval visionary allegory concerns a type of psychic experience that is by no means confined to the Middle Ages. This experience might well be expressed in terms of the archetype of pilgrimage and of the pilgrimage condition of man.[5] Representations of this archetype generally begin with a serious problem, a crisis, rather than with a paradisiacal situation. In fact, the time before the crisis may take on a paradisiacal character as the good time of personal stability, tranquility and integrity. The pilgrimage is a spiritual quest for a change, a transformation of oneself and relief from profound suffering, distress, anguish and illness. The pilgrimage begins as a response to a crisis. It may begin with a crisis of personal disintegration. It may be motivated by the remembrance of a lost integrity and by the hope of regaining it. The pilgrimage implies the refusal to accept the present condition of confusion and suffering as final; it implies the conviction that there is a way of transcending this condition, despite all the evidence to the contrary.

Piehler's study of allegory provides categories for interpreting the human pilgrimage condition and its archetypal character. It deepens our understanding of the process of psychic and spiritual redemption that underlies the human pilgrimage condition as a quest for personal transformation.

4. PRELIMINARY ANGUISH AND THE CHTHONIC POWERS

A preliminary anguish, an extreme emotional and psychic tension, characterizes the beginning of the medieval allegory and manifests the oppressive presence of the dark, chthonic, anti-rational powers.[6] It is in answer to the pilgrim's anguished prayer for help that a spiritual authority makes its appearance. Such help is necessary for confronting the dark and destructive forces of the psyche; for they must be named, analyzed and exorcised in order to liberate the pilgrimage from their lethal influence.

Towards the end of the fourth century, in Prudentius' *Psychomachia*, we are treated to an allegorical interpretation of the life of Abraham as the life of the spirit.[7] Just as Abraham was unable to have children before he overcame the savage rulers who took Lot captive, so we are unable to produce the fruits of the spirit until we have slaughtered the monsters dwelling within the heart enslaved to sin. The second part of the preface to this poem consists of an address to Christ, whose assistance in identifying the contending forces in the soul is considerably emphasized. The method of victory through the enlightenment and power of Christ consists in defeating the monsters through discerning them. Hence the double preface reveals the double purpose of Prudentius' allegory, which tells us something about allegorical methods in general. The correct analysis of the state of the soul is as important as the crushing of the evils one finds inhabiting it; otherwise, the evils are likely to return. The opening prayer of the *Psychomachia* indicates that the battle takes place within a mind under considerable stress. With Christ's aid and enlightenment we may look at the monsters face to face and recognize them for what they are. The two prefaces distinguish the roles of priest (prayer) and exorcist (liberation).

Medieval allegory is a mode of expressing and interpreting experience for the Christian pilgrim in his search for the mental states most productive of harmony with God. The pilgrim's search is aided by the figures of Nature, Reason, and Holychurch;[8] the pilgrim must heed them in order to attain the healing that he needs; he must be enlightened by them in order to recognize and vanquish the chthonic powers that beset him during his pilgrimage.

5. THE VISIONARY LANDSCAPE

A second important category for understanding the psychotherapeutic character of the medieval allegory is the visionary landscape.[9] Visible landscapes and locales represent invisible states of mind and mood. Such landscape symbolism appears in the basic psychic polarity of city and wilderness which arises out of man's experience of his environment. The society the city makes possible is the requisite of most ordered cultural life, a repository of traditional wisdom and a frame of reference for thought and speculation. Outside lie wilderness and ocean, not merely the symbols of the powers threatening human life, but the very place of their operation.

In ancient literature, the primary danger inherent in the wilderness is manifested and symbolized in its animal inhabitants. Because man has only uncertainly discerned their shapes and characteristics, their appearances are unpredictable and can hardly be distinguished from the internal menaces of the nightmare. At the frontiers of the unknown, the sleep of reason engenders monsters, warning man away from the hostile forces beyond his control. The monster embodies the terror instilled by the hostility of featureless terrain to the rational process.

A second major peril of the wilderness is the temptation from man to succumb to anti-rational self-indulgences of the body and spirit, unbridled sexuality or slothful daydreaming, away from the civilizing restraints of his community and its institutions.[10] In this context, the hero of ancient literature is the man who is able to internalize the psychic achievements of his community and to function in the wilderness as a rational and responsible human being. As the result of the hero's victories over the monster and the wilderness, it becomes possible for man to carry into the wilderness a city within himself; wilderness and the city are reconciled, the powers of nature are ruled by reason, the shadowy and pathless wilderness is illuminated by the light of reason, man's darker instincts are controlled through his enlightenment.

If the human pilgrimage situation contains elements of the wilderness and the city, both elements are reconciled in the landscape of the garden. Medieval allegory drew from the biblical Garden of Eden and the garden imagery of the *Song of Songs*.[11] This tradition recognized not only a physical paradise as the place where man was first created, but a spiritual paradise as every place where the soul is in a state of well-being or grace. This garden, in the psychology of landscape, symbolizes the true and comprehensive vision of reality enjoyed by those who are enlightened by the grace of God; it represents the ultimate and perfect state of psychic and spiritual integration in which man is at peace with himself, his neighbor and his Creator.

The visionary landscape describes the pilgrim's field of consciousness, the scope of his knowledge, the range of his interests. It corresponds in large measure with Bernard Lonergan's notion of horizon.[12] Within the horizon lie the objects that can now be seen: beyond it lie the objects that, at least for the moment, cannot be seen. For different standpoints, there are different horizons. For each different standpoint and horizon, there are different divisions of the totality of visible objects.

As the fields of vision vary with one's standpoint, so too the scope of one's knowledge and the range of one's interests vary with the period in which one lives, one's social background and milieu, one's education and personal development. In this sense what lies beyond one's visionary landscape is simply outside the range of one's knowledge and interests (meanings and values): one neither knows nor cares. But what lies within one's visionary landscape is in some measure, great or small, an object of interest and knowledge.

The quality of the pilgrim's consciousness changes as his visionary landscape (horizon) changes. Even within a given landscape (horizon) there are different levels of the pilgrim's consciousness. Lonergan affirms that they are successive, related and qualitatively different:[13] the empirical level of sensing, perceiving, imagining, feeling, speaking, moving; the intellectual level of inquiring, understanding, expressing what is understood, working out the presuppositions and implications of what has been expressed; the rational level of reflecting, marshalling the evidence, judging the truth or falsity, certainty or probability of a statement; the responsible level of concern with ourselves, our activities, our goals. And so we deliberate about possible courses of action, evaluate them, decide and carry out our decisions.

The visionary landscape is a category which concerns the pilgrim's conscious attentiveness, intelligence, reasonableness and responsibility as expressed in concepts, propositions, words, images, symbols. The medieval visionary allegory critically inquires for true meaning and value, sifting out what is illusory and false; its analysis is carried on chiefly in terms of imagery rather than abstact concepts, for its aim is to appeal not only to reason but also to feelings, emotions, instincts and all faculties that can be more directly affected by such imagery with its wide range of cultural connotations.[13]

6. THE SPIRITUAL AUTHORITY AND GUIDE

The pilgrim of the medieval allegory seeks a principle of authority by which his life may be enlightened and regulated. With the aid of a spiritual authority and guide, he finally achieves a psychic and spiritual synthesis in which the conflicting elements of his inner life are brought into harmony. The spiritual authority directs the pilgrim in a process of emotional and psychic integration in which obsessions, illusions and false desires may be purged both through the contemplation of true meaning and value as embodied in beneficial images and symbols, and through a therapeutic dialogue with the spiritual authority which enables the areas of disturbance to be related in an orderly way to the universal scheme of things. The spiritual guide helps the pilgrim to cleanse his mind and heart of all unauthentic thinking, desiring, imagining and feeling, as far as this is possible.

Alan of Lille's *Complaint of Nature* is an allegory in which the spiritual authority and guide is Lady Nature.[14] The opening depicts the poet not yet caught up in his visionary experience, but undergoing the intense inner turmoil that is the inevitable prelude to a spiritual journey or pilgrimage. The turmoil derives from inordinate sexual impulses. The process of healing starts with the contemplation of the created universe, ascending by degrees to the higher reality of the creating power. The assumption underlying Lady Nature's long and elaborate description of the natural world appears to be that the controlled contemplation of earthly creation and its order is in itself both calming and healing because it permits the object of the dreamer's (or patient's) obsessive attention to be viewed in relation to the general processes of the universe, and thus to be reduced to its natural proportions within his mental perspective. The order of nature is associated with the harmony of the psychic life; the notion "cosmos" denotes the moral as well as the physical order of things. When contemplated, such order may help to achieve an inner order, a healing enlightenment.

Lady Nature is Christlike as one who comes down to earth, rebukes and pleads with sinners, suffers ignominy at the hands of the wicked, and finally brings peace to the anguished soul. But her mere appearance does not rectify things; persuasion and threats are necessary to bring men to their senses. She must enlighten man's mind to free him from slavery to his rebellious instincts and passions.

Lady Nature engages in a therapeutic dialogue with the dreamer in a psychodrama directed to the healing contemplation of the natural universe characterizes the therapeutic process: the dreamer (pilgrim) must think rightly before he can be expected to act and feel rightly. The therapeutic dialogue is lengthy and elaborate because it is basically a spiritual exercise to enable a rational mind to overcome and regulate disordered emotions. The psychological strategy of this spiritual struggle is to identify, analyze and confront the evil forces with the forces of healing, and finally to repudiate and destroy them.[15]

Although the poet attempts to make the virtues more attractive than the vices, he is too careful a theologian to think that they can conquer by their own innate strength or attractiveness. Lady Nature, in view of the inability of the virtues to resist the vices, must send for her priest, Genius. Man conquers sin not through his unaided volition alone but with ecclesiastically mediated divine assistance; but for such assistance to be meaningful, he must first have rejected sin, so far as he can, on the natural level.

7. THE THERAPEUTIC DIALOGUE

The therapeutic dialogue, a major element in medieval allegory, developed from its classical form to constitute an enlightening rational dimension of the spiritual exercise through which the imagistic and symbolic elements were explicated and controlled and the specific problems of the pilgrim were alleviated as they were viewed in the perspective of the total pattern of human existence.[16] Therapeutic dialogue represented the indispensable role of right reasoning for the attainment of the pilgrim's (hero's) healing vision of reality. Through the dynamics of the therapeutic dialogue the medieval allegory functions as a mode of analysis whereby the different spiritual states of the pilgrim are examined, evaluated and constructively criticized with a view to personal healing and spiritual development.

8. DANTE'S PILGRIMAGE

The perfection of the medieval allegory is reached in Dante's *Commedia*.[17] Its comprehensiveness of vision enabled Dante to give more satisfying answers to the intellectual, spiritual and technical problems inherent in the allegories of his predecessors.

The *Commedia* opens with a restatement of the eternal conflict of man and monster appropriate to the psychological state of Dante as an individual and as representative of his time and circumstances, one living in a part of Christendom distant from the frontiers and the wilderness. The fierce beasts of his dark forest represent known species; they may hinder and frighten the poet rather than destroy him. They may prevent the inner peace that he desires, but they are not powerful enough to overthrow his reason. The presence of the sun and the delectable mountain as constituents of the landscape in the first canto show the state of mind of a man open to the possibilities of Christian salvation, but kept from it by his sinfulness. The animals represent those forces within Dante that impede his ascending the beautiful mountain, recalling the sacredness of Mount Zion, the holy mountain of the Lord.

Virgil is Dante's guide because he is the first man to descend into the underworld and to comprehend that place of archetypal darkness and confusion. Hence, Virgil may enable Dante to live with greater understanding and spiritual strength because he embodies that rationality which is adequate for intellectual comprehension (though not full mastery) of the sins of the underworld and the painful acquisition of human virtue, but which is not yet touched by divine grace. The special kind of enlightenment which Virgil brings to Dante is reflected in the landscape imagery which, previous to their encounter, evoked the chaos and confusion of the primal wilderness and now begins in the first dialogue of the poet to assume shape and identity, with talk of the city and the gate of St. Peter.

Dante learns that his spiritual journey with Virgil is under the protection of a special, unearned, divine grace manifested in Beatrice's plea to Virgil to come to the aid of the imperilled poet. Virgil sweeps Dante through the portals of hell, having convinced him of his fitness to face the realities of that chaotic world and to exert rational control over the dark powers. (The reader is meant to share this opportunity of imposing order on the underworld for himself. Moving with Dante through the afterworlds, he finds not only that the scheme of categorization encompasses moral judgments as a basis for classifying men in ideal landscapes, but that every type of human attitude, temperament and event is displayed in ordered succession.)

When Dante reaches the garden of the earthly paradise at the top of the mountain, a simple and natural image of convergence, we notice a concentration and convergence of basic images and their meanings: a higher viewpoint enables Dante to synthesize conflicting meanings.[18] The forest, for example, had beeen menacing and alien. In the forest of suicides Dante sees the fate of those who have ultimately lost their way in the forest: they have become trees themselves, suggesting the complete absorption of man's soul into the regressive forces that threaten him in the infernal manifestations of the forest. Here in Eden, however, man regains mastery over the forest, just as over himself; it is only now that he may hope to ascend to the true heavens.

The primary image of convergence in the *Paradise* is the garden or orchard. It embodies the harmonious conjunction of all previous landscape images and represents an authentic synthesis of their true meanings.[19] Dante links this image to the realms of the Lord in both heaven and earth.

As Dante journeys through his worlds of vision, the weight of his report is as much on his dialogues with the dead as on the description of the realms they inhabit. Most of his dialogues are related to the landscapes through which he passes in his spiritual pilgrimage from psychic dislocation to transcendence. His dialogues express the different phases of enlightenment in the process by which the evils within the soul are identified, analyzed, confronted and purged, and the corresponding virtuous qualities similarly identified in order to be accepted and personally appropriated by the visionary, with the aid of figures representing successively the operations of nature and grace. Dante links his therapeutic dialogue very closely with images and landscape. Typically, it is stimulated by encounters with specific persons and places and arises out of a progression of experience; each new phase is a preparation for the revelation of landscapes of a higher spiritual order.

The psychotherapeutic purpose of the *Commedia,* as defined in the letter to Can Grande (para. 15), is to remove those living in a state of misery and to lead them into a state of felicity. If Dante had ignored the miseries of earthly life in pure contemplation of the state of felicity, he would have failed in this purpose. The quest of personal salvation, for Dante, does not imply a turning away from the affairs of this world; hence, it is not surprising that even in the *Paradiso,* where we would expect the felicity of the blessed to be undisturbed by temporal preoccupations, Dante cries out against the wickedness in political and social life on earth. Genuine felicity is not achieved through escapism; the seeker after enlightenment is engaged in a struggle to close the gap between his knowledge and appropriate moral action.

9. THE CHRISTOTHERAPEUTIC PURPOSE OF SCRIPTURE

The categories which Piehler employs to explain the psychotherapeutic purpose and character of the medieval visionary allegory can be employed to point out a similar purpose in the Church's use of Scripture. The Gospels relate that the preaching of the apostles, unlike that of the Baptist, is accompanied by the healing of the sick. The content of the Mission Charge given in Mt. 10:5-15 contains seven imperatives that link preaching the Gospel with healing: (1) *Go . . . to the lost sheep of the house of Israel* (vv. 5-6); (2) *Preach as you go* (v. 7); (3) *Heal the sick* (v. 8); (4) *Raise the dead* (v. 8); (5) *Cleanse the lepers* (v. 8); (6) *Cast out demons* (v. 8); (7) *Take no gold nor silver* (vv. 9-10).

The Gospel is the good news of healing. It announces the healing event that is Jesus Christ, who during his lifetime healed people who were suffering physically, psychically and spiritually. Jesus Christ is the healing light. When he was presented in the Temple of Jerusalem the aged Simeon voiced on the part of the poor of Israel the recognition of Jesus as the promised savior and healer through enlightenment when he exclaimed:

> Now, Master, you can let your servant go in peace, just as you promised; because my eyes have seen the salvation which you have prepared for all the nations to see, a light to enlighten the pagans and the glory of your people Israel (Lk. 2:29-32).

Jesus is from the start acknowledged as the healer of the whole person. In the New Testament the same Greek word *sozein* is used to signify both saving (salvation) and healing or making whole. Jesus' saving activity is depicted as a symbol of the conferral of a far greater salvation than just the health of the body. Actually, the body-soul distinction as we know it is not a Hebrew but a Greek conception. Jesus viewed the human person as a unity and so to save and heal was to save and heal the whole person.

By his very nature, presence, and mission, Jesus is the healer *par excellence.* Secondly, he is the healer of the whole person and frees him from all the effects of sin. Thirdly, he is light and heals through his light. Fourthly, he crowns all the healing efforts of his lifetime through the great healing events of his suffering, dying, rising, ascending into heaven, and sending of his Spirit. He is the incarnation of the salvation (healing) of God. If the Lord is described as "the health of my countenance and my God" (Ps. 42:11), Jesus may be spoken of as the incarnation of the health and salvation of the Lord. It is he who is the good news of the Gospel, described as "the radiant light of God's glory" (Heb. 1:3) and as "the Way and the Life" (Jn. 14:6). In the prologue of Part III of the *Summa,* Aquinas says that Jesus our savior showed us in himself the way of truth through which we might attain eternal life. Hence, in the light of the scriptural stress on Jesus Christ as truth, the therapeutic character of the Gospel is seen in the radical healing available to us in Christ as the way and as the "light of the world" (Jn. 8:12). As light, Christ dispels darkness; as truth, he dispels ignorance; as life, he is inimical to disease in all of its forms. What Christ is gives his words and deeds their fundamental meaning and their definitive healing and enlightening power. Whatever Jesus says or does flows from what he is — the Word made flesh, "the same today as he was yesterday and as he will be forever" (Heb. 13:8-9).

Christ's full participation in the truth that is God is the source of meaning in all that he said and did. Every aspect of God's self-revelation in Christ has a healing and enlightening meaning and value for the lives of all men. Hence, it would be missing the point to look to the Gospel simply to acquire a notional knowledge about God or to learn what commandments and moral precepts must be obeyed. Such an approach to the Gospel fails to take Christ seriously as loving, healing truth whose words and actions unveil those existential life-giving meanings and values which will heal our mental, emotional, physical and spiritual diseases and which will communicate in a certain true fashion the light of the resurrection. Christ is The Unique Physician, the ultimate therapist, to be encountered in the Church's preaching of the Gospel.

The Gospel is meant to serve as a form of Christotherapy, of Christ's healing through the enlightenment of his word.[20] The Gospel is preached and read that we may be made whole and filled with the light of truth which frees us from the illnesses of body and soul that represent untruth, since they are caused by false attitudes, by false ways of life that are opposed to the Christ-meaning and the Christ-value. The therapeutic intent of the Gospel is to communicate the fullness of life which comes to the individual through a lived understanding of the Christ-meaning and a loving response to the Christ-value. This intent is implied by Jesus' affirmation that it is only the "sick" who feel their need for him (Lk. 15:2).

The preliminary anguish of the sick and the poor and the hungry, of those who weep now, initiates the spiritual pilgrimage and healing process that characterizes the authentic Christian response to the ultimate spiritual authority of Christ The Unique Therapist. The therapeutic dialogue of the Church with her Lord is found in the liturgical use of Scripture, which is not read for information but rather for healing and enlightenment. Whether the Gospel is read as a part of the liturgy or privately, it is meant to be read as a kind of spiritual exercise within the prayerful process of healing and enlightenment. There is a gradual transformation of the visionary landscape of those who are putting on the mind and heart that is in Christ Jesus. Paul affirms, in his prayer for the Ephesians, that knowledge and love merge into one in their perfection: "May Christ live in your hearts through faith, and then, planted in love and built on love, you will with all the saints have the power to grasp the breadth and the length, the height and the depth; until knowing the love of Christ, which is beyond all knowledge, you are filled with the utter fullness of God" (3:17-18).

The visionary landscape is gradually transformed in the process of conversion, as love and knowledge grow together, and the source of our thoughts, desires, and deeds becomes the same as that in Christ Jesus.

The conversion process that the Church's use of Scripture serves might be described in terms of the archetypes of pilgrimage and its existential moods: paradise (sacred garden and sacred mountain) and its mood of innocence, the wilderness (desert) and its mood of alienation, the pilgrim on the way (path) and his mood of aspiration and hope for recovering what is remembered as the foundational experience of integrity, peace and joy in God, with oneself and neighbor.[21] Remembering and hoping are the dynamic forces moving the pilgrim along his way, a way through the wilderness filled with threats and dangers.

For those who prayerfully participate in the spiritual exercise of the Gospel, there occurs a kind of therapeutic dialogue (Christotherapy) with Christ The Pilgrim who has once and for all completed the designated way of the Lord, who has confronted the ultimate evils that threaten the human pilgrimage through the wilderness situation of trials and temptations, who restores a paradisiacal innocence to sinful mankind by sharing his innocence on Golgotha, the sacred mount: "I promise you that today you will be with me in paradise" (Lk. 23:43).[22] It is in Jerusalem, Mount Zion, where redemptive history is fulfilled and where the disciples receive the power of the Holy Spirit. Through their preaching of the Gospel the absolute integrity (innocence) of the Lamb of God is made available to mankind for its healing and enlightenment.

The liturgical and private use of Scripture has a Christotherapeutic purpose for the human pilgrimage condition. Through the Scriptures Christ, The Unique Physician, communicates his enlightening and healing meaning and value to those who have faith in his absolute integrity. Through the Scriptures there is a remembering and a hoping which sustains the Christian pilgrimage process of putting on the healing heart and mind of Christ. The healing and enlightening power of the Risen Christ effectively transforms those engaged in the prayerful process of remembering Christ and his teaching in Scripture: "The Holy Spirit, whom the Father will send in my name, he will teach you all the things, and remind you of all that I have said to you" (Jn. 14:26). Through the gift of the Holy Spirit, the Father and Son communicate the healing and enlightening power of remembering, of fulfilling the command: "Do this in remembrance of me" (1 Cor. 11:24). Through the gift of the Holy Spirit the pilgrimage is possible; we receive the love to adhere to Christ and his Father, to live and to rejoice in their life-giving and healing presence.

10. THE METHOD OF ALLEGORY AND CHRISTOTHERAPY COMPARED

There are similarities in the therapeutic approach of the medieval visionary allegory and that of Bernard Tyrrell's *Christotherapy*.[23] Piehler's explanation of the therapeutic intention of allegory contributes to an understanding of the prayerful process of personal enlightenment and transformation that is Christotherapy.

11. ENLIGHTENMENT AS DIAGNOSIS

The medieval visionary allegory and Christotherapy are written for the consolation of those who are in need of healing and enlightenment; both offer their readers a kind of spiritual exercise that enables them to participate in a process of psychic redemption which, although sharing elements in common with modern psychotherapy, is wider in scope.

Although both focus on a process of healing that occurs in individual lives, attention is given to those environmental and social forces which both reflect and contribute to the interior landscape and spiritual state of the subject. Both recognize that much of the individual's physical, psychological and spiritual suffering is the result of environmental and social forces. Christotherapy seeks to remedy the existential ignorance that abounds not only on the individual level but on the group, national and international levels as well; it recalls Dante's remonstrance against the social and political evils of Italy (*Purgatorio* VI, 128) and his condemnation of false preachers (*Paradiso* XXIX, 127), which are intended for the psychotherapeutic benefit of his reader who is expected to react intelligently and responsibly to the challenges within his own visionary landscape.[24]

Both medieval visionary allegory and Christotherapy are concerned with the discovery or understanding of the meaning of the negative factors of one's life, the diseases and disharmonies which one experiences. Both assume that it is better to acknowledge our feelings regardless of how objectionable they are rather than ignore them. This enables us to know ourselves and understand and correct those things which are undesirable and harmful.

Existential diagnosis, the first form of Christotherapeutic enlightenment, involves our discovery of the negative, unrealistic, illogical and self-defeating thoughts that cause our emotional disturbances. Such discovery enables healing, the transformation of the mind and heart, freeing the mind from error and ignorance and the heart from false desires and values. Medieval allegory functions primarily as a mode of analysis in which the elements of one's visionary landscape must be diagnosed in order that one may know how to reject false meanings and values that diminish one's authentic existence and secure the true ones which ground human happiness.[25]

Visionary allegory and Christotherapy underscore the role of word, sight, dialogue and symbol in the therapeutic process. Christotherapy is achieved through the healing happening that is Jesus Christ, the Word of God, bearing the good news of healing. Christ's healing presence is concretely manifested by the sacraments, effective signs of his vital presence through his Spirit in the Church, which are expressed in symbols and words and administered in the Church.

Both allegory and Christotherapy recognize the role of a spiritual authority as an indispensable condition for the attainment of healing. This authority governs the healing process of the visionary and regulates his life. In Christotherapy, it is Jesus Christ who exercises his healing power on behalf of the whole person, the body and psyche as well as the spiritual; he is the spiritual authority who operates through his Spirit in human hearts and through his Church to heal those who are physically, psychically and spiritually ill.

12. ENLIGHTENMENT AS DISCERNMENT

Both allegory and Christotherapy assume the need for suprahuman aid in attaining the necessary enlightenment for a correct diagnosis of one's state of soul. The "existential discernment" of Christotherapy is that form of enlightenment which consists in understanding the positive directives and calls which God gives us as we work out our salvation; in terms of St. Paul, it is a matter of discovering "the will of God" and of knowing "what is good, what it is that God wants, what is the perfect thing to do" (Rom. 12:2). Existential diagnosis seeks to understand what is wrong with us; existential discernment seeks to understand what is truly good for us. Both forms of enlightenment are ordered toward our personal growth and transformation.

Religious conversion, the third form of Christotherapeutic enlightenment, is a multidimensional process, a change of mind and heart, a turning from sin, from idols, from an evil way of life. It involves a rejection of false values, attitudes, habits and a personal commitment in love and fidelity to God. It is the work of God who alone blots out our sins and endows us with the gift of a new mind and heart full of righteousness, love and truth.

Medieval allegory serves as a spiritual exercise which aids the reader in transcending his present spiritual state of distress; it aims at enlightening him by dispelling existential ignorance about the present malaise. The beginning of religious development is also ascetical in its impetus. As growth occurs there takes place a gradual shift from an authentic exercise of asceticism and self-discipline toward a self-surrender to the action of God in one's heart.

The *Spiritual Exercises* of Ignatius of Loyola, like the medieval allegory, are structured in imagery, content and analytical elements for progressive spiritual development; the insight of one phase prepares for the next. They also begin with a reflection on the crisis of sin and progress through the dynamic prayer (therapeutic dialogue with Christ) to further stages of enlightenment and transformation. They involve a series of contemplations and meditations whose prayer, images and symbols serve, in many respects, an intention analogous to that of their counterparts in the medieval allegory's therapeutic dialogue and visionary symbolism. Tyrrell cites the *Exercises* as a means of discerning what thoughts are the result of God's inspiration and providential guidance, noting that Ignatian discernment is rooted in the enlightening and healing word of God.

13. ENLIGHTENMENT AS DIVINE DIALOGUE

Just as in the medieval allegory it is through all therapeutic dialogue that the subject's specific problems are explicated, alleviated and viewed in the perspective of the total pattern of his physical, psychic and spiritual existence, so in Christotherapy it is by an active receptiveness to the word of God that the subject is enlightened and transformed into the image of Christ.

The therapeutic dialogue of allegory corresponds to authentic prayer in Christotherapy. All authentic prayer, whether one realizes it or not, is an encounter with God the Father through the mediation of his Son in the power of the Holy Spirit. It is a Christotherapeutic communion in love and knowledge and desire with the Love-Intelligence that is revealed in the Christ-event as Father, Son and Holy Spirit. It is a dialogue encounter of man with his God.

In all authentic prayer God is speaking to man about what concretely concerns him, and man's response must always be in terms of the concrete, of the particular imagery and symbols of his visionary landscape. In the authentic prayer of Christotherapy there is no room for an isolated I-Thou relationship which prescinds completely from other human beings and the cosmos in which man lives. Christotherapy involves the dynamics of the therapeutic dialogue as expressed in the concreteness of the individual's visionary landscape (horizon, field of consciousness).

Christotherapeutic dialogue involves listening: being alert, awake, attentive. Throughout Scripture we are exhorted to listen. One hears to the extent that one wants to hear. Hearing is not simply a passive act. Both God's actual speaking of his word to us and our active hearing of it in our mind and heart are required for spiritual hearing to occur. God speaks to us in his cosmic word, in his prophetic word, and once and for all in the Word made flesh. The Father wills that we listen to his Christ: "This is my beloved Son; he enjoys my favor. Listen to him" (Mt. 17:5).

Christotherapy affirms that God is constantly in dialogue with us in our own thoughts and desires; recognition of God, of healing and life, is the meaning of worship. Authentic praying is existential worship because it is never abstract but always concrete. Such prayer is a participation in healing through enlightenment because it is a communion in knowledge and love with the Three Who are One God, and love and knowledge shared between lover and beloved are the most powerful healing forces known.

Christ is the spiritual authority who enlightens our visionary landscape (field of consciousness) through the therapeutic dialogue that is authentic prayer. He enables us to discern the true meanings and values among the concrete constituents of our visionary landscape and employs all of them to communicate what we truly need for our growth and life. To the extent that we submit ourselves to his spiritual authority in authentic prayer, our visionary landscape changes; although the constituents may remain the same, they are interpreted differently, according to our personal transformation in Christ. We gradually share more of his vision of our landscape; we share his understanding and evaluation; we share his basic intention and spirit. The prayer of repentance implies such a change. It is the prayer of the pilgrim as he journeys in this life; it expresses loving sorrow for past sins and turning to God with trust in his merciful forgiveness.

The mysterious and just law of the Cross indicates one aspect of the Christotherapeutic change in the pilgrim's visionary landscape. Through this law the Father turns the effects of sin into a means for moral and religious self-transcendence. For the followers of Christ, sickness, suffering, and death need not be the cause of bitterness, hatred, and despair, but rather an opportunity for growth in hope and love. As Dante progresses in his spiritual odyssey, the forest, the animals and other elements of his visionary landscape are no longer menacing and alien; they are all integrated and reconciled in Christ's garden, the *bel giardino* of the heavenly hosts, where man is ultimately enlightened and healed through perfect communion with God. Participation in Christ's victory over sickness, suffering and death transforms their meaning.

14. Enlightenment for Growth: Mind-fasting and Spirit-feasting

The start of the spiritual odyssey in both the medieval allegory and Christotherapy is linked with disquietude. Existential diagnosis must be applied to the suffering and tension involved in the growth process. Through the existential diagnosis of disquietude and guilt, it may be understood that there is a call to go beyond certain learned but inadequate modes of life to more authentic, higher-level modes of existence. Both therapies rely upon suprahuman aid and the continual use of critical intelligence enlightened by that aid.

The prayerful process of mind-fasting corresponds to aspects of the visionary allegory. It aims at cleansing the mind and heart of all unauthentic thinking, desiring, imagining and feeling, as far as this is possible and God grants it. But to mind-fast effectively, it is first necessary to recognize just what unauthentic thinking and desiring are and why they are unauthentic. They are, in respect of Christotherapy, always in some way related to ignorance, darkness and delusion regarding true value and meaning. A first clue to the possible need for mind-fasting may be found in the subject's experience of a disease, accident or disharmony on some level of existence, whether physical, mental, moral, psychological or spiritual. An emotional disorder is often a sign of irrational beliefs in the diseased person; any disharmony in a person is a call to self-transcendence and possibly a symptom of the presence of unauthentic thinking and desiring. The medieval allegory begins with the experience of such a disorder.[26]

The second stage of the prayerful process of mind-fasting is reflective prayer or the prayer for understanding. In Christotherapy, the experience of internally or externally manifested disharmonies has valuable meaning for the subject suffering them. Once the proper meaning of the disease is understood and the existentially ignorant mode of thinking and desiring is corrected, the disharmony or disease vanishes. The prayer for understanding is a dynamic expression of the mind and heart seeking to understand the true meaning of an experience of disharmony. Analogous elements in visionary allegory are the therapeutic dialogues with a deity, a suprahuman figure (Lady Nature, Wisdom, etc.), a master of the spiritual life: i.e., the analysis of the symbolic elements from which the allegorical vision derives, with the aim of comprehending them to secure the reader's intellectual or emotional acceptance or rejection of these spiritual entities (ways of imagining, thinking, desiring embodied in symbols and personifications).

In the third stage of the prayer for understanding, it is necessary that the person who would receive the gift of a revelation of healingful meaning exist in a state of obediental receptivity. The revelation is the gift of understanding the existential meaning of the experienced disharmony that is symptomatic of unauthentic thinking and desiring; it is an existential diagnosis of the disease.

The fourth stage of the prayerful process of mind-fasting is the moment of demonstration, the actual living-out of the insight received on the level of revelation. If the revelation was correct and the mind-fasting properly carried out, the initial pathological disharmony should vanish and a state of harmonious integration should be achieved. Such is also the scope of the medieval visionary allegory, which concludes with the transformation of the visonary seeker after enlightenment through his attainment of true understanding, authentic thinking and desiring. The author of the allegory shares the psychotherapeutic process that he has undergone with his reader; he provides a type of spiritual exercise for the enlightenment and healing of his reader.

Spirit-feasting is an expression that Tyrrell coined to serve as a positive complement to mind-fasting. Through this process the positive gifts of enlightenment are actively received: right-knowing, right-aspiration or right-intention. It is a process of growth on the intellectual, moral, religious and psychological levels, involving participation in various forms of enlightenment. It is a matter of constant self-transcendence in a graced development of higher levels of self-realization and self-fulfillment. It is closely linked with the form of enlightenment called existential discernment and with those forms of enlightenment and prayer which focus on and delight in the positive and are nourished by the true, the good, the worthwhile, the beautiful and the divine. The medieval visionary allegory embodies the analogue of spirit-feasting in its analysis and contemplation of divine attributes, of human virtues, of the cosmic order and beauty of creation; such allegory admires and delights in the true, the good, the beautiful and the divine.

PART IV

Toward a Theology of Story

18

TOWARD A THEOLOGY OF STORY

There are many possible starting points for a theology of story. Jesus tells many stories to explain who God is, who he is, who we are. His many stories are all part of the one story that his life tells and which the evangelists retell. All the stories which Jesus and the evangelists tell derive from the story which Jesus' life tells. Their multiplicity of stories witnesses to the complexity of personal relationships with God, oneself and others, as well as to the unity or simplicity which Jesus has given his life by mastering its complexity. One story is not enough to explain the meaning of the story which Jesus' life tells about himself, ourselves, God and our personal inter-relationships; nevertheless, all these stories are told to contribute to our lived understanding of the Gospel truth, of the Good News of Jesus Christ's life story for us.

The fundamental presupposition of all these stories is that we are essentially storylistening and storytelling beings. We are storylisteners before we become storytellers. We learn who we are through the stories that we hear from our parents; and later, from the stories that others tell us about ourselves, about the world, and about God. We become aware of ourselves and of our interrelationships with others in our storylistening, whether or not we like or dislike what we hear. As storylisteners, we embark on our lifelong quest for our true story. Our storylistening is the precondition for our storytelling, both for the story that our lives will tell and for the many stories that we shall tell about ourselves and our world. We are storylisteners before becoming storytellers because we are affected both by stories lived and stories told by others before we become capable of putting together our own stories. Whatever stories we tell will have to emerge from our conscious, affective, critical reaction to our experience of the stories in which we live and breathe. The stories that we have heard, the stories that we are hearing, evoke a reaction at every level of our being that makes us aware of who we are in relation to the storytellers and their worlds.

We know and experience storytellers and their worlds in their stories. Our storylistening to their storytelling implies our awareness of ourselves as being affected by another, our being simultaneously in touch with both ourselves and another. The self-awareness of storylistening is dependent upon our awareness of another as storytelling; it is an awareness of ourselves as being aware of, in contact with, or affected by another. The who that we are is in some way identified or defined by the multileveled experience of the who that is the storyteller, inasmuch as our storylistening implies our self-presence as an affective presence to another.

Jesus is a storylistener before he becomes a storyteller. He is not a disembodied spectator of a world that is out there; rather, he is a storylistening participant in that storytelling world in which he lives. He is affected at every level of his being by his experience of storytellers. His being affected, negatively or positively, by the storytelling of others is part of what he knows about himself, the world, and God. The way and the degree in which Jesus is affected by what he experiences can vary greatly in his different storylistening situations, but he is never a purely passive or indifferent spectator in his act of storylistening. He is always present with presuppositions and expectations, his interests and his desires, be they implicit or explicit, and what he hears depends partially on these factors. Jesus' self-knowledge, his knowledge of his mission, his knowledge of his Father's will in the historical particularities of his daily experience, his knowledge of others and of the world, all are related to his storylistening and revealed in his storytelling.

Jesus' public storytelling, according to the Gospel accounts, begins rather late in life. After many years of storylistening, of actively sifting out the truth that many stories had to tell him about himself, the world, and God, Jesus is ready to embark upon his mission of public storytelling. Both his parables and the story which his life tells imply the knowledge which he has acquired through his years of storylistening. No less significantly, they imply the affectivity, the partiality, the angularity of vision and imagination through which this knowledge is filtered. Through storylistening, Jesus discovers his way to his true story; through storytelling, he shares it with others.

John's Gospel reflects upon Jesus' storylistening and storytelling from the cosmic perspective of the Storyteller who grounds the ultimate possibilities of all human storylistening and storytelling. Paraphrasing Tillich, the

Storyteller might be described as "the ground of story," the ground of every life story and the source of its courage to seek to become a truly good story. Pirandello, on the other hand, might have described us as incipient stories in search of the Storyteller, who can tell our true stories.

John's theology of the Word of God is an implicit theology of story. The Word expresses God's self-understanding. He speaks it coherently, meaningfully and truthfully within human experience. The experience of faith is one in which God is a speaker with something to tell, something comprehensible, something narratable about himself for us. God expresses himself in his Word or Story. Just as the Storyteller eternally expresses himself in his Word, so too he historically expresses himself in his same Story. The Prologue to John's Gospel might be loosely paraphrased as follows:

Fundamental to every life is story. The Storyteller, the giver of stories, calls forth every life to tell his truly good story. To say that the Storyteller was in the beginning is to say that there was the intention of a truly good story, a universal story embracing all life stories. All lives are created narratable, and there is no life that is created without the intention of its becoming a truly good story. Our life is the search for our true story within the Storyteller's universal story. Truly meaningful life stories shine out across the threat of absurdity, for absurdity has not destroyed them. Each life is created as an incipient story, for the Storyteller loves to tell truly good life stories and from the beginning has given the world its shape through them. But the world has not recognized his intention of telling truly good stories. Even man, the bearer of an incipient story, has rejected its promise. But all those who have responsibly accepted their incipient story and believe in its promise have been enabled to become the truly good life stories of the Storyteller. And this has happened not in the natural course of evolution or through our independent efforts at storytelling, but through the grace and demand of the Giver of life stories. For the meaning of the truly good life story has been defined in the story that a particular life has told, in which there was grace and truth; and we have seen in this life story our ultimate possibilities for the true story towards which every incipient life story moves — the glory of the true life story told and the glory of its Storyteller (Jn. 1:1-5, 9-14).

The pre-existent Word of God is the pre-existent intention of the Storyteller to tell his story. The storytelling and storylistening of Jesus reveals both the Storyteller and his intention for our discovery of the way to our true story. Reality is not absurd; it has a meaning which derives from the Storyteller's intention of telling a truly good story that embraces both our individual life stories and our universal story. The story which Jesus Christ's life has told defines faith's way to the discovery of both our own true story as individuals and the all-embracing story that gives its meaning to all the individual stories. The truth of Jesus' life story applies to every life story insofar as it derives from and reveals the Storyteller's true intention for the telling of every life story. Jesus' radical obedience, availability, openness and responsibility toward God are dimensions of his lifelong storylistening and finding of his true story. Jesus lives in receptivity to the felt presence of the Storyteller. "Not my will, but thine" Jesus prays in struggling to discern within the particularities of daily life the truth that the Storyteller's creative will intends for him to do in unfolding and realizing his true story. Because of Jesus' perfect receptivity, the Storyteller, the Father, is able to tell the story that he intends to tell in the story that Jesus' life tells: "The words I say to you I do not speak as from myself: it is the Father, living in me, who is doing this work" (Jn. 14:10). His story summons us to friendship: "I have called you friends, for all that I have heard from my Father I have made known to you" (Jn. 15:15).

We authentically remember the story of Jesus Christ by listening to the Storyteller as he did. Living in his Spirit, our lives retell his story: ". . . the Holy Spirit, whom the Father will send in my name, will teach you everything and remind you of all I have said to you" (Jn. 14:26). In both the Old and New Testaments, listening, hearing and remembering are connected with doing. Jesus blesses those who hear and do his word (Lk. 11:28). The sheep who hear his voice follow it (Jn. 10:16, 27). The man who hears and does his word builds his house on rock (Mt. 7:24ff.). On the Mount of Transfiguration Jesus' disciples hear the voice of the Storyteller saying to them: "Listen to him" (Mt. 17:5; Mk. 9:7; Lk. 9:35). Doing the will of God requires this fundamental attitude of obedient listening, hearing and remembering with regard to the story that Jesus' life is telling. To hear the apostles is to hear Jesus: "Anyone who listens to you listens to me; anyone who rejects you rejects me, and those who reject me reject the one who sent me" (Lk. 10:16). The Storyteller is truly heard in the life stories that he is telling. For Christian faith, the life story of Jesus Christ is normative for discerning such life stories. He is the human articulation of the pre-existent Word or Story of God for man· the Word as heard, the Story as told, the Will of God as done, in a normative, definitive. incontestably true way for mankind.

1. CHRISTIAN FAITH AND OUR TRUE LIFE STORY

Is there a true life story? Christian faith believes that there is. How is it found? The same faith believes that Jesus Christ is the way that the Storyteller would have us find our true life stories. He is "the way, the truth and the life" (Jn. 14:6). The Storyteller has told the story of Jesus Christ, that all who listen to him might have true life stories. It is in the goodness of Christ's life story that faith grasps what the Giver of all life stories intends for the fulfillment of every life story, what the Storyteller of life stories means by a truly good life story. Christ's life story reminds us that we are responsible for the story that the Storyteller is summoning us to tell; we are responsible for the quality of our listening, hearing, remembering, and doing. "Hear, O Israel: the Lord our God, the Lord is one; and you shall love the Lord your God with all your heart, and with all your soul, and with all your mind, and with all your strength . . . You must love your neighbor as yourself" (Mk. 12:29ff.). Faith lives in the constant remembrance of its obligation to love God, to listen for indications of his will, and to do it. The life story of Jesus Christ concretely defines what Christian faith means by loving God and our neighbor.

John's theology of the pre-existent Word implies that our true story derives from the Storyteller; his theology of the Word made flesh implies that the Storyteller is in his true story. The Spirit is where the Spirit acts. We are in our activity. The storyteller is in his storytelling and is known in it. The Storyteller, God, is a particular agent that can be known only as we know the life stories that he is telling, that he is calling forth in his creative grace and demand.

The Storyteller can be known in some way through every life story; for everyone is called forth by the grace and demand of the Storyteller to find his true story. Even resistance and indifference to this grace and demand disclose much about the Storyteller's intention that every incipient story become a truly good life story. Augustine's affirmation that our hearts are restless until they rest in God suggests the restlessness of the Storyteller in his demand that we get on with the business of discerning and realizing our true possibilities for the good story that he intends our lives to tell.

The Storyteller's restlessness is that of the shepherd and the housewife, portrayed in the fifteenth chapter of Luke's Gospel, who must find what they have lost. Like the father of the lost son, in the same chapter, he rejoices when his incipient stories find their way back to their true story. The restless concern of love for a single sheep, a single coin, for one of two sons, implies the Storyteller's love for every single incipient life story that he summons to find its true story. The love he bears for them is the opposite of indifference. It is bent on telling each story, not one must be lost; no incipient story is forgotten, it can always be retold. If we have lost the thread of our true story, the Storyteller has not. He is restlessly intent upon our recovering it. In fact, the recovery of lost threads for the retelling of our true life stories is the Gospel's Good News.

Because the awareness of self-existence and the awareness of God-existence are coextensive and virtually identical, we attribute restlessness both to ourselves as incipient stories in search of our true life story and to God as the Storyteller intending through his grace and demand that we find it. We experience this restlessness in the dynamics and structure of our consciousness.

188 SEEKING GOD IN STORY

Relying heavily on Lonergan, John Haught argues that the desire to know is the basic human drive and that it includes self-knowledge and self-acceptance; that it fans out and moves in diverse cognitional and intentional channels corresponding to the complexity of the knower, the other, and the world.[1] These various "intentional fields" are the sentient, the interpersonal, the narrative, the aesthetic, and the theoretic. Our religious belief is compatible with critical reason because our desire to know, in all its modalities, intends reality as opposed to illusion. Our stories of God are meant to help us find our true stories; there are real grounds for accepting and recounting them, insofar as they put us in touch with the truth of ourselves, others, the world, and God. Our religious awareness, as expressed in images and stories of God which present his unconditional acceptance of man, aids in satisfying the restlessness of our basic drive toward self-knowledge and self-acceptance: such stories of God encourage us to search for our true stories.

The storytelling and storylistening of faith implies the belief that we are called to truly meaningful lives in a universe that is essentially benign and comprehensible. The narrative quality of faith's experience posits coherence in the universe and a permanent meaning at the heart of things. Our ability to comprehend our experience in the spontaneous world-ordering act of storytelling implies that the world is comprehensible. Our experience of the world yields to the sequence of our narrative consciousness. We participate in distinguishable but interpenetrating levels of meaning, communicating a fullness of cognitive, affective, and imaginational experience drawn from a world that is intelligibly ordered and benignly open to comprehension. Our storytelling—and storylistening—lives intend a coherent universe on the premise that order ultimately prevails over chaos. Our ordering minds grasp the world as already ordered; and the persistent inability to participate in any story is in some cases a sign of psychic disorder or disturbance.

The story of Jesus Christ is that of the human image in which faith can see the life of God himself. Jesus is the man in whom faith sees what God is doing. As John Dunne puts it: "He understands what God is doing and he does what God is doing. By doing humanly what God is doing, he makes God's doings understandable to men and he makes it possible for them to go and do likewise."[2] His story invites us to believe in a Kingdom that is invisible on the basis of the signs of hopefulness in our experience of the visible. John asks how one can love God who is invisible if one does not love one's neighbor who is visible (1 Jn. 4:20): God's transcendent goodness is mediated by the finite.

Our basic faith, symbolized by the life story of Jesus Christ, is a responsible faith which gauges our responsiveness to the invisible God in terms of our responsibility for our own lives and those of our neighbors. Responsible faith not only sees God's image in Jesus Christ's life story of responsiveness to God and responsibility for others, but also goes and does likewise. The truth of the Gospel story demands that we be true to the exigencies of the human spirit and to its authentic possibilities as disclosed in the responsible freedom of Jesus Christ. His life represents Christian faith's interpretation of what it means to be true to the exigencies of the human spirit for the discovery of its true story; it is the key for understanding the meaning of personal authenticity.

The dynamic structure of life according to the Gospel truth involves both the gift which God discloses in the story which Jesus' life tells and our own responsibility for our particular choices. We are responsible for the stories that we attempt to make our own; also, for the human capacities we chose to make central to our actions and for the quality of their development. The Gospel story provides the context in which we can enlarge our world through the acceptance of its creative possibilities. It is faith's context for an ongoing recasting of our life story, with trust in the presence and future of an accepting God (storyteller) empowering us to cope with the multiple eventualities of our life (i.e. to tell our story).

The truth of Jesus Christ's life story is an answer for the questions of Christian faith in search of his true story. He reveals the questioner to himself: What he is looking for, what he is interested in, what he pays attention to, and why he is asking the question in the first place. The reasons and interests and concerns that determine what we are looking for partially determine what we see. We do not necessarily see what we are looking for, nor see only what we are looking for, but looking is the condition that makes seeing possible. As the answer to our quest for true stories, Jesus Christ illuminates the complexity of our dynamically structured questing experience, a whole whose parts involve sensing, inquiring, imagining, understanding, conceiving, reflecting, weighing the evidence, judging, deciding, and acting. In the concrete unity of sensibility and consciousness, knowledge and interest, knowing and desiring, truth and value are intrinsically and mutually conditioning aspects of our subjectivity in its adherence of faith to Jesus Christ as the way to our true life story.

Faith believes that the story which Jesus Christ's life tells is the way to our liberation from those elements in our questioning selves which hinder the finding of our true story: false ways of thinking and feeling about ourselves, others, the world, and God that motivate self-destructive decisions and actions. It believes that his story is the liberating way to our true story, to consciously and prayerfully participating in his storylistening and storytelling relationship with the Storyteller of all true life stories. The many stories which Jesus told, like this entire life story, invite us to put the whole of ourselves into his image of and feeling for ourselves, others, the world, and God, and to make the content of that image his own.[3] We are invited to share the same dynamic orientation that was Jesus' way of imagining and experiencing the world, retelling the truth of his story by re-imagining and re-experiencing it in his way. We are invited to accept his story as the structure or context for our faith's imaging and experiencing the stage of life as we move through the finite, the definite and the detailed in quest of our true story.[4]

Jesus Christ is the way to our true story not only by telling us truths, but also by providing us with meaningful images to educate our affectivity, seize our attention, hold our interest, motivate our decision and action to create new situations as further contexts for seeking and finding our true story for ourselves and others. He is the way to the true story for a genuine self, a genuine center of consciousness that has unified and integrated the whole life of sensibility in its relationship to the real, when no one part of the self has become the whole self, no one aspect of experience has been absolutized into the whole of experience, when no one actually has become the whole of reality.[5] Christ's freedom of the imagination, his openness to the totality of the self and the real, invites faith to follow his way of finding his true story.

A truncated and myopic view of the self and the real tends to define the self in relation to one univocal part of either the self or the real. Such a view impedes our ability to find our true story. Examples of such unfreedom abound. The gnostic or quietist tendency to become fixated or stuck at the point of contemplation, ideas, knowledge, and vision is a loss in our ability to move as free subjects through all the dimensions of the real in search of our true stories. Freedom in the balance and integration of the searching self is compromised by the gnostic hypothesis that the finding of our true story is in no way through involvement in the world, but rather through a special knowledge granted only to a few elect. Human development is stunted by the belief that knowledge as such, through itself alone, redeems us. Rationalists and idealists tend to fasten on the eternal truths that we must grasp in the story which Christ's life tells; they tend to overlook his feelings of compassion for the world, the power of his affectivity for transforming hopelessness into hope, unbelief into trust, indifference into caring. Romanticists, on the other hand, have the tendency to stress emotion, intuition and feeling at the expense of reason and the truth content of Christ's teaching; they tend to overlook that Jesus' teaching is quite distinct from the wild enthusiasm of hellenistic cults because it is never divorced from his constant seeking to know and do the truth of his Father's will. Individualists underplay the importance of their need for others in discovering their true story. Faith invites them to follow Christ's way of finding their true stories within the context of a covenant community. Activism, fundamentalism, legalism and other myopic views of the self and the real also tend to compromise our authentic following of Christ's way to the discovery of our true story.

Because we cannot do what we can in no way imagine, we need ways of imagining our true story in order to do what is necessary for finding it.[6] The story that Jesus Christ's life, death and resurrection tells provides believers with the way of imagining both their true stories and what they must do to find them. The story is filled with images that call us to a daily dying and rising in self-sacrificing love's lifelong orientation to its true story in the resurrection. Jesus has imagined a rich variety of paradigms for our understanding both of belief and disbelief, what must be done and what must be avoided in the search for our true stories. The whole of Jesus is in his images, both in those of his parables and in those of his entire life as the Parable of the Storyteller; his total personal resources go into making his images of the world and of our possibilities for truthful lives within it.

The story of God that emerges from the storylistening and storytelling of Jesus Christ tells how he imagined God and the world with the total resources of his human faculties, not only his seeing and hearing and touching, but also his history, his education, his feelings, his aspirations, his love and faith, insofar as they all went into the making of his images of God and the world.[9] His simplest images, therefore, are complicated; they are filled with the content that he has given them. Nothing comes nearer to defining us than our images of God and the world; they are not pure and simple, untouched by thought or desire or affectivity or context or faith. Our basic images are filled with our imagining, thinking, and feeling. We give an enormous content to the image of one we love. The basic images of Jesus' storylistening (with respect to the Storyteller) and storytelling (with respect to ourselves) enable Christian faith to affirm that God is love and loves us; the Storyteller's love is calling us forth to the goodness that Jesus Christ has found in his true story. The content of Jesus' basic images discloses to us discerning faith and love and the way to find the true story the Unbounded Love-Wisdom would have us tell.

The story which Jesus' life tells of God, man, the world, love, truth, evil, death and of everything else that is profoundly important for us, unifies the manifold of his experiences and his images and is mediated by them. His lifelong orientation towards his death and resurrection unfolds in the context of his maturing sensibility and in the content of his basic images. He knows himself and his world together, in his images. We know ourselves and whatever we know (God, persons, and so on) in relationship, be this relationship positive or negative, be it desire or interest, need or enjoyment, or any of their opposites. Our self-awareness is in relationship to the object of our knowing; it is awareness of this relationship in the concreteness of our images, symbols, and stories. The self and the real exist in relationship and can only be known in relationship. The conscious experience of the interrelationship is grounded in images (symbols and stories) and feelings about them. We are aware of ourselves being affected by the other; hence our self-awareness is an affective awareness of the other (God, persons, world, and so on). The story which Jesus' life tells discloses in many images, symbols and parables how he is being affected by the other (God, persons, events, the world). His lifelong orientation to the resurrection in dedication to God and existence for others is an affective orientation and presence to others. Jesus is affectively attuned to others in a concrete world where God is making his presence felt; he affectively responds to this felt presence in the detail of events and situations as it calls him forth to the consummation of his true story. He develops a feeling for his true story, a feeling which grows as he is able to imagine more sharply and concretely the truth of his story and the way it is to be told.

If the ultimate meaning of a process or movement or life story is seen in its outcome, then the unique outcome of Jesus Christ's life story tells Christian faith that he is a unique person. Resurrection experiences were not the usual outcome of a pious Jew's life story. The resurrection event expresses the ultimate truth of the entire life story of Jesus Christ and distinguishes it from every life story. If the beatitudes had seemed an outrageous formula for finding true happiness, now they would have to be taken seriously. In the light of the resurrection, faith would take seriously the entire life story of Jesus Christ, in all its historical particularities, its claims, its teachings, its concerns and deeds, its way of the cross.

The story which Jesus Christ's life-death-resurrection tell to faith empowers us with a new way of imagining ourselves, others, the world and God; therefore, it enables a new way of life or story, for we cannot do what we can in no way imagine. Jesus Christ transforms the consciousness and imagination of believers with a life story that overcomes the impotency of the human spirit for imagining and doing what the creative spirit of life-giving Love — the Storyteller that is his Father — empowers and demands for the resurrection of the just. His life story enables faith to imagine the way to our true story as one of dying and rising for others in the life-giving Spirit of his Love; therefore, it enables faith to experience and follow the way of that Love which survives death itself. Death is not the end of our life stories; it is only a part or movement within them. Pentecost celebrates the life-giving Spirit of Love which is and has the last word in the story which the life of Jesus Christ tells to faith. The life-giving Spirit of Love, the Spirit of the Storyteller, is both the first word and the last word, the alpha and the omega, the origin and outcome of his life story.

Life-giving Love, the Storyteller's creative Spirit — *Creator Spiritus* — inaugurates all life stories, summoning them forth from the primeval void depicted in the creation story of Genesis. It is the promise of our stories of which Ezekiel spoke: "I will put my spirit in you, and you shall live" (37:14). Our Storyteller is imagined as breathing his own life into our stories as individuals and as a people. His live-giving Spirit or breath, according to the image of Ezekiel, summons us to come forth from our graves. Just as God had once breathed into dust and made a living soul, he would breathe again his life-giving spirit into a people who had forfeited their life, and make them live again. The Storyteller is the Giver of life stories, not death stories. The Cross is the symbol of his life-giving love and the resurrection expresses its power to survive death. The Storyteller's life-giving Spirit of Love is recognized and experienced as having constituted or created Jesus Christ's entire life story for the community of faith which celebrates it as its own.

The Storyteller graces us with Jesus Christ's life-giving Spirit of Love, empowering us to step outside ourselves as he did in living according to the exodus-principle (departure) that created the way to his true story. Christian faith is summoned to a continual exodus of stepping outside itself in living for others. By voluntarily laying down his life for others, Jesus freely communicates the life that he has freely received. Our true story is ultimately a gift. All our own efforts to step outside ourselves can never suffice. He who only wants to give and is not ready to receive, he who only wants to exist for others and is unwilling to recognize that he for his part enjoys his life as the gratuitous gift of the Storyteller Creator, fails to grasp that we can only give what we have received from others and in the last analysis from the Other, the Storyteller Creator of every life story.

The story of the Church is that of the community of persons helping one another to find their true stories in the same way that Jesus Christ found his own. It communicates the Good News of the resurrection that the just are even now rising in the same life-giving Spirit of Love through which the Storyteller created Jesus Christ's life story for us. It proclaims that the Kingdom is coming wherever truly good life stories are being told by the life-giving Spirit of Love, expressing the Storyteller's will to be done in every life story.

The Storyteller Creator summons us to our true story through his *Creator Spiritus,* the Spirit of his life-giving love which created Jesus Christ's true story of life-giving love for us. Jesus Christ finds his true life story through the power of the *Creator Spiritus,* the power of both the Storyteller's love for him and of his love for the Storyteller. Faith is summoned to its true story by sharing in the filial receiving and fraternal giving that is Jesus Christ's story of life-giving love. We are summoned to recognize the Giver of life stories as our Father, the same Father who authored the life story of Jesus Christ. We are summoned to accept the gift of his *Creator Spiritus,* the same Spirit of life-giving love that impelled Jesus Christ to the gratuitous receiving and giving that culminated in the resurrection.

John's Gospel implies that the meaning of Jesus is grasped by faith only at the completion of his life story. Christian faith is born with the consummation and fulfillment of his story: "It is accomplished, and bowing his head he gave up his spirit" (Jn. 19:30). The death and resurrection of Jesus constitute the consummation and fulfillment of his life story, the revelation of his personal identity and the communicability of its true meaning through the gift of his Spirit and the Spirit's transformation of human awareness, affectivity, decision, and action. The Cross symbolizes the Christian community's liberating experience of the reciprocal love of God and man, of the Father and Son for one another and for ourselves. The meaning of Jesus of Nazareth — like that of every incipient story — emerges gradually; it is ascertained by Christian faith from the end, when all the evidence of that life story is in. A life story (not for dictionary) defines the meaning of a particular person, a meaning that is determined by what that person ultimately becomes.

Jesus of Nazareth is interpreted as Jesus the Christ on the basis of the personal transformation which his death and resurrection effected among his disciples. Their new interpretation discloses their personal transformation; for the interpretation interprets the interpreter. Christian faith is born in the experience of God's love and freedom for us in the life story of Jesus Christ, summoning our freedom and love to accept the gift of that life which culminates in the resurrection. The Christian community interprets itself on the basis of its experience of God's love for it in the life, death, and resurrection of Jesus Christ.

The life story of Jesus Christ is a lived interpretation of our basic self-others-world-God relationship. It disclosed Jesus' lived understanding of himself, others, the world, God, goodness, evil, freedom, unfreedom, life and death. The Christian community of faith lives through the gift of that love through which Jesus interpreted his fundamental self-others-God-relationship. The life story interprets its knowing and feeling and acting subject; it discloses this person's or this community's image and lived understanding of its fundamental relationships. The Christian community's experience of God's love is symbolized by the death and resurrection of Jesus Christ. It implies that the finding of our true story, or becoming our true self, is the achievement of divine love and freedom with the cooperation of human love and freedom, in the reciprocity of self-giving. This experience grounds the belief in the love and freedom which survives death, in the future resurrection of the just which has begun even now with the transformation of our lives through the power of God's love in Christ and ourselves.

2. RESPONSIBLE FREEDOM

The responsible freedom with which Jesus Christ lived out his life story orients his followers in their search for their own true stories. It implicitly indicts the belief that we are most free when in a spirit of Rousseauistic naturalism we let ourselves go in any direction toward which whim or uncontrolled instinct moves us. This is not freedom in an ethical sense, but sheer irresponsibility. Freedom is more than the capacity to do what we please; it is the capacity to do what is called for. If the finding of our true story is a question of responsible freedom in the interaction of God, self, and neighbor, we must be willing to discover and relinquish whatever compromises such freedom in our lives.

Jesus Christ structures our God-self-neighbor relationship of responsible freedom. His life story is what we mean by our responsibility before God for the quality of our life story and the life stories of our neighbors. From the perspective of his resurrection, we grasp the ultimate meaning of his life of responsible freedom as that which his gracious Father intends for our own. Responsible freedom towards God means being free to receive our true story from him in the way that Jesus was free to receive his; responsible freedom towards others means being free to share the true goodness of what we have received with others in the way that Jesus was free to share his true goodness. The God who entrusts us with the gift of life also empowers us to live it truthfully and care for others.

In certain critical circumstances of our lives, we especially experience our responsible freedom; almost despite ourselves, we then experience the demand that our life story be told truthfully and feel constrained to make decisions that we can no longer postpone, as though our life story were being forced out of us. We would prefer to absolutize some agreeable part of our story and to remain in permanent possession of it without ever really having to come to terms with the unknown risks and complexities that challenge our courage. We tend to inertia, and want to stop our life stories from being told any further once we have come to that part which we especially like. Perhaps Jesus' warning about trying to save one's life might be paraphrased in this context to the effect that we must not abandon the promise of our personal development in responsible freedom through interaction with God, self, and neighbor. Our life stories are not absolutely our own. The self is a gift, an incipient story that is summoned in grace and demand to exercise its responsible freedom in seeking and finding its true life story. The creative tension that we experience in the exercise of responsible freedom, having to make choices within the complexity of the human condition, is evidence of our being summoned to tell a truthful life story.

The courage to live out our life stories in responsible freedom is, in the Christian context, grounded in the God-self-neighbor images that we receive in the story that Jesus Christ's life tells us. His absolute trust in God, who had entrusted him with his life story and purpose (destiny or mission), empowers his followers to trust in God, in themselves, and in others.

Christian maturation is largely a question of learning to rely on the trustworthiness of God as the basis for our courage to meet the new challenging situations of life. Without such trust and courage, we despair of searching and of finding the story most appropriate to our true possibilities. The unfinished part of our selves, the part of our story which remains to be told, requires a basic trust in our God-self-neighbor relationships. Trust gives us the freedom to accept the summons to our true story, to the fulfillment of our God-given possibilities; it empowers our lives to tell the story that lies within their God-given response-ability, promise, and destiny. The failure to trust implies the loss of our true story.

Trust enables us to accept the challenge and responsibility of life; it is intimately linked with our drive to go out beyond ourselves, to develop our potentialities in becoming the selves that we are called by God to become. Through trust or hope we project our dreams and aspirations into a future which we believe to be given by God for both the fulfillment of our particular life stories and his universal, encompassing, story. Through our trust or hope we believe that, despite the worst evils in this ambiguous world, the loving creator God revealed in the life story of Jesus Christ is always before us, waiting to open a new possibility for our acceptance in responsible freedom. We have been given the awesome responsibility of sharing with God in the shaping of life stories, our own and others'. Although God opens the way, we are left free to decide whether we shall go the way of our true possibilities, and bring them to realization. Authentically Christian life stories develop with the confidence that God is with us, always opening a way in which we can responsibly follow.[7]

The Christian paradigm of trust or hope is the life story of a man whose message was rejected, whose gracious service was spurned, who was condemned as a criminal and subjected to a cruel death. Out of these grim happenings the Christian community experienced that God had indeed opened a new way for the development of our life stories in responsible freedom. Crucifixion and resurrection led to a new consciousness of God's absolute trustworthiness and creative power. Death itself could not put an end to the life that had fully entrusted itself to Him; nor could death set limits to his creative power in the achievement of the Risen Lord and his gift of the Holy Spirit, giving birth to the Christian community of faith.

A life story is its own interpretation, inasmuch as it gives expression to the understanding that a person has of himself, his situation, his role, the human condition.[8] A life story is a personal world mediated by meaning and motivated by value. It is the human spirit that constructs the meanings and responds to the motivating values in thought and word and feeling. The endless variety exhibited in life stories has its ground in the endless variety of ways in which persons understand themselves, their situation, and the human condition. Christian life stories are alike to the extent that they apprehend ultimate meaning and are motivated by ultimate value in their experience of the story which Jesus Christ's life tells of God and man and the world. They are alike to the extent that they entrust themselves to the trustworthiness of God with the responsible freedom with which Jesus Christ entrusted himself.

On the one hand, a Christian life story is one that has been inspired to trust in God as Jesus did; on the other hand, it is one that is always learning how to trust through the encouragement of others who are also learning through the gift of the Spirit and the message of the Christian community. We learn how to trust through trustworthy persons. The Christian community learns how to trust through its experience of the trustworthiness of Jesus Christ and his Spirit. It lives by its discernment between the trust-worthiness of a good conscience and the untrustworthiness of an unhappy conscience. It devotes its efforts to overcoming untrustworthiness (unauthenticity) and promoting trustworthiness (authenticity) in our basic human relationships.[9] It seeks to overcome untruthfulness and to promote truthfulness in our God-self-neighbor relationships. The truthfulness of Jesus Christ's life story is its truthworthiness, summoning us to follow him responsibly and freely, in making the truth and trustworthiness of God the center of our lives. His story communicates the grace and demand of freedom for the true story that every life is summoned to tell, a freedom that we do not normally and naturally possess, given our inclinations to be self-centered, self-concerned, self-important, self-indulgent, self-righteous, and self-willed.

The life story of Jesus Christ reveals a God who commits himself to our life stories and takes responsibility not only for initiating them but also for enabling their fulfillment. The incarnation and Passion express the extent to which God is coming out of himself in creative love, and actively sharing in our life stories: the cross symbolizes his liberating commitment to the true goodness of our life stories. God is personally and humanly involved in capacitating our responsible freedom for the story that his creative love intends each life to tell in its own and his own distinctive way.

Jesus' way of life discloses what he thought about freedom. The truth of his life story defines the specifically Christian way to freedom: "You will know the truth, and the truth will make you free" (Jn. 8:32). His story gives depth and definite content to our Christian understanding of freedom. He is not free from poverty, hardship, suffering, and those social and political forces which eventually send him to his death; but the New Testament does tell us that he was free from sin, from whatever separates us from our creative source in God, summoning us to our true life story. His freedom for death expressed his availability to God and enabled the community of faith to see the life-giving freedom of God himself, creating new possibilities for a qualitatively different way of life.

The Christian community of faith is an historical reality committed to the pursuit of Jesus Christ's way of responsible freedom in its God-self-neighbor relationships. Its authenticity is the resultant not only of the authenticity of its members but also of the heritage transmitted down through the centuries. In an ideal world, every member of the Christian community in all his words and deeds would be living with the authenticity generated by meeting the demands of intelligence, reasonableness, and responsibility. Inasmuch as this is not our world, authenticity cannot be taken for granted. Even if an individual Christian manages to be authentic in his following of Jesus Christ, one cannot exclude the possibility that elements of unauthenticity entered into the tradition of his particular religious communion.[10] Christians, therefore, both as a community and as individuals must live by discernment, questioning, and scrutinizing in their efforts to lead truthful lives and give a trustworthy witness to the God they confess in Jesus Christ. The righteousness that is the gift of God, as opposed to self-righteousness, motivates the Christian effort to overcome unauthenticity and to promote authenticity. The finding of our true story, in this context, is a lifelong enterprise. Even the gospel symbolizes existence as a field of pulls and counterpulls.[11] John's Gospel tells of a drawing that is a listening and a hearing: "Everyone who has listened to the Father and learned from him, comes to me" (6:45). The Father draws us: "No man can come to me unless he is drawn by the Father who sent me" (6:44). Jesus' power to draw men to himself is conditioned by the prior drawing of the Father: "And I shall draw all men to myself, when I am lifted up" (12:32). There are elements of light and darkness, of pull and counterpull, of the need of free choice to support the pull to our true story and to resist the counterpull to waywardness. Through the suffering and death of Jesus Christ, Christians have experienced God's pull to conversion, repentance, and authentic God-self-neighbor relationships. It is a pull that draws us away from the myriad attractions that distract the human spirit from the summons to its true story.

The individual person is not merely designated by his proper name. That name has a story to it. A person's name is a symbol for the world that lives in him, shapes him, and emerges in the dynamic structure of the free actions which tell his life story. Human decisions and actions have the dramatic quality of telling a story, even though the shape we give ourselves in the story that we are acting out is not entirely of our own making. The grammar of the individual person is not that of an indefinite noun or concept, but rather of a proper name with a particular story. A person is not a universal. To know who somebody is, it is not sufficient to say what he is; rather, we must know his story. In this respect, Stanley Hauerwas observes, a story can and does function like a proper name and vice versa:

For like the self, God is a particular agent that can be known only as we know his story. Too often it has been assumed that we can talk of God as if he is a universal — namely that the grammar of God is like the grammar of tree, towns . . . But the grammar of God is not that of an indefinite noun, but rather of a proper name.[12]

Agents are known through their stories. Inasmuch as every person is called into existence and summoned to his true story by the grace and demand of God, every life story obliquely tells us something about God. In the perspective of the resurrection, the Christian community of faith learns to speak of the Mystery which defines its existence and grounds its God-self-neighbor relationships in terms of Jesus Christ's life story. The liturgical prayer of the Christian community bears witness to what God has done in Jesus Christ, the correlative personal reality of God himself. From the earliest times the Church has prayed to the Father and to the Mediator of salvation, Jesus Christ. Insofar as prayer is the individual's acceptance of God's will to love and save him, it is also of grace; but to this extent it is always "in Christ and the Church" (Eph. 3:21), and therefore always bears an ecclesial character,[13] with the implication that we do not find our true life stories alone.

The dramatic action of the story which Christ's life told, and continues to tell, through the gift of his spirit in the Church is the story of God's love for us. The life story of Jesus Christ communicates the Good News of God's life-giving love for us. It specifies the Christian understanding of how God acts in his relations with mankind. Especially important, therefore, is prayerful reflection on the life and teachings of Jesus and on the action of the Holy Spirit in him, in his saints, and in the historical development of the community of faith. Through the gift of his Holy Spirit, the Christian community learns the prayer which characterized his perfect responsiveness to his Father. The dramatic action of the story which Christ's life told and continues to tell in his community of faith reveals the fullness of our God-given capacities for filial reciprocity with God (hallowing his name), for hoping in him (thy kingdom come), for realizing his love and his justice here and now in our private and public lives (thy will be done on earth), for communicating his true meaning (as it is in heaven), for sharing in his sustaining goodness (daily bread), for forgiving and being forgiven, and for coping with evil (lead us not into temptation).[14]

Freedom of mind and heart from bondage to anything that is not inspired by the Holy Spirit of Jesus Christ is sought in the prayer of the Christian community. To seek such freedom is to seek our true life story. Through the Holy Spirit given to us, we have the graced conviction of the Father's love revealed in his Son's crucifixion, death, and resurrection. Through the same Holy Spirit, we have the heartfelt realization that nothing can separate us from the love of God that summons us in Jesus Christ to the discovery of our true story. The Father's love that summoned Jesus Christ to the consummation of his life story empowers us with the heartfelt assurance of his present and future faithfulness; it frees us to make an integral assent to his saving work in Jesus Christ and to respond to his call for commitment by faith and love to the person of Jesus, to his message, and to the community of faith that proceeds from him. This healing and integrating commitment yields an enlightenment as we search for our true life story.[15] The enlightenment is mediated by God's love flooding our hearts through the gift of his Holy Spirit; it grounds our orientation towards God, ourselves, others, and the world in conversion from those forces that seek to frustrate God's saving summons to our true story. Our commitment to God in Jesus Christ is a commitment to finding our true life story through our commitment to others and the world with the same love that was and is in Jesus himself; consequently, it involves our prayerful discernment of our authentic gifts for serving others, allowing God to shape our lives in accordance with the service-value of particular gifts with which he has endowed us.[16] We must be affectively free to respond to what we have discerned to be the particular form of service to which we are being called by the promptings of divine grace. We are capable of self-deception, of rationalizations to avoid the demands of divine grace.[17]

The certitude of Christian hope is a sure tendency towards our true story.[18] It involves the tension of an anticipated initial possession of our true story and a confident waiting for the gift of its final realization. The present moment of our life story is experienced with confidence in God's unwaivering intention of drawing it to its ultimate fulfillment. Hope expresses our conviction that God is infinitely good and loving, the source of all values and the guarantor that all things will ultimately work together for his saving purpose. Hope is our response to the interior, striving, creative, guiding presence and power of God at the heart of our temporal reality, bringing all to good; it is equally our response to God as the absolute, eternal and the unfathomable ground of all reality, including time itself. God is the transcendent ground of hope. The lifelong response of Jesus to the transcendent reality of God defines the meaning of Christian hope. When his earthly life had been completed one could confidently speak of his life as a whole (and therefore of his person as such) as the revelation of God and ground of human hope. Jesus had freely acted, Christians would affirm, in response to God's call to him; his entire life story revealed God's claims to human hope in a way that depended on Jesus' full, imaginative and committed response.

3. PRAYER IN OUR SEARCH FOR OUR TRUE LIFE STORY

Prayer is one form that our Christian hope takes in our search for our true story.[19] Prayer is one dimension of our full response to the love of God which we now experience and whose fullness we seek in the consummation of our life story at the future resurrection of the dead, begun even now through our transformation by the gift of Christ's Holy Spirit. The prayer of Jesus and his community of faith is not confined to specific occasions of ritual or overt activity; rather, it expresses an orientation of life in the presence of God. Prayer expresses an awareness of God's reality which discloses itself in various ways throughout one's life story, so that one can accept every moment as a sacrament of value. Our various forms of prayer express our attitudes towards the reality of God: our attitudes derive from primary affective responses to the grace and demand of God which we experience in the historical particularities of our life story. Prayer is a particular way of being related to God in our search for fulfillment and renewal of life.[20] Prayer is a way of seeking to live in accordance with God's healing and enlightening will for our life story. If prayer expresses our need for help, it should also express our awareness that the help we receive may be other than what we had in mind; for God wills only what contributes to the discovery and realization of our true life story of filial communion with Himself and fraternal communion with others. Jesus Christ's prayer for community adumbrates the eschatological hope, "that all might be one, as thou Father in me and I in thee, that they all be one in us, that the world may believe that thou hast sent me." The prayer of Jesus expresses the Christian hope for a community that is one both by God's grace and by a consequent union of minds and hearts. Prayer is evidence of our communion with God in the Spirit of Jesus Christ: "God has sent into our hearts the Spirit of his Son who cries, Abba, Father" (Gal. 4:6).

The New Testament depicts the story of the Church as beginning in the communion of prayer. The Gospel of Luke ends in the temple where the apostles were "continually . . . praising God" (24:53; Acts 5:12). Community prayer prepares for Pentecost: "All, with one heart, were assiduous in prayer" (Acts 1:14). It also prepares all the great moments of the Church's life throughout the Acts of the Apostles, suggesting that communications is at the heart of what the Church is all about. The life of the Triune God, the basic reality on which the Church is founded, is a mystery of interpersonal communication in which mankind participates through Jesus Christ, the communicative self-expression of God the Father. Jesus Christ, the eternal Word, expresses God the communicator throughout his whole life story, and especially by the climactic events of his death and resurrection. He is the Christian paradigm of the freedom to pray, to direct our thoughts, affections, and acts to God, to cooperation with the action of God for the redemption of the world. The intercessory prayer of Jesus reveals that salvation is a question of both God's loving care for mankind and of our loving care for one another in the power of his Holy Spirit. His prayer, his conscious communion with his Father, is one of the ways in which the world is redeemed; it expresses his cooperation with the action of his Father for the world.

The Church is a communion which exists to bring all persons into communion with God and thereby to open them to communication with each other. Avery Dulles affirms that we may say that the Church is communications, if communications is seen as the procedure by which communion is achieved and maintained.[21] The Church is a vast communications network designed to draw persons out of their isolation and estrangement and to bring them individually and corporately into communion with God in Christ. Inasmuch as the entire life of the Church is a communications process, every major decision about the Church is implicitly a decision about communications.[22]

The Christian community derives from the experience of God's love in Jesus Christ. In loving as Jesus Christ loved, we have communion with God and with one another, living that divine and eternal reality which survives death itself (1 Cor. 13:8-13). The God that is revealed in Jesus Christ is experienced as a communicator who gives himself in love (cf. Rom. 8:32). The communion of the Father and the Son in the Spirit is at the heart of the Christian experience of love as communion, community, or communications. Through the experience of having been loved and cared for by God in Christ, the Christian community comes into existence, learning to accept and give this same love: "By this all will know you as my disciples: by this love which you will have for one another" (Jn. 13:35).

An authentically Christian life story is one of learning to accept and to give the love which Jesus Christ accepted and gave in such a rich variety of ways. We have an experience of this love before we come to analyze it and ask questions about it. The impact of this love guides the unfolding of our basic experience of the world and of ourselves; it motivates the prayer which characterizes Christian life in its basic affective response to the reality of God apprehended in such experience; it has lifelong implications as a call to a dreaded holiness in the authentic consummation of our life story. [23]

The experience of God's love inaugurates the situation of being in love that is an orientation to our true fulfillment. Prayer expresses our full response to the undeserved gift of God's love which we experience as sustaining us. Thanksgiving is the response of love for the goodness that God created for us and for whatever promises he holds out to us. The prayer of thanksgiving implies a conscious fellowship with the transcendent Giver of our life story, a grateful awareness of the Giver in his gifts, and particularly in the gift of our life story. Gratitude affirms the goodness of the Giver and the gift, of God, of his world, of our selves and other selves, of the universal story that is being told in the giving and accepting of gifts. Prayers of thanksgiving are the response of love to Love, the graced awareness that the love of God affirms us in every gift and that He is his own best gift. The worship of the Christian community is characterized by the prayer of thanksgiving for the gift of God's love, illuminated by the word of the gospel that announces that God has loved us first and has revealed that love in Christ crucified, dead, and risen.

The theology of story, like every Christian theology, is ultimately a reflection on the mystery of the divine love in its engagement with the world as revealed in Jesus Christ. It derives from the experience of a loving faith that matures within the context of the Christian community's commitment to the Father of Jesus Christ. The theology of story must meditate on the form of the divine love in the life-death-resurrection of Jesus Christ.[24] The Christian community interprets its experience of the divine love in terms of the Father who sends his Son to suffer and die that all that believe in him might have life through the gift of his love, the Holy Spirit, flooding our hearts. Love is the final test of faith's genuineness, the essential characteristic of the divine life (1 Jn. 4:8, 16), from which all fellowship with God in Christ is derivative. Although divine Love transcends its manifestations, it is only through them that it can be apprehended. Christians affirm that God is love on the basis of Jesus Christ's life story and every life story bearing witness to its basic truth and goodness.[25]

The Church understands the past out of the present in which it stands.[26] Its interpretation of its own experience grounds its interpretation of Jesus Christ's life story. *Kerygma, koinonia, diakonia,* and *eucharistia* express the Church's communal experience of the love of God, respectively, in listening to Christ as the Word of God, in relating to him as the center of all personal community, in serving him as Lord in deeds of service, and in celebrating his goodness in the joyful awareness of his risen presence.[27] The Church's present experience of the love of God provides the foundation for its interpretation of Jesus Christ's life story and person; in the light of its present experience of God's love, it continues to proclaim that Jesus Christ has risen from the dead and is communicating his Father's love to us through the gift of his Holy Spirit, uniting our life stories with his own in purpose and intention, and drawing them to their consummation in the resurrection of the just.[28]

Prayer expresses our responsibility for our life stories in the presence of God, a responsibility that cares for one's self and for one's neighbor. Intercessory prayer implies our conviction that the Giver of life stories cares for them, a belief whose foundation is our present experience of God's compassionate love enabling us to welcome the true meaning of Jesus Christ's life story, death, and resurrection. Prayer, the dialogue in our ongoing life story of our relationship with the Other, expresses our reciprocity with the divine Love that is creating our true life story and self. Love of God creates and sustains and unites life stories, summoning them to their ultimate fulfillment and goodness.

19

"SEEING GOD" IN HIS STORY

The story of Jesus Christ, communicated in our experience of his Church, is heard at different times. *Luke-Acts* underscores the historical relationship of the Age of Jesus and the Age of the Church in terms of the Holy Spirit which accounts for the birth of both. The Holy Spirit inaugurates the story which Jesus' life tells and empowers the Church to tell the same story from age to age.

Our Christian faith is rooted in historical life stories, both with regard to its origins in Jesus of Nazareth and with regard to its verification of the truth of its origins in our experience of the community of faith. The transcendence of God is mediated by and revealed in the life story of Jesus of Nazareth and his Church. Christian faith remembers Jesus as doing the truth in the particularities of the past; it follows him by doing the truth in the particularities of the present. The same truth which Jesus' life tells is retold by the faith of the community which remembers him and which shares the truth that he is by doing it with him in the present. The Christ story is the collective remembrance, group consciousness and common hope of the Christian people. It is the corporate autobiography of this people, told and retold, passed on from generation to generation, anchoring a whole way of seeing and of experiencing the world.

The historical dimension of the Christian faith is illuminated by the diverse levels of the story at its origins: (1) The lived story of Jesus of Nazareth, "the pioneer and perfecter of our faith" (Heb. 12:2), revealing God in the contingencies of a concrete history. (2) The lived story becomes the oral story when the Apostles preach the original kerygma after

Pentecost, interpreting the historical words and deeds according to the needs of their hearers. The primary way of sharing such an experience of the sacred is to tell the story, to draw others into the experience of its true meaning and value and, thereby, to unleash its power in their lives. (3) The story that has been lived and told becomes the written story of Matthew, Mark, Luke and John. The Gospels do not give us the words and deeds of Jesus in any strictly chronological sequence, nor even in the form in which they are preached in the second stage, but only in the form compiled and edited by the evangelists. They give us the truth which Jesus is and does, the truth that his life tells, as normative for the life of the Christian community in its fundamental orientation to the resurrection.

The authenticity of Christian life is judged in terms of a true understanding and doing of the truth that is told by the historically lived, spoken and written story of Jesus; consequently, the Christian community must guard against the possible devaluation, distortion, or corruption of its story which may occur when the words are repeated but the meaning is missed. Every generation must authentically appropriate the true meaning of the story and live accordingly: "If you know these things, blessed are you if you do them" (Jn. 13:17). The truth which Jesus knew and lived is saving only on condition that it is truly known and lived in a basic fidelity to the historical real of both the past and of the present.

In the tradition of the historical struggle between the true and the false prophets of Israel, Jesus clashed with the religious authorities with regard to the true meaning of Israel's religious heritage and its demands for doing God's truth in his own lifetime. Jesus criticized unauthentic interpretations of this heritage because such interpretations generated unauthentic lives. He summoned his contemporaries to conversion, to a personal authenticity in keeping with a true understanding of Israel's religious heritage and purpose. Authenticity of life, at both the individual and communal levels, evidenced fidelity to this heritage. Traditionally, the quality of Israel's life at every level had been interpreted as the index of its seeing God. Doing the truth with God verified the claim of seeing the one, true God: "Whenever the Israelites saw God they became virtuous. They saw him at the Red Sea and became virtuous. They saw him at Sinai and became honest . . . . They saw him in the tabernacle and became just."[1] Authentic lives evidence authentic vision. The excellence of man reflects the excellence of God. A truly good life bespeaks an authentic relationship with the living God, the source of all life.

Jesus condemned a religious formalism which distorted the meaning of Israel's religious heritage and purpose. He protested that the Sabbath was made for man and not man for the Sabbath. He did not reject Sabbath observance in its true perspective of fostering our basic self-other-world-God relationship; rather, he insted that the Sabbath was never intended to be an excuse for evading the doing of good for others in need. The beatitude of the pure of heart, who see God, is witnessed by the authenticity of their lives. It implies the authenticity of their self-image, other-image, world-image, and God-image; it implies the soundness of their corresponding feelings and actions.

Jesus' parables interpret his basic self-other-world-God relationship. The storyteller is in his stories; the interpretation interprets the interpreter. His parables communicate his orientation to doing the truth of God, to seeing God, in the particularities of the present. They are intended for our sharing his way of doing God's truth, for our participation in the orientation and outcome of his story, symbolized by the resurrection. The parables summon us to the resurrectional life of the Christian community through which the transcendent power of God intends the transformation of the world. The parables imply the tension of such a transformation in closing the gap between the weakness of man and the power of God. The Cross symbolizes the same tension of human finitude, limitation, and weakness which must be grasped, loved, and transformed by the powerful compassion of God.

The Christian faith does not see God in an abstract gnosis, in the way the gnostics claimed to have seen him in ecstatic visions. Rather, the distinctively Christian way of seeing God takes the form of the way of the cross, the experience of being grasped and sustained by the love of God in the daily struggle to respond to its demands. Our seeing God is not so much in our knowing but in our being known by God (Gal. 4:9). Our being grasped and sustained by the power of his love frees us to engage in the way of the cross, its difficulties, its risks, its challenges, its struggles: "He is not weak in dealing with you, but powerful in you. For he was crucified in weakness; but lives by the power of God. For we are weak in him, but in dealing with you we shall live with him by the power of God" (2 Cor. 13:3f.). The experience of being known by the power of God's love grounds the happiness of those who "hunger and thirst for what is right" (Mt. 5:5) in the particularities of their daily lives. The beatitudes which Jesus preaches express the spirit of his seeing God in his way of the cross.[2] The happiness of the resurrection in which his life culminates cannot be grasped apart from the cost of his love for others. At all times, from the Age of Jesus to the Age of the Church, the way to our true story in the power of God's love — our authentic self-other-world-God relationship — involves the kind of suffering and maturation that is symbolized by the Cross. The same Mystery defines the unfolding of every life story. Christian faith believes that the story of Jesus Christ and his Church discloses our true relationship to this Mystery as one which is grounded in its creative, sustaining and promising love for us.

Our seeing God as Jesus sees him is fostered by the authenticity of those virtuous lives within the Christian community who make the love of God visible to us as it was made visible in Christ Jesus. Paul writes to the Romans that those who love God are intended to become "true images of his Son, so that the Son might be the eldest of many brothers" (8:28f.). The motivating power of the perfect image of God's love in Jesus Christ (cf. 2 Cor. 2:4; Col. 1:15) is communicated from age to age by the many brothers whose lives are true images of that same love. The authenticity of their love is evidence of their seeing God in a true vision, and they reflect in the particularities of their lives the compelling goodness of that vision. Their internalization of the same love that is in Jesus Christ transforms and enlightens others. The love which sees God in doing what is right enables others to see God in doing what is right.

Paul's decision to follow Christ, motivated by his concrete experience of Christ in the Christian community that he was persecuting (Acts 9:5), reminds us of the psychological truth that all real decisions or conversions are linked with the concrete particularities of our experience and imagination.[3] While abstractions exist only in the mind, the decision to do something good, bad, or nothing, will have a relationship to the concrete; for what is good, always is concrete. We cannot do what we can in no way imagine; consequently, the importance of experiencing true images of God's love in Jesus Christ for following him in doing the truth. The image of God's love in Christ and his Church has transformed human lives in a way that philosophies of God cannot. [4]

The Christophany which Paul experienced at his conversion occurs in the traditional context of the Old Testament theophanies where God introduces himself by reference to a particular historical people. The compelling and transforming power of God is experienced in the living context of a believing people. He is seen among people whose authenticity enables us to see him. The truth of this vision is experienced, imaged, shared, and done; it involves participation in the life of a believing community and its story.[5]

20

OUR SENSE OF THE ENDING

Life stories have a beginning, a middle and an ending. Our sense of our story's ending, our basic faith concerning the ultimate meaning and value of our story, grounds our interpretation of and feeling for the entire story. The life story of Jesus Christ, with it final culmination in the resurrection, symbolizes the Christian sense of the ending of both our individual story and the universal. It expresses our belief that just as the Storyteller's *Creator Spiritus* of life-giving, story-giving love enabled Jesus to find his true story, so too it will enable us to find ours with the same love that survived the death of the cross in the resurrection.

There is a kind of love that we have for ourselves and others which does not survive death, which does not enable us to find our true story: "He who loves his life loses it, and he who hates his life in this world will keep it for eternal life" (Jn. 12:25; cf. Mk 8:35). We are free to reject the life-giving, story-giving love of the *Creator Spiritus* and its promise of the resurrection.

Matthew's story of the Last Judgment (25:31-46) expresses Christian faith's sense of the ending for every life story. It expresses a sense of responsibility for the incipient life stories that we have gratuituously received. We are responsible for our life story and those of others; in fact, we find our true story on the basis of our responsible love for others. The Son of Man is normative for distinguishing responsible from irresponsible life stories. The only truly good life story is one of responsible love; and the life story of Jesus Christ ultimately defines faith's understanding of that responsible love which survives death in the resurrection of the just. The experience of this love in the fellowship of the Christian community grounds our sense of the ending that awaits our stories and our conviction that they have been truly told when they have been truthfully lived according to the intention of the Storyteller's revelation of his life-giving, story-giving, responsible love in Jesus Christ.

Satan symbolizes that irresponsible love whereby we attempt to be our own little gods, creating our life stories independently of the Storyteller's grace and demand for life stories of responsible love for oneself and others: the illusion that a truly good life story can be found apart from the Giver of life stories and his intention for their fulfillment. Satan symbolizes the denial of the truth of things, which leads to deviousness, self-deception and missing the way to our true story.[1] He represents the way to an apparently good life story in the refusal to acknowledge and to accept the truth of his own reality in particular and of reality in general. Such denial is linked to the desire to master reality by the effort to destroy the truth which one finds repugnant. To have to behold the truth that has been denied is at the root of evasion and violence; however, the truth that has been denied does not go out of existence but remains expressive of itself to the great pain of the denier.

Satan is faith's symbol for what can go wrong with a life story. His expulsion from heaven and his being put on his own represents the risk of our own personal alienation from the grace and demand of the Storyteller for the discovery of our true story. Our egotism has the nihilistic character of making naught of everything except our own self-will. Satan symbolizes the absolutely separated and alienated personal existence in conflict with the truth of every other existence, inasmuch as he rejects the Giver of every life story in his demand for responsible love. His key-to-character statement might well be Sartre's "the other is hell" — for wherever he finds himself in creation, he can never really escape the context (hell) to which his primordial sin of irresponsible self-love has condemned him. What was created to become a truly good life story risks succumbing to the temptation of that irresponsible self-love which does not survive death in the resurrection of the just. The self-destructive character of rebellious pride consists in the attempt to tell one's own story independently of the Giver of life stories and his creative love.

There are apparently inexorable effects of evil — a king of contractual obligation — which Satan symbolizes. Jesus, on the other hand, represents a merciful escape clause from the evils which are expressed in the notion of a devil pact and its unmitigated contractual obligation. The devil pact is the reverse of the Covenant's contractual obligations with the living God and recalls the words: "No man can serve two masters: for either he will hate the one and love the other, or else he will hold to the one and despise the other. You cannot serve God and Mammon" (Mt. 6:19). Our life stories may be interpreted in the matrix of contractual obligations, with the assumption that every person has inevitably chosen to ally himself to the Giver of authentic life stories or to his adversary. Every person has placed himself under a higher power to obtain what he believes best in life, and is therefore contractually obligated to that power. We implicitly recognize that there is no way of independent existence which is completely safe and provided for; we cannot find our true story alone. Our search for our true story is doomed unless we seek it from the one and only Giver of authentic life stories and respond with responsible love to his life-giving, story-giving Spirit of creative love summoning us in grace and demand to lead truly good lives. The Good News of the Christ story illuminates our search for our true story, assuring us of the Father's love for us, of his approval and acceptance, and of his intention that his love within us culminate in the resurrection. The love of God for us, revealed in the resurrection of Jesus Christ, endows our life stories with a merciful escape clause from the apparent ultimacy of death, evil, and absurdity.

Our stories of God reflect our belief that our life stories, despite their finitude, are part of a universal story. Our life stories are called into existence and to fulfillment by the grace and demand of their Giver. The dynamic interrelationship and order of life stories is not an accidental happening, for every life story is summoned into existence and called to fulfillment by the same Giver of life stories and according to his intention of creating an all-embracing, universal story. Matthew's story of the Last Judgment discloses the Christian community's belief in a universal story within which every individual is held accountable for the quality of his or her life story. Although the times and cycles that govern our life stories are fixed, we have been endowed with freedom and responsibility for our choices and decisions within them. Each life story enjoys the significance of being derived from the Giver of life stories and summoned to its fulfillment within his universal story. Responsible love seeks its true story in attempting to discern and live in accordance with the will of God, with his love for us and its intention for our reciprocity in friendship: "No longer do I call you servants. . . .But I have called you friends" (Jn 15:15). Christianity proclaims that our authentic friendships with one another are the best evidence of our friendship with the God that Jesus Christ reveals as sharing his life with us.

Robert Heilman affirms that men not only write tragedy and melodrama but also, in quite nonliterary contexts, view human experience tragically or melodramatically.[2] Christianity interprets human experience and the precariousness of our search for our true story from the standpoint of tragedy rather than melodrama. There is a dramatic quality in the critical decision-making and action of every life story that is related to the subject's sense of the Mystery that defines it.

The tragic view of life stories respects their complexity. Man is seen in his strength and in his weakness; he experiences defeat in victory or victory in defeat; his will is tempered in the suffering that comes with, or brings about, new knowledge and maturity. With its inclusive vision of good and evil, tragedy never sees man's excellence divorced from his proneness to love the wrong; nor, on the other hand, does it see the evil that he does as divorced from his capacity for spiritual recovery.

The tragic view does not separate good and evil, treating them as independent wholes. It does not incline toward monopathic attitudes: toward a triumphal spirit, an unqualified hopefulness, a belief that good is chosen without anguish and integrity maintained despite danger; nor, on the other extreme, toward black despair of man's surviving against the villainy of other or of himself.

Tragedy is concerned with the whole person and his dividedness. The subject is caught between different forces or motives or values. His nature is dual and complex, and the different competing elements are simultaneously present and operative in his dramatic condition. Different competing elements endow the life story with risk and dramatic tension. We are drawn now this way and now that, and the awareness that is exacted is complex and troubling. Within the realm of literature it is tragedy that interprets the subject of the life story as suspended between salvation and damnation; consequently, it places primary value on the self-knowledge that concerns our possibilitie˙ of coming to salvation or damnation.

In melodrama, character is viewed as essentially undivided; the question of salvation or damnation does not arise. The subject of the life story is good or evil, hero or villain, angel or devil, victorious or defeated. There is no question of personal development or risk when good and evil are seen as independent wholes. Monopathic attitudes result: a triumphal presumptuousness, an unqualified optimism, a belief that good is chosen without effort and maintained without cost. On the other extreme, melodrama succumbs to total despair, whether of the world, of society, of one's ability to endure one's context or inner state. Everything is understood to contribute to a sense of ruin that is staggering because there are no apparent options. Hope is impossible. Whether intentionally or unknowingly, a part is taken for the whole, the complicating elements of character at the heart of a life story are eliminated or ignored. The melodramatic interpretation of human experience fosters either presumption or despair. Persons are either saved or damned.

The melodramatic obsession with one dimension of the truth to the exclusion of every other creates the illusion of possessing the whole truth while actually blinding ourselves to it. Melodrama is blind to conflicting evidence and intolerant of it; hence it seeks to destroy it. Fanatic obsessions, self-righteousness, pseudo-messianism, demonologies, Manichaeism and ideological hatred and violence are evidence of the melodramatic interpretation of life stories and history. Melodrama is not engaged in the quest for the true life story; it thrives on the illusion of already fully possessing it. Faith and hope do not enter into its sense of the ending to either the individual life story or history.

The Cross and Resurrection symbolize the sense of an ending with which the story of the Christian community begins and remains in existence. Even now the community experiences the promise of that life-giving, story-giving love which constitutes its sense of the ending intended both for its own story and that of the world: "Happy you who are hungry now: you shall be satisfied. Happy you who weep now: you shall laugh" (Lk. 6:21). The promised ending, disclosed in the community's foundational experience of the Cross and Resurrection, is now experienced in the unfolding of the Christian community's story: "Now is the acceptable time, this is the day of salvation" (2 Cor. 6:12). The story unfolds in the spirit of self-sacrificing, life-giving love which pervades the detailed complexity of our daily life: "Let him take up his cross daily and follow me" (Lk. 9:23). The Cross symbolizes the love which endures for others, the costly love that creates the authentic fellowship of the human community; without such love our stories are not authentic life stories.

The love which enables us to collaborate in the search for our true stories involves a daily dying and rising which John expresses with an image borrowed from the creative process in nature: "I say to you, unless a grain of wheat falls into the earth and dies, it remains alone; but if it dies, it bears much fruit" (Jn. 12:24). The community of Christian faith is summoned into existence and sustained by the creative power of God's love manifested in the costly love of the Cross. This foundational experience is prolonged, or re-experienced, from age to age as the constitutive experience of the Christian community. This love is the substance and promise of the Christian community's story. Paul describes it as that love which does not come to an end, which is the greatest of all divine gifts and without which we are nothing at all (1 Cor. 13:1-13). The Christian community's experience of this love finds expression in its teaching, fellowship, service and celebration.

The experience of the caring, compassionate, and sustaining love of God within the fellowship of the Christian community — symbolized by the Cross and Resurrection — enables faith to endure in the pursuit of its true story: "Your endurance will win you your lives" (Lk. 21:19).[3] Within the context of the anxieties that accompany finitude and the precariousness of human life, the foundational experience of God's sustaining love in Christ and Christian fellowship takes the form of patient love: "Love is always patient . . . . it is always ready to excuse, to trust, to hope, and to endure whatever come" (1 Cor. 4-7). The love which promises to survive death in the resurrection of the just, the culmination of our true story under God, is even now experienced as surviving absurdities, antagonisms, hatreds, persecutions, sufferings and the other forms of tribulation that assail it. Extrapolating from the experience of this love in the historical particularities of the present, the resurrectional faith of the Christian community is able to affirm that "Love does not come to an end" (I Cor. 13:8), that death is not the final intention of God for human life stories. Our sense of the end is not death; rather, it is that of a love without end. Just as we believe that the peace which Jesus gives is "not as the world gives" (Jn. 14:24), so too we believe that the end which he promises for our life stories is "not as the world gives" in death.

If our searching for our true stories involves struggle, our finding them implies completion. Faith is always reaching out for its true story and longing for its culmination; it matures in the tension between aspiration and achievement. In our aspiring and struggling for our true story, we experience the dynamics of story-giving Love's intention for our self-realization within the community of life stories that form the universal story. The presumption and despair that mark the melodramatic interpretation of human experience imply an alienation from life-giving, story-giving Love's intention for the fulfillment of our life stories. Presumption and despair are the attitudes of those whose sense of the end requires no searching to discern the will of God, no struggle to obtain the justice and peace of the kingdom, no aspiration for the achievement of righteousness.

The sense of an ending which pervades life stories is marked by a tension between the complacency which acquiesces in what is and must be and the concern (or solicitude) which does not stop at acquiescence, but contends for what is not yet but should be. This same tension appears in Christ's story and that of his Church. We are told that we can find rest for our souls by learning from him to be meek and humble (Mt. 11:29), and that we should not pay too much attention to tomorrow for life and food and drink and clothing (Mt. 6:26-34). On the other hand, we are given most pressing and urgent directives on the solicitude that we are to cultivate: we are to watch and pray (Mk. 13:33); we are to keep ourselves ready (Mt. 24:14); we are to strive to enter by the narrow gate (Lk. 13:24). Paul gives thanks for what he has gratuitously received; still, he insists that he is not content with receiving, but is stretching forward to the things that are before, pressing toward the mark (Phil. 3:13f), fighting the good fight to win the crown of justice (2 Tim. 4:7f). Peter, who on the Mount of the Transfiguration said that it was "good for us to be here" (Mk. 9:4) in prayerful contemplation, pursues the long road that led from Jerusalem to Rome in the unremitting effort to transform the world.

Both complacency and concern are technical words, employed by Frederick E. Crowe, which help us to understand our experience of the tension between the incipient, unfinished, life story that is and the final, complete life story that it must become, between the grace that is the gift of the self as story and the Giver of life stories' demand for its completion.[4]

The decision-making and action at the heart of our life stories bespeak orientations of our will and willingness, patterns of complacency and concern, that are not to be confused with smugness and anxiety. The pattern of complacency involves a quiet enjoyment of what is, an all's well attitude, a basic self-acceptance and approval of others. The pattern of concern refers to the good that can and should be accomplished. The attitude of concern is wholesome when it is based on our fundamental complacency, our consent to being, to the given state of affairs as a starting point for the completion of our unfinished life stories; when it is not wholesome, it becomes anxiety.[5]

Existentialism's stress on guilt, anxiety or despair contrasts with the Christian spirit of gratitude for the good that is motivating our faith in what it promises to become. Christian faith's complacency is the affective acceptance of the truth about all that is, as it is. That affective acceptance gives rise to a personal stability that puts us into harmony with reality as it is; it carries over into action. The experience of affective acceptance is even now a foretaste of the ultimate contentment which faith hopes to enjoy in the culmination of its true story. In the midst of his sufferings, Paul is able to affirm his fundamental complacency, his profound experience of God's love and acceptance:

> So far then we have seen that, through our Lord Jesus Christ, by faith we are judged righteous and at peace with God, since it is by faith and through Jesus that we have entered this state of grace in which we can boast about looking forward to God's glory. But that is not all we can boast about; we can boast about our sufferings. These sufferings bring patience, as we know, and patience brings perseverance, and perseverance brings hope, and this hope is not deceptive, because the love of God has been poured into our hearts by the Holy Spirit which has been given us (Rom. 5:1-5).

We extrapolate from our present experience of our life stories for our sense of their ultimate culmination. Extrapolating from our experience of the utter gratuity (grace) of our life story both in its origin and in its present unfinished state, we believe that its ultimate culmination will be no less gratuitous. Extrapolating from our present experience of the responsible love which is giving shape to our life story, we believe that its ultimate comprehensibility will be no less a question of such love. On the basis of this present experience, in the context of Christian fellowship, we embrace the Christ story as our own, as the articulation of our own self-understanding both as individuals and as a community. His Cross and resurrection make sense on the basis of our present foundational experience of the compassionate, caring, merciful love of God responding to human helplessness.

The Cross reveals the kind of love that survives death in the resurrection only on the condition that there is something of this love within our present experience of our fundamental self-other-world-God relationship. Helplessness and failure provide occasions for discovering whether anyone loves us. In this respect the resurrection symbolizes the answer of God to the question raised by the Cross. The New Testament emphasis on present conversion experience, Christian maturation and development, implies the dynamic orientation of fraternal love to the outcome symbolized by the Cross and Resurrection.

In John's Gospel, Jesus interprets the fulfillment of his life story in terms of accomplishing his Father's will: "My food is to do the will of him who sent me, and to finish his work" (4:34). He derives his sense of an ending from his relationship to his Father. His life story will reach completion when his Father's intention for it has been fulfilled. He receives his life story, his mission, his purpose and orientation from the Father who tells or intends it. The sustenance he draws from acting in harmony with his Father's loving intention (will) for him enables his life story to sustain others, as implied by his injunction: "Feed my lambs . . . Feed my sheep" (Jn. 21:15ff). Authentic Christian life stories will sustain others in the same way. They will share Jesus' awareness of the self as gift from the Father for others, as sustained by the Father to be of sustenance to others. The story of the Christian community is, therefore, intended to be that of a gift to others, of helping one another to find our true stories as they are "waiting in hope for the blessing which will come with the appearance of the glory of our great God and Savior Christ Jesus" (Tit. 2:13).

HOMECOMING

In his parable of the prodigal son (Lk. 15:11-32), Jesus understands homecoming as a beloved son's return to his father. John's Gospel interprets Jesus' life story as a homecoming: he is the pre-existent Word who is sent by the Father and returns to the Father. His journey to the Father is resonant of Israel's path to life as developed in both the Mosaic and exilic Exodus accounts. The journeys between Galilee and Samaria in which Jesus speaks the word of God as described in the "book of signs" are themselves signs of the journey to the Father which spans the entirety of Jesus' life, culminating in his final return as risen Son and Lord. These visible journeys are signs of Jesus' inner movement toward the Father; they also describe the quality of Christian experience as a homecoming which is not actualized in a moment, but in a life story.

The homecoming of Jesus Christ is both a process and a term that is not a return to the past; rather, it is a becoming into the future that is the gift of a participation in the Storyteller's own story for mankind. His homecoming is the dynamic passage into the future of our unfinished life stories; it is expressed in the continuum of his lived personal experience of his Father, whose story for us is the Good News which Jesus' life communicates both in the Age of Jesus and in the Age of his Church.

John's Gospel interprets Jesus' homecoming as a progressively more perfect communication of the Father's intention for the consummation of his life story, which creates the way for our own homecoming:

> Trust in God still, and trust in me. There are many rooms in my Father's house; if there were not, I should have told you. I am going to prepare a place for you, and after I have gone and prepared a place for you, I shall return to take you with me; so that where I am you may be also. You know the way to the place where I am going (14:2-4).

If home refers to our origins, where our life begins, Jesus is always at home in the world; for, wherever he is, he is one with his Father, the origin and ground and goal of his life story.[7] He has a radical sense of his home in his communion with his Father and of his homecoming in the accomplishment of his Father's will: "The Son can do nothing of himself, but only what he sees the Father doing" (Jn. 5:19). Home is being with the Father: "If you know me, you know my Father too. From this moment you know him and have seen him" (Jn. 14:6). The Father initiates and enables homecoming, showing us the way in the story he tells in Christ: "If anyone loves me he will keep my word, and my Father will love him, and we shall come to him and make our home with him" (Jn. 14:23). This story tells us that it is only by being in touch with our ultimate origins in the Father that we can hope to find our true story and return to them. (There is no story without origins, a beginning. The middle and conclusion of a story are intrinsically related to the beginning.)

Jesus employs the theme of home, homelessness and homecoming in his story of the prodigal son, implying the joy of the Storyteller in a happy ending, in a life story that ends well. Homecoming at the deepest level of our existence is the recognition and acceptance of the truth about ourselves and our ultimate environment or ground of existence (home, homeland, fatherland) which, in the context of the gospel message, is the Father of Jesus Christ. Homecoming is the reciprocity of mutual recognition and acceptance, a state where finally everything is as it was meant to be from the beginning.

Jesus' own homecoming, symbolized by his death and resurrection, tells us that we can even now experience the process of homecoming by sharing his relationship of reciprocity with his Father. The "Our Father" implicitly summons us to a community of universal sonship and brotherhood in the way that Jesus Christ's homecoming has disclosed this possibility to faith. The fatherhood and lordship of God denote a goodness that is known in our concrete experience of sonship and brotherhood, in the coherence of our feelings, words and deeds with the basic orientation of Jesus Christ's relationship of homecoming to his Father. The Christian community proclaims the Good News of homecoming in Christ's fulfillment of the Father's will for us, an enterprise of filial dependence and fraternal interdependence.

The life story of Jesus, the paradigm of homecoming for Christian faith, is both the Father's gift and the achievement of Jesus' effort and obedience. His homecoming is the process of living out his Father's will as it is given to him in the particularities of his daily experience. He becomes fully human by living our human condition sinlessly. His story is the drama of growth and development in cooperation with the grace and demand of his Father. In the Fourth Gospel we see that he is to be glorified by being lifted up when his hour comes. He receives his hour and his glory from his Father, but the way in which he goes to his glorification is anything but passive. The messianic hour brings to accomplishment the salvific plan of his Father. The Fourth Gospel interprets "the hour to pass from this world to the Father" (13:1) as the homecoming of Jesus Christ that is filled with his saving activity.

Homecoming involves both the vertical relationship of sonship and the horizontal relationship of brotherhood. After his homecoming in the resurrection, Jesus calls his disciples brothers (Jn. 20:17; Mt. 28:10). His homecoming transforms their consciousness; their mutual recognition and acceptance of one another now takes place at a much deeper level. Faith in Christ and the fulfillment of his Father's will are the foundation for achieving the prophetic dream of a universal brotherhood (Mt. 12:46).

The author of *Hebrews* affirms the impact of Jesus Christ's homecoming in terms of our sanctification and brotherhood: "For the one who sanctifies, and the ones who are sanctified, are of the same stock; that is why he openly calls them brothers" (2:11). The unity of brotherhood accrues from doing the Father's will; and the life story of Jesus Christ is faith's understanding of what it means to do that will.

In the New Testament Christians are called brothers about 160 times, and Jesus himself affirms that one who does the will of the Father is his own brother (Mt. 12:50; Mk. 3:55; Lk. 8:21). Brotherhood is the intention of the Father's will and evidence of its accomplishment.[8] In the context of Jesus' death and resurrection, we may see brotherhood as a kind of twofold communication: from the Father whose will is to be done and from Jesus Christ who does it. The outpouring of the Holy Spirit at Pentecost symbolizes the power of the twofold communication of life-giving, story-giving love (the Father's will or intention in Christ) for creating brotherhood (Acts 2:7-11, 33).[9]

The Giver of life stories, addressing us in grace and demand for responsible lives, is the underlying ground of unity or brotherhood. As source, ground and destination, he empowers the fulfillment of our life stories in a common enterprise through which individuals supplement one another in their efforts to achieve their fundamental aspirations. By reason of sharing basic common needs which cannot be attained alone, we have been predisposed by the Giver of life stories to share our lives with others, pooling our endowments and cooperating in the fulfillment of our needs. Our diversity predisposes us to fellowship, community and brotherhood: cooperation means that one must have something to give which the other lacks, and the latter must have a capacity to receive what the first has to give. Our self-knowledge and self-affection are correlative to our mutual knowledge and mutual affection. We have been capacitated and intended for such knowledge and affection by the Giver of life stories. Hugo Meynell writes: "All creatures arc known and loved by God; it is the special privilege of Christians that the knowledge and love is mutual, that they consciously share in the life of God and hope for a consummation of that sharing in the future."[10] Despite our intrinsic orientation towards brotherhood and home-coming, there is an element of precariousness; for while we develop little by little in understanding and love of ourselves and of one another, in both respects we are liable to corruption and regression as well as to development.

Our particular sense of the ending or culmination of our life stories derives from our basic faith, which interprets and unifies the manifold of our experiences on the premise that the ultimate issues of life are interpretable and not absurd. This basic faith addresses itself to questions about the ultimate nature and structure of reality and determines our notion of how we ought to behave.[11]

If "the sum total of necessary conditions for the coming into being of an individual, a species, a phylum or of life itself, are not logically or historically identical with the individual, or species, or phylum, or life itself,"[12] we are neither the absolute creators of our life stories, nor are we in full possession of them. We originate as gift, an incipient life story received from others, rarely able to account for more than the immediate others in the long and wide web of ancestors that have been the indispensable conditions for our existence.

In recounting our life story we are unable to remember all the biologically memorable individuals who have been the indispensable conditions for our biological reality. Our appearance, color, intelligence, shape, size, and temperament are influenced by our biological, cultural, and familial background. We have been called into existence through an ancestral web of life stories, into a particular world which, although presented to us for our free acceptance or rejection, we have not chosen for ourselves.

Our life story is not exclusively a matter of self-determination. It involves both our freely receiving what we have been freely given, and our freely giving what we have freely received. Our self-acceptance implies our willingness to accept the definite historical background from which our life story has been called forth; it implies our acceptance of a world which can never be worked over to such an extent that we are eventually dealing only with material that we have chosen and created for the telling of our stories. Ultimately, it also implies the acceptance of the Giver of all life stories in and through all his stories. An authentic self-acceptance implies both an acceptance of the universal story encompassing all our stories and a fully personal yes to their Teller, calling them forth in grace and demand.

The final judgment about the life stories within the universal story is possible only when all the evidence is in. The ultimate meaning of stories, whether of individuals or communities, emerges in their final outcome. Each new generation is a new framework for assessing the impact of former generations. As the meaning of life stories, events and movements continues to emerge, we become aware of how partial and incomplete our understanding of them was. We are always making new assessments of historical data (new histories) in the light of current developments. Similarly, the meaning of the Christ story and the Christian movement continues to unfold in the historical evidence of life stories bearing witness to it.

Hegel and Pannenberg, in different ways, have recognized that the complete understanding of a life story, event, or movement presupposes a grasp of their relationships to everyone and everything else in the continuum of history. Because every existent in this continuum is related to every other existent, its meaning is only partially ascertainable until its full context of relationships emerge at the end of history. Hence, Pannenberg affirms that God's historical revelation of himself (his story) will reach completion only at the term of the historical process in which it takes place. The fullness of human history derives from the grace and demand of the Storyteller calling it forth in the life stories which constitute it. The Church's belief in the general judgment implies that humankind, as a collective unity, has a story which comes under the Storyteller's judgment; it implies that the one total definitive state of man, as individual and as collective unity before God, is comprehensible and not absurd. The end of the universal story is fixed by the Storyteller; it is not merely arrived at. The final consummation which terminates history depends on the sovereign discretion and intention of God; it is not simply the result of a development immanent in the world. What is now ambiguous in an ambiguous world of ambiguous stories will resolve itself in the Cross God glorified with the resurrection. The Christian community celebrates the resurrection as Jesus' new way of being with us and with God, the fulfilled and fulfilling outcome of his life story for us experienced as the promise of God's love for our own stories with him.

21

CHRISTIAN FREEDOM

FOR A RENEWED LIFE STORY

Experiencing God's love in Christ means experiencing that we have been freely accepted, approved and loved, that we can and should accept ourselves and others with the same freedom. Salvation entails a joyful freedom in God and a relationship to others which expresses itself in many ways. The preaching of Jesus promises the fulfillment of human hopes, expectations and longings for a completely new freedom. In his inaugural sermon at Nazareth, Jesus announces that he has been sent to preach the good news concerning the liberation of captives and freedom for the oppressed (Lk. 4:18-19). His call to life concerns a liberation from anything that makes human life less than life and less than human; it touches all the dimensions of human life and existence. His historical concerns of healing, liberating and reconciling are still unfinished; consequently, his followers are identified by their participation in his same mission and purpose. The preaching of God's kingdom announces freedom for a completely new start: the blind are to see, the lame walk, the lepers are to be cleansed, the deaf hear, the dead are to be raised up and the poor have the good news preached to them (Lk. 7:22-23; Mt. 11:5-6). The freedom of Jesus Christ creates a new situation and context from which radically new human choices can be made here and now. His story creates a new people.

The freedom which Jesus offers is not the power to do with oneself and one's life whatever one wants; rather, it is the freedom to live as he lived. It is the freedom to believe and hope and love as he did. The freedom of Jesus lies in his life with God, lived as it was originally intended by God for man (e.g., Rom. 6:22). It reveals that the man who is truly free shows his freedom in being free for the service of God (1 Thess. 1:9) and his fellow man (1 Cor. 9:19). Jesus defines the Christian understanding of freedom by his life of loving receptiveness towards God and of loving responsibility towards his neighbor. His cross expresses both his relationship to God and to his neighbor in the consummate freedom of God and man. The life, death and resurrection of Jesus Christ reveals to Christian faith the freedom to become what by God's grace one can become by believing, hoping, and loving as Jesus did. The faith, hope, and love of Jesus enabled him to lose all in order to find all; for only he who is free to lose his life shall find it. Jesus' life and death for others is a free affirmation of a faith, hope, and love which survives death. He reveals the love that leads to life (1 Jn. 4:7-9). He is able to lay down his life for his friends because he is free.

One is not free to serve God if he is compelled to sin; still, man is meant to be free from this compulsion. There is no magical insurance against sin. The Christian is called to a constant struggle with sin (e.g., Rom. 6:12). As liberation from the compulsion to sin, freedom in Christ Jesus (Rom. 6:14, 18) opens up the hitherto impossible possibility of serving God (e.g., Jas. 1:25; 2:12). Jesus' freedom characterizes the new way of life in which man lives in accordance with the will of God: "the freedom which we have in Christ Jesus" (Gal. 2:4) enables Paul to speak of our "having been set free from sin" (Rom. 6:18). What previously separated God and man, and thus stood in the way of true humanity, is removed in the person of Jesus Christ. His freedom, his consummate availability for God and for others, is the way salvation exists in history; it reveals the new opportunity of human existence that grounds "the glorious liberty of the children of God" (Rom. 8:21).

Man's attempts at an absolute autonomy lead to the greatest bondage in which man misses what he is meant to be (Mt. 6:25; Jn. 12:15). True freedom exists when man is what he is meant to be. Jesus Christ's life, death, and resurrection defines for Christian faith the ultimate freedom that is available to man; it reveals the freedom to be what man is meant to be, a freedom that is gained as man denies himself (Mt. 16:24) in order to be free of himself for God and for others. Christian freedom consists in being available in loving readiness for the call and demand of God and neighbor. It develops in an atmosphere of acceptance, love, and trust. Our personal integration with God, with others, with ourselves, is a question of our being free for others; and the way that this is accomplished is defined for Christian faith by Jesus.

Death reminds the Christian that his existence is given. Freedom from death means that he believes in the promise of a future which lies in Christ, beyond himself and his own death. The assurance that nothing more can stand between him and God (Rom. 8:38) and that death is overcome can liberate man from the fear of death. Freedom from such fear is rooted in the fact that the free man does not belong to himself (cf. 1 Cor. 16:19). He belongs to him who has set him free (cf. Rom. 6:18). The gift of freedom is bound to the giver: "For all things are yours . . . and you are Christ's and Christ is God's" (1 Cor. 3:21). Consequently, not even death can separate man from Christ; for the Church enjoys the continued experience of the Risen Christ's presence and of union with him (cf. Rom. 6:4-6; Gal. 2:20). Those who experience that their lives belong to, are in the posession of, the one who has survived death can no longer believe that death is the utter annihilation of their existence. They implicitly recognize that the quality of their own lives is defined in and through their personal relationship to God in the Risen Christ. They are maturing in the freedom to believe and hope and love as Jesus did. They are participating in the meaning of the resurrection as a passage into a new life that they can know only in faith and hope in the God who raised Jesus from the dead.

The freedom which Christian faith knows in Jesus Christ reveals God's involvement with the world, with human joy and sorrow, with human excellence and weakness. The Holy Spirit and the power of God ground the finite freedom of Jesus, disclosing to faith the freedom that is present "where the Spirit of the Lord is" (2 Cor. 3:17), in our response to the particular demands of the historical real. The freedom of Jesus Christ defines our understanding of Christian maturation as the life-long process of becoming free to do what the Spirit of the Lord calls for at any moment. It is in fidelity to this Spirit that Christian freedom is experienced as our being able to respond to the grace and demand of God for doing what is right, for becoming what God intends us to become. To the extent that the Spirit of the Lord governs our lives we are becoming free from whatever counters God's intention for our personal maturation; we are becoming free for whatever promotes its realization in our choices, decisions, and actions. Under the influence of the Spirit of Christ, Christians are enabled to grow in freedom and responsibility both for what they do and for who they are.

The freedom which Jesus exercised, like that of every person, was not indetermined; for at no stage in life does a person exist in isolation from or independent of the real. We are tied to the real in a multiplicity of ways through all the dimensions of sensibility. Even in doing what we want we are being determined by something. Freedom as indetermination is an illusion. Jesus exercised a finite freedom within a horizon of infinity in a way that was sinless; for he neither absolutized its impotence and its finiteness (inertia) nor its power and dynamism (pride) to infinity. He was free of cowardice and arrogance, of cynicism and presumption. The exercise of his freedom was devoid of evil, either as a lack of being (meaninglessness) or as a perversion of being; rather, it communicated to faith the confidence to act like a son in God's presence (cf. Eph. 3:12; Heb. 3:6; 1 Jn. 2:28), recognizing that our existence is his gift and that our freedom is meaningful only in relation to the Source from which it ultimately derives and to which it ultimately tends. There is no authentic freedom in our giving to a creature the importance that should belong to God alone; for the only possible result of this must be a terrible distortion of our existence. The Chrisian believes that he belongs to the Lord and that his freedom is destined for the resurrection (1 Cor. 6:12-14); consequently, he must resist the temptation to found his life upon himself, upon creatures, and to understand life and give it meaning in terms of finite creatures alone, to the exclusion of that ultimate meaning which has been revealed in Jesus Christ. Speaking of the perversion of man's life through sin, Paul points to idolatry as the source of the trouble: "They exchanged the truth of God for a lie and worshiped and served the creature rather than the Creator" (Rom. 1:25).

Every person lives by some faith or other which enables him to make sense of his own life, of others, of the world, of suffering and evil, of God. Perhaps it is more correct to say that his faith is the way he is able to find — rather than to make—sense to his life and to that of others. Our faith may be described as our image, idea, understanding, working hypothesis, or vision of ourselves, of others, of the world, of suffering and evil, of God. It underlies the choices, decisions, and actions whereby we forge our relationship to reality and define our character. Although society has a role in shaping our faith and our character, there remains the fact of the individual's freedom and responsibility for the self that he is. Only true faith does in fact lead to authentic selfhood, to community, to making more and more sense of life in the world; an inadequate or illusory faith eventually proves itself, whether in the individual or in the community, to be sterile and even self-destructive. Christians believe that the faith which governed the entire life and death of Jesus Christ is the true faith which authentically integrates our lives with God and neighbor and enables us to attain the freedom which culminated in his resurrection. The true faith leads to true freedom: "The truth has set you free . . . if the Son sets you free, you will indeed be free" (Jn. 8:32, 36). And true freedom is the work of God's grace and man's free obedience, the integration of divine and human freedom, which faith affirms to have been achieved in Jesus Christ.

The view of freedom which derives from faith's understanding of Jesus Christ is opposed to the gnostic or ideological view which tends to see the theoretical at the expense of the practical, to put freedom pure and simple against definite responsibilities and concrete obligations. The freedom of Jesus Christ is not indetermination; his relationships, in all their multiplicity and variety, are ultimately determined by his loving responsiveness to the creative and liberating demands of God's will for him and for others. Christian freedom implies a state of mind which tries to see things as a whole and in a perspective admitting varying degrees of importance; it maintains a balanced perspective even at the expense of clear-cut, simple solutions, and it does not imply a flight from complexity and responsibility.

The freedom of Jesus Christ is both the gift of God and that which he earned by mastering the complexity of his life. He exercises his freedom in a way that reveals to faith what God can do with human finitude when it is perfectly responsive to his creative and liberating will. To know Jesus Christ is to know the meaning of divine and human freedom: what God freely accomplished when man freely responds to him. Again, it is our knowing that God loves us that frees us to love him, our neighbors, and ourselves. The certainty that "he first loved us" frees us to make others as important to us as ourselves; it frees us for a love which survives the finitude of death in the promise of the resurrection.

What the Christian means by freedom in God or man is articulated by the life, death, and resurrection of Jesus Christ in whom faith grasps what God intends man to become in the reciprocity of his personal freedom. In the faith and obedience of Jesus Christ emerges the paradox that the man who asserts his autonomy loses it through self-idolatry; while the man who lives in obedience towards God is set free from the very things that are most oppressive and distorting, and becomes most responsibly his true self in the service of others: "Whoever would save his life shall lose it; and whoever loses his life for my sake and the gospel's will save it" (Mk. 8:35). Christian freedom is outgoing in its responsiveness to God and to others in relation to God. Freedom is exercised as Jesus Christ exercised it when it is for the benefit of others. The ultimate freedom which one has in Jesus Christ means a concern for others, for what may help or hurt them. The gift of God's freedom in Jesus Christ finds its proper expression in personhood and peoplehood; it involves a relationship with God in Jesus Christ in which God acts to bring men fully to himself as individuals in a community. Through faith Christians hold fast to the liberating power of God in Jesus Christ; their holding fast is by God's power, at work through the presence of the Spirit of the Lord within them as individuals and as a community (cf. 2 Cor. 3:17).

If we understand sin as alienation from oneself, alienation from one's fellows, alienation from society, alienation from the whole scheme of things or from God, then the grace of God's freedom in Jesus Christ can be expounded as the overcoming of alienation and as the reconciling of what has been separated or disrupted. Through the risen Christ we derive our power to be freed from those forces which alienate us from ourselves, from others and from God. The perfection of authentic friendship among human persons and between them and God is a goal which Christian faith believes cannot be realized without the capacitating gift of God's liberating love. There can be no self-fulfillment apart from the fulfillment of the community in which the existence of the self is set; consequently, freedom from egoism is required in order that we be free for communion with God and neighbor in the way that Jesus sets forth and enables us to follow in the presence of his Spirit. This is the way of Jesus' self-giving love toward God and others. The resurrection experience of his disciples is the liberating coming to be in them of that faith and hope and love towards God that Jesus preached and lived. The Spirit of Jesus' faith and hope and love is poured out upon them in the experience of the risen Christ. This is the liberating, community-building Spirit, giving birth to the Church, the community of faith, hope and love, through the power of the risen Christ enabling our personal integration as individuals with God and one another. The *koinonia* of Christians communicates the *agape* that is God in the freedom of the risen Christ. Such love is a vital sign for Christian faith of authentic participation in the new freedom of the new life of the risen Christ; for the Resurrection is not a resuscitation or revivification, as in the Fourth Gospel's account of Lazarus, but a totally new and different kind of life involving a radical change and transformation of the life that existed in history.

The freedom of Jesus Christ's life, death, and resurrection reveals to faith God himself, welcoming and exigent towards the human person, summoning and empowering the actualization of a free human community of free human persons. It reveals the reciprocity of freedom between mankind and God in which we accept him as absolutely trustworthy and give ourselves to him in love, and through him give ourselves to one another, struggling to overcome obstacles to the full human and spiritual development of the human community. The freedom of the electing God and elected man is revealed to faith in Jesus Christ as the ultimate ground for the liberation of the human community through an ongoing process of many conversions and renewals. This is the freedom of that charity which Paul designated to the Corinthians as the "yet more excellent way." There is nothing that it cannot face; "there is no limit to its faith, its hope, and its endurance" (1 Cor. 12:31; 17:7). Through the commitment of love to the human and spiritual development and welfare of others, the Christian shares in Jesus Christ's way of freely shouldering the burden of personhood for the meaningful peoplehood of the human community under God.

Christian freedom may be described in Pauline terms as our dying with Christ in order to rise with Christ and live in Christ, sharing in his life, in his love, in his mission, in his power. Our living with the freedom that is in Christ involves our sharing in his creative, reconciling, healing work for the transformation of all creation, when "God will be all in all" (1 Cor. 15:28). The freedom which follows Jesus' way of the cross is that of an unconditional love and commitment which endures in the face of the apparently irreconcilable, the contradictory, the absurd, despite our mortal, creaturely, and human propensity for fear and distrust. It is the freedom to carry the pain of the world in one's heart, and yet remain a sign of hope to others. It is freedom from the fear of a conversion that will destroy the comforts of a spiritual status quo. The freedom of the cross is that of unconditional love's courageously facing controversial situations in the struggle for doing the truth. It is operative within the human condition where more or less opposed perspectives move in their contention towards consensus and are opposed by fresh perspectives as they approach it; where the fundamentally dialectic nature of human knowing challenges our responsible doing of what truly contributes to the personhood and peoplehood of ourselves and others. It is opposed to that conditional commitment which, being impatient, operates by threat and ultimatum, and which keeps the option of defection open as a protection against the consequences of overcommitment.

To the extent that Jesus Christ is the directive spiritual force of the individual Christian, the local congregation, or the Church, Christians are being progressively freed for loving and truthful lives (cf. Jn. 8:31-33). Christian fellowship is the enduring sacrament of the risen Christ's abiding presence among those whom he is liberating for loving and truthful lives; it is the extension of the risen Christ's life and power for our personal integration as individuals and as a people under God and with God. As the service of God in spirit and truth, Christian fellowship implies a dialectic of voices, unified by a common body of fundamental truths and a common commitment of faith, engaged with one another in an effort to make more manifest the full implications of Christ's gospel. It promotes personhood by encouraging individuals to reexamine honestly their own commitment to Christ through the Church; it promotes peoplehood by bearing with one another charitably while courageously examining elements of disharmony for their meaning in order to attain such harmony as is needed. Authentic Christian fellowship implies the freedom to tolerate and even to benefit from the differences of opinion aimed at discovering truth; for it fosters efforts to release the person to his full Christian potential for a truthful and loving life. Our authentically knowing that God loves us frees us to love him, our neighbors and ourselves truthfully. When Christian fellowship is authentic, it is an expression of such knowing and its liberating impact upon our lives; it evidences the qualities which marked Jesus' lifelong orientation towards the resurrection, suggesting that our own lives are dynamically sharing in this same orientation.

In Jesus Christ the community of faith recognizes the dignity and lasting worth that the freedom of God's love gives to finite, definite, limited man and the humble quotidian realities of his world. The freedom of God, which Christians believe is both present and available in Jesus Christ, is humanly known and experienced in the finite, the definite, the limited, the temporal. It is not a freedom from the particularities and finitude of the human condition; rather, it is the freedom of God's love for and within that condition. The gift of God's freedom in Jesus Christ offers no escape from the complexity, conflicts, and creative tensions of the human institutions and structures, whether sacred or secular, by which men define themselves in their various relationships and capacities, and in which they both conserve and learn the full import of their values. It is within the complexity of human institutions, especially as they are pressed by time, change and adversity, that the authenticity of our Christian freedom for self-expending commitment is put to the test. The freedom of God defined by the cross of Jesus Christ does not offer us a haven of invulnerable living; rather, it is the freedom of the Suffering Servant and Wounded Healer, empowering us with the same Holy Spirit of freedom to act likewise. It is in the definiteness, concreteness, limitedness, and finitude of the Cross that faith grasps the meaning of God's freedom.

Our notion of Christian freedom is conditioned by our understanding of the resurrection. If we view the resurrection exclusively as an event that we are waiting for after the completion of our historical life-span, we risk lapsing into a quietism which ignores the concrete demands of our social context for justice and compassion, a gnosticism which assumes that knowing about the resurrection is as good as participating in it, and a Manichaeanism which believes that the world cannot be redeemed. The authentically Christian experience of the risen Christ as a present reality brings redemption, not despair; it brings a saving faith, hope and love for the world. To despise the world in the wrong sense is to miss the point of the resurrection and to despise onself; for to despise the world is to despise time and change, the necessary dimensions of personal development for our participation in the redemptive impact of the resurrection.

If, on the other hand, we view the resurrection of Jesus Christ in continuity with his lifelong orientation of loving dedication to God and self-expending existence for others, we may recognize the crucial importance of our contemporary participation in this same orientation and hope for its same culmination. The selfless love of God and neighbor, the freedom of the Christ-oriented person for others, bears witness to the resurrection as a present reality transforming our lives through the gracious release of God's power in love, which enables the attainment of their intended significance in Christ. Such love emerges in the Christian's intellectual and spiritual courage in the face of the cross-purposes, internal contradictions, multiple perspectives and unanticipated consequences that result as much from the time-bound mysteriousness of man's environment as from his perversity and short-sightedness.

Christian fortitude manifests the freedom and power of the risen Christ's self-giving, sharing, and suffering love. In the crucified Christ and in Christian martyrs, fortitude is not the virtue of the stronger but instead that of the seemingly vanquished; it entails the willingness to struggle, to suffer and, if need be, to die because of our authentic love for others. It is an illusion to believe that we can be consistently faithful to the grace and demand of God without having to risk something for it. What is risked, if the occasion arises, may be something less than life itself: tranquility, possessions, honor, or face saving. What is required may be the acceptance of death at another's hands. The freedom of the risen Christ is a victory over death that is not won without suffering and self-sacrifice. To know the power of the resurrection is to share in Christ's sufferings (Phil. 3:8-15); such concrete knowledge of Christ is ordered to our final assimilation to him in the resurrection from the dead. This is the voluntary suffering on behalf of others that communicates the healing power of God's compassion in the Passion and Resurrection of Jesus Christ and in all those who are faithful to his Way of the Cross.

22

THEOLOGY AND AUTOBIOGRAPHY*

A cynical appraisal of linking theology with autobiography would be: here we go again. After brief but intense affairs with secularity, play, and revolution, theology has found a new partner. This time the choice has been shrewd. It is not a fad or the burning concern of a burning few but an in-season, out-of-season bandwagon, the always-relevant, ever-fascinating *me*.

A more moderate and more accurate appraisal would be: linking theology and autobiography is the latest and most promising form of the general enterprise of relating theology to lived experience. Rationalism, ideas without discernible existential import, still plagues theology. The practical and unavoidable question of all theological activity is: "Does it make a difference? If so, how?" Despite a clear understanding of this problem and a firm resolve to do something about it, the gap between Christian existence and Christian theology remains. Wolfgang Beinert situates the problem historically.

Theology, once unified, divided into disciplines, and exegesis and dogmatics separated. Moral theology soon separated from dogmatics, asceticism and mysticism were assigned minor roles in priestly training. Great theologians were no longer saints and saints were no longer great theologians; sainthood was no longer a category in dogmatics. Theology degenerated into a mere school subject and Christian piety became a wilderness of indigestible fancies. Hence moderns think of Christianity as

*This article by John Shea is reprinted from the June 16, 1978 *Commonweal*.

a shallow and unbeneficial pursuit . . . ("Theology and Christian Existence," *Theology Digest,* Summer, 1977, pp. 105-106)

Contemporary theological activity is keenly aware that it is easier to run from rationalism than it is to actually arrive at life.

The drive to make theological reflection an integral component of the life process is more than a bid for popularity. It stems from faith's concern with the question of salvation. Faith's ambition and its natural home is to be where everything is at stake, where life hangs in the balance, where serious loss and gain are the outcome. Today the locale of salvation is not relegated to death and after-life possibilities. All of life is understood as an ongoing redemptive process. As such, faith seeks to be present and formative to the decisions that influence personal and social life. The person of faith is convinced that it makes all the difference. Theology is the effort to explain and explore this critical difference. It seeks to understand how faith and the symbols of faith enter into the transformation of human life.

The phrase "theology and autobiography" in the title of this article is not a strict designation. It does not mean a concentration on autobiography as opposed to biography, history, or myth. Rather it points to a series of ideas, side-by-side insights that cluster around the relationship between religious self-understanding and story forms. At any given moment we may be telling our own story or someone else's, the traditional stories of our community or of someone else's, a fictional blend or the closest we can come to hard fact, a mythic, apologetic, actional, satiric, or parabolic story (to use Crossan's distinctions); but no matter what the form of the story is, a similar process is at work. In the telling we ourselves are told.

The teller is present in his tale in at least two ways. Gertrude Stein has shrewdly observed:

> Everybody's life is full of stories: . . . They are very occupying, but they are not really interesting. What is interesting is the way everyone tells their stories. If you listen, really listen, you will hear people repeating themselves. You will hear their pleading nature or their attacking nature or their asserting nature.

More importantly, the content of the stories we choose to tell and retell betray the convictions, values, and conducts we prize and deplore. Storytelling seems to be a human activity which excludes disinterestedness. In fact, a recent approach to Christology attempts to study how the parables Jesus told reveal his identity. Since we are never far from our stories, our stories become a way of getting at us.

Not only the stories we tell but those we hear and read are often quickly translated into our own life situations. James Olney (*Metaphors of Self: The Meaning of Autobiography,* Princeton University Press, 1972) thinks that autobiography is the form of literature which "most immediately and deeply engages our interest." The reason for this is that "it brings an increased awareness, through an understanding of another life in another time and place, of the nature of our own selves and our share in the human condition." At least one reason why certain stories interest us is that they come close to home and yet are an invitation to journey. In other words, a story engages us because it is both similar and dissimilar. "A story . . . must reach me on some level to which I can respond, but it must also 'stretch' me, pull me beyond where I now am." (Robert McAfee Brown, "My Story and 'The Story' " *Theology Today,* July, 1975.) This perspective of approaching stories from the way they reflect and influence our self-understanding is not meant to reduce the many dimensions present in a story to the single dimension of self-reference. It is simply the recognition of the intense involvement of the self in the stories it tells and hears and the attempt to explore the nature and scope of that involvement.

This widened focus on autobiography is one of many avenues into the recent, vast, and highly diverse literature on theology and story. Some of the theologians who have contributed to this discussion are: R. Richard Niebuhr, John Dunne, Harvey Cox, Michael Novak, Sam Keen, James Wm. McClendon, Jr., Gregory Baum, Wesley Kort, John Navone, Robert McAfee Brown, Louis Cameli, Johann Baptist Metz, James Cone, Dominic Crossan, Amos Wilder, James Barr, Sallie TeSelle. (For an excellent survey from an academic viewpoint consult George W. Stroup, III "A Bibliographical Critique" *Theology Today,* July, 1975, pp. 133-143.) Some insights of the formation of the self through story are captured in key recurring themes, catch phrases which suggest the power and possibility of this approach.

1. The title of an article by Stephen Crites, "The Narrative Quality of Experience" *(Journal of the American Academy of Religion,* Vol. XXXIX, 1971), establishes the anthropological foundations for the relationship between religious self-understanding and story. All experience is inescapably temporal. Each moment is a "tensed unity" of past, present, and future. Therefore the linguistic form most appropriate to this basic given of human existence is narrative. In fact, in order for life to be creatively negotiated, a person must live out of a narrative infrastructure. Even philosophers like Sartre, who proclaim a meaningless existence where each moment is alien to every other, are secretly supported by a narrative pattern which enables them to courageously accept that existence. (Cf. John Haught, *Religion and Self-Acceptance,* Paulist Press, 1976, pp. 148-52.) Narrative is an inherent quality of experience and so a primal form of human discourse.

Dominic Crossan escalates the story form into a metaphysical principle. (*The Dark Interval,* Argus Press, 1976.) All is story. There is no reality which is independent of our constructive imagination. What we think is an objective description of what is "out there" is really a story, one possible way of imagining. Crossan emphasizes this point by contrasting the classical and modern mind-sets. The foundational story of the classical mind runs:

Once upon a time there were people who lived on rafts upon the sea. The rafts were constructed of materials from the land whence they had come. On this land was a lighthouse in which there was a lighthouse keeper. No matter where the rafts were, and even if the people themselves had no idea where they actually were, the keeper always knew their whereabouts. There was even communication between people and keeper so that in an absolute emergency they could always be guided safely home to land.

The modern version reads: "There is no lighthouse keeper. There is no lighthouse. There is no dry land. There are only people living on rafts made from their imaginations. And there is the sea." Crossan's conclusion is that "the classical mind says, that's only a story, but the modern mind says, there's only story."

The perspectives of Crites and Crossan attempt to rescue story from second-class intellectual citizenry. Story is not merely that inferior form which antedated the clarity and precision of conceptual thinking. Story is the continual and fundamental way humans appropriate encountered reality. Also story does not fade when speculation soars. On the contrary it both points the direction and sets the limits of thought. In the past theological rescues have often led to theological crownings. The last becomes first with remarkable regularity. Whether the case for story is overstated or not, it is compelling enough to pursue. After all, it does seem that we are all under the sentence of Scheherazade. We tell our stories to live.

2. Sam Keen's remark that "telling stories is functionally equivalent to belief in God" suggests an inescapable religious dimension to storytelling. (*To A Dancing God,* Harper and Row, 1970.) The very act of storytelling is an implicit affirmation of ultimate meaning. Storytelling raises a person out of the "randomness" of the moment and inserts him into a larger framework. It points to what is holy and sacred, which is now defined as "that irreducible principle, power, or presence which is the source and guarantor of unity, dignity, meaning, value and wholeness." Charles Winquist philosophically elaborates this insight by contrasting the act and content of storytelling. "What is absent in many modern stories is a *content* of positive affirmation. What is present even in relating a story of nothingness is a positive *act* of affirmation . . . . The escape from meaninglessness is achievable through the transcendence of act over content." ("The Act of Storytelling and the Self's Homecoming," *Journal of the American Academy of Religion,* Vol. 42, 1974.) True existential atheism is not telling a godless story but having no story to tell.

Keen volunteers his own story as an example of this "subterranean theology." As a small boy Keen watched his father carve a monkey from a peach seed. The boy asked for the "creation," but his father said that this one was for his mother; he would carve one for him later. Years passed and both father and son forgot the promise. Then one day in a conversation with his father Keen suddenly found himself saying, "In all that is important you have never failed me. With one exception, you kept the promises you made to me—you never carved me that peach-seed monkey." Not long after that conversation Keen received a peach-seed monkey in the mail. Not long after that his father died. "He died only at the end of his life." For Keen this story creates a world of promises made and kept. ". . . a peach-seed monkey has become a symbol of all the promises which were made to me and the energy and care which nourished and created me as a human being. . . . I discover a task for my future; being the recipient of promises, I become the maker of promises." The holy has been affirmed, not on the basis of scriptural or ecclesiastical authority, but in the development of Keen's own life story.

Keen developed his perspective in explicit dialogue with the death of God movement. Part of his agenda was to find an alternate religious language to God-language. In an atmosphere more amenable to God-language his maxim might easily be reversed—to tell a story of God is functionally equivalent to believing in the human person. Stories of God are not tales of a supernatural person but the way birth-and-death-bound people relate to the Mystery they find themselves within. To tell a story of God is to proclaim a pervasive purpose in which humankind shares. The immediate criticism is that stories of God are thieves of the human. They take what is finest about us and project it skyward. But once the interpenetration of the human and the divine (not their separation) is the context of the stories, their real meaning surfaces. The Christian stories of God include the ultimate worth and salvific possibilities of the human world.

3. "God made man because he loves stories" is the conclusion to Elie Wiesel's often quoted story about stories. Whenever misfortune threatened the Jews, Rabbi Israel Baal Shem Tov would retreat to the forest, light the fire, say the prayer, and the misfortune would be avoided. In the passing of time this task fell to a second Rabbi, who knew both the place in the forest and the prayer but not how to light the fire. Nevertheless the misfortune was avoided. A third Rabbi knew only the place: the prayer and the fire had been forgotten. But this too was enough and the misfortune was avoided. Finally the task fell to Rabbi Israel of Rizhyn, who knew neither the place nor the fire nor the prayer. All he could do was tell the story. "And it was sufficient."

Storytelling is more than a delightful and engrossing activity. From a religious perspective it is a redemptive undertaking. Stories are one way we come into contact with the ubiquitous yet elusive presence of the sacred. This contact is probably the ultimate reason why we "believe in" a story. It has, in some way, grasped us and mediated to us the power of the sacred. We find that in relating to reality through the story we are healed and renewed. This power of story to effect what it tells is captured in a delightful Hassidic tale passed on by Martin Buber.

> My grandfather was paralyzed. Once he was asked to tell a story about his teacher and he told how the holy Baal Shem Tov used to jump and dance when he was praying. My grandfather stood up while he was telling the story and the story carried him away so much that he had to jump and dance to show how the master had done it. From that moment, he was healed. This is how stories ought to be told.

4. One way of redemption through story is the interaction of personal experiences with the stories the community holds to be sacred. Elie Wiesel's own life travels this path. His most recent work, *Messengers of God,* is a reworking of the traditional Old Testament stories in the light of his own experience and a reappropriation of his own experience in the light of the traditional stories. His telling of the Isaac story is a case in point. Isaac, like Wiesel himself, is a survivor of a holocaust. God ordered his slaughter then relented. Yet the name Isaac means laughter. The story of Isaac is a tale of the affirmation of life in the face of the despair and nihilism of holocaust. As Wiesel tells the story, his own story is taken up and moved beyond madness and murder.

> Why was the most tragic of our ancestors named Isaac, a name which evokes and signifies laughter? Here is why. As the first survivor, he had to teach us, the future survivors of Jewish history, that it is possible to suffer and despair an entire lifetime and still not give up the art of laughter.
>
> Isaac, of course, never freed himself from the traumatizing scene that violated his youth; the holocaust had marked him and continued to haunt him forever. Yet he remained capable of laughter. And in spite of everything he did laugh.

As in any genuine dialogue both the communal and personal stories are transformed in the mutual process of listening and speaking.

A second example of the healing effects of relating personal and communal stories is John Haught's suggestion that the foundational Christian story can move us beyond self-deception. (To concretize this discussion consult Stanley Hauerwas and David Burrell, "Self-Deception and Autobiography: Theological and Ethical Reflection on Speer's *Inside the Third Reich," The Journal of Religious Ethics,* Spring, 1974.) Self-deception is one of the most baffling of human phenomena. Our desire to know ourselves as we really are is suppressed. This restriction of the drive to know is often the result of guilt. "The flight from insight into self would not occur did I not already somehow know that my actual condition is painfully distant from an ideal toward which I aspire but which I also seek to evade." In this situation we create cover stories which carefully screen out all input that does not reinforce them. One way beyond this torturous and self-defeating circle is to situate ourselves in the story of God's unconditional acceptance of humankind. Within this foundational narrative framework of acceptance the need for cover stories dissolves and the dynamic urge to know is released. The sacred story of the community becomes the freeing context for individual biographies.

5. "The long narrative corpus of the Old Testament seems to me, as a body of literature, to merit the title of story rather than that of history." (James Barr, "Story and History in Biblical Theology" *The Journal of Religion,* January, 1976, p. 5.) Statements like this indicate a revolution in the academic understanding of the sacred writings of Christianity. In the recent past the dominant method of investigation was historical. Did it really happen was the popular and insistent question. But the recognition of Scripture as basically a story form suggests a new approach. The guiding question becomes: what picture of self, others, nature, history, and God does the story suggest? This is part of Paul Ricoeur's meaning: "The sense of a text is not *behind* the text [its historical origins] but in front of it [the world it opens up]." The suggestion is that scripture is most adequately prosecuted by neither history nor science but by the quality of the world it creates, the dangers that lurk within that world, and the possibilities that world holds out.

Dominic Crossan has outlined five relationships between story and forms and our phenomenological world. These relationships are extremely helpful in understanding the story approach to religious self-understanding. "Myth establishes world. Apologue defends world. Action investigates world. Satire attacks world. Parable subverts world." Although all five story forms are found in scripture, myth and parable are particularly important.

A story functions mythically by structuring consciousness, encouraging attitudes, and suggesting behaviors. In the first moment the mythic story configures experience so that certain elements are highlighted. It calls attention to certain patterns present in the encountered reality and entices the person to relate to that reality through those patterns. In its second moment mythic stories embody and promote values. Donald Evans catches this aspect in the Christian creation myth.

In the biblical context, if I say 'God is my Creator' I acknowledge my status as God's obedient servant and possession, I acknowledge God's gift of existence, and I acknowledge God's self-commitment to me. *(The Logic of Self-Involvement,* London: SCM Press, 1963, p. 158.)

Finally, myth provides a broad directionality for action but not a guide to the complexities of concrete situation. To move within the myth of the loving God suggests a lifestyle of care but it does not assure the ability to care or the knowledge of what the "caring thing" is in any situation. A story functions mythically when it establishes the world in which we live and move and have our being.

Two recent attempts which trace concrete activity to its mythic foundations are Michael Novak's *"Story" in Politics* (The Council on Religion and International Affairs, 1970) and Stanley Hauerwas and Richard Bondi's "Memory, Community and the Reasons for Living: Theological and Ethical Reflections on Suicide and Euthanasia" (*Journal of the American Academy of Religion,* No. 44, Sept. 1976, pp. 439-452). Both articles emphasize that behavior cannot be fully comprehended apart from its underlying mythic story. Novak's suggestion is that the U.S. should understand the basic story it is working out of before making foreign policy decisions. Hauerwas and Bondi argue that the Christian story of life as a gift and our need to live in communities of trust create a world where euthanasia and suicide are alien choices. Mythically functioning stories are integral to self-understanding and activity.

Stories which function parabolically are not about the making of worlds but about the clash of worlds. Every attitude and behavior is grounded in a vision of reality. We work out of pre-conceptions, unexamined biases which both encourage and forbid. Parables take aim at these presuppositions and dominant directions. Their goal is subversion. They penetrate to the core of what we unquestionably hold and question it. For example, the parable of the Good Samaritan shatters the world of Jewish cultural expectation where every Samaritan is evil. In the shattering is the invitation to construct another world. (For an excellent survey of the history of parable research, which focuses on the story of the Good Samaritan, consult Norman Perrin, *Jesus and the Language of the Kingdom,* Fortress Press, 1976). In the Christian Scriptures stories function mythically to establish our powers and insights and parabolically to subvert our false consciousness and call us to "go beyond."

As with most new directions in theology each insight in the area of religious self-understanding and story forms raises multiple questions. If story is the linguistic form essential to temporal existence, how do we define it "clearly enough" to use it systematically? How is story related to concept? How should the various story forms be distinguished and discussed? How is a story verified or falsified? Telling a story may be an implicit affirmation of God but is it an adequate one? How does the reality of God explicitly influence our lives and how does God's language explicitly enter our stories? Isak Dinesen may say, "All sorrows can be borne if you put them into a story or tell a story about them," but how exactly does this healing go on? If it is not magic, we must explore how story reconciles the past, envisions the future, and redeems the present. The relationship between narrative and history in the Bible needs to be extensively explored. Some observers think that in the next thirty years literary criticism will have the same revolutionary impact that form redaction criticism has had in the last thirty years. What shape does the hermeneutical problem take when processed through story categories? How does scripture, if it does, function mythically and parabolically today? Theology, because it dwells on transcendence, atrophies on answers and thrives on questions. Religious self-understanding through story forms is a live option.

Although "theology and autobiography" has immense potential for the classroom (cf. Elena Malits, "Theology as Biography" *Horizons,* Vol. 1, No. 1, pp. 81-87), its natural environment is the grass roots community. Story is a perspective close enough to the street to be the way the "ordinary Christian" (non-professional theologians) reflects. In the parishes and neighborhoods life stories are unfolding in dialogue with each other and the larger Christian story. If the Christian peoples are to reflectively own their lives, this process must be articulated and celebrated. In the present situation theology cannot be done in the university and then passed on to the parish. Each community must relate its experiences to the Christian symbols and so tell their story for their time and place.

The relationship between ministry and theology has always been strained. Ministry appears concrete, action-oriented, practical. Theology appears speculative, couched in technical jargon, in many ways a private preserve. Yet from the perspective of story forms and religious self-understanding, ministry and theology are inseparably linked. The minister is the facilitator, catalyst, and resource for the ongoing story-telling process. (Cf. Louis Cameli, *Stories of Paradise: The Study of Spiritual Autobiographies and the Formation of Today's Stories of Faith,* Paulist Press, 1978.) He/she initiates the type of question or perception which will lead to a faith appropriation of their experiences. He/she helps the people hear and clearly articulate the religious, theological, and ecclesiological dimensions of their situation. He/she becomes a theological resource, relating the contemporary situation to Christian perspectives and values. This is the concrete way of Christian story-telling and a direction for pastoral theology.

The general area of "theology and autobiography" is rich in insights and possibilities. It will undoubtedly be developed in many directions. But perhaps its outstanding quality is one few associate with theology. It is interesting. Whitehead once remarked: "In the real world, it is more important that a proposition be interesting than that it be true. The importance of truth is that it adds to interest." The interest in who we are and what we must be about as we move through life and life moves through us is both a path to truth and the task that comes with breath. In Elie Wiesel's language: "When he opened his eyes, Adam did not ask God: 'Who are you?' He asked: 'Who am I?' "

23

CONTRIBUTORS TO A THEOLOGY OF STORY

Julian N. Hartt, in his book *Theological Method and Imagination* (New York: Seabury Press, 1977), argues that story is possibly the most effective way of expressing theological truths; however, he insists that the New Testament faith is not just a story. It is also a "strenuous effort" to show how the import of the story must be understood and, above all, made effective in one's life. That requires not only storytelling but serious theologizing. At the root of both is the human exigency to make sense of life. Narrative is an inherent quality of meaningful experience and so a primal form of human discourse with regard to our basic self-others, world-God relationship. Hartt is among the growing number of scholars who are attempting to build a bridge between our lived experience and theology, between our life stories and the Gospel story, the foundational story of Christian faith.

This chapter surveys what certain scholars are saying about the relationship of faith and theology to story; it surveys some of their insights into the formation of the self through story which suggest the power and possibility of this approach for enhancing our religious self-understanding.

Storytelling can be understood as a participation in several distinguishable, but interpenetrating, levels of meaning, communicating a fullness of cognitive, affective, and imaginational experience. Through stories we move in and out of worlds of meaning in a way that recalls what H. Richard Niebuhr wrote, over thirty years ago: "Man lives in two worlds and when he tries to make his home in one alone something goes wrong with him. Our race, like that of the migratory birds, cannot live and perform all its

240

functions in one climate but must undertake a periodic flight to another homeland." Indeed, says Niebuhr ". . . the life of man, the migratory being, into whose structure the law of a seasonal movement is written, is thwarted and distraught by confinement to one world, whether it be the world of sight or the realm of the spirit."[1]

Our stories reveal the quality of our lives: "An unhappy life is like a bad book," writes the English novelist Charles Morgan; "it runs hither and thither and carries within it no assurance of form. And the chief difficulty of living is the difficulty we all have in perceiving what the form of our life really is or indeed that it has a form." A bad book is structurally unsound, lacking the integrity of form and coherence; its author has failed to integrate in a reasonably satisfying way the components of his story. Such a book does not meet the exigencies of intelligence and reason. The same exigencies are criteria for judging the quality of the story which our life tells. We not only have histories; we are our histories, and we make our histories. Our individual stories, according to Mary McDermott Shideler, belong within the larger and longer stories of our families, societies, cultures, the human race, the divine order, and they are not always good as stories.[3] As human beings we are storymakers. Our stories are open-ended and must have continuity as well as coherence. We have liberty within the constraints of the tools of our lives, but we cannot control how and when the story ends. To live in the light of death is to live under the aspect of eternity and so we can contemplate the form of our lives.

1. JAMES WM. MCCLENDON JR.: BIOGRAPHY AND STORY

How life stories can remake today's theology is the theme of James Wm. McClendon's book *Biography as Theology*.[4] McClendon suggests that narrative or story is a means of expression uniquely suited to theology. Biography, a form of story, is in intention a true story. It occurs, according to McClendon, in earliest Christianity; the *Confessions* of Augustine, the *Acts* of the apostles and martyrs, and the various *Gospels* tell stories. If biographies are the smallest discrete units in which experience can be reported, experience is to be understood in the durational form of a narrative. McClendon believes that philosophers have perhaps misleadingly assigned a cognitive priority to the compressed, the non-durational, the abstracted products of actual and durational experience, when they have asked whether we can have an experience of God.[5] The life-experience of a religious person is understood better when it is treated as experience with God.

The current rebirth of interest in story and theology, the new openness to religious myth as an indispensable means of human expression, is based on the recognition that human experience necessarily has a narrative form.

Stephen Crites, for example, shows that the time-defying strategies of modern intellectual work (conceptual abstraction; phenomenological contraction of attention) cannot dispense with this necessary form, so that the "sacred stories" by which people live their lives are representative of the dwelling places of all human beings: we all live in some story or other.[6]

Every culture or tradition lives by the compelling stories of its heroes. The Church singles out some of its members as saints, as deserving special honor and emulation, because they are creative models of Christian life. They illuminate new ways of being Christian, new ways of accepting and understanding Christian life. Their lives awaken new insight into the values of their tradition. Biographical theology would seek to discover the features of such lives. The doctrine drawn from these life stories, if it is compelling, is so because of its prior embodiment in them.[7]

Biographical theology would investigate the images which give compelling Christian lives their characteristic flavor.[8] It would recognize the importance of certain "holy images" and their metaphoric force as a mode of inspiration. Different Christians are conditioned and formed by different sets of images within the larger manifold of their tradition. Biographical theology would attend to the images which converge in a particular life, shaping that life, and through that life exerting an impact on others. Lives are known through their dominant images linking them with their creative sources (their "scripture" and "tradition") and their creative possibilities (the influence these lives may have on the lives of others). Saints belong to communities of the past and shape communities of the future; their images are an important means of their communication. No life is lived without images and symbols; no life story can be understood adequately without attending to them. They are a clue to character; they help us to discover the vision, the central or formative convictions, of our subjects.[9] Their convictions are affective and volitional as well as cognitive. They represent the basic quality of the self's cognitive and affective involvement with the world. Autobiographical theology attends to convictions which govern particular lives and groups to discover which ones we must live by; such convictions about existence and reality will always be mediated by images and symbols.

For a biographical theology the center of attention must be the lives themselves, or more accurately, the impact of the life of Christ in those lives.[10] The stories of the saints' lives are understood as a part of the life of Christ. His life is the shared life of those he redeems. They are in Christ and Christ is in them (Gal. 1:22; Rom. 8:10). The saints' lives tell that story; hence, biographic theology must take account of the Church.

2. *John S. Dunne: Life Stories and Stories of God*

A search for God in time and memory carries John S. Dunne on quests and journeys through life stories, through ages of life, through stories of God.[11] Such a journey is compared to the writing of an autobiography or to the composition of a personal creed. Autobiographical writing brings time to mind. We begin by trying to recall in as much detail as possible our past. As we begin to articulate our past, we find that our story could be told in different ways, depending on the particular future we thought it was leading to. We would think of the possible relationships between our past and future. Unable to foresee the actual events of the future and to recall the entirety of the past, we should have begun to focus on our life as a whole, on all its dramatic elements: the plot, the characters, the thought content, the modes of expression, the setting. Examining the span from birth to death, we should be made to wonder how our life fits into our times, whether it is a typically modern life story. We might ask whether our life finds a parallel with other lives, how far it is our own story and how far it is the modern story.

Our composing a personal creed would set us searching for God in memory. We must consult our memory and our own anticipations to know what God really is to us, to know what we personally believe and act upon. We should ask ourselves about our mental image of God, what God once was to us, what he is to us, what we expect of him. We should ask about how happy or unhappy, how certain or uncertain, we are. We compare our findings with those of others. The pursuit of our own personal issues enhances our ability to appreciate other lives with a sympathetic understanding of them. We pass over from the standpoint of our life to those of others, finding resonances, and returning, enriched, to our own standpoint. Many things in our own life become known to us only when resonances of this kind are generated by the process of passing over, which tends to bridge the gap between personal and public knowledge by giving a personal seeking and finding something of the communicability of public knowledge. Such a process gives a wider context to questions that would be treated in an autobiography and in a personal creed.

Dunne considers what is involved in bringing the lifetime to mind both from a biographical and an autobiographical standpoint. With this background he passes over to the life of Jesus, going from the finished life described by the four Gospels to the unfinished life as it might have appeared to Jesus himself and his disciples before his death. Dunne then brings to mind "deathtime," the time encompassing the lifetime. He reconsiders the finished life of Jesus. Then he considers various historic forms which the life story has taken in the Christian era: first the story deeds in the New Testament, especially in the writings of Paul; then the story of experience in the *Confessions* of Augustine, the prototypical autobiography and classical model of the search for God in time and memory; and then the modern story of appropriation in the writings of Kierkegaard.

Dunne examines varieties of religious experience in life stories of the modern era from Luther to Kierkegaard; then he examines varieties of secular experience from Rousseau to Sartre. He relates these two kinds of experience to the disappearance of human mediators between man and God, the medieval "lords spiritual" and "lords temporal." Dunne takes a cue from Luther, who compares hell, purgatory and heaven to despair, uncertainty and assurance, in order to treat the modern cycle of religious experience as a kind of divine comedy, in which the modern seeks to find his way from the hell of despair and the purgatory of doubt to the heaven of assurance. Dunne deals with the cycle of secular experience by examining each of the ages of life as they appear in modern autobiography where childhood is more than the traditional prelude to the "years of discretion," where youth is prolonged beyond that in previous epochs, where manhood comes rather late in life, and where old age was a rare attainment in past history.

After examining the life stories, Dunne considers the stories of God told in the modern era. These are tales of how "once there was a God," "now there is no God," "someday God will be." Dunne seeks to discover what it is about the modern life story that makes the human lifetime seem a pause in God's time. He compares and contrasts with the God of Jesus, the God whom Jesus called "Abba," with the dark God in modern tales of God, the God hidden in the darkness, what it would be for a contemporary to relate to the dark God as Jesus related to Abba.

The hint to an answer to the question Dunne raises is found in Dunne's method of passing over by sympathetic understanding to others and coming back to a new understanding of ourselves. This method describes man's making contact with Jesus. By passing over, a man becomes a contemporary with Jesus, and by coming back to himself from this, Jesus in turn becomes contemporary with him. This is the way we discover the shape of the life story in other ages, the story of deeds, and the story of experience, and coming back from this to our own time is how we discover by contrast its current shape, the story of appropriation. Dunne believes that this is how the modern epoch makes up for the loss of spiritual and temporal mediation, for passing over to others makes them mediators between ourselves and God, and yet coming back to ourselves from them places us once again in the modern situation of unmediated existence. Passing over avails us of the time and memory of others, and coming back leaves us our own time and memory enriched. In this process we go from man's time and time of life stories, to God's time, the greater and encompassing time which is that of the stories of God, and we experience companionship with God in time. Thus searching through time and memory, we discover in this the greater dimensions of man, those which reach beyond the self and the individual life story, and become aware of the compassionate God and Savior underlying all.

In his first book *The City of the Gods,*[12] Dunne was engaged in passing over to cultures where he compared cultures in terms of their answers to death. Dunne's concern with death led him to an interest in the life story in *A Search for God in Time and Memory,* where he studied the different standpoints, biographical and autobiographical, from which a life can be understood. He became engaged in passing over to lives. In his book *The Way of All the Earth,*[13] Dunne becomes engaged in passing over to other religions where the influence of the first and second phases appear in his effort to correlate the life story and the story of mankind.

3. ROSEMARY HAUGHTON: THE DRAMATIC STORY OF SALVATION

Storytelling has a dramatic quality, for action is always a part of a story. Our actions tell a story and take place through a form which narrative consciousness attempts to represent. Action, the structuring of our present and future relations, is at the heart of the dramatic story which faith tells. Rosemary Haughton recognizes the dramatic quality of the story of salvation in her book, *The Drama of Salvation,* where she seeks to clarify what we mean by "salvation."[14] Her study of drama is a means of exploring this basic tenet of Christianity. She incorporates her insights under the chapter headings of "The Raw Material; The Play; The Role; Actors, Audience and Language; The Denouement." She affirms that the stories of life, death, and eternity can be saving statements only when dramatized. By showing the inherent nature of drama as something happening in, to, and between people, she tries to help us understand that the very nature of salvation is something inexpressible, yet dramatically ever-present. She leads us through the process of experiencing the meaning of salvation by way of the dramatic form, and the dynamics of action.

Without stories there is no knowledge of the world, of ourselves, of others, and of God. Our narrative consciousness is our power for comprehending ourselves in our coherence with the world and other selves; it expresses our existential reality as storytelling and storylistening animals, acting and reacting within our particular world context, overcoming the incoherence of the unexamined life. One man's story is another man's point of departure. We live on stories; we shape our lives through stories, mastering the complexity of our experience through the dynamic of our structured knowing, a whole whose parts involve many distinct and irreducible activities: seeing, hearing, smelling, touching, tasting, inquiring, imagining, understanding, conceiving, reflecting, weighing the evidence, judging.[15]

4. WILLIAM F. LYNCH: STORIES AS IMAGES OF FAITH

The work of William F. Lynch reminds us that the way we imagine faith conditions our understanding of the stories of faith. Every story is a story of faith if we imagine faith as the most primary and elemental force in human nature, a force which precedes what we ordinarily call knowledge and all the forms of specific knowing, a force that is uneducated and needs education by knowledge of every kind, by people to every degree, and ultimately by Christ.[16] This primal, powerful, turbulent and broad force of belief, according to its goodness or falseness, shapes or mis-shapes the lives of persons and society. This force, together with the powerful experiential elements that belong to it, should be imagined as moving historically into and up to a religious context, taking on the form of religious stories, especially under the educating action of the promises of God and the reactions of men.[17] It remains integral to religious faith as its body.

Faith is a central force which grounds all human culture and knowledge. There is no human life without beliefs, orientations, and expectations. Faith precedes knowledge, providing a structure or a context or a paradigm within which we experience or imagine the world.[18] To imagine the world is to experience it. Faith, as a way of imagining the world, is also a way of experiencing it. Faith has an identity and seeing power of its own as a world within which we imagine or experience. The form that our imagining takes is of crucial importance. The way we imagine anything is exactly what leads to the creation or the solution of a question. The forms that our faith takes determine the quality of our lives at every level. There are no pure appearances or pure facts uncolored by the way we imagine and the way we believe. There is no pure image or pure experience into which the whole of ourselves does not enter. Our imagining and thinking fills our basic images of God, man, woman, child, death, home, friend, enemy, here, ourselves, mother, father, and so on.[19] We give an enormous content to the image of one we especially love, to the image of what we especially value.

The Gospel story of Christ is imagined and experienced differently. It meets with varying degrees of acceptance, rejection, and indifference. Even though it educates the broad primal faith of those who accept it, the quality of its impact will vary. Despite discernible regularities, Christians imagine Christ differently. William Lynch implies this with his fundamental understanding of imagination as referring to the total resources in us which go into the making of our images.[20] These include all our faculties, all our resources, not only our seeing and hearing and touching but also our history, our education, our feelings, our wishes, hopes, aspirations and dreams, love, hate, faith and unfaith. Our simplest images are complicated. Nothing comes nearer to defining persons than their images of God, of the world, of others. We define ourselves by the content we give our images, by our imaginations, by the way our primal faith experiences and imagines the world and its particulars. We are not without responsibility for our images and the content which we have given them. One group has a way of imagining another group. There is no pure image (fact, story, experience) unqualified by abstraction or thought or context or attitude or faith.[21]

Faith generates and demands active imagining: "it is always asking us to put the expected (of the promise of God) together with the historical forms of the unexpected."[22] Through its ironic imagination, faith is able to recognize the relationship between the promise and the apparently contrary form in which the promise is realized. It knows that the promises will be kept, even if it does not know in what form. Christ's irony re-imagines our poverty, weakness, and suffering. It is to these weak parts of ourselves that his promises are made and his revelation is given. Christ redeems us by transforming our images of these parts in ourselves, this weakness, suffering and death.[23]

The story which Christ's life tells communicates the central force of his faith's radically new way of imagining and experiencing the world.[24] Christ re-imagines, re-views, re-cognizes, and re-patterns Israel's image of the world (of God, of ourselves and our relationships). The whole of Christ gets into his image of the world (of God, of himself, of life, of death, of the past, of the future, and so on). Christ's radical re-imagining of the world expresses the power and quality of his faith. The existence of the Christian community is evidence of its creative, revitalizing, liberating and enlightening impact; is evidence of Christ's new way of imagining and experiencing the world.

The Gospel writers communicate the world which Christ has re-imagined; they communicate the richness of content that he has given basic human images. To retell the story of Christ is to re-imagine it. The whole of the Gospel writer gets into the images of the story that he tells. There is a way in which he embodies it before he writes it. Because his faith is embodied, it is imaginable. The story that Christ's life tells activates the Gospel writer's imagination. His retelling of the story is directed to making active imaginers out of us, implicitly inviting us to put the whole of ourselves into Christ's image of the world and to make the content of that image our own. We are invited to share the same dynamic orientation that was Christ's creative way of imagining and experiencing the world; we are invited to accept his story as the structure or context for our faith's imagining and experiencing the stages of life as we move through the finite, the definite and the detailed in quest of insight, understanding or vision. We do not grasp the significance of faith's experience apart from the shape and content of our images. We are unable to grasp the real possibilities for hope, reconciliation and conversion apart from faith's re-imagining, re-viewing, re-cognizing and re-patterning the images present to our consciousness.

The meeting of the ordinary and the unexpected which characterizes God's words is a pattern of every good story. William Lynch's notion of the ironic quality of faith's imagination helps to explain the meeting of the ordinary and the unexpected in stories of faith.[25] He explains that irony deals with the very opposite of appearances, and that its main task is to keep opposites together in a single act of the imagination (or story). Thus if we ask what is power and who has it, appearances will say that the powerful have power. The ironic imagination of faith, on the other hand, in the sermon on the mount in the Gospel of St. Matthew says the opposite. Faith's stories move below appearances into existence. The usual quality of irony is the unexpected coexistence, to the point of identity, of certain contraries.[26] The irony of faith's stories recognizes that those who, at least at heart, are spiritually free of this world's enormous goods possess forms of real power and freedom.

5. JOHN DRURY: THE SPIRIT OF STORYTELLING

In his article, "The Spirit of Storytelling," John Drury affirms that we live on stories.[27] Our appetite for them is the same as that of our ancestors. Drury relates this appetite to Scripture's affirmation that we do not live by bread alone, but by every word that proceeds from the mouth of God. Our appetite for stories derives from the Creator. As storylistening and story-telling beings, we have a created appetite for God's words, for the stories that he tells in the lives of others. It is an appetite for news from elsewhere which shows us our way about in the here and now, a conjunction of the strange and the familiar. It can hardly be a coincidence, Drury concludes, that these divine messages or signals are for ever taking the form of stories.[28] Religions abound in stories of faith. The story of Jesus is the central message of the Christian faith, and this story has the character of Good News for everyone, a new story that is good news, the Gospel. And since God does not confine his activities to the religious sphere, Drury believes that it is more than likely that he speaks to his secular children through the stories which are as essential to their life as bread.[29]

6. JAMES BARR: THE BIBLE READ AS STORY

A key concept of biblical theology is that of revelation in history: The locus of divine revelation lies in the events of the history of Israel as recorded in the Old Testament. James Barr examines this concept and concludes that the Old Testament should be read as story, not as history.[30] The long narrative corpus of the Old Testament merits the title of story rather than that of history; put another way, it seems to merit entirely the title of story but only in part the title of history. Barr believes that the basic revelation of God, in the sense of the initiation of communication between God and man, is not in the Bible, nor narrated in the Bible, but is presupposed by the Bible. From the beginning it assumes that we know who God is and that he is in communication with man. What we learn about God in the Bible is not the first contact with deity, it is new information about a person whom we already know.[31]

The Bible, read as story, serves as a means of expressing — revealing — revelation, though indirectly it can be said that the Bible (story) is the locus of revelation, for it is the expression which the Israelite tradition has in fact formed, the way in which it wants to speak on the basis of that which it has heard and learned. This would imply that the reading of the story is the way to meet the God whom they met, and this might mean that the explication of the story for itself, as a story, is the right form for biblical theology.[32]

7. C. S. LEWIS: STORIES OF LONGING FOR GOD

The true beauty of Northern and Mediterranean myths enthralled C.S. Lewis, who maintained that the *mythos* of the New Testament transposed their best visions into another key.[33] In Lewis' mythopoeic novel *The Last Battle,* the noble worshipper of a pagan god discovers in a moment of apocalyptic revelation that all along he has actually worshipped Aslan, the divine lion, without knowing the real name. For Lewis there are no immediate experiences of God, for all we know of him is mediated through some created thing: people, stories, symbols, images, history, ritual.[34] The excellence of the creature is evidence of the Creator. In *Arthurian Torso,* Lewis affirms that "Every created thing is, in its degree, an image of God, and the ordinate and faithful appreciation of that thing is a clue which, truly followed, will lead us back to him."[35] Lewis' faith imagined and experienced the world as the reflection of its creator, bidding us through the concreteness and particularity of creation to be one with him. As Lewis puts it in a paragraph which he pencilled on a fly-leaf of his copy of von Hügel's *Eternal Life:*

It is not an abstraction called humanity that is to be saved. It is you . . . your soul, and, in some sense yet to be understood, even your body, that was made for the high and holy place. All that you are . . . every fold and crease of your individuality was devised from all eternity to fit God as a glove fits a hand. All that intimate particularity which you can hardly grasp yourself, much less communicate to your fellow creatures, is no mystery to him. He made those ins and outs that he might fill them. Then he gave your soul so curious a life because it is the key designed to unlock that door, of all the myriad doors in him.[36]

Lewis believes that all our storytelling of Shangri-La, El Dorado, Narnia, and the like, are splashes of Godlight in the dark wood of our life.[37] These stories are evidence of that object of our longing which really exists and is really drawing us to itself.[38] These stories imply a faith imagining and experiencing the possibility of this world's ultimate fulfillment.

8. J. R. R. TOLKIEN: THE CHRISTIAN STORY AS EUCATASTROPHE

The Christian story, according to J.R.R. Tolkien, is the greatest possible news.[39] The Gospels contain a fairy-story which, Tolkien affirms, embraces the essence of fairy-stories.[40] They contain many marvels, including the greatest and most complete eucatastrophe: "the good catastrophe, the sudden joyous 'turn' . . . a sudden and miraculous grace."[41] The Christian story has entered history and the primary world; the desire and aspiration of sub-creation (storymakers are "sub-creators") has been raised to the fulfillment of creation.[42] The birth of Christ is the eucatastrophe of man's history. The resurrection is the eucatastrophe of the story of the incarnation. This story begins and ends in joy. It has pre-eminently the "inner consistency of reality."[43] There is no story ever told that men would rather find was true, and none which so many sceptical men have accepted as true on its own merits. The story which Christ's life and the Gospels tell possesses the storymaker's excellence which enables that state of mind called "willing suspension of disbelief."[44] God is implicitly compared to a storymaker, whose divine art in telling his story in Christ enables us to suspend our disbelief and willingly accept and enter into the Secondary World where the magic spell of his authentic presence is experienced. Unbelief inhabits the Primary World and looks at the Secondary World from outside. The eucatastrophe of the Christ story is the ultimate possibility for the storytelling and storylistening animal that is man. The archetypal fairy-tale, the story that God tells in Christ, is the most beautiful, moving and significant experience open to man. God calls all men to make a "willing suspension of disbelief" in order to enjoy the full impact of his storytelling. His storytelling is an invitation to enter into a new world of conscious cognitive and affective experience. Tolkien implies that we experience the Primary World at its deepest level only when we have made the willing suspension of disbelief whereby we enter into the wonderful and gracious Secondary World where the Gospel story is heard and believed. This is the world of deeper knowledge and clearer vision where the Holy Spirit guides the sons and daughters of God (Rom. 8:14).

9. MICHAEL NOVAK: RELIGIOUS STUDIES AND STORY

Michael Novak intends his book *Ascent of the Mountain, Flight of the Dove* to serve as an introductory text to the field of religious studies, which he describes as "a full articulation, through systematic, historical and comparative reflection, of a person's way of life.''[45] Novak believes that all persons have religious experiences or a religious drive which seeks the underlying meaning which alone can give sense and provide order to the myriad actions and activities each person performs through his daily life. This basic drive pervades all our other drives, interests and desires. Religious studies attempt to come to grips with all integrative world views, especially those with explicit reference to the divine. Religion, for Novak, is the acting out of a vision of personal and human community; it is constituted by the most ultimate, least easily surrendered, most comprehensive choice a person or society acts out. Religion is the living out of an intention, an option, a selection among life's possibilities.

Religion is related to story: a narrative that links sequences, a structure for time which links actions over time. Every life tells a story; to act is to be the author of a life story. We are born into a culture that has its own stories and we grow up among persons who possess their particular stories. Our life stories, however unique, are linked to and conditioned by these encompassing stories; in fact, they cannot be told without them. Myth, when speaking of others, is a set of stories, images, and symbols by which human perceptions, attitudes, values, and actions are given shape and significance; however, when we speak of our own culture, the ordinary sense of reality performs the same function. Although we inherit the myths of our culture, we need never be completely or greatly inhibited by it; we are able to discard these myths in the selection of our own desired and much preferred values. Inasmuch as we are capable of selecting and choosing, so too we carry the responsibility to become conscious of the story we are actually living.

Self-knowledge, Novak finds, resembles ignorance more than knowledge. The more I try to understand who I am, the more I become a mystery to myself. Ambiguities, perplexities, contradictions—all tend to frustrate my self-understanding; still, I manage to form some image of myself, which serves as a guide to my self-identity. The image, or self-interpretation, can become subject to growth, mutation, and change. Self-deception may enter into our lives; nevertheless, tragedy, calamity, or necessity challenge us to recognize the truth of ourselves. Unexpectedly, our genuine convictions emerge for all to witness.

Though some would say religion is believing in doctrines, Novak believes that it seems better to envision religion as the telling of a story with one's life; for there are countless ways of living out the same doctrines. Action defines a person's story. In this weak sense every person is religious. The completed lives of persons trace out a story, whose implications reveal what they took the world in which they lived to be, who they thought they were, and what in their actions they actually cared about.

Action is a declaration of faith, implicitly revealing our way of imagining the shape of the world, its ultimate purpose, the significance of our own role. We act before we are clear about our ultimate convictions. Our actions, reflected upon, reveal what we really care about more accurately than our words or aspirations we should like to care about. Action reveals being. For Novak, I am what I do.

"Religious" has, therefore, two different senses. In its most neutral sense, it means that a life story is a declaration of identity, significance, role, place: all action is the living out of a story in a cosmos. In its second, more normative sense, religion is the awareness of the story dimension of life: it is an awe, reverence, wonder at the risk of human freedom. It is the awakening from the merely routine, pragmatic round of actions to a sense of being responsible for one's identity and the involvement with the identity of others. Therefore, the two basic religious questions for Novak are: Who am I? Who are we, we human beings?

A third interpretation of the word "religious" exists. Not only does a person live out a story, not merely is he aware of the alternatives which he is choosing, but he also adds a religious interpretation to what each and others are doing. Each person interprets the operations each is performing (of wonder, inquiry, commitment, longing) as signs that each of us is in the presence of God. We address the moving power and presence of existence as "thou." We see the world in the metaphor of persons, rather than things. We place the name or the letters of God to this Thou (un-nameable, but known in the same way).

Although this third meaning is often taken to be the traditional meaning of religious, Novak suggests that it is wiser to take the first meaning as our basic term, where in fact persons live out a commitment, select their own identity. In religious studies, one ought to study all such possibilities, including the un-reflected, self-satisfied, pragmatic one. These people raise no metaphysical questions; in one sense, they live in a pre-religious state; in any case, each person can become aware of the story each is telling with his life. Without this self-awareness, religious studies are pointless.

To uncover our life story we ask: What are the experiences of my life which, when I look back upon them, most tell me who I am? This emphasis on experience is important because the original fullness often lies buried in memory and the search for the self takes place largely through memory.

In summary, to tell a story with one's life is simply to act. One may be the author or reader; creating it, shaping it, or looking back afterward. It is well to remember also that the image of the story in our consciousness may not be like what we are actually living out. The more integrated a life, the more the complexity of elements within it work toward a single direction.

A story not only links actions, it also recounts a struggle. The key struggle of life is psychic transformation: a breakthrough in the way one perceives events, imagines oneself, understands others, grasps the world, acts. A story, therefore, links transformations and standpoints (the subjective context in which a view is held, the orientation of a person at a given point in time). A standpoint, more concretely, is a complex of past experiences, a range of sensibilities, purposes, structures, passions, judgments, values, goals, decisions.

Underlying all propositions are frameworks of experience, imagination, and remembered or projected action. Wisdom, the ability to go to the heart of the matter in concrete situations, is a discipline of experience, imagination, and story; it is acquired slowly.

The drive in us to move from standpoint to standpoint in our quest for broader and deeper understanding gives birth to Novak's metaphor of ascending the mountain. From each new height a new viewpoint is realized, more comprehensive, from a different angle, of fresh clarity. The climbing requires determination, will, endurance, patience, steady efforts. However, effort is not everything; for life is also grace and gift. Novak reminds us that so many of the best, deepest, and most important turns in our lives were not exactly of our own choosing and effort, but came to us as gift: "the flight of the dove."

Novak identifies two types of story, the descriptive and the critical. We can use the category story in a descriptive way (every person who has ever lived a story) or in a critical way (we can ask, have I found the story that is most appropriate to my own possibilities?). Am I being true to myself, to my times, to my possibilities? My life story ought to be proper to me and no one else. It ought to be appropriate to my times and to my own best possibilities. There are suitable (true) and unsuitable (false) stories to live out. We may judge our sense of reality to be inadequate, our life to be false. Our actions have within them an implicit story of the world, implicit ontological choices. For those who are religious, the world is interpreted as in some way personal, some way a conversation between human persons and the Thou. The religious person does not imagine himself to be the central point even of his own universe; he struggles to discern what is intended for him, for the achievement of his true life story as grace and demand, as divine gift and human effort.

10. JOHN SHEA: ENVIRONMENTS AND FEELINGS OF A LIFE STORY.

John Shea's book, *Stories of God* (Chicago: Thos. More Press, 1978), explores the basic contours and substratum of story. The human life story unfolds in the rich and intricate interweaving of the self and its multiple environments. A common set of environments forms the context of every life story: (1) the self, our most immediate environment; (2) family and friends, the primary locale of human development; (3) society and institutions; (4) the non-human universe, the physical environment influencing our psychic make-up. Human experience is the reciprocal flow between the self and its environments; it is interpreted according to the symbolic structures of our mind, according to principles and patterns of interpretation which the input of our environments suggests. Because of the dynamic interrelating of human experience, it is misleading to speak of the merely subjective or strictly objective.

Shea does not limit human experience to what the senses are capable of delivering; rather, he understands it as the pervasive atmosphere of all human development. The human person could be defined as the sum of his experience, the complex of his relationships with his own self, others, society, and the universe. The relationships with our environments are not 'something' we have, but 'something' through which we come to be; they are constitutive of our life stories, of who we are, not extras which we could well do without.

There is a very distinctive and important More, another relatedness to human experiencing. This is not a fifth environment, but a dimension present and available in every environment. It is not experienced separately, but is encountered as the depth of every interaction of the self with its environments. It has been called the Transcendent, the Ultimate, the Sacred, the More, and so on. Our words do not so much define it as acknowledge its presence. This transcending yet permeating reality is the dimension of Mystery.

Feeling is the way that we perceive Mystery; it is both cognitive and affective. A popular misunderstanding reduces it to emotionality. Feeling perceives Mystery by participation; it is the way that the total person appropriates Mystery as the ground of value and as the ultimate context in which the particular meanings of our life necessarily subsist. We are intimately involved with Mystery as the permeating context of our being and activity. Our awareness of that involvement comes through a feeling perception which engages the entire person. There can be no observing of Mystery from outside our environments because there is no outside that can serve as a vantage point for a better look. Our awareness of Mystery is always and inevitably from within.

Our felt relationship to Mystery is ambiguous: "Our dwelling with Mystery both menacing and promising, is a relationship of exceeding darkness and undeserved light. In this situation and with this awareness . . . we gather together and tell stories of God to calm our terror and hold our hope on high."[46] At other times, we feel that Mystery either grounds or undermines our deepest hopes and loves.

11. STANLEY HAUERWAS: THE NORMATIVE FORCE OF NARRATIVE

The narrative of story, according to Stanley Hauerwas, is a means of expression uniquely suited to Christian theology in order to remind us of the inherently practical character of theological convictions.[47] A story is a narrative account that binds events and agents together in an intelligible pattern and is a form of understanding that is indispensable for understanding ourselves. If we are to learn to speak of God, Hauerwas believes that we must learn to speak of him in stories and to do it truthfully.

Hauerwas illuminates the meaning of an authentically Christian life story in terms of the formation of character.[48] He affirms that any fundamental change in the nature of the self can be understood as a change in character. Such a change means that our behavior and action are formed and directed by certain fundamental beliefs and reasons rather than others. To have one's character formed as a Christian is not different from having one's character formed as a non-believer. The difference, according to Hauerwas, is not in how one's character is formed but in the actual orientation the Christian's character assumes because of the particular content of that which qualifies his agency. To be a Christian is to have one's character determined in accordance with God's action in Jesus Christ. The determination, Hauerwas concludes, gives one's life an orientation which otherwise it would not have; it marks a real change in our mode of being and existence. To be so qualified cannot be translated into a particular set of actions to be followed, though it may conclude such actions; rather Hauerwas characterizes it as an orientation that gives direction to our mode of being (agency) by ordering that which we do and do not do. Such an orientation has substance inasmuch as it is formed from our beliefs, reason, and action, interacting to give our life order and moral substance. Loyalty to God's act in Jesus Christ implies the actual determination of our agency and the kind of person we become as a result.

In *Truthfulness and Tragedy* Hauerwas develops the notion of story as an analytic tool for locating major problems with the standard account of moral rationality represented by the philosophical version of the narrative which has dominated Western culture since the Enlightenment: the story of the solitary individual confronting decisions equipped only with the power of free choice.[49] Hauerwas employs the notion of story for determining which narrative or set of narratives has normative force for the stories which engage the lives of the individuals and communities. He suggests that such normative force should be connected with the possibility of making claims to truth for the distinctive shape and commitments of Christian life. The narrative that has normative force for the stories of Christians, that which shapes Christian convictions, is that of God's dealing with his people in both Covenants. The truth of this narrative is a normative force in the lives of those whose convictions are actually being shaped by it.

12. DAVID TRACY: THE CATEGORY OF THE CLASSIC

Certain stories are classics. David Tracy defines a classic as any text, event or person which unites particularity of origin and expression with a disclosure of meaning and truth available, in principle, to all human beings.[50] A classic, as distinct from a period piece, is always public, never merely private. Tracy holds that most public statements achieve their public character by providing arguments, evidence, warrants that, in principle, are available to all reasonable persons. A claim to public status is ordinarily vitiated by claims to purely personal belief, taste, preference, or opinion. Although we know that someone holds to a particular belief, we do not know why we should share that meaning if the speaker does not provide recognizably public argument for his audience.

A classic contains three major components: (1) a major expression of one person's experience and understanding. That person may be expressing principally a new and highly individual experience and set of meanings or may, as a social self embedded in a particular community or tradition, be expressing principally that tradition's experience and self-understanding. (2) If the experience and self-understanding are sufficiently intense and integral and, (3) if a mode of expression (whether it be a text, gesture or style of life) be found appropriate to express the experience and its meaning, then a classic expression does occur.

There exist in our history, Tracy maintains, classic texts, events and persons — the saints and witnesses — which we must always retrieve through new interpretations. For the Christian theologian there exists, above and beyond even our greatest classics, the classical text, event, and person — Jesus as the Christ. When Christian theologians announce that the Scriptures are the ultimate norm of Christian theology, they mean, Tracy believes, that all the Christian classic texts are finally to be judged by that one classic text. When we reflect upon all the classic events and persons of Christian history, we also recognize that the event of the person of this Jesus as the Christ, the event of this proclamation of Jesus Christ as Lord must be and remain the classic, the decisive and public, manifestation of reality. For the Christian that text, event and person speaks what truly lies immeasurably high above us — the reality of the mystery of God as Pure Unbounded Love and Power; the reality of the radical call to a life of authentic humanity — a life of love; the reality of the manifestation that the final power with which we must deal is, in fact, neither cosmic speculation, nor anxiety, nor sentimental journeys, nor death, nor sin itself, but the unyielding, gracious power of that love.

The personal intensity of the experience of that love within the Christian community implies a unity of order which is analogous, not univocal or equivocal, and which encourages members to help one another in finding the proper genre — the form of a style of life — which can somehow manifest the meaning of that love which lies for each of us immeasurably higher than we dare to imagine, and which resonates to the fundamental law of our true self.[51] Tracy believes that if each of us can encourage the rest of us, in the power of that love, to find one's own proper genre with the dual risk of a personal intensity and a drive to genuine publicness, then the disclosive and transformative meaning and truth of Christianity will produce more classics — more texts, more events, more persons — that will, by their own dynamism, leave the realm of the private and enter that of the public.

13. THEODORE W. JENNINGS: STORY AS PATTERN OF PARTICIPATION IN THE WORLD

A specifically human existence entails consciousness, a way of being characterized by participating in, but also by transcending, the surrounding world. Through storytelling we express our patterns of participation in and our transcendence of circumambient reality. Theodore W. Jennings affirms that our reflection upon that world is conditioned by and grounded in the images and symbols whose meaning emerges within the structure of our stories.[52]

Faith also has its stories, with their images and symbols, to express its consciousness of the sacred presence by virtue of which all the dimensions of our existence have significance and value. Faith tells stories which express the relationship of our experience to the generative power from which it springs and to which it owes its existence. Faith narrates its interpretation of human existence. Through the concreteness of its imagery and the universality of its intention, the story which faith tells makes a claim on its audience to understand its existence and the world in a particular way. The storytelling of faith seeks to express and make effective the presence of the sacred in such a way as to represent, orient, communicate, and transform the existence of the world.[53]

The stories which faith tells are answers to basic questions about the purpose of life and of the world. They situate us within a pattern of meaning interpretative of life and death, nature and history, work and play, individual and community. They orient our lives, appealing to every level of our existence in order to recreate an experience like that which led to the creation of the story. They express insights into the fundamental images and symbols of our experience; they are concretized expressions of a vision of reality and of an affective response to reality.

14. ANDREW GREELEY: EXPERIENCED MEANING AS KEY TO STORY

The stories which faith tells us are not fully understood until their meaning is experienced. They bear on our existence and cannot be grasped unless they are embodied. As David Burrell says, "Before we can possess what we have glimpsed, we must undertake a style of life which embodies some of the syntax of the new language adumbrated in the original insight."[54] The storytelling of faith presupposes the unity of thought with life, of language and belief with personal, public existence; it functions to open the multiple dimensions of our lives to the fullness of their potentialities before God.

Our religious knowledge, according to Andrew Greeley, is first expressed in dense, complex, multi-layered, polyvalent symbols, pictures, rituals and stories.[55] Creed, code and cult flow from the basic world-view, the fundamental interpretative scheme, expressed at this primal level of our consciousness. Our intuition of the real is the primal and revelatory religious phenomenon which gives rise to the religious symbols and stories which ground creed, code and cult. We reflect on the meaning of faith's stories and symbols only after we have lived the renewed life which they have communicated. Our reflection seeks to explain what the religious experience, embodied in the story and in our lives, really means. Theological reflection derives from experiences which reveal to us the world of meaning beyond the everyday, the world which gives rise to the stories of faith, and to the images and symbols which mediate their meaning for the fullness of our experience.

The stories which faith tells speak to us at many levels because they are in experience and a record of an experience with meaning for every dimension of human existence; they concern that reality which originates and sustains everything that is and will be, which intersects with every level of human consciousness and imagination. These stories are open-ended because they have an unspecified number of potentialities for articulation left for us to explore in emerging situations and contexts. We cannot, however, arbitrarily read meanings into them and claim to have the same or basically similar experience as that of the author, his tradition and community. The stories are not merely conceptual propositions; rather, they record an experience which can bring new illumination. This happens only when our experience shares an historical, psychological and existential continuity with the original experience which gave birth to the religious stories and symbols. It is also possible to receive illuminations from the religious stories and symbols that were but dimly perceived or not perceived by those who first had the experience.[56]

Religious symbols and stories are addressed to the whole person: heart, head, imagination and feelings. They appeal to that realm of being where we know affectively. What Archibald MacLeish has written about poems in this respect applies equally to religious symbols and stories: "no man who comes to knowledge through a poem leaves the feel of what he knows behind, for the knowledge he comes to is the knowledge of that *feeling life* of the mind which comprehends by putting itself in the place where its thought goes — by realizing its thought in the only human realizer — the imagination."[57] And to the degree that we achieve such realization, we have initiated a new self-understanding and thus acquired that margin of transcendence towards a fuller humanity which the religious story compels us to "try out." We are unable to give full assent to the possibilities religious stories present to us unless they are commensurate with our deepest sense of ourselves. Religious stories invite us to extend our sensibilities, to share some intuition about what constitutes the ground of experience and its vital possibilities, to consider what is beyond the limits of immediate perception.

Religious stories and symbols mediate a form of otherness, a sense of things not quite our own, which nevertheless resonates with our sense of what the nature and meaning of human existence really is.[58] They present the possibility of wholeness and redemption from the hell of self-division through reunification with the ground and substance of our being and the being of All That Is.

15. T. PATRICK BURKE: THE THEOLOGIAN AS STORYTELLER

Relating theology to lived experience, T. Patrick Burke offers three theses concerning the nature of theology: (1) In general, theology has been the translation of a story into philosophy in order to preserve the story, which is thought to be necessarily meaningful. (2) This procedure is not defensible, for it subverts both story and philosophy, and the meaningfulness of a story depends on other assumptions. (3) A theology will best serve its tradition not by determinedly ascribing meaning to it, but by evaluating it critically in the light of experience.[59]

Burke criticizes a traditional conception of theology: the starting point of theology is loyalty to a particular tradition which at all costs must be preserved. With the Semitic religions the essential tradition is a story. Burke believes that the assumption is mistaken that a story can be the foundation on which a religion rests. If the story is thought of as in some sense historical, then a special divine significance is ascribed to a past event. But Burke holds that such an ascription is always an act of interpretation, and the basis for the interpretation can only lie in the present, in our personal experience. It is our interpretation of our own experience of life that provides what Burke believes to be the foundation for our interpretation of history; consequently, we can understand the past only out of the present in which we stand.

If the story is regarded as a myth, and therefore as something that did not happen, Burke believes that its value is that of a symbol, and that it can only meaningfully symbolize aspects of our experience of life. In either case the basis of a religion cannot be the story, but must be that which gives the story its significance: our general assumptions about the nature of the world and experience (our philosophy).

Our interpretation of experience, of history, and of myth raises the question of human authenticity; and this, according to Bernard Lonergan, is never to be taken for granted.[60] Lonergan affirms that even if anyone manages to be perfectly authentic in all his own personal performance, still he cannot but carry within himself the ballast of his tradition; and down the millennia in which that tradition developed, one can hardly exclude the possibility that unauthenticity entered in and remained to ferment the mass through ages to come.[61]

16. CHARLES E. WINQUIST: STORY AS ACT OF AFFIRMATION

Winquist finds the importance of storytelling for self-understanding in the act by which storytelling is made possible; for only after we see how storytelling is possible and valorize the act can we critically pursue the story of our lives.[62] Even in relating a story of nothingness, there is present a positive act of affirmation. This implies that the act of knowing can be distinguished from the content of knowing. The active response of our desire to know bespeaks our dynamic involvement in the full context of experiencing that transcends the achievement of any particular content. Analysis of content in storytelling attends only to the objective pole of the word-event; but, our analysis of the act of knowing in storytelling centers on the dynamic unity of the subject-object relationship.

Storytelling is an act of thinking expressing the power of affirmation; the meaning which it communicates is to be sought both in act and in content. Storytelling is an action that requires a content for its realization; and neither can be examined in isolation from the other. The act of knowing in storytelling has primacy over the content of the known to the extent that the achievements of understanding are preceded by those of experience.

Our storytelling, our asking questions, our building paradigms are activities in which meaning is embedded before it is attached to objective abstractions. Storytelling is a reaching outwards toward a depth of meaning in the reality of our experience that encompasses both actuality and possibility; for the actuality of a story embodies possibility and encourages a concern for a complexity of meanings. Storytelling implies both our transcending of past events and our orientation towards future events. The meaning we derive from the past becomes a question we put to the future; our ability to understand the past equips us to cope with the future, through a meaningful frame of reference open to new possibilities. Storytelling is the power to make sense of our experience, of our relationships, of our potentialities. As such, it reveals the reality of our becoming in a movement towards an unconditional horizon.

The storytelling of faith involves homecoming that is not a return to the past; rather, it is a becoming into the future that is the gift of participation in God's own story. Homecoming is the dynamic passage into the future of our unfinished selves seeking fulfillment in the unlimited promise which God's overarching story holds for us. Homecoming is never completed because there is always a dimension of possibility that awaits its future actualization.[63] With the storytelling of Christian faith, our homecoming even now grasps this future moment.

The meaning of our storytelling can be ascertained in a transcendental inquiry. Such inquiry discloses structural possibilities which can be weighted with the richness of dramatic narratives, poetic images, psychological recollections, or theological projections in the discernment of a concrete story. The construction of a story, according to Winquist, is an experimental beginning that can lead to the uncovering of an archetypal story, the overarching story of God grounding the existence and intelligibility of every other story.[64] Novelists, philosophers and theologians tell stories in order to find a story. Their stories are experiments in possibility, relative, and bound by the limits of their originating circumstances.[65] But the movement of understanding reaches beyond the content of the story in the consciousness of new relationships. The evolving story is increasingly free from the limits of its origin. The story reaches toward both the primordial beginning and the eschatological end as it is retold in the language of an enlarging consciousness.[66] Storytelling, according to Winquist, reaches towards theological understanding.[67] Because stories seek an understanding that surpasses the scope of their content, the theologian is responsible not only to the originating consciousness of a religious community, but also to the expansion of consciousness. Our storytelling implies our longing for God and his "archetypal" story grounding the possibility of all storytelling. We learn to tell our personal story in our movement toward his story.[68] Our desire to know ourselves implies our need to participate in his story. It is the framework within which faith both achieves its conscious self-understanding and is called beyond it in the recognition of its existence as a personal relationship with Pure Unbounded Love-Wisdom, The Storyteller empowering the truthfulness and goodness of every story.

17. WESLEY A. KORT: NARRATIVE ELEMENTS AND RELIGIOUS MEANING

Why do narratives so often contain or imply religious or religiously suggestive meanings? Wesley A. Kort believes that the answer can be derived from a study of the nature of narrative.[69] Kort holds that both the writer and the religious person have similar interests and images of wholeness, totality, and cosmos. Their conscious construction of such images is achieved through the dominant unity-creating properties of narrative: through temporal structure or the ordering of time; through image, symbol, epiphany; through the orientation of language in both the narrator and the religious person toward the inexpressible, towards silence. Through these properties language is called forth by namelessness; and above language stands the image of the perfect speaker (narrator) of the perfect word.

Kort's method is that of isolating the elements of narrative to demonstrate the kind of religious meaning each tends naturally to draw to itself or by which each tends naturally to be enhanced, and to extend the discussion of that element out into its corresponding moment of religious life. He examines basic elements of narrative and the actual or potential religious meaning which they contain. Narratives are the creation of meaning through setting, character, plot and tone; consequently, Kort's four chapter titles relate one of these elements to its religious correlative: 1. Atmosphere and Otherness; 2. Character and Paradigm; 3. Plot and Process; 4. Tone and Belief.

The narrative quality of consciousness and its expression is characterized by elements which converge with the religious quality of consciousness and its expression. Kort would seem to imply that the dynamic structure of knowing that is operative in secular storytelling is also operative in faith's storytelling. He affirms that the elements of narrative stand to the characteristics of religion like two walls of a canyon stand to each other, separated but with structural matching points.[70] Our grasp of the dynamics of narrative can illuminate its counterparts in religious life and thought; it can help us to appreciate the resources whereby we are empowered to create entire worlds of meaning, expressing our radical orientation to a Being, Power and Value that is always beyond our control and comprehension. We have a narrative power for expressing our relationship to this transcendent reality, which is some way in our world, somehow made available, or to some degree accessible. Narrative form is given to this radically transforming relationship, expressing the reality of both its unique benefit (grace) to our lives and its demands upon us (personal and social responsibility).

Reflection on narrative's atmosphere (setting) suggests to Kort the givenness of our transcendent context; reflection on character leads to consideration of human possibilities (characters are paradigms of them); reflection on plot is suggestive of social, psychic, or natural processes and their ultimate ends; reflection on tone is related to testimony, affirmation and belief. There, aspects of human experience are related to the religious experience of receiving, hoping in, and responding to the power, being, or value of that Ultimate Reality which cannot be controlled and comprehended, made available in religious forms, and fundamentally determining our life in the world. The tone of our narrative consciousness and its expression is our "world-view" or "sense of life" or "intention"; it is the quality of our response to the world characterized by the images derived from experience which constitute an a priori, subjective horizon, within which we see ourselves and the world in their relationship.

The act of storytelling is an openness to the other and its possibilities that is based on a priori affirmations of the self and the other; it presupposes the intelligibility of the real despite the fact that Ultimate Reality is beyond our finite comprehension. Plot as an element of storytelling is related to natural processes and religious ritual; it suggests that we are not fully in control as to what kind of story we make our lives out to be, that human freedom, at every level of secular and religious consciousness, is always within limits, structures or some form of order. A story is an ordered account that reflects the order and coherence of existence itself. Narrative plot implies that our experience of time is not incoherent and meaningless.[71] Resemblances between narrative and religion are seen as extrinsic without, unfortunately, coming to grips with the narrative consciousness of the knowing subject which explains the intrinsic quality of the dynamism grounding these resemblances. The dynamic structure of knowing that is operative in the secular storyteller is operative in faith's storyteller as well.

18. JOHN HAUGHT: STORY AS CONTEXT FOR BELIEF IN GOD

John Haught tells us that if storytelling brings to light the power for creating meaning in confronting the facts of our experience, the persistent inability to participate in any story is often symptomatic of psychic disturbance and the experience of meaningfulness.[72] Our need for meaning primordially expresses itself in the narrative mode. Storytelling satisfies this need and desire by intending an intelligible, coherent, meaningful world. Our myths and stories of God witness to our spontaneous conviction that order prevails over chaos, that reality is intelligible. They imply our will to believe that the world is ultimately intelligible and that the absurd is not the last word.

Our desires for meaning and for knowledge strive to join our narrative expression with our will to believe. They give rise to the stories that provide the context for belief in God. The dynamics of our desire to know uncover a meaning which anticipates some form of narrative expression. This occurs even though our desire to know leads through apparent meaninglessness. The dynamics of both the desire to know and the will to believe in God merge in their intention of an intelligible world. The meaningfulness of such a world is experienced, lived and felt within some narrative framework; for life without story would be experienced as absurd.

Story links our feelings with the reality of ourselves. Story is the integrating structure that organizes our feelings and forms a sense of continuous identity with our past and our future. Story brings a temporal context of meaning to the immediacy of the moment; otherwise, we would be forever losing our grip on the reality of our own identity with the passage of discrete moments. Mental balance involves keeping in touch with the narrative sequence underlying our thought. The impulse to tell or retell stories gives the lie to claims that the world is absurd; for it is a way of ordering the world which implies that the world is intelligible. The dynamics of narrative consciousness in storytelling intend a coherent universe and disclose our world-ordering impulse and power.

A spontaneous narrative consciousness persists and functions on the premise that there is a permanent meaning at the heart of things. Its resurgent tendency to shape the world with myth and story, despite every obstacle, implicitly affirms that the universe is not absurd. Ordering the world at a spontaneous level of storytelling implies that the search for coherence in the universe is not futile; it testifies to a primal conviction that reality lays itself open to being ordered in a comprehensible way, and that this would not take place if there were a primal conviction that reality is absurd. The spontaneous world-ordering acts of storytelling involve a primal consciousness that is so intimately one with its world that it has not yet made the theoretical distinction between the subject and its world. Such spontaneous primal thinking does not need to question whether the universe in itself is intelligibly ordered, for ordering (subject) and recognizing the world as already ordered (object) become different only to theoretical judgment. The spontaneous narrative consciousness involves an order that is also the order of the totality embracing both subject and object.[73]

Narrative activity intending a meaningful world is the ontological ground for affirming that we are empowered to create such a world. Human vitality takes the form of intentionality; it is given to creating meaning and to affirming its own identity. Animal vitality, on the other hand, simply acts according to inalterable biological routines. Narrative consciousness is ultimately rooted in the ontological power of being or Being-itself (God). Our participation in this power grounds our ineluctable need to order the world through stories. The dynamic of narrative consciousness postulates the supremacy of an intelligible universe over an indifferent one, of meaning over absurdity, of being over non-being. The persistent workings of our narrative consciousness postulate our participation in the power of meaningful being over and against the void, the possibility of new meaning revising our sense of reality and relating us in new ways to the world. Our will to believe in an intelligible world activates our narrative consciousness and the worlds of meaning that it opens up to us. Reflection on our narrative consciousness becomes the basis for our awareness of our desire to know and the postulate of a rational universe, a world-to-be-known in a questioning and critical way. Our narrative consciousness (the dynamic of storytelling) posits that there is intelligibility to be grasped in the world; otherwise we would not have sought it out. There would be no storytelling without the anticipation or foreknowledge, however vague, of some story to be told. And we would not continually revise our stories (and histories) if we did not anticipate some further intelligibility. Storytelling is undertaken on the premise that the real is comprehensible, meaningful, intelligible. (Even our question about the intelligibility of the real posits intelligibility as the horizon of our questioning).

The parables of Jesus, the oral tradition of the Church which preceded the writing of the New Testament itself, involve that prior narrative-religious self-involvement which grounds Christian theological reflection. They represent that religious knowledge of God that is essentially symbolic and therefore laden with sentient, interpersonal and aesthetic overtones; they represent the way believers have accepted the congruity, value and validity of their belief. Theology is no substitute for the sentient, interpersonal, narrative and aesthetic cognition of the sacred apprehended in the symbols of primal awareness; rather, it must respect the cognitional worth of these patterns of religious experience in which the meaning of the sacred enters into our consciousness.[74] Theology reflects from within the theoretic pattern of consciousness upon the pre-theoretical fields of religious awareness and meaning. It reflects upon the religious story in which we participate, in which we are aware of the reality of God; it does not and cannot require total disengagement from the narrative mode of awareness in religious life.

Haught affirms that questions of meaning, value and validity spontaneously arise when we are told a story.[75] They are usually only implicit in our response to a story. We tend to approach stories of God with the same pattern of questioning.

The question of congruity asks whether the story fits my experience. What does it mean? Does it integrate elements and episodes of my experience into a coherent whole? Does it strike me or interest me in any way? Or is it meaningless and alien to my concerns? If it does not move me, I shall probably be indifferent to its value and truth claims, but, if it awakens my sensitivities, I might inquire about these claims. Through the resonance of feeling, the story is in some way *my* story and may serve as a vehicle of self-knowledge.

The question of value asks whether the story corresponds to what I consider worthwhile. Does it conform to my sense of what is good? for myself and others? Would it be morally and socially responsible to appropriate its vision?

The question of validity asks about the reasonableness of its point of view. I might find the story entertaining and valuable and still wonder whether it is true, whether there are real grounds for accepting it. Are the religious claims of the story reducible to desires, feelings and moral commitments, or do they have a truth content that transcends their aesthetic or moral appeal? It is unlikely that the inquiry about the truth of a religious story can seriously begin before there has been some spontaneous appropriation of its content in a pre-theoretical way. The stories about Moses, Jesus or Buddha may mean nothing to a person in terms of his feelings and desires; hence, he may never have experienced the need to ask whether there are reasonable grounds for these stories. Each Gospel is a reflection of the early Christian community's self-understanding articulated in the particular way it recounts the story of Jesus; each is written to establish a congruity between the once-and-for-all truth of the story which Jesus' life has told and the particular readership to which that Gospel is directed.

Our world is able to be reached as our world only through some story.[76] The intentionality of most of our conscious life is pre-theoretical in nature. We relate to the world through feeling and mood, through moral concern and in instinctive interest in beauty. Storytelling (our narrative mode of intentionality) expresses our feelings and concerns; it symbolizes what we consider to be ultimately fulfilling and the ways in which to achieve it. Our religious insights suffuse the world given to us by our stories of God as well as the world given to us by our sentient, interpersonal and aesthetic patterns of experience. The sense of the sacred first took hold of religious man's consciousness within these pre-theoretical fields of meaning; in fact, the world of the sacred becomes transparent only in them. Stories have the capacity to articulate the richness of intentional activity by catching the links between human actions and responses that are inherently particular and contingent; they have the capacity to keep our world together by binding contingent events and free agents in an intelligible pattern. Narrative form expresses the intentional nature of human action; hence, it especially lends itself to the expression of our desire for that essentially religious meaning which integrates our lives.

19. HUGH JONES: FAITH AS BELIEF IN AN OVERARCHING STORY

Hugh Jones examines faith as a belief in an overarching story.[77] A universal story, a linear sequence with a beginning and an end, is assumed to exist as the ultimate context within which each life story receives its ultimate ground and meaning. To know God is compared to knowing the overarching or universal story, that is, to participate in it. The belief that there is an overarching story is a confession of faith that reality is ultimately comprehensible, meaningful and good. This confession of faith is uttered in relation to our experienced historical circumstances: "We simply cannot greet the biblical Lord except we greet the sticky human story which is the only means he has given us to speak of him at all.'''[78] Our personal stories, our more or less adequate explanations, our attempts to interpret and shape our world are thus taken up into a more encompassing idiom. God, as it were, has his own story. He is a giver of stories, someone to be greeted, someone working out his purpose in real contact with our experience, endowing it with the ultimate intelligibility of his own overarching story, which enters but is not reducible to the stories of Israel or the Church. His decisive story overarches, interprets, judges, sustains and calls forth our stories and is obliquely known in them.

Jones detects four overlapping uses of story-language in the writings of James Barr and James Wharton: (1) story as a descriptive category; (2) story as a way of remembering one's life-story; (3) story as a form of explanation; (4) story as an overarching interpretation of life.

20. *EDWARD K. BRAXTON: STORY MEDIATING MYSTERY*

Religion, for Edward K. Braxton, is characterized by stories of faith. Religion results from the change in one's horizon that follows upon religious experience. The unthematized religious experience is one of ultimacy, of mystery, of the known-unknown; it involves one's feelings, affectivity and intentionality. Through a complex of narratives, myths, rites and symbols, this experience of the ultimate is communicated to others and incorporated into a people's history and tradition. These are the vital mediators which both occasion and nurture theological reflection. These non-discursive symbols at the primal level of human life contain a fullness of meaning that cannot be exhausted in discursive language. Braxton affirms that although this complex of narratives, myths, rites and symbols is concrete and descriptive, its elements are not merely in the world of common sense; they are not simply to be called upon at the end of the theological process to communicate with and motivate simple people.[79] The relationship between religious narrative, myth, rite and symbol, on the one hand, and theology on the other, ought to be complementary and dialectical and not competitive and supplantive.[80] Although religion and theology are distinct, they are complementary; for the values which a religion proposes to a culture are the result of the interpretation or misinterpretation of a people's experience.[81] Theology reflects upon the significance and value of religion in a culture; it reflects upon that complex of narrative, myth, rite and symbols that is essential to religious life within a particular culture. Theology's intellectual pattern of consciousness and experience must do more than merely acknowledge the fact of religious narrative patterns in the context of the polymorphic nature of human consciousness and the patterns of experience. Theology must ask whether faith's narratives, myths and symbols serve as heuristic structures mediating the meaning of ultimate mystery. Braxton believes that it must ask whether there is not a way in which they contain the plentitude of meaning rather than merely potential meaning.[82]

21. URBAN T. HOLMES III: MINISTRY, IMAGE AND STORY

Treating of image and story in his book *Ministry and Imagination,* Urban T. Holmes III describes story as a way of seeing in the dark.[83] Story is a narrative account (a constellation of images) of certain events that are related to time; it has a plot and *dramatis personae.* History is a species of story. Story is by intention a narrative symbol of the content of our awareness, of the meaning we give our experience.[84] In their inception, stories are an imaginative way of ordering our experience; they express our sense of reality.

The Gospels are open stories because they are capable of providing an essential ongoing nurture for the human spirit.[85] They invite us to be open to the present word of God so that our personal stories will be those always expanding with the horizons of our knowing. There should be a creative tension between our story and the Gospel story, contributing to our personal growth and development.

A story lives first in the lives of people. It preserves past events in a way that those events still have meaning for us. Stories can be personal, or they can be cultural, historical or universal. In one sense, no story is exclusively personal, for the story that constitutes our personal vision is drawn from our most intimate communities and beyond. Holmes argues that there is within the nature of story a discrete quality which can be clearly identified in terms of person, culture, history and the ultimate; and yet there is a movement through all categories which is characterized by certain common motifs.[86] He believes that the personal story is anecdotal, because, like the original Greek root of the world *anekdoros,* it is "unpublished," "secret," as compared to the common property of the community.[87] Anecdote indicates, for Holmes, the story as the expression of the idiosyncratic process of shaping the individual's vision. The stories we tell and the way we tell them reveal our character; they reveal our prevailing attitudes, our way of seeing things, our vision or subjective intentionality. A man's character is formed by his vision. Although society has a role in shaping the vision and character of the individual, there remains the individual's responsibility for the self that he is and its actions. There is an interplay between the corporative narrative of the individual's cultural, historical and religious context and that of his personal life story. The corporate narrative provides common images which the individual uniquely embodies in his own life story, vision, character and action. A uniqueness of style within a common vision results whenever there is a truly personal appropriation of the corporate narrative.

In moving from personal to folk stories, Holmes' focus changes from the process (the individual appropriation of a series of images) to the content (the nature of the images themselves).[88] Folk tales, fables, fairy tales, legends, sagas and myths are all forms of story which in their manifest and latent content engage the levels of culture, history and universality. These many forms of story are drawn into the subjective intentionality of the person, into his own life story, to be qualified by insights that are peculiarly those of the individual. Holmes believes that all these stories may have theological validity to the extent that they serve as signposts which help us to read or to hear our way to the gracious presence of God in our lives.[89] Man is drawn to the experience of God through inspiration, imagination and metaphor, through the metaphor of a story. The problem of theology, for Holmes, is how the stories I am told in this age (your story), the story by which I am living (my story) and the biblical story (God's story) can be brought together in one unified intention.[90] The conjoining of these stories is the prerequisite of effective living in the Christian community.

In the story we put ourselves into relation with the things of life; we are saying what those things mean in relation to ourselves.[91] We weave the common and significant events of our lives into a plot in which we triumph over death, the apparent end of our life story. We remember in story a transcending of death in our lives; we express our relationship to our life and death. Our personal story reveals our ability to grasp a meaning for our lives as well as the way we grasp that meaning. Holmes affirms that the ministry aims at conjoining our vision with the vision of God in Christ to work for the kingdom in love for one another and all mankind in the telling of the human story, and hence God's story.[92] The concern of the ministry is that the story of Jesus, the Good News of Pentecost, be held in remembrance so that today we see the presence of God within our individual stories.[93] The Church preserves and communicates the authentic story of Jesus; and its ministers proclaim what it remembers of Jesus' singular relationship with God and of Jesus' death as a part of God's vision to unite all mankind to himself. The Church invites all men to share in the story God has told in Jesus, the story that indicates the way to the Father: "So now, my friends, the blood of Jesus makes us free to enter boldly into the sanctuary by the new, living way which he has opened for us through the curtain, the way of his flesh" (Heb. 10:19-20).

The task of the ministry, for Holmes, is to find ways of conjoining *our* contemporary story and *my* personal story to the story of Jesus.[94] Holmes believes that the Holy Spirit moves in the conjoining of visions: Jesus' story, your story, my story, and their relationship under the vision of God.[95] This process involves a dying to self and an openness to God. The Church tells us the story of Jesus to bring us to expect the abiding presence of God in our lives, to make us conscious of the presence of God soliciting us into being his sons in the Son.[96]

22. HARVEY COX: RELIGION AS STORY AND SIGNAL

Harvey Cox entitles the preface to his book *The Seduction of the Spirit* "Religion as Story and Signal."[97] He holds that religion provides one of the main ways of meeting the human need to tell and hear stories. Religions begin as clusters of stories, embedded in song and saga, rite and rehearsal, parables and anecdotes, allegories and fables, that convey the teaching of each religion's holy men.

As vehicles for religious expression, two kinds of stories are especially important. The first, according to Cox, is autobiography or testimony, the first-person account of the teller's struggle with the gods and the demons; it begins inside the speaker and says, "This is what happened to me." Testimony is a primary mode of religious discourse which celebrates the unique, the eccentric and the concrete. In an age which is suspicious of the particular and the irregular, autobiography is especially valuable in reclaiming personal uniqueness; in an age of externality it uncovers the interiority of my story.

People's religion is what Cox calls the second religiously significant mode of storytelling; this is the collective story of a whole people. Like popular music and folk medicine, Cox believes that this religion is usually mixed with superstition, custom and kitsch; it is a kind of corporate testimony which specialists and professionals view with suspicion; it includes both the folk religion of ordinary people in its unsophisticated form and the popular religion that occurs outside formal ecclesiastical institutions. People's religion, our story, expresses a collective interiority.

Neither testimony nor folk expression, there is a third type of religion which is coded, systematized, controlled and distributed by specialists. Though this form of religion still bears certain marks of a story, it is actually a system of what Cox calls "signals." Most world religions are a mixture of story and signal. Understanding of the distinction between story and signal helps us to grasp the nature of contemporary societies. Stories reflect those forms of human association which blend emotion, value and history into a binding fabric, whereas signals make possible large-scale and complex types of human association where such binding would not be possible. Stories amplify, eliciting emendations and embellishments from their hearers, and often telling us more about the narrator than about the plot. Signals specify, cuing a single patterned act and telling us nothing about the signaler. Stories enrich the store of common recollection and stimulate shared imagination, whereas signals permit us to move around in systems that would not survive if all human communication had to be deep and personal. Stories are enhanced by literary and local color. Signals must be clear, attempting to transmit one unequivocal message and to discourage all but one response. Stories convey multiple layers of meaning all at once and can be told and interpreted in different ways. Stories serve many functions.

All societies, according to Cox, need both stories and signals. They need both the autonomous activities people engage in without anyone else's planning these activities and also the impersonal procedures that make possible the constant flow of ideas, goods and persons. Cox believes that religions serve their purposes best when they include both the spontaneous personal aspect and the inclusive consensus on value and vision that makes whole civilizations possible. A proportion must be maintained between story and signal, between people's faith and clerical religion. Institutionally programmed forms of activity should be balanced with random, capricious and inwardly initiated forms of human action.

The swamping of stories by signals concerns Cox because signals are a less human form of communication. He notes that animal language consists almost entirely of signals — the screech, the bark, the howl — but persons are storytellers, and without stories we would not be human. Cox asserts that through our stories we assemble our pasts, place ourselves in a present and cast a hope for the future; without them we would be bereft of memory or anticipation. We create innumerable stories and find endless ways to recount them.

Religion today, according to Cox, is not fulfilling its storytelling role. Although it should be the seedbed of stories, it has become top-heavy with signals and systems; without stories there is nothing to systematize at both the individual and corporate level. Religion, for Cox, is that cluster of memories and myths, hopes and images, rites and customs that pulls together the life of a person or group into a meaningful whole. It gives coherence to life, furnishes a fund of meanings, gives unity to human events and guides people in making decisions; as its Latin root suggests *(religare)*, religion is what binds things together.

Cox identifies the three components of every religion. A religion tells us where we came from, and in connection with that often tells us what is wrong with us, and how we got that way. Our myths of origin, creation and fall express this part of religion. Second, religions present some ideal possibility for humankind: the blessed condition of salvation. They portray what it means to be fully free or integrated or saved. Holy people personify this ideal. Third, a religion tells us how to get from our present fallen state (of being sick, alienated, lost, or captive) to what we can be or ought to be or already are if we only knew it. This is what Cox calls the "means of grace."

With this definition in mind, Cox thinks that the signal clusters of the mass media can also be understaood as religion. TV shows and magazine ads show this with myths and heroes that guide decisions, inform perception, provide examples of conduct, identify our transgressions, and hold up models of saintly excellence. Mass-Media culture, for Cox, is a religion with its own sacraments and promised bliss. The behavior models that mass-media images promulgate often directly contradict the life goals Christianity celebrates. Cox sees the mass media and Christianity as competing value systems, competing for the same loyalities. He sees the mass media as disguised forms of religion. He is aware that life is a never-ending series of choices among conflicting values and disparate beliefs, and that when we do not make those choices ourselves, someone is always ready to make them for us. His book is therefore concerned with three forms of religion: testimony, people's religion, and the value patterns of the mass media.

When signals begin to pose as stories, when control cues pretend to be something other than what they are, there occurs what Cox calls the "seduction of the spirit." Seducers employ the language and gesture of dialogue, trust, intimacy and personal rapport with a skill that is employed to subvert both intimacy and human community; they use the natural needs and instincts of another for their own selfish ends; they callously exploit others into becoming unwitting accomplices in their own deception. Cox defines the seduction of the spirit as the calculated twisting of people's natural and healthy religious instincts for purposes of control and domination. It abuses religion by enlisting people in their own manipulation. The seducer wears the garb of the storyteller: what he tells sounds like a story, but it is really a line or a cover.

Cox believes that after centuries of enlightenment and skepticism man is now evangelized, catechized and proselytized more than ever; but he does not perceive the process as a religious one. Some are critical of religion in the narrow sense, but they remain vulnerable to religions they do not recognize as such. The actual stories of men and women and the shared memories of living groups must not, according to Cox, be silenced by seductive signals. Cox urges us to become partisans instead of onlookers; he feels that religion in our time can best restore the balance that our culture needs between story and signal by being partisan, by supporting the storytellers against the signalers. He warns that people's religion is in danger and testimony is discouraged, that without these forms of story-telling we would cease to be human. Religion must become corrective and critic; it must free persons and groups from manipulation or seduction by massive organizations, prepared programs and external signals; it must help us find our own place within the cosmos, our proper role in history and our appropriate relationship to the holy; it must help us test our powers and come to terms with our limitations, to recognize at a very basic level of our being that our story is one among many, to become critically and reflectively religious in our reappropriation of our religious heritage.

Testimony, the primal human act, involves telling my story in a world of people with stories to tell. It attempts to construct a common world that fuses authentic interiority with genuine community. Although subject to debasement and trivialization, the telling and retelling of my story (testimony) is a form of reaching out to the worlds of others in an attempt to create our world.

Interiority distinguishes the person from the robot. A person selects, digests, orders, decides, responds — all on the basis of an interchange between his own interior life and the culture; the automaton lights up instantly to every cue relayed to it from the control board. Human interiority requires love and community; it breaks the barrier between the inner and outer worlds through storytelling and storylistening, through giving our testimonies and listening to the testimonies of others. We weave stories into our story; we select the worlds of others for our own; we learn to experience our lives in new ways through our experience and interpretation of other individuals, communities, and cultures. Our hunger for community corresponds to our need for a place to tell our stories, to learn how all life might be lived differently or more fully.

24

NARRATIVE THEOLOGY AND ITS USES

The value of narrative theology might best be expressed in terms of some of its uses. This chapter will review briefly some proposals for the use of narrative theology.

MORAL THEOLOGIANS

Given that Jesus Christ and his story have always formed the basis and center of Christian theologizing, Enda McDonagh believes that aspects of the Christian message may be more fruitfully pursued and understood in the narrative and historical mode.[1] The development of theology as story or biography should enrich moral theology.

The moral theologian's work, according to McDonagh, is implicitly autobiographical; it reveals his preoccupation and course of life. Such a relationship between theologial issues and concrete experiences discloses a first stage understanding of theology as autobiography. The further understandings depend on the interaction between these experiences of his life story, theological reflection on them and the transformation (or other) effects on the author's further living and thinking, acting and praying, on the whole integrated life or *bios* of which the *graphe* must be composed.

The moral theologian's deepest commitments provide the material for autobiography as theology, even though they only find an indirect expression in his professional writings. The theme of conversion best describes such commitment: the change of heart, *metanoia,* to which Jesus summoned his followers, and the centering of that heart (Mt. 6:21), by which he indicated that

274

they were to be judged, enable us to plot the graph of our Christian and human life stories.

Conversion as a continuing process does not affect the moral theologian in a vacuum because it is not simply or primarily conversion to intellectual systems or moral values and patterns of living; rather, its appropriate and ultimate term is only in another personal reality. Conversions in consciousness (pre-reflective or reflective), in commitment, and in action find their true meaning and fulfillment in relationships of conversion to other personal realities, human or divine, whether through face-to-face or structural relationships. Such a personally grounded understanding of conversion defines the true autobiographical structure of growth in theological understanding and of the final limits of that growth.[2] Friendship is central to autobiography and conversion as social; for the direction of the theologian's conversion is towards the establishment or emergence of friendship in the kingdom of God.[3]

Paul Steidl-Meier, in rethinking the social components of Church ministry, avails himself of the approach of narrative theology. He has found that far too much of contemporary theology is unreadable and fails to employ models that adequately address contemporary social reality and social ministry. Steidl-Meier, in his quest for ordinary language and adequate paradigms for analysis, concludes that the best way to attain such an objective is to pay explicit attention to the language of narrative and to the significance of human stories for theology: "In this way my own work relates directly to a companion volume, *Tellers of the Word,* by J. Navone and T. Cooper (1980)."[4]

Steidl-Meier affirms that the questions which sociology pose concerning the theology and social teaching of the Church ask about the guiding values and ideas that serve as a basis of Christian union and how these contrast with other groups and their bases of union. It examines a religion's view of ultimate reality and meaning — what that religion calls the "end-state" — which also confers meaning on the present. An end-state means a global, all-encompassing vision of reality and is rendered concretely visible in the stories and religious symbols that constitute a religious tradition. Stories and symbols render ultimate reality concrete, and so provide the grounds for theological reflection, which articulates the meaning of the end-state as expessed in stories and symbols and specifies the types of behavior — the moral virtues — that are consistent with the end-state.[5]

The matter of competing interpretations of the stories of a religious tradition emphasizes for Steidl-Meier that religion is dynamic. For example, some see the exodus story or the symbol of the cross as a demand for liberation and the willingness to undergo the suffering that marks the struggle. Or it may be interpreted as the journey of withdrawal from the fleshpots of the world and the consequent crucifying of the flesh by continual abnegation.

Steidl-Meier concludes that no particular theology or interpretation of religious story and symbol is ever neutral regarding social order. In fact, what is taking place in the Catholic Church is a critical theological reflection on the very adequacy of systems of interpretation of the Christian story and symbol.[6]

Questions regarding value judgments, norms, or criteria of social relations raise issues of ultimate meaning and reality.[7] The narrative-historical method and the critical-rational method are, for Steidl-Meier, the most fundamental methods for probing ultimate reality. The narrative-historical method represents the most far-reaching and broadly-based approach to human meaning; as such, he believes that it is far richer than either empirical-behaviorist or critical-rational methods. The narrative-historical method seeks to recapture an entire flow of experience in its retelling or artistic representation. Its most fundamental language is that of stories or myths, which in turn yield paradigms or models for reality. In this way, the narrative-historical method does not, for example, merely add up the number of hungry in the world and tabulate the various indicators; rather it presents an overall interpretation of the reality as either good or bad with reference to ultimate reality and meaning. Thus, stories are told of oppressors and liberation, of sins in a previous life and cycles of deliverance, of individual excellence and free economic activity. This method symbolically presents ideal types or heroes who are models for reality. The paradigm of reality is presented in historical, literary, and artistic forms in which ultimate reality and meaning are effectively symbolized and serve either to legitimate present behavior or to denounce it in a prophetic way. Such method marks an improvement over behaviorist empiricism because it provides a basis for discussing the full meaning of human experience; yet it does not yield clear and distinct notions of norms and criteria for human behavior. It tends to be more descriptive than explanatory.

The aim of the critical-rational method is to explain underlying interrelations and causes. This method in its transcendental aspects probes the critical foundations and the very possibility of knowledge itself. Both Rahner and Lonergan employ the transcendental method. They focus on dynamic categories of the human being. Rahner's focus emphasizes the dynamic structure of human persons who pose the question of their own being. Lonergan begins with the human experience of knowing and seeks to delineate the dynamic and transcendental structures (activities rather than concepts) of human knowing that serve as the critical foundations of all human knowledge. The main fruit of the rational method is in the critical awareness that leads to relentless probing of the coherence of one's own approach and questions both the validity of and interrelations among one's own assumptions, axioms, postulates, and propositions. It leads to the questioning of the questions themselves, to the probing of their adequacy, and to the analysis of experiential data to determine both their relevance and their validity as evidence. Rational method is concerned with the critique method. The narrative theology of Steidl-Meier's companion volume, *Tellers of the Word,* employs both the narrative-historical and critical-rational methods.

Stanley Hauerwas is another of the moral theologians who have taken up the question of the experiential roots of narrative and the relationship of the human life-story to lived convictions. In his study of the nature and formation of Christian character, Hauerwas argues that narrative is a perennial category for understanding better how the grammar of religious convictions is displayed and how the self is formed by those convictions.[8] He believes that the meaning of character is to be found in narratives and that these narratives are a form of explanation. For Hauerwas, a story is a narrative account that binds events and agents together in an intelligible pattern and in so doing offers a description and explanation of why things are the way they are.[9] In Hauerwas' argument, narrative is a necessary form for describing the intentionality of human action.[10] He raises the issue of self-deception and the question of criteria for determining the truthfulness of a human story.

For Hauerwas, stories are the key to Christian ethics. He focuses on the distinctive story of Jesus, which must become our own guiding story and find expression in the Christian community. This story outlines the path of Christian discipleship.

Hauerwas develops an ethics of character that stresses the gradual self-formation of the moral agent, which is often overlooked by moral philosophers, who concentrate on decisions and the norms that guide them. The integrity and continuity that lend shape to our character cannot be ignored. Character formation is a question of a gradually developing consistency that places our moral decisions in a personal context. Our morality does not emerge at occasional moments of decision. Our Christian life is more than a series of existential decisions or moments of obedience to a clear command of God. The normative virtues that give consistency to the self as Christian are found in the Gospels' story of Jesus. Essential to consistent character is a *way of life,* a concrete pattern of expectations that guides commitments. The Christian way of life is shown in the story of Jesus. We are called to follow his way faithfully. Such fidelity both shapes the characters of individuals and procedures in the distinctive community called the Church.

The Gospel of Mark exemplifies how the story defines the disciple when it recounts the collision between Peter's understanding of the Christian way of life and that of Jesus. Peter first acknowledges that Jesus is the Christ and then immediately rejects Jesus' description of the way of suffering and death that lies ahead (Mk. 8:27-9:1). Peter had learned the name but not the story that determines the meaning of the name.[11] He had a different story for the title "The Christ," who was in his mind the victorious Messiah who would achieve God's purpose without the suffering of self-sacrifice. Jesus' way must become that of his disciples as well (Mk. 8:34-36).

The story of Jesus' impending suffering and death challenges the truth of Peter's existence and exposes the emptiness of his ambitions. Either this story changes Peter and the other hearers so that they embark on that fateful journey, or else they cease to be Jesus' disciples. The concreteness of the story is that of Jesus' own life; it cannot be resolved into a general teaching on self-sacrifice or an abstract ethical theory on the difficulties of a virtuous life. The message is inseparable from the person of Jesus. We cannot learn the truth of the Kingdom without following the way of the King whose love governs life in the Kingdom.[12] The life story of Jesus defines the way of God's ruling love as the way of the cross.

The messianic expectations of Peter were a "counter-story" to the way of life embodied in Jesus. The dominant story of the would-be disciple clashes with that of the master. The costly demands of the Gospels clash with our innate tendency to make immediate self-satisfaction the ultimate norm of our life. We cannot have a completely private life-story: our way of life is always determined by a specific community to which we are loyal. We learn how to be virtuous by the example of others in the community. Their witness inspires us to be virtuous. Every way of life has its own story; the Christians' community is the story of Jesus. His story shapes our self-understanding and that of the community. What we do and how we do it are ultimately rooted in a way of life that his story has shaped for us. His story defines his community and inculcates the virtues that help his disciples navigate the complexity of human life envisioned by it. The goodness and truth of the story is judged by the kind of people that its community produces. The authenticity of our lives manifests the truthfulness of the story that we are living.

Sallie McFague addresses the moral dynamics of story by selecting *parable* as the basic revelatory medium for learning what it means to act as a disciple of Jesus. Parable is an extended metaphor that shocks the reader into new meaning and calls for a response of commitment.[13] Parable is the central expression of the teaching of Jesus. The parables of Jesus jar us out of a familiar world into one with new, compelling possibilities. The story of Jesus is an extended parable because it concretely embodies the shocking love of God, placing our familiar compromises and mundane expectations in a new context, empowering us to move from compromise to commitment. Parable is the literary expression most appropriate for a religion founded on incarnation, the embodiment of infinite graciousness in a concrete life. The Gospels and parables are not histories but re-enactments of the good news — dramatic narratives that "say" the same thing that the big story, the story of Jesus' passion, death and resurrection, says.[14] "If we say," writes McFague, "as I would want to, that Jesus of Nazareth is *par excellence* the metaphor of God, we mean that his familiar, mundane story is the *way,* the indirect but necessary way, from here to there . . . Metaphoric meaning is a *process,* not a momentary, static insight: it operates like a story, moving from here to there, from 'what is' to 'what might be.' "[15]

William C. Spohn, S.J. employs the expression "narrative ethics" in his book *What are they saying about scripture and ethics?*[16] Spohn affirms that Christians turn to Scripture to discover more than the right thing to do; they want to act in a way that responds to the God of their lives. Systems of ethics begin with a fundamental principle or value. The Gospel begins with a person who claims that he himself is the "norm" we are to follow: "Come, follow me." Spohn is concerned with the morally revealing dimensions of biblical symbols, narratives, parables, poems, and how they color our reading of the rules and principles in Scripture.[17] The use of Scripture in Christian ethics must be rooted in the history of the covenant people and the One it reveals.

Spohn considers six different ways of using Scripture for moral guidance. In his fifth way, "Call to Discipleship," moral questions are answered by referring directly to the New Testament story of Jesus Christ.[18] To be disciples Christians ought to embody their Master's distinctive way of life. The most important literary expressions here are story and parable. The story of Jesus claims to be the truth of our lives, so we either have to let it redefine our own identity or dismiss that claim as false. Prior to questions of action is the question of character. Do we have a coherent sense of self at the core of our identity? Unless the Gospel story redefines the person's character, he or she cannot follow the way of life proper to the disciple. Letting the story of Jesus serve as the pattern of our own lives will conflict with the basic assumptions of our secular culture, which has its own story, one quite different from that which should be lived out by the Christian community.

The most practical use of New Testament material for moral guidance is the discipleship that deliberately patterns actions on those of Jesus Christ. Employing the symbols of Scripture challenges the self-understanding of the agent and demands discernment to discover an appropriate response to God acting in our history. Discipleship, for Spohn, begins with the conviction that the most appropriate path is the one already blazed by Jesus and that the Christian must creatively embody that way of life in all situations.[19] The moral question "What ought I to do?" is recast in more particular terms: "How should I act as a disciple of Jesus in these circumstances?" Spohn examines authors who take a mediated approach, turning to the story of Jesus: Gospel parables and moral norms to chart the path for the contemporary disciple.[20]

Spohn concludes from his study that Scripture issues a call to discipleship. The Christian finds a new pattern for morality in the shape of the life of Jesus Christ. Neither the secular culture nor general human experience provides insight into the life of discipleship unless scrutinized in terms of the particular values found in the Gospel story. The incarnation is not an endorsement of all that is humanly good but a radical break with the fallen condition of humankind. The Gospel story of Christ provides the normative story for the Christian, a lived pattern of meaning that can enable the Christian to face life truthfully. "Character" is self-understanding become dynamic, making action integral with one's deepest commitments. The person of Jesus is the Kingdom come, the truth about God's way of acting in the world. That truth is learned through the living witness of the Church and is embodied in the distinctive Christian virtues that reshape the agent's character.[22]

William Kirk Kilpatrick, professor of educational psychology at Boston College, underscores the importance of stories of wisdom for teaching morality. Long before the Greeks learned their ethics from Aristotle, they learned them from *The Iliad* and *The Odyssey*. When Christianity swept the world, it was the Gospel story, not the Christian ethic, that captured human hearts. Still later, people learned how to behave well by hearing accounts of the lives of saints and stories of Arthur, Percival, and Galahad. Not only were these stories good teaching devices, but our own lives are best understood as stories. An individual is more than just an individual self. The individual belongs to an ongoing tradition, a family story or a tribal story. We cannot identify ourselves without bringing in the whole family history. We are defined by the story of which we are a part.[23] We each play an irreplaceable part in a cosmic drama, a story in which some of the strands only come together in eternity. In such a story, what you do counts infinitely.[24] A traditional incentive to moral behavior was the conviction that we are part of a story that begins before us and goes on after us, but whose outcome we may influence. The important thing was to play our part well in the ongoing enterprise to which all belonged.[25] Certain things are expected of those who want to play a part in the Christian story. The main reason that you cannot extract ethical principles from Christianity and set them up on their own is that Christianity is *not* an ethical system. It is not meant to be a prescription for good behavior, although good behavior is one of its side effects. It is a true and good life-story. Consequently, it makes no sense to talk about keeping the Christian ethic and ignoring Christ. The story is mainly about Christ: who he is and what he has done. Without him it makes no sense. You cannot separate the message of Christ from the person of Christ and simply pretend that his words could be put into any good person's mouth.[26] How would it sound if Dante had said, "I am the Resurrection and the Life?" Or if Churchill had said, "Before Abraham came to be, I Am"? That is not their story. Those lines belong to only one Person.[27] Doing the right thing is no guarantee that good consequences will follow. Our role is to play our part faithfully and as best we can see it, not to foresee the future. The traditional morality of character gives us good people as models and asks us to act like them: it provides us with stories to live by.[28]

FUNDAMENTAL THEOLOGY

The contribution of four American Lonerganian theologians is the basis for Robert Peevey's doctoral dissertation *Narrative Theology: A Contribution to Fundamental Theology.*[29] Peevey's study centers on the work of John Haught, Michael Novak, John Navone, and John Dunne.[30] Peevey finds in the works of these writers a series of insights and foundational ideas of relevance to the problem of divine revelation and human experience. He finds that their work is a valuable guide for clarifying the relationship between human experience and the process of that revelation whereby God enters and transforms human history. He suggests that they provide valuable pointers in deepening our understanding of the particularity and universality of divine revelation.

Peevey finds that the work of John Haught and Michael Novak highlights human experience as an "encounter" with a pre-given reality.[31] Experience is the product of something encountered and also of our being able to receive it. Pre-given reality is a foundational component of human experience, which is always in consequence a dialogical reality. We are open to pre-given reality through our foundational consciousness, through which we are aware of the whole situation in which we are immersed, which is the basis of any insight into that situation. Peevey's focus on foundational consciousness puts the primacy on being and our encounter with being through our intentional activity as opposed to the personal mediation of experiences in narrative and theoretic consciousness. In narrative consciousness the subject is present in the world in an historical manner, relating to himself as a meaningful whole, and himself to reality as part of the whole. In theoretic consciousness the subject searches for objective insights and consequently detaches himself from reality in a critical conscious manner.

The sustained reflections of Dunne and Navone on the "journey" theme imply that human experience is the result of an ongoing process that takes time and has a temporal structure; such experience will of necessity be influenced by the selective operations taking place within human memory, as well as the person's anticipations of, and overall intentionality towards, the future.[32]

All four theologians illuminate the narrative mediation of human experience. Haught attends to how the person's complex mode of being in the world is modified by any modification in his narrative self-understanding: for our moods and interpersonal relationships are so intimately linked to the narrative pattern of experience that if the latter is dramatically altered, the former tend to change also. This centrality of narrative derives from the power of narrative to give unity and meaning to the complex totality of human experience and thus to direct human attention toward significant persons and events in experience. Navone attends to the existential influence of narrative ending or conclusion: the individual lives the present according to the conclusion he anticipates. Consequently, a change in our sense of the ending colors our approach to the present. The journey metaphor illustrates the centrality of the ending.[33] When life is lived as a journey, the individual structures his approach to experience according to a set of basic symbols. A pivotal symbol is that of *home.* In the journey toward a more human and fuller existence, the individual is a *pilgrim* who is *journeying* toward his true home, which in turn gives sense to his *self-renunciation, courage,* and *remembering.* Michael Novak attends to the process of change in narrative consciousness. This process passes through the three stages of *breakdown, breakthrough,* and *reintegrating.*[34] In the first stage the inauthenticity of one's narrative self-understanding is put under such a strain by one's repeated contact with authentic reality that human authenticity demands its rejection (breakdown). There follows a process of waiting and searching, in which the person exists essentially in an attitude of receptivity, ready to make his own a narrative which is capable of giving authentic meaning to his lived experience. When the individual encounters the authentic narrative structure (breakthrough), there follows a process of reintegrating his experience according to the principles of understanding and feeling which the narrative encourages (reintegration).

A particular value of Dunne's narrative theology lies in his focus on the various stages of the historical unfolding of divine revelation within the personal, historical, and transcendent parameters of human existence.[35] These categories enable us to reflect on the experience of divine revelation from three perspectives: "personal experience," or what is happening within and to me; "historical experience," or what is happening to my life; "transcendent experience," or what is happening to my vision and knowledge of God and his world. Revelation entails the transformation of our experience and understanding of each of the three parameters. "Revelation" and "salvation" are complementary and interchangeable terms for describing the whole process of our experiencing the divine self-communication. The four Lonerganian narrative theologians concur that divine revelation is a process that unfolds within human experience and that it consists of the transformation of human experience into revelatory experience. "Knowing God," in a biblical sense, is such an experience; it derives from seeking and doing his will.

Divine revelation presupposes a particular attitude to human experience. Dunne shows that divine revelation only unfolds within human experience when life is lived as an authentic struggle with the Mystery that underlies the contours of all our finite experiences. Such struggle expresses this attitude as an affirmation of and personal involvement with the Mystery. We do not equate human experience with divine revelation. Although we can affirm that divine revelation is a process which unfolds *within* human experience, this unfolding only occurs when the individual is brought to approach his experience in a particular way.[36]

The narrative theologians Peevey studies agree that the universality of divine revelation derives from the universal salvific will of God who comes to man in a mysterious way, offering him the gift of salvation, in and through persons, experiences, and the cultural symbol systems concretely available. The universality of divine revelation from the point of view of man derives from the fact that human experience is common to the human race. Its three basic components — "encounter," and "approach," and "narrative understanding" — are significant in clarifying the universality of divine revelation.[37]

Encounter: Granted the universal salvific will of God, the individual's encounter with pre-given reality is equivalent to the providential guidance of the experiences in which he is immersed and of the relationships in which he participates. This suggests that God is continually guiding people into experiences and relationships which are healing and enlightening.

Approach: Human choice is always somehow active in what we conceive as important and worthwhile. As such, the individual's approach to his experience is part of the mystery of human freedom. However, we can look for the unfolding of divine revelation where the human person searches for authentic understanding of his experience, strives for self-integration, or hungers for self-surrender.

Narrative Understanding: The relationship between the individual's approach to experience and his understanding of experience is not a simple one. Narrative understanding does not necessarily condition our approach to experience as, for example, the existence of insincere Christians demonstrates. Nonetheless, we can expect a person who approaches his experience with authenticity to be attracted to "narratives" which enlighten his experience of and encourage his search for authentic understanding, self-integration, and self-surrender.

Narratives can also be viewed from the point of view of their social influence. As publicly available, narratives have the social effect of encouraging particular attitudes through their diffusion of symbols within society at large. As such, narratives which encourage an authentic understanding of and approach to human experience contribute to the diffusion of divine revelation.

Dunne associates the experience of divine revelation with the experiences of self-integration and self-surrender.[38] Wherever a person experiences the gift of a renewed wholeness as opposed to a previous inner alienation or a renewed personal relationship as opposed to a previous enmity — in that situation we have an authentic human experience of divine revelation or grace.

These experiences prepare us for the realization of our supernatural call to share the interpersonal divine life of the Trinity.

The particularity of Christian revelation is rooted in its irreducible historical specificity: the Son of God was made man at a particular time and place, so that God has a human life-story. The Incarnate Word is the Incarnate Life-story of God, the ultimate meaning and goodness of the universal human story. Peevey finds two elements in Christian particularity common to the four narrative theologies: first, the structure of the Christian standpoint and, second, the specificity of its historical content.

The structure of the Christian standpoint is based on the self-revelation of God in Christianity as a revelation of absolute personal love (God is love, 1 Jn. 4:8). The absoluteness of this love is turned toward all humankind in all the parameters of our existence (personal, historical, and transcendent) as unrestricted divine concern and call to responsibility. The self-revelation of God as absolute love is totally gratuitous and can in no way be concluded from reflection on our limited imperfect experiences. Once God's personal love has been revealed, however, it enables us to construct an anthropology which confirms humankind's deepest longings and possibilities. Thus, only Christianity can fully explain the human search for authentic understanding, self-integration, and self-surrender.

The specificity of Christianity's historical content is expressed in the Christian community's confession of faith that Jesus is the Christ in and through whom God liberates his people and establishes his kingdom for the ultimate fulfillment of all humankind.[39]

INTRODUCTION TO RELIGION

The category of story or narrative is employed as an introduction to the study of religion in general and perhaps Christianity in particular. Sam Keen's *To a Dancing God,* Harvey Cox's *The Seduction of the Spirit,* Michael Novak's *Ascent of the Mountain, Flight of the Dove,* Robert Roth's *Story and Reality,* John Shea's *Stories of God,* and a collection of essays edited by James B. Wiggins, *Religion as Story,* are recent examples of attempts to describe religion and Christian faith by means of the category of narrative.[40] In each case "narrative" is used to describe and explain the location of religion in human experience and the meaning of "faith" in relation to a person's encounter with other people and the world. The "religious dimension" of human experience is interpreted as having something to do with the narratives people recite about themselves or the narratives they use in order to structure and make sense out of the world. Narrative is both the form for the interpretation of that reality which is the source of religion in human experience and a means of communicating to and sharing it with others. The category of narrative or story provides the link between personal experience and religious symbols.

Stephen Crites' article, "The Narrative Quality of Experience," which is one of the earliest and most signficiant pieces of narrative theology,[41] argues that one of the conditions for being human is the possession of the capacity for having a history, and that the formal quality of experience through time is inherently narrative.[42] That is, the form which active consciousness assumes in its experience of the world is narrative form, which suitably expresses "the tensed unity" of the three modalities of past, present, and future.[43] In order to understand the primordial status of narrative in human experience (and in that sense its "religious significance"), we must concentrate not simply on the "mundane stories" which people recite, stories which are set within a determinate world and frame of consciousness and by which people explain "where they have been, why things are as they are, and so on."[44] Rather we must also attend to what Crites calls "sacred stories," not so much because gods are commonly celebrated in them, but because men's sense of self and world is created through them.[42] Sacred stories provide consciousness with a sense of orientation in life and a pre-conscious apprehension of reality. For Crites, the narrative quality of experience has three dimensions: the sacred story, mundane stories, and the temporal form of experience itself.[46]

The German discussion of the use of narrative in theology began slowly, but in recent years it has produced a number of important essays.[47] Initially the topic seemed to be of interest only to American theologians; but clearly, such is no longer the case. The German discussion, like the one taking place in the United States, has focused on two major issues: the relationship between narrative and doctrinal theology and the reinterpretation of traditional doctrines by means of the category of narrative. One important contribution to this discussion is the small volume by Dietrich Ritschl and Hugh O. Jones, *"Story" als Rohmaterial der Theologie.*[48] Also of significance have been essays by Harald Weinrich and Johann Baptist Metz and a recent book by Josef Meyer zu Schlochtern.[49] Ritschl's essay is particularly important for his discussion on the relation between story and human identity, the nature of story, its form and function, and the relation between story and theology. Attempts to reconstruct the meaning of Christian doctrines in the light of the cateogry of narrative have been Hans Frei's *The Identity of Jesus Christ,* Eberhard Jüngel's *Gott als Geheimnis der Welt,* and Edward Schillebeeckx's *Jesus: An Experiment in Christology.*[50]

CHRISTIAN RELIGIOUS EDUCATION

Narrative also plays a role in what Thomas Groome terms Christian religious education by "shared praxis": "a group of Christians sharing in dialogue their critical reflection on present action in light of the Christian Story and its Vision toward the end of lived Christian faith."[51] Groome details five components of this process. After asking questions which elicit from participants a personal statement in regard to the topic under discussion, he proposes leading them to critical reflection, that is, "using critical memory to probe the biography of the self."[52] This movement, "telling one's story," leads to the telling of the Christian Story and Vision, by which Groome means "the whole faith tradition of our people however that is expressed or embodied."[53] He makes plain that the Story embraces narrative, but transcends it; the Story is found in more sources than narrative. The fourth movement juxtaposes the Christian Story with that of the participants (what he terms a "present dialectical hermeneutic"), and thus provides a way of engaging in the knowing of the community. The fifth movement, in turn, juxtaposes the Christian Vision (a metaphor for the "comprehensive representation of the lived response which the Christian Story invites and of the promise God makes in that story") with that of the participants.[54] In other words, it is an occasion for decision about the appropriate way of response in faith.

Groome retains praxis as a technical term to avoid any suggestion that theory can be bracketed out of the business of living. Praxis can embrace all in which we are engaged in the now of our existence. This includes the whole tradition of academic theology. The potential of that now is discovered, explored, named, and actualized within a conversation with the story of the Christian tradition and the constructing of a vision for the future. Groome's shared praxis pedagogy seeks to honor a way of knowing that is relational, reflective, and experiential, and that holds in fruitful tension past and present for the sake of reshaping the future.

James W. Fowler studies the Christian story in stages of faith. Deeply indebted to structural developmentalists Jean Piaget and Lawrence Kohlberg (because faith is a way of knowing) and to psychosocial developmentalist Erik Erikson (because faith is relational), Fowler has proposed that there are six basic structuring styles or ways of composing and maintaining a meaningful orientation of faith. Fowler has thus focused on attempting to identify basic structures of faith shared by all humans, regardless of their particular religious affiliation; his identification of six sequential and invariant stages in the development of faith is a way of naming what happens in the lifelong process of giving form to our affirmations about our experience taken as a whole.[55] Fowler's stages have apparently provided religious educators with a useful heuristic tool. His six stages are rather widely known and used, and have been more fully disseminated through his major exposition, *Stages of Faith*.[56] Fowler recognizes the educational value of human life stories; his theory is grounded in the lives of particular people growing in faith.

BIBLICAL THEOLOGY

Charles Homer Giblin, S.J., states the case for the relationship between story or narrative and biblical theology.[57] All four Gospels are narratives, that is, they are basically stories. The fact that the term "story" covers epics and dramas as well does not diminish its importance in the study of narrative. Nor should the further problem concerning "gospel genre" distract one from the need to affirm that "story-form" is an issue central to literary criticm of the narrative-style Gospels. "Gospel," according to Giblin, covers literary genres/forms other than narratives and so "gospel genre" must be regarded as an analogous concept.[58] For it can hardly exclude Paul's preaching, especially his speech in Rom. 1:16 to 8:39, which is an argumentative exposition based on the attested fact of Jesus' death for us and his transforming bodily resurrection. That attested fact determines "the Gospel" — whatever literary forms the latter assumes. Even among the four Gospels its literary form/structure is analogous. Mark presents only its "beginning," and that as a kind of apocalyptic manifesto. Luke recasts it as a kind of religious history. John seems to present it as the latest eschatological theophany, the final and definitive manifestation of God as the Father and his Son Jesus Christ, who communicate the Spirit and provide everlasting life to believers.

Giblin affirms that stories always deal with persons, what they do and/or say, how they interact, where, when, and so on.[59] One cannot tell a story without at least personifying the chief actors. Their interaction determines the plot-line of the narrative and the meaning of the whole story. As a story moves to its climax, the author's presentation of its chief characters may be expected to prove critically important for the audience's perception of its relevance to themselves. Accordingly, one may expect a given evangelist to disclose his theology in terms of his chosen medium, the story, particularly as he brings the narrative to its climax and more closely interrelates the actions of the chief character, Jesus, both with those of his disciples and with those of his adversaries. Giblin concludes that the passion-resurrection narrative functions as the lodestone of every one of the story-form Gospels; the passion in particular stands out as the climatic "conflict" or "confrontation" in the plot-line of the Gospels.[60] Robert C. Tannehill's study of the function of a narrative role calls our attention to the major axis of any Christian, evangelical (i.e. gospel-form) communication, namely, the relation of Jesus to his disciples as realized through the passion-resurrection.[61]

The discovery of narrative and its role in Scripture is obviously not a recent development. For some time biblical theologians such as Gerhard von Rad, Oscar Cullmann, and G. Ernest Wright have pointed to the crucial role played by different forms of *Heilgeschichte* and narrative history in Scripture.[62] Yet it is only recently that the genre of narrative and the question about its function in the context of the whole of Scripture have received concerted attention. Among those who work primarily with the Old Testament, the narrative structure of the Pentateuch and the possibility of canonical criticism have been major topics of conversation. Among interpreters of the New Testament, questions about the very nature of "gospel" as a literary form/genre and the structure of particular Gospels have generated a considerable body of literature.

Amos Wilder argues that the narrative mode is uniquely important to Christianity, for when the Christian in any time or place confesses his faith, his confession turns into narrative.[63]

For James Barr, the Old Testament should be read as story, not as history; put in another way, it seems to merit entirely the title of story but only in part the title of history.[64] Barr believes that the basic revelation of God, in the sense of the initiation of communication between God and man, is not in the Bible, nor narrated in the Bible, but is presupposed by the Bible. From the beginning it assumes that we know who God is and that he is in communication with man. What we learn in the Bible is not the first contact with deity, but new information about a personal God we already know.[65] The Bible, read as story, serves as a means of expressing — revealing — revelation, though indirectly it can be said that the Bible (story) is the locus of revelation, for it is the expression which the Israelite tradition has in fact formed, the way in which it wants to speak on the basis of that which it has heard and learned. This implies that the reading of the story is the way to meet the God whom they met, and that the explication of the story for itself, as a story, is the right form for biblical theology.[66]

Because the Bible is mostly narrative of one kind or another, narrative theology is concerned with a new evaluation of biblical stories. From the seventeenth century onwards, attention was concentrated on whether the Bible was historically accurate, and the question asked was whether or not the narratives were "historical." In the context of narrative theology it is now thought more appropriate to say that the biblical story is "history-like"; that it is not a simple reportage of history, but it is also not a fictional story having no contact with history

This approach leads to other possibilities of assessing the "truth" of a story rather than arguing that it is true as a record of historical events. It may also, or indeed instead, be "true to life," because it awakens in the reader or hearer a response rising out of a perception that authentic human experience has been deepened by the story. Or the story may contain teaching about life or a vision of the future which inspires a particular reaction or way of living in the present, as well as communicating information about the past. Thus an interpretation of the Bible in terms of narrative theology would be conceded with its truth in all these dimensions rather than just in terms of "Did it really happen?"

It is the question of the characteristic elements of narrative which occupies contemporary scholarship most actively today. The reason for this rests not in purely literary interests alone, but in theological and philosophical ones as well. For it is recognized that the narrative mode constitutes the founding medium of Christian religious perception, first in the metaphorical narratives (parables) of Jesus himself, then in the *kerygma* (proclamation) of the early Church and later in the Gospels. From such a perspective, the tendency among scholars is to define narrative as the relating of an event in which there is a build-up *(desis)* and a release *(lysis)* of tension, or to define it as a plot with a beginning, a middle, and an end. The significance of narrative is reflected in the proliferation of articles, monographs, and books concerning "story," a word which has become as commonplace as "history" was twenty years ago.

SPIRITUALITY

James Wm. McClendon's work on the relationship between biography and theology implicitly raises questions of interest for spirituality. The theological examination of the lives of others is what McClendon calls "biographical theology."[67] He describes the proper task of theology as the study of how individuals and communities embody those convictions that are at the core of the Christian faith. In order to examine those convictions as lived realities rather than as mere propositions, theology must be at least biography. As such, the object of theological reflection is the embodiment of the convictions of the Christian community in singular or striking lives.[68] McClendon examines specific biographies and attempts a brief explanation of how we should understand the relation between convictions and biography.

McClendon investigates the images which give compelling Christian lives their characteristic flavor.[69] Such "holy images" and their metaphoric force express a mode of inspiration. Different Christians are conditioned and formed by different sets of images within the large manifold of their tradition. Lives are known through their dominant images linking them with their creative sources (Scripture and tradition) and their creative possibilities (the influence these lives may have on the lives of others). Saints belong to communities of the past and shape those of the future. No life is lived or understood without images or symbols.[70] They are the clue to character and help us to discover the central convictions of our subjects.

Louis John Cameli's study of classical and modern autobiographies of faith attempts to draw together some intuitions about spirituality as a study and as a formative process.[71] Cameli focuses on four individuals: Augustine, Teresa of Avila, Thérèsa of Lisieux, and Thomas Merton, presenting their personal stories of paradise and drawing on the role of the behavioral sciences to clarify their perspective for the contemporary world. Cameli studies spirituality by way of autobiographies, offering general and particular questions for a critical reading. He attempts to show that spiritual autobiographies are particular stories about a single story of faith, God's relationship with his people. When individual stories are truly heard in their specificity through study, then one can begin to understand certain convergent lines which relate the stories to a single involvement of the authors and ourselves in a story of faith. To understand the story of faith requires another process of study which explores the nature of faith, its levels, and its dynamics. Cameli envisions spiritual direction as ministry to the stories of faith.[72]

CONCLUSION

This brief survey of the uses of narrative theology presents examples of the impact it is having in different areas of theological endeavor. No attempt has been made to give full coverage to the major writers in each field; nevertheless, representative selections have been made which should suffice to communicate the value of narrative theology as a contribution to the entire theological enterprise.

Notes for Chapter 1

[1] A study of dialogue in the theology of St. John appears in Dominic Crossan's book, *The Gospel of Eternal Life* (Milwaukee: Bruce, 1967).

[2] The ideas of this section are developed in the book that I have coauthored with Thomas Cooper, *Tellers of the Word: Nine Moments in the Theology of Story* (New York Le Jacq Publishing Co. Inc., 1981).

Notes for Chapter 2

[1] Other terms have been used to designate the material that we have called here "conflict stories." The term *Streitgespräche* (controversy dialogues) was used by Martin Albertz and Rudolf Bultmann. Martin Dibelius used *Paradigmen*. Vincent Taylor used *pronouncement stories*. Sometimes *controversy stories* was used in English as a general designation.

[2] The following conflict stories are those designated by such as Arland J. Hultgren in *Jesus and His Adversaries* (Minneapolis: Augsburg Publishing House, 1979), pp. 26–27:

1) *There are eleven conflict stories in Mark, usually with parallels in Mathew and Luke:*

2:1-12:	The Healing of the Paralytic (Mt. 9:1-8; Lk. 5:17-26).
2:15-17:	Eating with Tax Collectors and Sinners (Mt. 9:10-13; Lk. 5:29b-32).
2:18-22:	The Question About Fasting (Mt. 9:14-15; Lk. 5:33-35).
2:23-28:	Plucking Grain on the Sabbath (Mt. 12:1-8; Lk. 6:1-5).
3:1-5:	Healing on the Sabbath (Mt. 12:9-13; Lk. 6:6-10).
3:22-30:	The Beelzebul Controversy (Mt. 12:22-32; Lk. 11:14-23).
7:1-8:	The Tradition of the Elders (Mt. 15:1-9).
10:2-9:	On Divorce (Mt. 19:3-9).
11:27-33:	The Question About Authority (Mt. 21:23-27; Lk. 20:1-8).
12:13-17:	Paying Taxes to Caesar (Mt. 22:15-22; Lk. 20:20-26).
12:18-27:	On the Resurrection (Mt. 22:23-33; Lk. 20:27-40).

2) *There are two conflict stories in the special Lukan material:*

13:10-17:	Healing the Crippled Woman on the Sabbath.
14:1-6:	Healing the Man with Dropsy on the Sabbath.

3) *There are three conflict stories in Matthew based in part on Markan and Q materials:*

12:38-42:	The Refusal of a Sign (in part from Mk. 8:11-12 and Q; Lk. 11:29-32).
22:34-40:	The Double Commandment of Love (in part from Mk. 12:38-42 and Q; Lk. 10:25-28).
22:41-46:	The Question About David's Son (in part from Mk. 12:35-37).

4) *There is one conflict story in Luke based in part on Markan material:*
    7:36-50: The Sinful Woman at Simon's House (in part from Mk. 14:3-9).
5) *There is one conflict story in Q:*
    Mt. 12:22-32; Lk. 11:14-23; The Beelzebul Controversy (see Mk. 3:22-30).
[3]Conflict stories, obviously, are but one way for the evangelists to express Jesus' struggle. The story of the demoniac in the Capernaum synagogue, for example, expresses the demons' sense that in Jesus they have met the victor in the cosmic conflict between good and evil: "You have come to destroy us, haven't you?" (Mk. 1:24).
[4]See the treatment of Christian conversion in the eighth chapter of my book, coauthored with Thomas Cooper, *Tellers of the Word: Nine Moments in the Theology of Story* (New York: Le Jacq Publishers, 1981).
[5]The incapacity to enjoy seems to be connected with the incapacity to love. Some do not enjoy anything enough to be able to forget about themselves. The first thing we read about God in the Bible is that he made something and thought it was good. St. Thomas writes of the love of benevolence or friendship; that by it, the person who loves desires for the person loved *the same goods that he desires for himself* "as for *another self.*" And so the lover desires to give to the beloved the same things that have been the objects of his own love and enjoyment. See, e.g., *ST.* I-II. q. 27. a. 3.

Notes for Chapter 3

[1]The Church felt, from the start, that it needed all four Gospels. The Syrian Church had compiled the four Gospels in a continuous narrative, in the *Diatessaron* (c. 150 A.D.), that became the standard text of the Gospels until the fifth century, when it gave way to the four separate Gospels. The experience of the Syrian Church implicitly corroborates the functional utility of four separate "manuals" for four distinctive moments of Christian life.
[2]Self-transcendence for the catechumen wishing to follow Jesus involves knowledge of oneself as a sinner. Mark 21f. catalogues the sins that render us incapable of authentically loving others as Jesus did. The prayer of the blind beggar, Bartimaeus — "Jesus, Son of David, have mercy on me" (10:48). . . "Master, let me see again" (10:52) — captures the spirit of this Gospel's basic function in awakening within us our sense of need for the deliverance that is available to us in Jesus Christ, in his new way of "seeing" our basic self-others-world-God relationship.
[3]The sacramental character of Jesus is seen as Healer in Mark, as Church in Matthew, as Illuminator in Luke, and as Word in John. He is the healing presence of God's love in the Church enlightening the world with regard to its ultimate meaning. He is the healing grace and demand of that love which enables all those who receive it to become the sons of God (Jn. 1:12). The terminology and episodes of the Gospels indicate that Christian life is one of growth and maturation. God *is* perfect; we are summoned to *become* perfect through and in the power of his love in Jesus Christ and his Church.
[4]Although a conversion may begin easily or suddenly, living it out runs into many obstacles. The Gospels contrast the suddenness of the discovery of the treasure in the field with the mustard seed's slow and mysterious growth. See Luigi M. Rulla, "The Discernment of Spirits and Christian Anthropology," in *Gregorianum* 59 (1978) 3, pp. 537–569. Rulla treats of progress in Christian living in relation to personal dispositions on a conscious and unconscious level. Two persons may be sub-

jectively committed to Christ, but one may be less free because of an unconscious need for affective dependency, then he will be less effective in communicating the altruistic love of Christ.

⁵See Bernard Lonergan, *Method in Theology,* p. 291.

⁶With respect to our fundamental self-others-world-God relationship, the gift of God's love is operative when we truly imagine the potentialities (as well as actualities) of ourselves, others, and the world in the spirit of that self-transcending love, and act accordingly.

⁷Throughout the New Testament there are texts that imply gradualism in Christian development (e.g. 1 Cor. 2:6, 14:20; Gal. 6:6; Heb. 6:6; 2 Pt. 3:16). Forbearance, forgiveness, and patience are the qualtiies of a love that redeems by enduring with hope. There is a perfectionism, on the other hand, that is closely related to hatred, that clashes with the transcendent love which Jesus' life and death have manifested to Christian faith. . . . That only the perfect have the right to exist, to acceptance or approval, is an un-Christian attitude. This attitude is implicit, at times, among those whose melodramatic view of Christianity leads them to restrict the appellation of "Christian" to the perfectly well-adjusted or mature Christian. Perfectionism, fanaticism, exclusivism, intolerance, and radical impatience are forms of self-righteousness and egocentricity. The work of Jesus symbolizes redemptive love's acceptance of finitude.

⁸William M. Thompson, *Christ and Consciousness* (New York: Paulist Press, 1977) p. 50.

⁹*Ibid.,* p. 51. Two false hermeneutical principles: The Principle of the Full Head, implicitly Hegelian, that one must know everything before one can know anything; the Principle of the Empty Head, that one must have no presuppositions in order to read a text objectively. (Lonergan coined the expression for the latter principle.)

¹⁰For the writers of the New Testament books, as for Christians today, Scripture is a means to Christian living. The purpose of Scripture is perverted by those who would make it an end in itself (e.g. esoteric scholarship, fundamentalists, etc.). Union with God and neighbor in the foundational experience of Love as gift received and given is both the origin and goal of the New Testament. There is a way of merely repeating the parables that betrays them. Our following Jesus means that we must learn to tell parables that radiate the meaning of God's love within our own creative lives. See Frederick H. Borsch, *God's Parable* (London: SCM Press, 1975).

¹¹The ecclesial experience of the gift of God's love in Jesus Christ is commensurate with the experience of its demand for oneness, holiness, catholicity, and apostolicity. The experience of such love evidences itself in the Christian imagination's search for concrete ways to achieve unity, righteousness (authenticity), comprehensiveness, and a faithful continuation of the Church's purpose of sending forth witnesses to the gift of God's love in Christ. The gift of God's love is witnessed by the active reception and declaration of it in Jesus and his community. They declare, share, preach, and teach it in word and deed. They suffer for it.

¹²See John Navone, "Christ, the Beatitude of God," *The Furrow* 29 (Nov. 1978), pp. 698–701.

¹³William P. Loewe, "Lonergan and the Law of the Cross; A Universal View of Salvation." *Anglican Theological Review* LIX (April, 1977), p. 170.

¹⁴*Ibid.,* p. 172.

¹⁵See Bartholomew M. Kiely, S.J., *Psychology and Moral Theology: Some Lines of Convergence,* Pontifical Gregorian University Press, Rome, Italy, 1980, pp. 197, 207, 210–11, 265.

¹⁶William P. Loewe, "Lonergan and the Law of the Cross," p. 172.

Notes for Chapter 4

[1]Bernard Lonergan, *Method in Theology* (London: Darton, Longman & Todd, 1971), p. 267.

[2]Bernard Lonergan, "Mission and Spirit," in *Experience of the Spirit,* Peter Huizing and William Bassett, eds. (New York: Seabury Press, 1974/76), p. 77.

[3]Lonergan, *Method in Theology,* p. 116.

[4]Frederick E. Crowe, "Eschaton and Worldly Mission in the Mind and Heart of Jesus," in *Eschaton: A Community of Love,* Joseph Papin, ed., (Villanova, Pa.: Villanova University Press, 1971), p. 118.

[5]Frederick E. Crowe, "The Power of the Scriptures: Attempt at Analysis," in *Word and Spirit: Essays in Honor of David Michael Stanley, S.J., on his 60th Birthday,* Joseph Plevnick, Ed. (Toronto: Regis College Press, 1975), p. 338.

[6]Lonergan, *Method in Theology,* p. 130.

[7]*Ibid.,* pp. 282f.

[8]*Ibid.,* p. 73: "Incarnate meaning combines all or at least many of the other carriers of meaning. It can be at once intersubjective, artistic, symbolic, linguistic. It is the meaning of a person, of his way of life, of his words, or of his deeds. It may be his meaning for just one other person, or for a small group, or for a whole national, or social, or cultural, or religious tradition."

[9]*Ibid.,* p. 107.

[10]*Ibid.,* p. 112. To say that the dynamic state of religious conversion, which occurs in the immediacy of the subject's consciousness, is "conscious," is not to say that it is "known": "For consciousness is just experience, but knowledge is a compound of experience, understanding, and judging" (p. 106). Lonergan notes that what is conscious but not objectified seems to be the meaning of what some psychiatrists call the unconscious (p. 34, n. 5). Other related concepts: the preconscious, the subconscious, the infrastructure within knowing, unreflective consciousness.

[11]William P. Loewe, "Lonergan and the Law of the Cross: A Universalist View of Salvation," *Anglican Theological Review* 59 (April, 1977), p. 170.

[12]*Ibid.* Loewe underscores the role of the imagination for this task of expressing and communicating Jesus' identity in all its forcefulness. Those who contributed to the formative tradition of the New Testament constructed dramatic narratives: "Guided by their interest in conversion and redemption, they enriched and reshaped their memories of Jesus' words and deeds with appropriate images drawn from the Hellenistic world and above all the Old Testament. The one who died on the cross became the prophet who was to come, the Messiah, the Suffering Servant, the Lord, the Son of God. Each image placed at the service of Christian faith a wealth of symbolic power evoking the meaning incarnate in Jesus." This meaning is that of the dynamism of God's gift of his love exerting its creative pressure on every human consciousness, independently of the human subject's religious conversion.

[13]Biblical passages with a strong exhortatory content are termed paraenetic. The proclamation of Christ (kerygma) and paraenesis are related to each other as gift and task, indicative and imperative, and, in the realm of theological reflection, as dogmatics and ethics. The promise of the Good News is the foundation and presupposition of the claims of paraenesis (See Rom. 1-11 with 12-15).

[14]Avery Dulles, *Models of the Church* (Garden City, N.Y.: Doubleday & Co., 1974), p. 47. Dulles notes that for Aquinas the Holy Spirit is the principle of unity in the Church, that the humanity of Christ and the sacraments can be communicators of the grace of God. The external means of grace are instruments of the uncreated grace, that is, the Holy Spirit of Christ and the Father. The external means are,

therefore, secondary and subordinate to their foundation in the self-gift of God, the Holy Spirit.

¹⁵*Ibid.,* p. 187: Dulles affirms that of their very nature institutions are subordinate to persons, structures are subordinate to life. Without calling into question the value and importance of institutions and structures, he believes that this value does not properly appear unless it can be seen that they effectively help to make the Church a community of grace, a sacrament of Christ, a herald of salvation, and a servant of mankind. External expressions of the fundamental experience of God's gift of his love are called into existence by the gift, and exist for its service and communication.

¹⁶See "Trinity," in Karl Rahner and Herbert Vorgrimler, *Theological Dictionary,* Cornelius Ernst, ed., tr. by Richard Strachan (New York: Herder & Herder, 1965), p. 471: "From that experience of our faith which the Word of God himself (Jesus-Scripture) gives, we can therefore say that God's absolute self-communication to the world, *as* a mystery that has approached us, is in its ultimate originality called Father; *as* itself a principle acting in history, Son; *as* a gift bestowed on us and accepted, Holy Ghost. This 'as,' which is ordered to us, is really the self-communication of God 'in himself': the triplicity affirmed is thus a triplicity of God in himself."

¹⁷In terms of Old Testament imagery, the two moments of religious experience might be symbolized by the creative power of God that is operative in both chaos and cosmos, in prestructured and structured reality, in darkness and in the light. Urban T. Holmes, III, *The Priest in Community: Exploring the Roots of Ministry* (New York: Seabury Press, 1978), employs this symbolism in his study of the function of the priest. Because our minds are finite, Holmes believes that the order we make of disorder, the cosmos we make of chaos, is inevitably an incomplete representation (p. 16). Again: "If we abandon the image of chaos or the abyss as surrounding us we will inevitably make idols of our representations of the experience of God. . . . We never get rid of the abyss. It is within human history. Our personal consciousness arises from the infinite, dark void of our unknowing. Chaos is the source of our creativity. . . . Our consciousness — our reality, our meaning, and our truth — is made from and rises from the abyss, from chaos" (pp. 18f.). Our symbols, metaphors, myths, and stories are employed to represent our experience of the presence of God within our own inner wilderness (pp. 88f.). The task of the priest is to illuminate our consciousness from out of the darkness (p. 91).

¹⁸Harvey Egan, "Christian Apophatic and Kataphatic Mysticisms," in *Theological Studies* 39 (September, 1978), p. 405. This article is the source for what appears here on these two mysticisms.

¹⁹*Ibid.,* pp. 422f.

²⁰*Ibid.,* p. 424.

²¹*Ibid.,* p. 426.

²²See Bernard Lonergan, *Method in Theology,* p. 360, where he affirms that the ideal basis of society is community, and the community may take its stand on the religious principle that is God's gift of his love, that forms the basis for dialogue among those who experience religious conversion. The Christian principle, upon which community may take its stand, conjoins the inner gift of God's love with its outer manifestation in Christ Jesus and in those that follow him. Such is the basis for Christian ecumenism.

²³Harvey Egan, *art. cit.,* p. 420. Egan affirms that man's supernaturally elevated and Christ-anointed transcendence has Mystery for its destination; Truth illuminates it; God's Love draws it.

[24]See John Haught, *Religion and Self-Acceptance* (New York: Paulist Press, 1976), p. 44. Haught affirms that the world of the sacred becomes transparent only in the primal patterns of consciousness, in the immediacy of the sentient, interpersonal, narrative, and aesthetic fields of religious insight. It is within these primal fields of meaning that a sense of the sacred *first* takes hold of religious man's consciousness. They are pretheoretical fields of religious insight in which the knower is so united with the known that what is later called "subject" and "object" constitute an original, still undifferentiated whole. In the theoretic pattern, or *second* moment, of religious consciousness the desire to know the real leads the subject to detach himself in a reflective way from the object known in order to know it as it is in itself, apart from subjective moods or aesthetic bias. The subject goes beyond descriptive and seeks explanatory knowledge of the world of the sacred.

[25]Thomas Cooper, "Communicating the Incommunicable," *The Clergy Review* (May, 1977), p. 191.

[26]Karl Rahner, "Experience of Self and Experience of God," in *Theological Investigations,* vol. XIII (New York: Seabury Press, 1974–75), pp. 122–132.

[27]Thomas Cooper, *art. cit.,* p. 188. Cooper affirms that awareness of my limitations, however unthematic, implies an awareness of the Unlimited. Awareness of my relativity, be it ever so unreflective, implies an awareness of the Absolute, an awareness of Truth and Goodness which precedes and makes possible every subsequent act of understanding the true or willing the good.

[28]*Ibid.* The New Testament symbolizes the transcendent realm of God by presenting Jesus as God's self-revelation. The kataphatic and apophatic elements of the Love we experience are implicity in his name and title: Jesus Christ. To follow him is to do what he does with respect to God's gift of his love: he communicates (the kataphatic dimension of *incarnate* meaning) the Incommunicable (the apophatic dimension of his orientation to a Love that transcends our very appetites). The New Testament thematizes the meaning of its central image (Jesus Christ) and affirmation as redemptive.

[29]Eric Voegelin, "The Gospel and Culture," in *Jesus and Man's Hope,* ed. by D. G. Miller and D. Y. Hadidian (Pittsburgh: Pittsburgh Theological Seminary, 1971), p. 90. This passage is quoted from Bernard Lonergan, "Theology and Praxis," in *Proceedings of the Thirty-Second Annual Convention,* Vol. 32, Luke Salm, ed. (Toronto: The Catholic Theological Society of America, 1977), p. 9. What Voegelin affirms as the purpose of Jesus' charge in Matt. 16:20 finds its counterpart in the messianic secret of Mark's Gospel. Absolute fidelity to his Father's will, the fullness of his being drawn by the transcendent power of his Father's love and goodness, is what manifests him as fully Messiah, fully Son of God.

[30]William Johnston, *The Inner Eye of Love: Mysticism and Religion* (San Francisco: Harper and Row, 1978), p. 68. This is the distinction of Bernard Lonergan between faith and belief in *Method in Theology,* pp. 188ff. Faith is the knowledge born of religious love (p. 115). However obscure, it is a love that necessarily brings enlightenment. The inner light of faith leads to the outer word of proclamation.

[31]*Ibid.,* p. 69. It is not the prerogative of Christians alone, for God loves all men and desires them to be saved (1 Tm. 2:4): consequently, it shines in the hearts of all who sincerely seek the truth. Johnston believes that modern religious plight centers on the search for the authentic superstructure that will satisfy the inner longing for the infinite.

[32]*Ibid.,* pp. 65–66, 70.

[33]Lonergan, *Method in Theology,* p. 78. See Charles C. Hefling, Jr., "Liturgy and Myth: A Theological Approach Based on the Methodology of Bernard Lonergan"

in *Anglican Theological Review* LXI (April, 1979) 2, p. 213. Hefling affirms that "the gospel's Saving Tale of divine Incarnation, Death and Resurrection is a great *eikon,* a hierophanic revelation of divine reality" that in Lonergan's terms has its source in transcendence (Voegelin's "Beyond"), and its foundations in interiority (Voegelin's *nous, psyche,* consciousness). The function of hierophany, for Hefling, is to provide in sensible image, the *eikon,* that sparks the insight which allows us to articulate our conscious experience of intending, and being drawn toward, the divine (p. 212). For both Voegelin and Lonergan, the divine is what is ultimately intended in every operation of intentional consciousness, the restlessness that continues to raise questions of truth and of value even when questions about the world of space and time have been put to rest (p. 211).

Notes for Chapter 5

¹William V. Dych, "The Logic of Faith," *America* 140 (March 19, 1979), p. 219.
²John Drury, *Angels and Dirt* (London: Darton, Longman & Todd, 1972) p. 50.
³*Ibid.*
⁴Bernard Lonergan, *Method in Theology* (London: Darton, Longman & Todd, 1971), p. 9. See also T. Patrick Burke, "The Theologian as Storyteller and Philosopher," *Horizons* 4/2 (1977), p. 207.

Notes for Chapter 6

¹See Robert M. Doran, "Aesthetics and the Opposites" in *Thought,* LII (June 1977), 205, p. 120. The author explains that the human subject is a Protean commingling of opposites: spirit and matter, archetype and instinct, intentionality and body. The operator of their progressive integration is the human soul, or psyche, or imagination. The three are the same for Doran, who attributes his notion of imagination to Heidegger's *Einbildungskraft* in *Kant und das Problem der Metaphysik* (Frankfurt: Klostermann, 1951). The German word denotes the art of forming into one. Soul, when undifferentiated, is the defective operator of personal disintegration. The differentiation of soul or imagination is, for Doran, as arduous a task as that of spirit or intentionality.
²John Navone, *Towards a Theology of Story* (Slough, U.K.: St. Paul Publications, 1977), pp. 105-114 (reprint of my article, "A Theology of Darkness, Terror and Dread" in *Theology,* LXXX (Sept. 1977), 677, pp. 348-353).
³Existential consciousness begins in feelings. See Bernard Lonergan, *Method in Theology* (London: Darton, Longman & Todd, 1971), pp. 37f. Feelings are liable to an opaqueness surpassing that of the cognitional process, according to Doran, *art cit.,* p. 121.

Notes for Chapter 7

¹Hannah Arendt, *The Human Condition* (New York: Doubleday Anchor, 1958), p. 181.
²*Ibid.,* p. 286.
³Stanley Hauerwas, "Story and Theology," in *Religion in Life* XLV (1976), 3, p. 347.
⁴David Burrell, *Analogy and Philosophical Language* (New Haven: Yale University Press, 1973).

[5]Stanley Hauerwas, "Story and Theology," p. 347.
[6]See John F. Haught *Religion and Self-Acceptance* (New York: Paulist Press, 1976), pp. 37f.
[7]Michael Novak, *The Experience of Nothingness* (N.Y.: Harper & Row, 1971), pp. 23f.
[8]Maxwell Anderson, *Off Broadway* (New York: William Sloane Associates, 1947), p. 19.
[9]See David Tracy, *Blessed Rage for Order* (New York: Seabury Press, 1975), pp. 207-11. Tracy's remarks on the need for fiction are most relevant.
[10]John Navone, *Communicating Christ* (Slough: St. Paul Publications, 1976), p. 45.

Notes for Chapter 8

[1]Ludwig Wittgenstein, *Philosophical Investigations,* tr. by G.E.M. Anscombe (Oxford: Basil Blackwell, 1967), pp. 50-51e, no. 129.
[2]Russell Kirk, *Enemies of the Permanent Things* (New Rochelle, N.Y.: Arlington House, 1969), pp. 111ff.
[3]The word 'literature' in the context of this article is intended to refer to the whole world of creative artistic expression, of the reality experienced by authors and directors and presented in their writings, plays and films.
[4]Richard R. Niebuhr, *Experiential Religion* (New York: Harper & Row, 1974), p. 76.
[5]Geoffrey Preston OP, "Fiction and Poetry in the Bible," in *New Blackfriars* (July 1972), pp. 300-1.
[6]Stanley Romaine Hopper, discussing the primacy of metaphor in meaning, points to the hiddenness of reality. "Within the limits of our finite perceiving it must be grasped in perspective and conceptual modes, that is to say mythically, metaphorically and symbolically" (S. Romaine Hopper, "The Poetry of Meaning" in *Literature and Religion,* ed. Giles B. Gunn [New York: Harper & Row, 1971], p. 227).
[7]The importance of this recognition is underlined by Vincent Buckley's reference to Mircea Eliade's "The Sacred and the Profane." According to Eliade, "A hierophany is 'anything that manifests the sacred'; and so we must get used to the idea of recognizing hierophanies absolutely everywhere, in every area of psychological, economic, spiritual and social life . . ." (Vincent Buckley, "Specifying the Sacred" in *Literature and Religion,* p. 61).
[8]Wittgenstein, *op. cit.,* pp. 50-51e, no. 130.
[9]Amos N. Wilder, "The Uses of a Theological Criticism," in *Literature and Religion,* p. 43.
[10]J. Mitros SJ, "Patristic Views of Christ's Salvic Work," in *Thought* (Autumn 1967), vol. 42, p. 444.
[11]John Navone, *Everyman's Odyssey: Seven Plays Seen as Modern Man's Quest for Personal Integrity* (Seattle University Press, 1974). Much of what has been said here on the subject of myth is a reworking of the Preface to this work.
[12]Ian T. Ramsey, *Models and Mystery* (Oxford, 1964), p. 65.
[13]George H. Tavard, "Christianity and the Philosophies of Existence," in *Theological Studies* 18 (March 1957), pp. 4f, notes that the analogical conception of the Christian man as developed by the Greek Fathers opened the way for the application to the natural man of a philosophy of analogy. This systematizes the idea that man is made to the image of God. Analogy is the philosophical way of

defining the correspondence between God the Creator and his creatures. For Tavard, it means this: the being which man enjoys is neither identical with, nor heterogeneous to, the being of God. Instead, their relationship is analogical. Being is one, yet it develops intrinsic differentiations according to how it is actualized. Those differences are related one to another according to a scheme of proportionality. If we conceive of being as a relation between existence (that which is) and essence (the way it is), the connection between this existence and this essence corresponds to the connection between that existence and that essence. Being is realized proportionally at all its degrees.

Notes for Chapter 9

[1]*Mental Growth through Positive Disintegration,* London: Gryf Publications, 1970.
[2]*The Great Wall of China,* New York: Schocken Books, 1946, p. 265.
[3]*Earlier Writings,* Philadelphia: Westminster Press, 1953, p. 259.
[4]The "Christ-self" is an expression coined by Bernard Tyrrell, S.J., in his course *Christotherapy: Healing through Enlightenment.* It is the self that makes the Father the vital center of his consciousness just as the Father was and forever is the center of the consciousness of Jesus. Among the dimensions of transformation into the Christ-self, according to Tyrrell, are the sacramental, the moral, the ascetical, the ontological, the illuminative, and the mystical. Tyrrell has coined other expressions of the self: the "anti-Christ-self" refers to everything in man that is opposed to Christ: the "perfect Christ-self" is the glorified self one is called eternally to be in the resurrected state or in the "beatific vision," which participates in the inner life of God as Triune: the "zero-self" and the "Hell-self" refer to the definitive and lasting rejection of the exigencies of the self and the Christ-self. The "authentic self," the "true self," is the self insofar as it is understanding, rational, responsible, loving: the "anti-self" is the caricature of the true self, characterized by disease, disharmony, ignorance, sin. The "present self" is self-explanatory. Tyrrell notes that when to the failure to obey the natural exigencies of the spirit there is added a rejection of the light of Christ, the anti-Christ-self appears.

Notes for Chapter 10

[1]Mircea Eliade, in *Myths, Dreams and Mysteries* (New York: Harper Torchbook, 1960), 59, studies the nostalgia for paradise in primitive traditions about a primordial epoch when men knew nothing about death and enjoyed immortality, spontaneity, freedom, and a marvelous communion with the gods. As a result of the fall, the rupture between heaven and earth, the paradise condition came to an end and the painful longing for its restoration began.
[2]In the Judaeo-Christian tradition paradise is located in three times: paradise of the primeval age is described in the Yahwist narrative of Genesis (2:4 to 3:24), in Isaiah 51:3, in Ezekiel 31:8, etc.; paradise in the eschatological age occurs in the writings of the Old Testament prophets, such as Isaiah 11:6-11, and is vaguely situated in 'latter times'; paradise in the present age is assumed to have been taken up to heaven after its removal from earth (Apocalypse of Baruch 4:6), and Jesus refers to the temporary abode of the just after their death (Lk. 16:23).
[3]See John Navone, *Everyman's Odyssey: Seven Plays Seen as Modern Myths About Man's Quest for Personal Integrity* (Seattle University Press, 1974). The preface

treats of dream and myth; the second chapter is a study of *Streetcar Named Desire*.

⁴See Norman Cohn, *The Pursuit of the Millennium* (New York 1961). He studies visions of the future and ideal societies.

⁵A prior concern of the Christian community in the earliest times was a true understanding of the meaning and value of many kinds of psychic and charismatic phenomena. Many of these experiences were assigned to the Spirit of God; others were assigned to false spirits. The community prayed for light to understand such experiences with faith in its Lord, "the light of the world" (Jn. 8:12), the healing light, "the radiant light of God's glory and the perfect copy of his nature" (Heb. 1:3), which dispels the darkness and ignorance that is inimical to the human spirit. Authentic discipleship is bipolar: it bespeaks both a liberation from false dreams (false values, ideals, dehumanizing obsessions) and a healing sharing in the authentic vision or world view of Christ. The process of liberation from the false dream implies the discovery and understanding of the negative forces, diseases, in one's life (and society); it also implies the recognition of God's summoning inspirations and providential guidance to a deeper sharing in the authentic values, attitudes and habits of Christ, the incarnation of man's dream of ultimate and enduring communion with God.

⁶Paul Ricoeur ("The Hermeneutics of Symbols and Philosophical Reflections," in *International Philosophical Quarterly* 2 (1962), p. 195) has shown how the New Testament symbolics of evil and purgation include psychic strata that go down into primordial human archetypes. He observes that the long way back of reflection on the successive layers of the great cultural symbols can alone match psychoanalysis and co-operate with its regressive exploration.

⁷Amos N. Wilder, "Myth and Dream in Christian Scripture" in J. Campbell, ed., *Myths, Dreams, and Religion* (New York: Dutton, 1970), p. 68 notes that the New Testament contains many dreams, visions and auditions which indicate the deeper dynamics of human awareness, and suggests that they are pervaded by an eschatological consciousness, by the sense of world-transformation in course and ultimate goals within reach. These goals are social and cosmic as well as individual. The entire *Book of Revelation* consists of visions and auditions which represent a mythopoetic reading of the contemporary historical events and experiences of the Christian community. Dreams, visions, auditions, trances, epiphanies, theophanies, raptures to heaven are dramatizations of existence, the imaginative media of world-representation animated by that sense of crisis and world-metamorphosis that pervades the New Testament; they are, according to Wilder (p. 71), what the psychology of religion might describe as expressions of supranormal ecstatic, mystic experience.

⁸See Rollo May, ed., *Symbolism in Religion and Literature* (New York, 1960). May believes that symbols are 'mothered' by the archaic, archetypal material in the unconscious, but 'fathered' by the individual's conscious existence in his immediate struggle.

⁹See John Dunne, *A Search for God in Time and Memory* (London. Macmillan, 1967). Dunne develops the notion of autobiographical criteria for the life story.

¹⁰William Lynch, "The Imagination and the Finite," in *Thought* 33 (Summer 1958), p. 209, speaks of "images of limitation," which correspond to the concrete and historical expression which the dream within a man must necessarily take.

¹¹Avery Dulles, in *Myth, Biblical Revelation, and Christ* (Washington & Cleveland: Corpus Books, 1969), offers a useful survey of the essential elements of myth. He notes that the numinous presence which myth discerns behind the world of phenomena is portrayed in personal terms.

¹²See Maude Bodkin, *Archetypal Patterns in Poetry: Psychological Studies of Imagination* (London 1951). She analyses archetypal patterns in sacred and profane literature.

¹³See Philip Wheelwright, "The Archetypal Symbol" in *Perspectives in Literary Symbolism,* Yearbook of Comparative Criticism, vol. 1, ed. Joseph Strelka, 2nd ed. (University Park & London: The Pennsylvania State University Press, 1972); also Mircea Eliade, *Patterns in Comparative Religion* (New York: Sheed & Ward, 1958; Meridian Books, 1963).

¹⁴See Northrop Frye, *Anatomy of Criticism* (Princeton University Press, 1957), esp. pp. 100-12, 131-60; cf. "The Archetypes of Literature" in his *Fables of Identity* (New York: Harcourt Brace and World, 1963; Harbinger paperback).

¹⁵See John Navone, *A Theology of Failure* (New York: Paulist Press, 1974). The fifth chapter, "Man Fails," treats the archetypal contrast in the symbolism of the garden and the wilderness.

¹⁶See Robert B. Heilman, *Tragedy and Melodrama: Versions of Experience* (Seattle & London: University of Washington Press, 1968) for his comments on these two plays (pp. 120–22) and on William's use of myth (pp. 92 3).

¹⁷See William Lynth, *Images of Hope* (Baltimore: Helicon, 1965). He links hope, sanity, and fantasy, and sees in them the beginning of religion.

¹⁸Thomas Porter, *Myth and Modern American Drama* (Detroit: University of Detroit Press, 1969), maintains that significant plays are part of that process by which a community interprets its own experience: its origins, its institutions, its history and its values. He affirms the mythic qualities of the world view embodied in a play.

¹⁹See Hans Meyerhoff, *Time in Literature* (Berkeley, 1955). He considers aspects of time in literature that are excluded from the scientific analysis of time in space.

²⁰Schubert Ogden, *Christ without Myth* (New York: Harper, 1961), p. 24. There are cultural, psychological and spiritual realities which underlie myth as the symbolic expression of truths about man's own life and thought.

²¹The Christian believes that in and through Christ the dream of paradise is fulfilled, that through his full recognition and acceptance of Christ's meaning and value he too shall receive Christ's assurance: "I tell you that this day you shall be in paradise with me" (Lk. 23:43).

Notes for Chapter 11

¹See William F. Lynch, *Christ and Apollo: The Dimensions of the Literary Imagination* (New York: Sheed & Ward, 1960), p. 150. Lynch's description of analogy applies to the relationship between the written script and its re-enactment according to the potentialities of diverse actors. He affirms that existence is analogous. It is never the same act of existence. It is a completely new fact; it must be new; for it must adapt itself completely to the new materials which it confronts, adapting itself in its bone and heart to the bone and heart of each new subject of being, each new part of the total organism. So too with an analogical idea, with our inward thinking about being. The work, the thinking of it, is never done. The process of adaptation is eternal. We can never come up with one logical core and say it will satisfy the requirements of all subjects. Only the proportion is the same; but the two parts of the proportion are always changing. The act of existence is always different; so too is the possibility, the material into which it enters. (The Word of God has different existences in the different individuals [and communi-

ties] in which it exists; it exists as qualified according to the potential of those who receive it.) See George H. Tavard, "Christianity and the Philosophies of Existence," in *Theological Studies* 18 (March 1975), pp. 4-5. Tavard explains that the being which man enjoys is neither identical with, nor heterogeneous to the being of God. Instead, their relationship is analogical. Being is one, yet it develops intrinsic differentiations according as it is actualized. Those differences are related one to another according to a scheme of proportionality. If we conceive of being as a relation between existence (that which is) and essence (the way it is), the connection between this existence and this essence corresponds to the connection between that existence and that essence. Being is realized proportionally at all its degrees. (The one Gospel truth is realized proportionally in individual Christians and in separate Christian communities.)

[2]Bernard Lonergan, *Method in Theology* (London: Darton, Longman and Todd, 1971), pp. 28.

[3]Edward Bozzo, "Jesus as Paradigm for Personal Life," in *Journal of Ecumenical Studies* 11 (Winter 1974), pp. 45-63.

[4]This does not mean that it fails as drama.

[5]For a related problem see John Navone, *History and Faith in the Thought of Alan Richardson* (London: SCM Press, 1966), p. 47.

[6]The divisions among the Christian churches might also be explained in terms of Hugh Dalziel Duncan's principle that "Social order is achieved through resolution of acceptance, doubt and rejection of the principles that are believed to guarantee such order" (in *Human Communication Theory*, Frank E.X. Dance, ed. [New York: Holt Rinehart and Winston, Inc., 1967], p. 253). Duncan believes that the question of social order or unity is not how to eliminate doubt and rejection, but how to resolve them. This requires that means must be provided to express openly and freely love, doubt and rejection. When we cannot communicate with a real other, Duncan believes that we create fantasy others; for even in the dream we must communicate. The dream is a drama, and, like all drama, it is an act of communication in which we struggle to make some kind of order out of problems in relationships. Dreams and fantasies arise out of blocks in communication. Perhaps the breaking away of Christian communities from the central authority of the Church can be interpreted in this context: a breakdown of communications for resolving conflicts and the consequent pursuit and realization of new dreams of Christian fellowship. Visions of the future represent a search for ways to complete an action in the present. And since the present is always problematical, it is only through such visions of the future, as well as the recaptured past, that we organize action in the present. Protestant churches, by their very existence, imply new interpretations of the past, of the primitive church, which are incompatible with that of the Roman Church; they also imply a new vision of the future that seeks to resolve the conflicts and problems of the present. See also E. Bozzo, *op. cit.,* pp. 43-63.

[7]John Gardiner, *Self-Renewal: The Individual and the Innovative Society* (New York: Harper and Row, 1963), p. 38. Gardiner affirms that such a trait enables an individual to tolerate internal conflict and suspend judgment in the presence of unanswered question. A tolerance for ambiguity enables one to endure unresolved differences with tranquillity and patience as one analyzes the differences in search of a resolution.

[8]The crucial importance of *how* we express ourselves, as opposed to what we express, is recognized by Kenneth Burke in *The Rhetoric of Religion: Studies in Logology* (Boston: Beacon Press, 1961). Burke is concerned with how words about society persuade us to act in certain ways in our social relationships. *How* we

express ourselves *is* a determinant of *what* happens to us in our social relationships. We do not relate and then talk, we relate in talk, and the forms of talk available to us and the spirit with which they are employed determine how we relate as social beings. Society not only exists *by* transmission, *by* communication, but *in* transmission, *in* communication of the significant symbol. For Christians, communication in Christ and the Gospel truth give existence to the Christian community; nevertheless, the distinctiveness of *how* Christians communicate Christ and in Christ can be either a source of enrichment or of division and conflict among Christians. *How* Christians communicate determines how they relate; how they distinctively embody faith in Jesus Christ determines how they relate as denominations and as individuals within denominations. We must create models of the Christian as communicator as others have created their models of man (e.g. psychologists, sociologists, etc.); and such models must respect distinctiveness among Christian communicators.

⁹Vincent Taylor, *The Names of Jesus* (London, 1951).

¹⁰Joseph Mitros, "Patristic Views of Christ's Salvific Work," in *Thought* 42 (Autumn 1967), p. 414.

¹¹The form of action and passion in the God-and-man relationship can be illuminated by dramatic models. Forms of drama have been used by Aristotle and Kenneth Burke, and to a lesser extent by Freud and such anthropologists as Lord Raglan in their models of social interaction. A dramatic model involves an action, a struggle between hero and villain over some principles of social order, a cast of characters, a group of community guardians (as in the chorus) who comment on the actions of the players, and an audience who accept, reject or doubt the value of the acts of the hero and villain as a way of upholding social order. And finally, there is some kind of ultimate appeal to a great transcendent principle of social order, whose mystery and radiance resolves all conflict. The Gospels offer such a dramatic model of the God-and-man relationship in Christ's struggle to redeem mankind; the Fathers of the Church express the work of Christ with similar models.

¹²Hugh D. Duncan, "The Search for a Social Theory of Communication," in *Human Communication Theory*, p. 254, affirms the importance of re-enactment of those principles of order that are believed necessary to the survival and continuation of a society. Social order, he holds, is created in social drama through intensive and frequent communal presentations of roles whose proper enactment is believed necessary to community survival. These principles are never given once and for all. Myths of origin are not simply acted out in one great moment of social birth. The visions of futures that are guides to action in the present are never 'engraved' for all time in the minds of the community. They must be done with great conviction and intensity, using all the resources of self, if these principles are to retain their hold over us. Duncan's views have obvious implications for the existence of the Church and life according to the Gospel truth through faith's daily re-enacting the authentic meaning and value of the Christ-event in the present moment of history.

¹³John Navone, *Themes of St. Luke* (Rome: Gregorian University, 1970). The ninth chapter treats of the Christian's summons to represent the life of God in mercy and other perfections of God, pp. 95-100.

¹⁴E. Bozzo, *art. cit.,* p. 458.

¹⁵E. Bozzo, *art. cit.,* p. 458.

¹⁶See Avery Dulles, *The Church is Communications* (Rome: Multimedia International, 1970), pp. 6-8. See also Vernon Ruland, *Horizons of Criticism.* (Chicago:

American Library Association, 1975). This brilliant assessment of religious-literary options views *religion* and *literature* not as substantives, but primarily as adjectives, adverbs, dimensions of one integral process of human experiencing. His focus is on a single consciousness, experiencing poetically-religiously, more or less as a pervasive style of being. The experience is symbolized in religion and analyzed in theology.

[17]Gerhard Ebeling, "Die Evidenz des Ethischen," p. 344, quoted by R.W. Funk, in *Language, Hermeneutic and Word of God* (New York: Harper and Row, 1966), p. 220.

[18]See Bernard Tyrrell, *Christotherapy* (New York: New Seabury Press, 1975). The fourth chapter, "Mind-Fasting and Spirit-Feasting," explains the implications of effective repentance.

[19]William F. Lynch, *Christ and Apollo*. The sixth chapter, "The Analogical," is germane to this concept.

[20]David Burrell, "Indwelling: Presence and Dialogue," in *Theological Studies* 22 (March 1961), p. 16. Burrell affirms that every friendship between God and an individual is unique, because the love of God is received by unique individuals. Its expression is unique, because the active receptivity of the gift of God's love ever seeks expression among those who have received it. Although the receptivity and the expression (complacency and concern: cf. F. Crowe's three articles, "Complacency and Concern," in *Theological Studies* 20, March, June, September 1959) are the created effects of God's gift in us, they differ in that God works the first one alone, but the second along with us and in virtue of the first (p. 17). We are his friends, radically, because all that Christ has heard from his father he has made known to us (Jn. 15:15); we are his friends authentically only if we respond to this revelation of Love by faith and love, which means holding fast to his commandments (1 Jn. 5:1-5). In that case, the eternal possession that God has of us is historically unfolded in a multiplicity of ways and persons. The ground of this friendship is that "He has first loved us"; being loved comes before loving, consent to God's love for us is the source of any concern for his glory. This friendship must be lived out in the presence of the person to God, where he is loved with an eternal love, where "those whom he has foreknown he has also predestined to become conformed to the image of his son" (Rom. 8:29). The Good News is that Christ summons man to respond to this predilection of eternal presence—man's presence to God's eternal love and wisdom—from within his properly historical self. Man never was and never is absent from God; however, God will ordinarily be present to many only intermittently, as a prevailing intention seeking varied and multiple expression, within the limits of the human consciousness' ability to sustain the presence of another.

[21]Bernard Lonergan, *De Verbo Incarnato* (Rome: Gregorian University Press, 1960). He sees the historical mission of Jesus as that of making the ineffable more and more effable. The idea is developed in *Eschatology,* Daniel Onley, ed., based on Lectures of David Tracy (Washington, D.C.: Catholic University of America, 1967), pp. 183-5.

[22]Don Fabun, *Communications* (Beverly Hills: Glencoe Press, 1968), p. 4.

[23]*Ibid.*

[24]*Ibid.,* p. 5; see William F. Lynch, *Images of Faith: An Exploration of the Ironic Imagination* (Notre Dame, Indiana: University of Notre Dame Press, 1973). For Lynch the imagination is the mode in which we experience and manage the world, and faith is a form of imagining and experiencing the world, more specifically an activating paradigm that moves through the stages of man's life and is above all

ironic. Irony is the imagination's capacity for holding together contraries (the two most widely separated members of a single class or species). Lynch affirms that there is no single way that faith imagines the world because there is no incontrovertible evidence for one paradigm over another.

[25]*Ibid.,* p. 8.

[26]See Andrew Greeley, *The Persistence of Religion* (New York: Harper and Row, 1974), p. 173. Religion is man's view of ultimate reality, a view learned in community and generating community, a view which demands the involvement of the whole man and thus embodies itself in myth and produces, in some form or other, a sense of the numinous or the transcendent.

[27]Michael Novak, "Culture & Imagination," in *Journal of Ecumenical Studies* 10 (Winter 1973), pp. 138-40.

[28]*Ibid.,* pp. 134-8.

[29]*Ibid.,* p. 131.

[30]Richard R. Niebuhr, *Experiential Religion* (New York: Harper & Row, 1972), p. 78. Religion, for Niebuhr, arises as human reaction and answer to the state of being affected totally (p. 31).

Notes for Chapter 12

[1]Our myths are concerned with our meaning, asking 'Who are we?' They examine three organically related questions: 'Where do we come from?,' 'Where are we bound?' and 'What must we do now to get there?' These are the problems of Creation, Destiny and Quest. Living myths would redeem and renew a living heritage by reaffirming its basic truth and value within a new context and by rejecting spurious interpretations of this heritage. They touch on man's basic relation to the world and fellow men, on his original roots, his future possibilities and destiny; they supply a symbolic memory, a symbolic hope, and an allegorized account of the perils of the way. See William E. Hocking, *Goethe and the Modern Era* (Chicago, 1949), pp. 279-80. Hocking states that men must remember their traditional wisdom to retain their identity and to be united in their sense of destiny on their journey. Myth supplies a symbolic memory of such wisdom. The perennial appeal and vitality of myths derives from the analogous character of human experiences and situations in all civilizations. Myths draw on the underlying correspondences that unite mankind and enable their creation, communication and comprehension.

[2]See Carl Kerenyi, in *Essays on a Science of Mythology* by C.G. Jung and C. Kerenyi (New York, 1949), p. 5. Myths offer paradigms of recurrent scenes in the human drama. Harry Slochower, in *Mythopoesis* (Detroit, 1970), pp. 17-18, explains the link between the universal schema of the myth and its temporal or story sequence in terms of the Four Causes: the mythic pattern provides the formal and final cause, while the historical content operates as the material and efficient cause.

[3]The 'Christ-self' is an expression coined by Bernard Tyrrell in his book *Christotherapy* (New York: Seabury Press, 1975), ch. 3, "Self, Christ-Self and Self-Image." It is the self that makes the Father of Christ the vital center of one's consciousness of Jesus; the "anti-Christ-self" refers to everything in man that is opposed to Christ.

[4]Northrop Frye, "The Archetypes of Literature," in *Myth and Method,* pp. 159-60. The importance of the god or hero in the myth, according to Frye, lies in the fact

that such characters, who are all conceived in human likeness and yet have more power over nature, gradually build up the vision of an omnipotent personal community beyond an indifferent nature. It is this which the hero regularly enters in his apotheosis. The world of apotheosis thus begins to pull away from the rotary cycle of the quest in which all triumph is temporary. Hence if we look at the quest-myth as a pattern of imagery, we see the hero's quest first of all in terms of its fulfillment. This gives us, Frye asserts, our central pattern of archetypal images, the vision of innocence which sees the world in terms of total human intelligibility. It corresponds to, and is usually found in the form of, the vision of the unfallen world or heaven in religion. We may call it the comic vision of life, in contrast to the tragic vision, which sees the quest only in the form of its ordained cycle. In the comic vision the human world, according to Frye, is a community, or a hero who represents the wish-fulfillment of the reader. In the tragic vision the human world is a tyranny or anarchy, or an individual or isolated man, the leader with his back to his followers, the bullying giant of romance, the deserted or betrayed hero. All divine, heroic, angelic or other superhuman communities follow the human pattern.

[5] *Group Psychology and the Analysis of the Ego,* St. Ed. 18 (London, 1955), p. 122.

[6] See Thomas Mann, "Freud and the Future," in *Essays of Three Decades* (New York, 1947).

[7] *The New World Philosophy* (New York, 1961), pp. 136-37. Also Harry Slochower, "Symbolism and the Creative Process in Art," in *American Image* 22 (Spring-Summer 1965).

[8] *Essays on a Science of Mythology,* 5.

[9] The 'timeless meaning and value' imply the fixity and permanence of the human dynamism and its structure which is fulfilled by fidelity to the transcendental precepts: Be attentive, Be intelligent, Be reasonable, Be responsible, and Be decisive about what has authentic meaning and value. Before these precepts are ever formulated in concepts, they have a prior existence and reality in the spontaneous, structured dynamism of human consciousness. See Bernard Lonergan, *Method in Theology* (London: Darton, Longman and Todd, 1970), p. 20. The transcendental precepts are permanent because the existence of the human spirit is permanent. Attention, intelligence, reasonableness, responsibility and decision are to be exercised not only with respect to the authentic meanings and values of the existing situation but also with respect to the subsequent, changed situation. Thus finding the inadequacies and repercussions of the previous venture to improve what is good and remedy what is defective. Change itself makes it likely that new possibilities will have arisen and old possibilities will have advanced in probability. Change begets further change: mythopoesis begets mythopoesis. The sustained observance of the transcendental precepts makes these cumulative changes an instance of progress, which proceeds from originating value, from subjects being their true selves by observing the transcendental precepts intrinsic to the exigencies of the human structure in all ages.

[10] Priests, prophets, poets, seers, leaders and artists attempt to spell out in their concrete situation, in the critical context of their historical moment, how the eternal exigences of the human spirit are to be authentically met. They must be men of vision to envision how this is to take place. Every man experiences the exigences; however, not everyone has the creative imagination and intelligence to work out something of true value in his concrete context. This is where human finitude is painfully experienced. Human suffering is not always caused by human malice; much of it results from the slowness of the human mind and community to arrive at intelligent and effective solutions to problems.

[11]*Creative Writers and Day-Dreaming,* St. Ed. 10 (London, 1959). Dreams reveal the dreamer's self-image, his expectations for the future, his imagined solutions to pressing problems, his thoughts, desires, impulses, memories, concerns and mood. They reflect the dreamer's view of the nature and meaning of life, the quality of relationships and the degree of relatedness. They express the dreamer's personality structure, his subjectivity, his attitude towards life. Jung regarded dreams as the most authentic, most autonomous and purest product of the unconscious psychic process, and therefore presenting our subjective state as it really is.

[12]*Ibid.*

[13]*The Interpretation of Dreams,* St. Ed. 4 and 5 (London, 1953).

[14]Ernst Kris, *Psychoanalytic Explorations in Art* (New York, 1952), p. 25: "Creative artists in our day are wont to use free association as a training ground for creative thinking or as an independent mode of expression, and some among the surrealists have assigned to their work the function of thus making explicit what had previously been implicit."

[15]William F. Lynch, *Christ and Apollo,* (New York: Sheed & Ward, 1960), p. 133. The entire sixth chapter, 'The Analogical' (pp. 133-60), is especially relevant.

[16]Carl Jung, *Psychology and Religion* (New Haven, 1938), p. 45.

[17]Northrop Frye, "The Archetypes of Literature," in *Myth and Method: Modern Theories of Fiction* (Omaha: University of Nebraska Press, 1960), p. 159. Frye holds that the quest-myth is the central myth of literature in its narrative aspect. To understand this myth as a pattern of meaning, he starts with the workings of the subconscious where the epiphany originates, in the dream, free expression of the inner dynamic of man.

[18]The function of myth is to adapt the individual to the group according to *The Psychoanalytic Study of Society,* Vol. III, ed. Warner Muensterberger and Sidney Axelrad (New York, 1964).

[19]Harry Slochower, *Mythopoesis* (Detroit, 1970), p. 34.

[20]*Ibid.,* p. 36.

[21]Northrop Frye, "The Archetypes of Literature," in *Myth and Method,* pp. 159-60. Also p. 54, note 4.

[22]Just as the science of history develops in terms of new histories, of new interpretations of historical evidence, so the transformation and development of individuals and societies must be understood in terms of a new self-understanding which entails both a new history and a new vision of the future. Because man cannot help expressing himself, his new self-understanding will inevitably emerge in a wide variety of forms and symbols. It will be revealed in his pictures, stories, songs and myths; for these imply his sense of true meaning and value, his self-orientation for the attainment of such meaning and value, and his accompanying mood. Reinterpretations of experience signal both personal and social transformation; new myths, new histories, new ways of telling stories about men bespeak new men and new societies. They generally arise in periods of personal and social crisis, when our traditional understanding proves inadequate and a higher viewpoint is required. In periods of cultural transition prophets and artists would redeem the values of the past and present through symbolic forms structured to the fulfillment of human aspirations.

[23]Alan Richardson, *An Introduction to the Theology of the New Testament* (New York: Harper & Bros., 1958), p. 12: "In this book . . . the hypothesis is defended that Jesus himself is the author of the brilliant re-interpretation of the Old Testament scheme of salvation ('Old Testament Theology') which is found in the New Testament."

[24]Maude Bodkin, *Archetypal Patterns of Poetry* (Oxford, 1934), p. 334.

[25]Sigmund Freud, *Psychopathology of Everyday Life,* St. Ed., Vol. 6 (London, 1960), p. 84.

[26]See Franz Ricklin, *Wishfulfillment and Symbolism in Fairy Tales.* Nervous and Mental Disease Monograph Series No. 21 (New York, 1915).

[27]*Sex in Psychoanalysis* (New York, 1956), p. 15. Freud was an artistic storyteller, and *The Interpretation of Dreams* employs metaphorical analogies, according to E.S. Tauber and M.R. Greene, *Prelogical Experience* (New York, 1959).

[28]See Daniel E. Schneider, *The Psychoanalyst and the Artist* (2nd ed., New York, 1954).

[29]See R.G. Collingwood, *The Principles of Art* (Oxford, 1945).

[30]See Ernest Cassirer, *The Logic of the Humanities* (New Haven, 1961).

[31]See Lawrence S. Kubic, "The Distortion of the Symbolic Process in Neurosis and Psychosis," in *Journal of the American Psychoanalytic Association,* 1, 1953, pp. 59-85. Kubic holds that because symbols are ambiguous man is vulnerable to neurosis and psychosis.

[32]William F. Lynch, *Christ and Apollo* (New York: Sheed and Ward, 1960), p. 133.

[33]Harry Slochower, *Mythopoesis* (Detroit: Wayne State University Press, 1970), pp. 22-24.

[34]John Navone, "The Myth and Dream of Paradise," in *New Blackfriars 55* (November 1974), pp. 511-16.

[35]See Otto Rank, *The Myth of the Birth of the Hero* (New York, 1959). Also Lord Raglan, *the Hero* (London, 1936). Moses is an archetypal hero, who clashes with the authorities (Pharaoh), is pursued by the Egyptian army in the Exodus from Egypt, and journeys for forty years before beholding the Promised Land.

[36]The two volumes, Luke-Acts, tell the story of Jesus and his Church in terms of the Journey. The Gospel of Luke recounts the journey of Jesus from Galilee to Jerusalem (the City of Peace, a paradise symbol); Acts of the Apostles recounts that of his apostles from Jerusalem to Rome and the ends of the earth.

[37]Leslie Fiedler, "Archetype and Signature," in *The Sewanee Review,* 60 (Spring, 1952), pp. 253-73, implies a kind of homecoming for the mythopoeic writer as well as for the hero at the completion of the work. Fiedler affirms that the poet, in deed as in word, composes himself as maker and mask, in accordance with some contemporaneous *mythos* of the artist: "In the Mask of (the poet's) life and the manifold masks of his work, the poet expresses for a whole society the ritual meaning of its inarticulate selves; the artist goes forth not to 're-create the conscience of his race,' but to redeem its unconsciousness. We cannot get back into the primal Garden of the unfallen Archetypes, but we can yield ourselves to the dreams and images that mean paradise regained" (p. 273). The poet's expression stamps his personal signature upon the archetype; hence, mythopoesis, implicitly, is a clue to an event in the poet's psyche, the arena in which *Dichtung* and *Wahrheit* become one. The event is a form of self-transcendence and transformation objectified by the completion of the mythopoesis.

[38]Nietzsche somewhere notes that the more a tree grows towards the sun, the deeper do its roots reach into the earth. The Latin *altus* means both 'high' and 'deep.' Christ's descent into Hell is prior to his resurrection. Human greatness is not achieved without great suffering and many forms of death.

[39]See Bernard Tyrrell, *Christotherapy: Healing Through Enlightenment* (New York: New Seabury Press, 1975). The existentialist myth expresses the value of homelessness. The individual is 'thrown' into existence, has no parents and produces no offspring; hence, there is no question of rehabilitation. Beginning with 'Nothing,' its

goal, for some, is the nothingness of death. In this respect, there is an ironic sense of homecoming in the existentialist myth, despite its aim of affirming the individual's unconditioned freedom from systems, essences, and any type of organized control, and of accepting the resulting homelessness and anguish as final.

[40] John Macquarrie, "Word and Idea," informally published paper given at the International Lonergan Congress (St. Leo, Florida, 1970), p. 7.

[41] Geoffrey Preston OP, "Fiction and Poetry in the Bible," in *New Blackfriars* 53 (July, 1972), p. 300. Preston notes in Jesus the qualities of a creative artist.

[42] *Ibid.*, p. 300. See Anthony Battaglia, "Autobiography and Religion," in *Horizons* 2 (Spring, 1975), 1, pp. 61-73.

[43] *Ibid.*, pp. 305-6. See Sallie TeSelle, "Speaking in Parables: A Study," in *Metaphor and Theology*. (London: SCM Press, 1975). This extraordinary insightful study treats of theology and story, of autobiography as the unity of life and thought.

Notes for Chapter 13

[1] Mark R. Hillegas, *The Future as Nightmare* (Carbondale, Ill.: Southern Illinois University Press, 1967). This book surveys literary works which describe nightmare states, where men are conditioned to slavery, where earthly life is threatened with worldwide or cosmic disaster.

[2] Apocalyptic writings of the Bible attend to such topics as the warfare between the children of light and the children of darkness, the radical separation between heaven and hell, the awfulness of the catastrophes which are reserved for the end times, affirming that the divine kingship cannot be avoided. It will be established in terror, dread, horror and cataclysm.

[3] Johannes Metz, quoted in Walter H. Capps, *Time Invades the Cathedral* (Philadelphia: Fortress Press, 1972), p. 92, affirms his "creative militant eschatology": "God is the pressure for maturity exercised upon men who recognize that heaven and hell are real possibilities." Metz's interest in "the last things" is a major focus of his concern for the care of the world. Fear of the Lord inspires such care.

[4] Bernard Tyrrell, *Christotherapy* (New York: Seabury Press, 1975), p. 129. Tyrrell affirms that there is a healing meaning in the death of Jesus which is available to every person as he faces death. Jesus shows that fear, anxiety and apprehension in the face of suffering and dying are natural feelings, not to be ashamed of, because physical disintegration is an enemy of man's unity as inspirited flesh and is naturally repugnant. But Jesus also shows us that if properly understood and participated in, physical disintegration can be the pathway to a higher mode of integration, that of resurrection.

[5] Louis Bouyer, *Christian Initiation* (New York: Macmillan, 1958), p. 112, affirms: Christianity asserts quite unambiguously that neither the individual nor the collective salvation of humanity is possible either on earth or in any possible prolongation of the present state of affairs. Christianity is, as they say, eschatological. That is, it rests on a belief in the end of time. It asserts that human history must end in catastrophe, that it will be interrupted by the supremely miraculous event, the return of Christ and the universal judgment and resurrection. After that, but only after that, the salvation of humanity will be possible.

[6] Richard R. Niebuhr in *Experiential Religion* (New York: Harper and Row, 1972) writes of "Fearing" (pp. 83-95), of religious man as a fearing being that is familiar to us directly and through a quantity of literature about dread, melancholy and

anxiety. He believes that Kierkegaard is for most of us the modern prophet of the religious and Christian meaning of dread, and that his book *The Concept of Dread* has been the stimulus for much theological reflection on the tonalities of our existence. Niebuhr believes that dreading and fearing is far too conspicuous and pervasive a characteristic of existence in our world to be called epiphenomenal. Dreading men, he notes, apprehend something positive, the world of power that is in part antecedent to each one of us, that is a defining and limiting field of existence, that is not mine or ours, an ambience over which we have no rights, a reflection of our own poverty and weakness. Dreading is a revelation of infinite energy and of environing, shaping power that approaches us on alien terms. It reveals what Coleridge called the "sacred horror" of existence, in *The Friend, The Works of S.T. Coleridge,* vol. 2, p. 464.

[7]*Ibid.,* pp. 90-91. Niebuhr distinguishes four elements in fearing/dreading as presented by selected writers: (1) the sense of powerlessness in the presence of power that one is unable to annex to oneself or to master; (2) one's personal existence experienced as aimless, outside any fixed coordinates, and the opposing world as an environment of randomness; (3) a sense of guilt for this idleness and impotence, for foundering and stagnation; (4) a sense of the world as inimical or disgusting.

[8]Mircea Eliade, *The Myth of the Eternal Return,* tr. by W.R. Trask (Princeton, N.J.: Princeton University Press, 1971, Bollingen paperback printing), p. 102.

[9]*Ibid.,* p. 103.

[10]*Ibid.,* pp. 139-162.

[11]*Ibid.,* p. 150.

[12]*Ibid.,* p. 150.

[13]Michael Novak, *The Experience of Nothingness* (New York: Harper and Row, 1971). Novak explores the technical concept of "horizons," pp. 27-29.

[14]*Revelation Theology: A History* (New York: Herder and Herder, 1969), pp. 177-78.

[15]William C. Marrin, "The Kingdom—Models and Meaning," *Bible Today,* 87 (December 1976), pp. 990-994 *passim.*

[16]Stanley Hauerwas, "The Significance of Vision: Toward an Aesthetic Ethic," *Studies in Religion* (Summer, 1972), pp. 26-49.

[17]*Ibid.,* p. 36.

[18]*Ibid.*

[19]Iris Murdoch, "Vision and Choice in Morality," *Christian Ethics and Contemporary Philosophy,* ed. Ian Ramsay (New York: Macmillan Co., 1966), p. 202.

[20]James W. McClendon Jr., *Biography as Theology* (Nashville: Abingdon Press, 1974), pp. 30ff.

[21]David Shapiro, *Neurotic Styles* (New York/London: Basic Books, Inc., 1965), pp. 118f.

[22]Louis Dupre, *Transcendent Selfhood* (New York: Seabury Press, 1976), p. 43.

[23]Magda B. Arnold, *Feelings and Emotions* (New York: Academic Press, 1970), pp. 173-177.

[24]*Ibid.,* p. 177.

[25]Bernard Lonergan, *Method in Theology* (London: Darton Longman and Todd, 1972), pp. 30f.

[26]Maurice Nicholl, *The New Man* (Baltimore: Penguin Books, 1967), pp. 118f.

[27]I have extrapolated the distinction between "dependent" and "foundational" from Gerald O'Collins' application of it to revelation in his book, *Theology and Revelation* (Cork: Mercier Press, 1968), pp. 45-50.

[28]I owe this insight to William V. Dych, S.J.

[29]Our images may be at any point on the spectrum between these extremes.

Notes for Chapter 14

[1]Ernest Ferlita, *Film Odyssey* (New York: Paulist Press, 1976), 4f. Ferlita distinguishes between plot (visual/aural reality) and meaning (spiritual reality).

[2]The Latin word for homeland or native country is fatherland *(patria),* the place where our father(s) dwells, our origins.

[3]Every biblical travel story has its heroes. When we choose or create heroes, we tell one another how we see the world and what we take to be the most important things in our lives. Through the heroes, the leaders of the biblical travel stories, we announce to one another who and what we truly are, or hope to become. Biblical heroes were not detached and sublime members of a ruling class; they came from the people, they interacted with the people.

[4]The travel story of his homecoming, like every journey, has three parts: a beginning, a middle, and an end. There are different starting points for determining the threefold division; and there are different levels at which the journey may be considered. From the standpoint of the Christian community's travel story, Christ is the Alpha, the Way, and the Omega. He is the Pre-existent Logos, the Incarnate Word, the Risen Christ. He begins from Galilee, follows the Way of the Lord through Palestine, and finishes his work in Jerusalem. The Christian follows Jesus' "way to life" (Acts 2:28). He is obedient to the injunction: "Let him take up his cross daily and follow me" (Lk. 9:23). There is a threefold temporal dimension to Jesus' journey: "It is necessary for me to be on my way today and tomorrow and the day following, for it is impossible that a prophet should die outside Jerusalem" (Lk. 13:33). Jesus is sent by the Father and returns to the Father as the first of many brothers. He is the New Adam, recalling another journey pattern: Paradise Lost (Garden), the Desert Wilderness, and Paradise Regained. Israel had experienced its homecoming (the Return) after its Babylonian Exile (587-537 BC). Egyptian tyranny, a desert wandering, and entrance into a Promised Land had marked its first homecoming. The Parable of the Prodigal Son involves a travel story with three phases: a rupture of relations with and a departure from the Father, "exile" and riotous living in a foreign land, remembering and returning to the Father. In the parable, the return to the Father includes the notion of the land where he dwells (fatherland). Such homecoming implies mutual recognition and acceptance, and that state where we are most ourselves, where we have life most fully.

[5]Ernest Ferlita, *Film Odyssey,* puts the biblical words for sin in the context of journey narrative.

[6]Christ is the Lord of the travel story which the life of the Christian community tells. He is the goal of human development. In Augustine's words: "He is our native country." He is the criterion of Christian development, for "He made himself also the way to that country" *(On Christian Doctrine,* tr. D.W. Robertson, Jr., [Indianapolis, 1958], p. 64). The Christian grows both in Christ and to Christ. As Augustine remarks in *Christian Doctrine* (p. 13), the Christian life is "a journey or voyage home." Life as journey also appears in Luther: "For it is not sufficient to have done something, and now to rest . . . this present life is a kind of movement and passage, a transition . . . a pilgrimage from this world into the world to come, which is eternal rest" (quoted by Gerhard Ebeling, *Luther: An Introduction to His Thoughts,* tr. R.A. Wilson [Philadelphia, 1970], pp. 161f).

[7]The power of growth involves the quality of our vision, of our way of seeing and of feeling about the world and ourselves. In *Revelation Theology* (New York: Herder and Herder, 1969), Avery Dulles describes three "mentalities," or ways of viewing revelation (pp. 177-180).

Notes for Chapter 15

¹Ernest Ferlita, *Film Odyssey* (New York: Paulist Press, 1976), p. 4f.
²David Tracy, *Blessed Rage for Order* (New York: Seabury Press, 1976). Throughout this book, Tracy explains "limit-experience" and "limit-language."
   Tracy asserts "that the concept 'limit' can be used as a key (but not exhaustive) category for describing certain signal characteristics peculiar to any language or experience with a properly religious dimension" (p. 93). Certain features of human existence "can be analyzed as both expressive of certain 'limits' to our ordinary experience (e.g., finitude, contingency, or radical transience) and disclosive of certain fundamental structures of our existence *beyond* (or grounding to) that ordinary experience (e.g., our fundamental trust in the worthwhileness of existence, our basic belief in order and value)" (p. 93).
   There exist limit-situations in the world of the everyday wherein a human being ineluctably finds manifest certain ultimate limits or horizons to his or her existence (p. 105). Limit situations refer to two basic kinds of existential situations: either those boundary situations of guilt, anxiety, sickness and the recognition of death as one's own destiny, or those situations called "ecstatic experiences" of intense joy, love, reassurance, or creation (p. 105). In both, negative or positive, we experience our own human limits (limits-to) and also recognize some disclosure of a limit-of experience. Negative experiences reveal our basic existential faith or unfaith in life's very meaningfulness, while positive experiences are truly "self-transcending" moments which cannot be stated adequately in the language of the ordinary and everyday (p. 107).
   For these basic limit-situations of our lives (as both limit-to and limit-of) a language re-presentative of the basic faith disclosed in moments of crisis and ecstasy seems appropriate (p. 119). The signal peculiarity of *religious* language is its character as a limit-language disclosive of such limit-experiences and of a possible mode-of-being-in-the-world. It seeks to discern *the* meaning of life with universal significance and total commitment. An "odd-language" is thus required since we need to *qualify* our normal object language to the point of infinity in order to express a *total* commitment and a *universal* significance.
   To do this, the NT "consistently modifies the traditional use of the language of proverbs, eschatological sayings, and parables through such procedures as intensification, transgression and 'going to the limits' of language" (p. 124). These modifications through such means as paradox and hyperbole extend language "to the point where the course of ordinary life is broken; and intensification of everyday life emerges; the unexpected happens; a strange world of meaning is projected which challenges, jars and disorients our everyday vision precisely by both showing us the limits to the everyday and projecting the limit-character of the whole" (p. 130). It challenges us that the "odd, mysterious, indeed scandalous limit-experience the gospel proclaims is an authentic human possibility" (p. 133).
³*Ibid.*, p. 146.
⁴Hannah Arendt, *The Human Condition* (New York: Doubleday Anchor, 1958), p. 181; Robert Scholes and Robert Kellog, *The Nature of Narrative* (London: Oxford University Press, 1966), p. 239, affirm that the people who make the interaction of events draw us to stories: "Quality of mind (as expressed in the language of characterization, motivation, description, and commentary) not plot, is the soul of narrative. Plot is only the indispensable skeleton which fleshed out with character and incident, provides the necessary clay into which life may be breathed."
⁵*Ibid.*, p. 286.

⁶Stanley Hauerwas, "Story and Theology," in *Religion in Life,* 45 (Autumn 1976), p. 347.

⁷*Ibid.* Only through narrative (stories) can we catch the connections between actions and responses of persons that are inherently particular and contingent. The intentional nature of human action creates the space that demands narrative as the form to account for the connection and intelligibility of action. Story is a necessary way of re-expressing reality true to the form of human action.

⁸*Ibid.,* p. 348. See Elena Malits, David Burrell, Stanley Hauerwas, "Theology as Biography," *Horizons* I (Fall 1974), pp. 81-87.

⁹*Blessed Rage for Order,* pp. 220f.

¹⁰*Ibid.,* p. 221. "Man strives in his seeking, but never finds" (Eccles. 8:17), but Jesus announces that "He who seeks, will find" (Mt. 7:8). Underlying all human restlessness is a seeking for God, but often this search fails and must be set right.

¹¹John F. Haught, *Religion and Self-Acceptance* (New York: Paulist Press, 1976), p. 37. Haught examines "the narrative field" of human consciousness as one of the five intentional fields. These are simply ways of reaching out for and allowing the world to come into consciousness in ways corresponding to its and the subject's depth and richness. The other four fields are the sentient, interpersonal, aesthetic and theoretic. The story by which we live is the integrative element of our experience determining the specific tone of all four fields of our awareness.

¹²See Stephen Crites, "The Narrative Quality of Experience," *Journal of The American Academy of Religion,* XXXIX (1971), pp. 291-311.

Crites affirms that stories give qualitative substance to the form of experience because it is itself an incipient story (p. 297); that our consciousness grasps its objects as a whole; that without memory, our experience would not have coherence, for our consciousness would be locked in a momentary present, in a disconnected succession of perceptions which it would have no power to relate to one another (p. 298). To narrate is to recall a background of antecedents, causes, and conditions.

¹³*Ibid.*

¹⁴*Religion and Self-Acceptance,* p. 37.

¹⁵*Ibid.,* pp. 89f.

¹⁶John Navone, "Three Aspects of the Lucan Theology of History," *Biblical Theology Bulletin* 3 (1973), pp. 115-132.

¹⁷See *Religion and Self-Acceptance,* pp. 90f.

¹⁸See John Navone, "The Gospel Truth as Re-enactment," *Scottish Journal of Theology* 29 (July-August) 4, pp. 311-333.

¹⁹Michael Novak, *The Experience of Nothingness* (New York: Harper and Row, 1971), p. 87. Action cannot take place except through form; action is the structuring of our present and future relations. It is always part of a story, and hence part of a myth. Every myth relates to structures against which it plays its own counterpoint. See Herbert Fingaret, *Self-Deception* (London: Routledge and Kegan Paul, 1969).

²⁰Bernard Lonergan, *Method in Theology* (London: Darton, Longman and Todd, 1972), p. 27. The meaning of love for Christians is not a vague abstraction; it is defined by the entire story which the life of Jesus of Nazareth has told and which the Risen Christ continues to tell in his Church. The meaning of Christian love, as found in such a statement as "God is love," cannot be abstracted from the life story which revealed it and defined it. To do so would distort it.

²¹*Religion and Self-Acceptance,* p. 74. Haught affirms that religious stories have as their normative function that of allowing a continual expansion of reality sense, of the "world."

²²See *The Experience of Nothingness,* p. 24.
²³*Ibid.,* pp. 23f.
²⁴Stanley Hauerwas, "The Ethicist as Theologian," *The Christian Century* (April 23, 1975), p. 409.
²⁵L.O. Mink, "History and Fiction as Modes of Comprehension," *New Literary History* I, 3 (1970), pp. 557-558.
²⁶See *The Experience of Nothingness,* p. 22.
²⁷*Ibid.,* p. 23.
²⁸*Ibid.,* p. 27.
²⁹*Ibid.,* p. 84.
³⁰*Ibid.,* p. 68.
³¹Michael Novak, *Ascent of the Mountain, Flight of the Dove* (New York: Macmillan, 1973) treats of the presuppositions of autobiography as a way into the study of religion, affirming that we keep the experience of chaos at bay by supporting one another in bringing intelligibility to the world through cultures, societies, institutions and organized religion. To the extent that we insist that the world is meaningful and live accordingly, we have religion. The chapter headings of his book: The Voyage; Autobiography and Story; Cultures; Societies and Institutions; Organizations. He states, "For me religious studies has two focal points: (1) All integrative world views whatever; (2) especially, world views with explicit reference to the divine . . . My basic theorem is that all human action necessarily implies a view of the world in which it occurs, of the self, and of their relations" (pp. 211f).

Notes for Chapter 16

¹Gabriel Marcel, *Home Viator* (New York: Harper and Row, 1969), p. 153.
²Frank M. Buckley, "An Approach to a Phenomenology of At-homeness," *Duquesne Studies in Phenomenological Psychology: Volume I,* ed. by Amadeo Giorgi, William F. Fisher, Rolf Von Eckartsberg (Pittsburgh: Duquesne University Press, 1971), pp. 198–211.
³Maurice Merleau-Ponty, *The Visible and the Invisible* (Evanston: Northwestern University Press, 1968), p. 263.
⁴Frank M. Buckley, *op. cit.,* p. 198.
⁵*Ibid.,* p. 206.
⁶*Ibid.*
⁷*Ibid.*
⁸*Ibid.,* pp. 206f.
⁹*Ibid.,* pp. 20f.
¹⁰Gaston Bacheland, *The Poetics of Space* (Boston: Grossman Publishers Inc., Beacon paperback, 1969), p. 4.
¹¹Frank M. Buckley, *op. cit.,* pp. 200f.
¹²*Ibid.*
¹³*Ibid.*
¹⁴*Ibid.,* p. 206.
¹⁵*Ibid.,* pp. 208f.
¹⁶*Ibid.,* p. 208.
¹⁷*Ibid.,* p. 208; see William Lukjpen, *Existential Phenomenology,* Revised ed. (Pittsburgh: Duquesne University Press, 1969), p. 266.

[18]A. van Kaam, *Existential Foundations of Psychology* (Pittsburg: Duquesne University Press, 1966), p. 16.

[19]Frank M. Buckley, *op. cit.,* p. 209.

[20]*Ibid.*

[21]*Ibid.*

[22]*Ibid.*

[23]Richard R. Niebuhr, *Experiental Religion* (New York: Harper and Row, 1972), p. 85, n. 2.

[24]*Ibid.,* pp. 87f, pp. 91f.

[25]Bernd Jager, "Theorizing, Journeying, Dwelling," *Duquesne Studies in Phenomenological Psychology,* Volume II, ed. by A. Giorgi, C. Fisher, E. Murray (Pittsburgh: Duquesne University Press, 1975), p. 235.

[26]*Ibid.,* p. 236.

[27]Jager quotes Herodotus in *History of the Greek and Persian War* (New York: Washington Square Press Inc., 1963) I, 30, p. 97; *ibid.,* p. 237.

[28]Jager quotes H. Koller in "Theoros und Theoria," *Glotta, Zeitschrift fur Griechische Sprache:* Band 36, 1958, Göttingen, p. 283.

[29]Jager quotes Plato in *The Laws,* tr. by R.G. Bury (Harvard University Press), Vol. II, p. 505.

[30]*Ibid.,* p. 506.

[31]*Ibid.,* p. 240.

[32]*Ibid.*

[33]*Ibid.,* p. 243.

[34]*Ibid.,* p. 249.

[35]*Ibid.*

[36]*Ibid.,* p. 250.

[37]*Ibid.*

[38]*Ibid.*

[39]*Ibid.,* p. 251.

[40]*Ibid.,* p. 253.

[41]*Ibid.,* p. 255.

[42]*Ibid.,* p. 257.

Notes for Chapter 17

[1]Paul Piehler, *The Visionary Landscape: A Study in Medieval Allegory* (Montreal: McGill-Queen's University Press, 1971). This work is the source for most of what is here affirmed on medieval allegory.

[2]*Ibid.,* p. 5.

[3]*Ibid.*

[4]The relevance of Piehler's categories to Bernard Tyrrell's *Christotherapy: Healing Through Enlightenment* (New York: New Seabury Press, 1975) is of primary interest in this study.

[5]The notion of archetype in this study is not used in a strictly Jungian sense, but in a somewhat broader sense; the notion of pilgrimage is not explicitly used by Piehler.

[6]Piehler treats of this first category, the preliminary anguish (psychic crisis) on pp. 7, 15, as a prerequisite for visionary allegory, p. 84.

[7]*Ibid.,* pp. 27, 30.

[8]*Ibid.,* p. 37.

[9]Piehler treats of the psychology of landscape, pp. 72ff; landscapes of vision, pp. 69-83; landscape and dialogue, pp. 84-110.

[10]Dr. Nicolas Beets, in "Dynamic Psychology and the Liberation of Man," *Faith and Freedom* (Spring, 1974) XXVII, p. 98, relates the psychic illness of man to a wilderness condition. He affirms the power of a therapeutic liberation that ". . . will ultimately lead people out of the wilderness that invades the *territorium* of our inner life. The exploration of this inner wilderness, darkness, chaos — and the facing of my own bewilderment is a precondition for the liberation of man." He speaks of the psychotherapist's leading his patient into the jungle of his (patient's) own inner life to help him confront the confusion of his wilderness condition.

[11]Piehler treats of garden symbolism, pp. 75, 77f; in *Genesis* and *The Song of Songs,* p. 98; the paradise garden, pp. 77-79; Earthly Paradise, pp. 130f; the Park of the Good Shepherd, p. 107; in the *Paradiso* of Dante, pp. 131-133.

[12]Bernard Lonergan, *Method in Theology* (London: Darton, Longman and Todd, 1972), p. 236.

[13]*Ibid.,* p. 9.

[14]Piehler, p. 20.

[15]*Ibid.,* pp. 46-67; "Alan's Vision of Nature" is one example of the Spiritual Guide.

[16]Piehler treats of the therapeutic dialogue, pp. 62-67; its role in allegory, p. 19.

[17]Piehler devotes a chapter to Dante's *Commedia,* pp. 111-143.

[18]*Ibid.,* pp. 124, 140. The mountain suggests a more ample view of reality that enables a mastery of complexity (forest) and an enlightenment view of the forest below, pp. 112f.

[19]*Ibid.,* pp. 131-133.

[20]The expression "Christotherapy" is taken from Bernard Tyrrell's *Christotherapy: Healing Through Enlightenment* (New York: New Seabury Press, 1975).

[21]Philip Wheelwright studies the archetypal symbolism of pilgrimage and its related images in his article, "The Archetypal Symbol," *Perspectives in Literary Symbolism (Yearbook of Comparative Criticism,* vol. I), J. Strelka ed. (University Park and London: The Pennsylvania State University Press, 2nd printing, January 1972), pp. 237-240. He notes three main moods that mark the characteristic symbols of pilgrimage: innocence, alienation and aspiration (p. 237).

[22]*The Spiritual Exercises* of St. Ignatius Loyola have a Christotherapeutic purpose which may also be analyzed in terms of Piehler's categories. There is a preliminary anguish for one's personal sins, the therapeutic dialogue with Christ, the spiritual authority throughout the entire prayerful process of the *Exercises,* and the changing visionary landscape terminating in the "Contemplation to Attain Divine Love," where one attends to the loving presence of God working in every element of one's visionary landscape for one's well-being.

[23](New York: New Seabury Press, 1975). The genre of travel literature as a guide to the spiritual life and ascent of the mind to God or truth has spread widely since Philo and Gregory of Nyssa, or the life of Moses and the Exodus, or even the journey structure of Luke's gospel. The Western vocabulary for spiritual growth as journey (*poreia*) and ascent (*anabasis*) came into use as early as Hesiod and Simonides. In our time, Rober Pirsig records a philosophical and spiritual journey (development) in his book, *Zen and the Art of Motorcycle Maintenance.*

[24]See Una Kroll, *TM A Signpost for the World* (London: Darton, Longman and Todd, 1974). This book on Transcendental Meditation contains much that might be compared with the therapeutic elements of the visionary allegory. In the Maharishi Mahesh Yogi's description of consciousness, the pilgrim who wishes to attain union with God must pass through the gateway of Transcendental Medita-

tion. Among the affinities between Christianity and Transcendental Meditation is the insistence on the necessity for a spiritual guide on the way to God. The guru, or spiritual master, has always been an important figure in Hinduism. Catholic mystics are no less insistent upon the need for an experienced guide. Early Christians flocked to seek advice of the desert fathers. The therapeutic dialogue with the spiritual guide is a means for making spiritual growth in diagnosing the true meaning and value of the particular elements in our "visionary landscape," in our consciousness of our interior life, of our changing social, historical contexts. Kroll quotes Abishiktananda *(Prayer* [London: S.P.C.K., 1967], p. 43): "Nobody should ever engage in it (prayer) without the help of a sure guide — the guru — that is somebody who himself has trodden the path, has been granted at least a glimpse of the goal and is prudent enough to lead others." The path to the ultimate encounter with the Father in the oneness of the Holy Spirit is not without its risks; hence, obedience to and dialogic openness with a spiritual director has been a traditional norm for spiritual development in both Catholic and Orthodox traditions. Contemplative awareness of God involves a cosmic consciousness that has affinities with the concept of the "visionary landscape" (our existential context) that nourishes and specifies our consciousness.

[25]Many insights of both Piehler and Tyrrell are corroborated by John Dollard and Neal E. Miller in *Personality and Psychotherapy: An Analysis in Terms of Learning, Thinking and Culture* (New York and London: McGraw-Hill, 1950). The suffering that results from ignorance is described in the case of neurosis: "The victim feels a mysterious malady . . . The neurotic is mysterious because he is *capable* of acting and yet he is *unable* to act and enjoy . . . The therapist confronts a person who is miserable, stupid (in some ways), and who has symptoms . . . Neurotic misery is real—not imaginary" (p. 12). The neurotic is miserable because he is in conflict. Generally two or more strong drives are operating in him and producing incompatible responses. Strongly driven to approach and as strongly to flee, he is not able to act to reduce either of the conflicting drives; hence, they remain dammed up, active, and nagging. Though obviously intelligent in some ways, he is stupid (ignorant) insofar as his neurotic conflict is concerned. Though he is sure that he is miserable and is vocal about his symptoms, he is vague and ignorant about what it is within him that could produce such painful effects. He cannot describe his own conflicts; nor can the therapist immediately spot these areas of ignorance. The conflicting drives which afflict the neurotic person are not labelled: "He has not language to describe the conflicting forces within him" (p. 15). He has no insight into his problem: "Since the neurotic cannot help himself, he must have the help of others if he is to be helped at all. . .He feels that someone should help him, but he does not know how to ask for help since he does not know what his problem is. He may feel aggrieved that he is suffering, but he cannot explain his case" (p. 15). His symptoms are the most obvious aspects of his problems. These are what he is familiar with and he feels he must get rid of them. His phobias, inhibitions, avoidances, compulsions, rationalizations and psychosomatic symptoms cannot be integrated into the texture of intelligent, responsible social relations. He believes they are the basic disorder; he would like to confine the therapeutic discussion to getting rid of the symptoms. The symptoms do not solve the basic conflict, but they mitigate it. They reduce neurotic misery. They keep the neurotic away from those stimuli which would activate and intensify his conflict (p. 16). The spiritual guide in the medieval allegory and in the case of Christotherapy offers a deliverance from such misery and suffering through the enlightenment of the therapeutic dialogue and its analysis of the problem concerning whose causes the sufferer is in ignorance.

[26]The preliminary anguish that occasions the spiritual journey may be described in part by Joseph Mendel's *Concepts of Depression* (New York: John Wiley & Sons, Inc., 1970, pp. 6-12). The central symptoms of depression are sadness, pessimism, self-dislike, feelings of hopelessness, futility, emptiness, meaninglessness, the loss of energy, motivation and concentration. There is an inability to accomplish tasks, a feeling that "the joy has gone out of life." There is a decrease in bodily movements, gestures, communication. Movements are slow, as if a tremendous effort were involved; there is little attempt to initiate or engage in discussion. Often the patient becomes mute. In extreme depression, there are often suicidal thoughts, threats and attempts. The field of one's consciousness ("visionary landscape") does not yield any source of joy, hope, faith, inspiration; either there is no consciousness of true meaning and value, or there is no consciousness of the possibility of participating in it.

Notes for Chapter 18

[1]John Haught, *Religion and Self-Acceptance* (New York: Paulist Press, 1976).

[2]John Dunne, *The Way of All the Earth* (New York: Macmillan, 1972), p. 86.

[3]See William F. Lynch, *Images of Faith* (Notre Dame: Notre Dame University, 1973), 1973, p. 16.

[4]See William F. Lynch, *Christ and Apollo* (New York: Sheed & Ward, 1960). Lynch argues that the Christian imagination is analogical. The Christian understanding of finding one's "true story" is neither univocal nor equivocal, but analogical.

[5]See Stephen Crites, "The Narrative Quality of Experience," *Journal of the American Academy of Religion* 39 (Sept., 1971), pp. 291, 309. Crites affirms that the formal quality of experience through time is inherently narrative. The self in its concreteness is indivisible, temporal, and whole, as it is revealed to be in the narrative quality of experience, as an activity in time.

[6]See Clifford Geertz, "Religion as a Cultural System," in Donald Cutler (ed.), *The Religion Situation* (Boston: Beacon Press, 1968), p. 643. Geertz defines religion as (1) a system of symbols which acts to (2) establish powerful, pervasive, and long-lasting moods and motivations in persons by (3) formulating conceptions of a general order of existence and (4) clothing these conceptions with such an aura of factuality that (5) the moods and motivations seem uniquely realistic.

[7]John Macquarrie, *The Humility of God* (London: SCM Press, 1978), p. 13.

[8]Bernard Lonergan, "The ongoing genesis of methods," *Studies in Religion/Sciences Religieuses* 6 (1976-77), p. 347.

[9]*Ibid.,* p. 353.

[10]*Ibid.,* pp. 348f.

[11]Bernard Lonergan, "Theology and Praxis," in Luke Salm, F.S.C. (ed.), *The Catholic Theological Society of America: Proceedings of the Thirty-Second Annual Convention,* Vol. 32 (Bronx, N.Y. 10471: Catholic Theological Society of America, 1977), pp. 8, 13.

[12]Stanley Hauerwas, "Story and Theology" in *Religion and Life* 45 (Autumn, 1976), p. 347. Hauerwas does not claim that stories are necessary for articulating everything about our existence, but that they are indispensable for those matters that deal with the irreducible particular. Our stories reveal the world which we inhabit. They are indispensable for expressing the nature of two such particulars as the self and God. We learn of God through others' stories of their relationship with him.

[13]Karl Rahner and Herbert Vorgrimler, *Theological Dictionary,* art. "Prayer,"

Cornelius Ernst, ed., Richard Strachan, trans. (New York: Herder & Herder, 1965), p. 370. Alan Richardson writes that Christian prayer is possible only if we believe in the God whom Jesus called Father, not the clockmaker God of the deists, or the Absolute in whom all differences are reconciled, or the 'problem-solver' or Aladdin's Lamp of popular misconception. See A. Richardson, ed., "Prayer," *A Dictionary of Christian Theology* (London: SCM Press, 1969), p. 263.

[14]John Navone, "A Theology of Darkness, Terror and Dread," *Theology* 80 (Sept. 1977), p. 352.

[15]See Donald L. Gelpi, *Experiencing God: A Theology of Human Experience* (New York: Paulist Press, 1978), p. 62. Gelpi's book elaborates a foundational theology that implicitly explains what we mean by the process of searching for our true life story in response to the grace and demand of God.

[16]*Ibid.,* pp. 246-249.

[17]See Karl Rahner, *Christian at the Crossroads,* tr. by V. Green (London: Burns & Oates Ltd., 1975), p. 46. Rahner gives some examples of self-deception: (1) the effort of eudemonist or stoical intent to hasten and force the reconciled integration of our lives in our private existence, instead of patiently and confidently enduring the changing and the unpredictable, the contradictory and the unforeseeable, and renouncing all desire to cook our history up by our own recipes; (2) to believe that we can live in the social dimension by means of a ready-made ideology, whatever it might be, which would make us the absolutely sovereign planners of our future, instead of being weary but hopeful pilgrims constantly searching for the way to the absolute future so that then, when we have found it, we can appropriate it to ourselves in grace and undeservedly.

[18]See Juan Alfaro, *Christian Hope and the Liberation of Man,* translator not indicated (Rome and Sydney: E.J. Dwyer, 1978). This book treats of the certainty of hope as the inner grace of confidence in the love of God revealed in Christ, as a certainty lived in insecurity and risk, involving the inner tension of Christian existence. This book offers a foundational theology for theological reflection on Christian life stories.

[19]Life stories might be examined in terms of the traditional division of the spiritual life into the purgative, illuminative and unitive ways. The first stage of purgation is one in which one seeks to separate oneself from attachment to pleasures of the world, purify oneself morally and mortify the self until one is wholly surrendered to God. The illuminative stage is one in which the soul finds itself in an affectionate union with Christ, as a living personal presence. And the unitive stage is one in which one passes beyond knowledge and analytical thinking, to a state which cannot be grasped by thought, and yet is believed to unite one with true reality in a way which somehow is even beyond the grasp of the emotions.

[20]Prayer might be examined in terms of the threefold structure which Keith Ward attributes to language about God in his book, *The Concept of God* (Glasgow: Collins, Fount paperback, 1977), p. 37. Such language is revelatory, enshrining paradigmatic revelatory experiences; it is charismatic, functioning in ritual contexts to relate one to sacred powers; and it is exemplary, specifying a set of roles or attitudes which are appropriate responses to reality, and which extend to the whole of one's experience.

[21]Avery Dulles, *The Church is Communications* (Rome: Multi-media International, 1970), p. 6. See also Jerome Hamer, *The Church is a Communion* (New York: Sheed and Ward, 1964).

[22]Avery Dulles, *loc. cit.*

[23]See Bernard Lonergan, *Method in Theology* (London: Darton, Longman & Todd, 1972), p. 113.

²⁴See J.K. Riches, "What is a 'christocentric' theology?" in *Christ, Faith And History: Cambridge Studies in Christology,* S.W. Sykes and J.P. Clayton, eds. (Cambridge, London, New York: Cambridge University Press, 1972), p. 23. Riches remarks that the actions, events, words which make up the biography of a love cannot be equated *tout court* with that love. Love, in this respect 'transcends' its manifestations. On the other hand, how can it be known apart from the words, actions, and demeanor of the lover? Riches affirms that the subject of theology is the revelation of the glory of the divine love in Jesus Christ (pp. 226f); that theology is possible only on the basis of a loving response to the revelation in Christ, which response is in turn only made possible by the divine love itself (p. 228); that theology has the task of meditating on the form of the divine love, to present it in such a manner that the pattern and shape of God's engagement with the world become clear, and in a way which shows the centrality of this in the form of Christ (232f).

²⁵See Robert M. Doran, "Aesthetics and the Opposites," *Thought* 52 (June 1977), 205, contributes to our understanding of the life story in terms of the meaning that he gives James Hillman's expression, soul-making. See James Hillman, *The Myth of Analysis* (Evanston: Northwestern, 1972) and *Revisioning Psychology* (New York: Harper and Row, 1975). Doran affirms that soul-making begins when I discover, identify, and accept previously submerged feelings. This perhaps necessary beginning introduces into human living new ranges of schemes of recurrence that represent in effect the elaboration of soul. Soul-making is akin to the Hegelian enterpise of Geist's recapturing of its own evolution, though it occurs on the plane of realism. It is telling a story, first perhaps by repeating the story that has been going forward without one's being able to tell it as it is, but then by creating the story as one lives it, creating it in all its richness and variety and patterns of differentiated response. Soul-making, for Doran, is life and not therapy. It is living the dream forward, as a living symbol, a symbolic man or woman, and yet as removed from the symbol one is by a detachment from both inner states and outer subjects (p. 123).

Doran affirms that soul-making is dramatic; it is the mediation of immediacy by a story. It is the elevation to storytelling of a story that already was going forward without being told very well. And it is also the elevation to storymaking, to self-constitution, of a story that otherwise would continue without being either made or told. Soul-making is the mediation by meaning of the dramatic component in the struggle for authenticity in one's knowing, one's doing, and one's religion (p. 124).

²⁶See T. Patrick Burke, "The Theologian as Storyteller and Philosopher," *Horizons* 4/2 (1977), 207-215.

²⁷See Kevin O'Shea and Noel Meehan, *A Human Apostolate: Theology and Education for a Christian Life-Style* (Melbourne: Spectrum, 1971), 74.

²⁸"Story" is the basic dimension of a person's life into which all the other aspects are integrated. St. Francis' life, for example, is not above all "happy," or "Italian," or "medieval." Above all, it is St. Francis' life implying that persons are responsible for their life stories.

Notes for Chapter 19

¹H. Strack and P. Billerbeck, *Kommentär zum NT aus Talmud und Midrasch,* I (Munich, 1922-8 and 1956, 2nd. ed.), p. 213, quoted in *Encyclopedia of Biblical Theology,* III, Johannes B. Bauer, ed., see Rudolf Schnackenburg, *Vision of God* (London and Sydney: Sheed and Ward, 1970), p. 951.

²The Sermon on the Mount is best understood when the Beatitudes are seen in the instance as affirmations of Jesus about himself (Mt. 5:3-11; Lk. 6:20-26).
³See Irving L. James and Leon Mann, *Decision Making* (New York: The Free Press, 1977), p. 15. Attention is called to the concrete emotional influences on human knowing and deciding: "Man is not a cold fish but a warm-blooded mammal and, not a rational calculator always ready to work out the best solution but a reluctant decision-maker beset by conflicts, doubts and worry, struggling with incongruous longings, antipathies, and loyalities, and seeking relief by procrastinating, rationalizing, or denying responsibility for his own choices."
⁴Bernard Lonergan, *Method in Theology* (London: Darton, Longman & Todd, 1971), p. 27. The vivid images of our concrete experience are intimately related to our decision-making. The closer to concrete experience or to vivid images our knowing comes, the more likely our attention is seized and our emotion aroused. Drama, narrative, poetry and parable owe their force to the use of concrete language and vivid images.
⁵The community of faith shares Jesus Christ's motivating power which images the love of God for the world to the extent that it is available to this love for the world. If Jesus is the Parable of God's love, every authentically Christian life story is such a parable, sharing a continuity of purpose and intention, summoning its hearers to decision.

Notes for Chapter 20

¹See David Bakan, *The Duality of Human Existence* (Chicago: Rand McNally and Co., 1966). Also John Navone, "Satan Returns," *Sign* 54 (Sept. 1974), pp. 11-17.
²Robert B. Heilman, *Tragedy and Melodrama: Versions of Experience* (Seattle and London: University of Washington Press, 1968) provides the basis for this distinction. Frank Kermode, *The Sense of an Ending: Studies in the Theory of Fiction* (New York: Oxford University Press, 1967) is implicitly relevant for an approach to eschatology.
³See Schyler Brown, *Apostasy and Perseverance in the Theology of Luke* (Rome: Gregorian University Press, 1969).
⁴Frederick E. Crowe, "Complacency and Concern in the Writings of St. Thomas," in *Theological Studies* 20 (1959). This article appears in three installments which followed its first appearance in a brief, popularized form in *Cross and Crown* 11 (June 1954), pp. 180-190.
⁵See Garrett Barden and Philip McShane, *Towards Self-Meaning* (New York: Herder & Herder, 1969), pp. 55-62, 78. Also, the closing chapters of Frederick E. Crowe's book, *A Time of Change* (Milwaukee: Bruce, 1968).
⁶John Dunne, *The Way of All the Earth* (New York: Macmillan, 1972) pp. 89f.
⁷Jesus' life story is received from his Father: he is sent by the Father on a mission and lives for its accomplishment. The Father is understood as having his own life and his own story to tell about our ultimate environment or home.
⁸Peace is one expression of a God-given homecoming: "Peace I leave to you, my own peace I give you, a peace the world cannot give, this is my gift to you" (Jn. 14:27). The peace of a good conscience, of being "right" with ourselves and the Ultimate Truth of things, implies that God himself — the Ultimate Truth of things — is the basis of our peace or homecoming.
⁹According to Matthew's Gospel, the whole past of Israel is relived in the relationship of Jesus and his disciples as he communicates to them an understanding of the

kingdom of heaven, and this recapitulated past is prologue to the future struggles of the Church among all nations. See Charles H. Giblin, "Theological Perspective and Matthew 10:23b," *Theological Studies* 29 (1968), pp. 637-661. Also his "What is the Gospel?" *Thought* XLV (Summer 1970), p. 233.

[10]Hugo Meynell, "The Holy Trinity and the Corrupted Consciousness," *Theology* LXX (May, 1976), p. 148. This is not inconsistent, according to Meynell, with God's giving the gift of his love in and through other religious traditions. He notes Bernard Lonergan in *A Second Collection,* pp. 174f, to affirm: "But if the Spirit who is God's love is the Spirit of the Son, and the Son is made man, those who receive the Spirit explicitly through the Son do have a special privilege," p. 148.

[11]See Andrew Greeley, *What a Modern Catholic Believes About God* (Chicago: Thomas More Press, 1971), pp. 18-21.

[12]Daniel W. Hardy, "Man the Creature," *Scottish Journal of Theology* 30 (1977) 2, p. 123.

Notes for Chapter 23

[1]H. Richard Niebuhr, "Towards a New Other-Worldliness," Theology Today, 1 (April, 1944) 1, pp. 78, 81.

[2]Charles Morgan, *Reflections in a Mirror,* Second Series (New York: Macmillan, 1947), p. 95.

[3]Mary McDermott Shideler, "The Story-makers and the Story-tellers," *Religion in Life,* 45 (Autumn, 1976) 3, p. 351.

[4]James Wm. McClendon, Jr., *Biography as Theology* (Nashville: Abingdon Press, 1974).

[5]*Ibid.,* p. 190.

[6]Stephen Crites, "The Narrative Quality of Experience," *Journal of the American Academy of Religion* (Sept. 1971), pp. 291-311.

[7]James Wm. McClendon, Jr., *op. cit.,* p. 192.

[8]*Ibid.*

[9]*Ibid.,* pp. 193-195.

[10]*Ibid.,* p. 198. See Gerald O'Collins, "A Neglected Source for the Theology of Revelation," *Gregorianum* 57 (1946) 4, pp. 757-768. "Dependent" (rather than "Foundational") revelation is examined in terms of Christian autobiographical material.

[11]John S. Dunne, *A Search for God in Time and Memory* (London: Macmillan, 1967).

[12](New York: Macmillan, 1965).

[13](London: Sheldon Press, 1973).

[14]Rosemary Haughton, *The Drama of Salvation* (London SPCK, 1976).

[15]Bernard Lonergan, in *Collection: Papers by Bernard Lonergan,* ed. by F.E. Crowe (New York: Herder & Herder, 1967), p. 222. Human knowing is a formally dynamic structure that puts itself together, one part summoning forth the next, till the whole is reached. The process is conscious, intelligent, and rational. Story-telling is a form of the dynamic structure of knowing and its distinct activities. It leads from experience through imagination to insight; it expresses understanding (interpretation of experience) and judgment *(Ibid.,* p. 223).

[16]William F. Lynch, *Images of Faith: An Exploration of the Ironic Imagination* (Notre Dame, Ind.: Notre Dame University Press, 1973), pp. 9-10.

[17]*Ibid.,* p. 10.

[18]*Ibid.,* pp. 4, 7, 12, 14.
[19]*Ibid.,* p. 18.
[20]*Ibid.,* pp. 18f.
[21]*Ibid.,* pp. 18f.
[22]*Ibid.,* p. 22 and p. 155.
[23]*Ibid.,* pp. 160f.
[24]William Lynch, *Images of Faith,* p. 14, outlines four aspects of the Hebraic-Christian faith as prime imaginer of the world. (1) It is a paradigm within which we experience or imagine the world. (2) It is not a passive but a creative paradigm, one that activates the imagination. (3) It is a moving paradigm that will not be understood until it has moved through all the stages of the life of man and, in the same act, all the stages of the life of Christ. (4) It is an ironic paradigm.
[25]William Lynch, *Images of Faith,* pp. 84f.
[26]*Ibid.,* pp. 84f.
[27]John Drury, "The Spirit of Story-telling," *Theology 79* (March, 1976) 668, p. 78.
[28]*Ibid.*
[29]*Ibid.* See also in *Angels and Dirt: An Enquiry into Theology and Prayer* (London: Darton, Longman & Todd, 1972), John Drury has much to say about story in his second chapter, "The Old Curiosity Shop" (pp. 39-57). The Church draws on its biblical stories of God to show us our way about, to indicate some of the possibilities of life and some of its limitations. It tells stories of its saints who forgave their enemies so we can see how it is done and what happens when we do it. Story is both a direct and an indirect means of communication. It is direct, Drury explains, in the sense that it overcomes the abstract remoteness of precepts and ideas; at the same time, it is removed from us precisely because of this. The story will always be about someone who is rather different from me and set in more or less different circumstances. Its directness satisfies; its remoteness teases. The story which the apostles told is one with which we have never finished; it is told repeatedly and each time we lay our own lives and stories alongside it.

Drury recalls that Edwin Muir saw his own life as a narrative on the two levels of individual difference and shared mystery, calling them story and fable (p. 50). Our story marks us off from others. Fable is always impinging on our life story; in the realm of fable we share our deepest connections with one another. Muir is an instance of the convergence of the individual story and the archetypal story or 'fable' in the biography of one man. We live on our ability to understand other people, to lay their stories alongside our own in a community of interest which acknowledges the differences (p. 55). We come to know ourselves indirectly by knowing others. To be religious is to acknowledge that one is always in the presence of the other — God. We learn about that "Other" by understanding others who live(d) in his presence. The tradition of the Church consists in stories of others who illuminate the way in which we hope to walk with the Other.
[30]James Barr, "Story and History in Biblical Theology," *The Journal of Religion* 16 (January, 1976) 1, p. 5.
[31]*Ibid.,* p. 16.
[32]*Ibid.*
[33]Corbin Scott Carnell, *Bright Shadow of Reality: C.S. Lewis and the Feeling Intellect* (Grand Rapids, Mich.: William B. Eerdmans Publishing Co., 1974), pp. 134f.
[34]*Ibid.,* p. 135.
[35]*Ibid.,* p. 163.
[36]*Ibid.*

[37]*Ibid.*, p. 164.

[38]*Ibid.*, p. 137. See C.S. Lewis, *English Literature in the Sixteenth Century* (Oxford: Clarendon Press, 1954), pp. 356f.

[39]J.R.R. Tolkien, "On Fairy-Stories," *The Tolkien Reader* (New York: Ballantine Books, 1966), pp. 71-72.

[40]*Ibid.*

[41]*Ibid.*, p. 68.

[42]*Ibid.*, pp. 71-72.

[43]*Ibid.*

[44]*Ibid.*, pp. 36-37. See John E. Zuck, "Tales of Wonder: Biblical Narrative, Myth, and Fairy Stories," *Journal of the American Academy of Religion* 44 (1976) 2, p. 299.

[45]Michael Novak, *Ascent of the Mountain, Flight of the Dove* (New York: Harper & Row, 1971), p. xii.

[46]John Shea, *Stories of God* (Chicago: Thomas More Press, 1978), pp. 38ff.

[47]Stanley Hauerwas, "Story and Theology," *Religion and Life* 45 (Autumn 1976), pp. 339-350.

[48]Stanley Hauerwas, *Character and the Christian Life: A Study in Theological Ethics* (San Antonio: Trinity University Press, 1975), pp. 227f.

[49]Stanley Hauerwas with Richard Bondi and David B. Burrell, *Truthfulness and Tragedy: Further Investigations in Christian Ethics* (Notre Dame: University of Notre Dame, 1977).

[50]David Tracy, "Theological Classics in Contemporary Theology." This paper was the Annual William Rossner Lecture delivered Nov. 15, 1977, at Rockhurst College, Kansas City, Missouri. It appears in abbreviated form in *Theology Digest* 25 /4 (Winter 1977), pp. 347-355.

[51]The classic, according to Tracy, challenges us to look above and beyond ourselves to our 'educators,' allowing them to transform us, refusing to be satisfied with a mere repetition of past achievements, and risking a genuine retrieval (reinterpretation and reapplication) of its meaning in this new situation demanding new application. Mere repetition of the classic leads to decline and decadence. Modern retrievals and new applications can themselves achieve classical status, challenging and transforming the horizons of contemporaries.

[52]Theodore W. Jennings, Jr., *Introduction to Theology: An invitation to reflection upon the Christian Myths* (Philadelphia: Fortress Press, 1976), p. 18.

[53]*Ibid.*, p. 57.

[54]"Reading The Confessions of Augustine: An Exercise in Theological Understanding," *Journal of Religion* 50 (October, 1970), p. 332.

[55]Andrew Greeley, *The Mary Myth* (New York: Seabury Press, 1977), p. 28. See the second chapter.

[56]*Ibid.*, p. 50.

[57]A. MacLeish, "Crisis and Poetry," an address delivered before the Yale Alumni convocation in the Arts and Sciences, 7 October 1960; quoted by Maynard Mack, "To See It Feelingly," *Publications of the Modern Language Association* 86 (May 1971), p. 373.

[58]Giles Gunn, "Threading the Eye of the Needle: The Place of the Literary Critic in Religious Studies," *Journal of the American Academy of Religion* 43 (June 1975) 2, p. 181.

Gunn affirms that religious forms purport to define what truly is the case no matter how the facts may appear, while literary forms purport to suggest what might instead be the case if the facts were other than they obviously are. The first deals in what are claimed to be ontological givens, the second in what are rarely meant to be taken as anything more than hypothetical possibilities (pp. 169f).

[59]T. Patrick Burke, "The Theologian as Storyteller and Philosopher," *Horizons* 4/2 (1977), 207-215.

[60]Bernard Lonergan, "The Ongoing Genesis of Methods," *Studies in Religion, Sciences Religieuses* 6/4 (1976-77), p. 349.

[61]*Ibid.*

[62]Charles E. Winquist, "The Act of Story-telling and the Self's Homecoming," *Journal of the American Academy of Religion* 42 (1974), p. 103.

The act of storytelling has a subjective pole (the storymaker) and an objective pole (the story-material of experience). Jesus, as storymaker, communicates his spirit in the concreteness of his parables. Those who grasp and welcome their meaning share his spirit. The storyteller is in his stories; and they are a part of the overall story that his life tells.

[63]Charles E. Winquist, "The Act of Story-telling and the Self's Homecoming," *Journal of the American Academy of Religion* 42 (1974) 3, p. 110.

[64]*Ibid.,* p. 111.

[65]*Ibid.*

[66]*Ibid.,* p. 112.

[67]*Ibid.*

[68]*Ibid.,* p. 113. Sam Keen, *To a Dancing God* (New York: Harper and Row, 1970), p. 86: "I will suggest that telling stories is functionally equivalent to belief in God, and, therefore, 'the death of God' is best understood as modern man's inability to believe that human life is rendered ultimately meaningful by being incorporated into a story."

[69]Wesley A. Kort, *Narrative Elements and Religious Meaning* (Philadelphia: Fortress Press, 1975).

[70]*Ibid.,* p. 111.

[71]*Ibid.,* p. 62. Kort affirms that plots are images of recognizable processes, particularly of growth or dissolution. Fictions are the imaginative act of unifying time into a concord. Richard F. Dietrich and Roger H. Sundell, *The Art of Fiction* (New York: Holt, Rinehart and Winston, 1967), p. 48: "The conventional plot assumes that life is not meaningless, that the universe is essentially rational and causal."

[72]John Haught, *Religion and Self-Acceptance* (New York: Paulist Press, 1976), p. 120. Haught's sixth chapter grounds this section.

[73]*Ibid.,* p. 123.

[74]*Ibid.,* p. 140.

[75]John F. Haught, *Religion and Self-Acceptance* (New York: Paulist Press, 1976), pp. 7-9.

[76]*Ibid.,* p. 40. Giles Gunn, "Threading the Eye of the Needle," *Journal of the American Academy of Religion* 43 (June 1975) 2, p. 170, calls attention to the fact that religious and literary forms are narrative to the degree that both presuppose in Lionel Trilling's words, that "life is susceptible of comprehension and thus of management" (Trilling, *Sincerity and Authenticity* [Cambridge: Harvard University Press, 1972, p. 135] by virtue of our capacity for perceiving meaningful connections between beginnings and ends. In this case a beginning is not conceived of simply as the first of a series of events but rather as the originator of those that follow, and ends are viewed less as "the ultimate event, the cessation of happening" than as "a significance or at least the promise, dark or bright, of a significance" (*Ibid.,* pp. 135-36). To the narrative mind, Trilling continues, "the tale is not told by an idiot but by a rational consciousness, which perceives in things

the process that are their reason and which derives from this perception a principle of conduct, a way of living among things" (*Ibid.,* p. 136).

[77]Dr. Hugh Jones, "The Concept of Story and Theological Discourse," *Scottish Journal of Theology* 29 (1976) 6, p. 427.

[78]James Wharton, "The Occasions of the Word of God: an unguarded Essay on the Character of the Old Testament as the Memory of God's Story with Israel," *Austin Seminary Bulletin* (Faculty Ed.), September 1968, p. 5.

[79]Edward K. Braxton, "Bernard Lonergan's Hermeneutic of the Symbol," *Irish Theological Quarterly* XLIII (June 1976) 3, p. 197.

[80]*Ibid.,* p. 196.

[81]*Ibid.,* pp. 196f.

[82]*Ibid.,* p. 195. Lonergan's notion of heuristic structures and the known-unknown (the permanence of mystery) is seen as a context for a theological appreciation of faith's narratives, myths and symbols.

[83]Urban T. Holmes III, *Ministry and Imagination* (New York: Seabury Press, 1976), p. 165.

[84]*Ibid.,* p. 166.

[85]*Ibid.,* pp. 167f.

[86]*Ibid.,* p. 169.

[87]*Ibid.*

[88]*Ibid.,* p. 171.

[89]*Ibid.,* p. 176. Holmes likens fairy tales to the Gospel in their telling of a power that does not belong to the person who uses it, and yet over which the person has some control. Legend is a hagiographic story. Saga focuses on the tragic hero. Myth is a self-conscious cosmic story with roots in universal motifs such as death and resurrection, conflict and vindication, expulsion and return, integration and transformation, incorporation and assimilation, opposition and individuation.

[90]*Ibid.,* p. 177.

[91]*Ibid.,* p. 178.

[92]*Ibid.,* pp. 177, 183.

[93]*Ibid.,* p. 184.

[94]*Ibid.,* p. 185. There is no problem in identifying the story of Jesus in the New Testament. It is celebrated in the liturgical year of the Church and told in many literary forms. Holmes finds a greater problem in identifying our stories. Although he makes no explicit mention of the problem, it is clear that self-deception, ignorance, inattention and misunderstanding can occur.

[95]*Ibid.,* p. 190. God's story becomes my story by your-story-in-God being told me in various ways. We "facet" God's story in terms of multiple stories from our culture. We see how the contemporary world relates its story to God's story. We re enact God's story in our liturgy and in our lives. There is a need of communicating Christian meaning to take into account three stories: Jesus', the culture's mine.

[96]*Ibid.,* p. 191. That world of Judeo-Christian faith revealed in biblical narratives has both a confessional and a didactic (or catechetical) character. The narratives are confessional in bearing witness to the truth and meaning of what has been experienced; they are didactic (or catechetical) in attempting to involve the reader in the same experience so that it also becomes his lived experience.

[97]Harvey Cox, *The Seduction of the Spirit* (New York: Simon & Schuster, 1973).

Notes for Chapter 24

[1]Enda McDonagh, *Doing the Truth* (Dublin: Gill and Macmillan. Notre Dame, Ind.: University of Notre Dame Press, 1979) 1.

[2]*Ibid.,* 4-7.

[3]*Ibid.,* 9-13.

[4]Paul Steidl-Meier, *Social Justice Ministry* (New York: Le Jacq, 1984) p. xv.

[5]*Ibid.,* 5.

[6]*Ibid.,* 7.

[7]*Ibid.,* 35-37.

[8]Stanley Hauerwas, with Richard Bondi and David B. Burrell, *Truthfulness and Tragedy* (Notre Dame, Ind.: University of Notre Dame Press, 1977) 8. See also Hauerwas' other books, *Character and the Christian Life: A Study in Theological Ethics* (San Antonio: Trinity University Press, 1975); *Vision and Virtue: Essays in Christian Ethical Reflection* (Notre Dame: Fides, 1974); *A Community of Character* (Notre Dame: University of Notre Dame Press, 1981).

[9]*Ibid.,* 76.

[10]*Ibid.,* 75.

[11]*A Community of Character,* 48.

[12]*Loc cit.*

[13]Sallie McFague, *Speaking in Parables* (Philadephia: Fortress Press, 1975) 157.

[14]*Ibid.,* 36.

[15]*Ibid.,* 32-33.

[16]William C. Spohn, S.J., *What are they saying about scripture and ethics?* (New York/Ramsey: Paulist Press, 1984) 147.

[17]*Ibid.,* 1.

[18]*Ibid.,* 15 and ch. 5, "Call to Discipleship," 89-105.

[19]*Ibid.,* 89.

[20]*Ibid.,* 89-105.

[21]*Ibid.,* 104.

[22]*Ibid.,* 132.

[23]William Kirk Kilpatrick, *Psychological Seduction* (Nashville/Camden/New York: Thomas Nelson Publishers, 1983) 107.

[24]*Ibid.,* 109.

[25]*Ibid.,* 110.

[26]*Ibid.,* 117.

[27]*Ibid.,* 118.

[28]*Ibid.,* 119.

[29]Robert Peevey, *Narrative Theology: A Contribution to Fundamental Theology* (Rome: unpublished doctoral dissertation for the Theology Faculty of the Gregorian University, 1983).

[30]Peevey selects eight works from these four authors for the realization of his goal: John Haught, *Religion and Self-Acceptance* (New York: Paulist Press, 1976); Michael Novak, *The Experience of Nothingness* (New York: Harper & Row, 1970) and *Ascent of the Mountain, Flight of the Dove* (New York: Harper & Row, 1971); John Navone, *Towards a Theology of Story* (Slough, U.K.: St. Paul Publications, 1977), *The Jesus Story: Our Life as Story in Christ* (Collegeville, Minn.: The Liturgical Press, 1979) and *Tellers of the Word* (New York: Le Jacq, 1981); John Dunne, *The Way of All the Earth* (London: Sheldon Press, 1972), *Time and Myth* (New York: Doubleday, 1973) and *Reasons of the Heart* (New York: Macmillan, 1978).

[31]Peevey, *Narrative Theology: A Contribution to Fundamental Theology* 280.

[32]*Ibid.*, 283.

[33]*Ibid.*, 284f.

[34]*Ibid.*, 285.

[25]*Ibid.*, 287.

[26]*Ibid.*, 290f.

[27]*Ibid.*, 294-6.

[38]*Ibid.*, 296f.

[39]*Ibid.*, 298-300.

[40]Sam Keen, *To a Dancing God* (New York: Harper & Row, 1970); Harvey Cox, *The Seduction of the Spirit* (New York: Simon and Schuster, A Touchstone Book, 1973); Michael Novak, *Ascent of the Mountain, Flight of the Dove* (New York: Harper & Row, 1971); Robert P. Roth, *Story and Reality* (Grand Rapids: Eerdmans, 1973); John Shea, *Stories of God* (Chicago: Thomas More Press, 1978); James B. Wiggins, Ed., *Religion as Story* (New York: Harper & Row, 1975).

[41]Stephen Crites, "The Narrative Quality of Experience," *Journal of The American Academy of Religion* 39/3 (September 1971) 291-311.

[42]*Ibid.*, 291.

[43]*Ibid.*, 301.

[44]*Ibid.*, 296.

[45]*Ibid.*, 295.

[46]*Ibid.*, 305.

[47]For a brief summary of the positions of a few of the figures in the German discussion see Bernd Wacker, *Narrative Theologie?* (Munich: Kösel, 1977).

[48]Dietrich Ritschl and Hugh O. Jones, *"Story" als Rohmaterial der Theologie* (Munich: Kaiser, 1976).

[49]Harald Weinrich, "Narrative Theology" and Johann Baptist Metz, "A Short Apology of Narrative" in *The Crisis of Religious Language,* eds. Johann Baptist Metz and Jean-Pierre Jossua (New York: Herder and Herder, 1973) 46-56 and 84-96. Josef Meyer zu Schlochtern, *Glaube-Sprache-Erfahrung* (Frankfurt: Peter Lang, 1978).

[50]Hans W. Frei, *The Identity of Jesus Christ* (Philadelphia: Fortress Press, 1975); Eberhard Jüngel, *Gott als Geheimnis der Welt* (Tübingen: J.C.B. Mohr [Paul Siebeck], 1977); Edward Schillebeeckx, *Jesus: An Experiment in Christology* (New York: Seabury Press, A Crossroad Book, 1979).

[51]Thomas Groome, *Christian Religious Education: Sharing Our Story and Vision* (New York: Harper & Row, 1980) 184.

[52]*Ibid.*, 211.

[53]*Ibid.*, 192.

[54]*Ibid.*, 193.

[55]James Fowler and Robin Lovin, eds., *Trajectories in Faith* (Nashville: Abingdon, 1980) 120.

[56]James Fowler, *Stages of Faith* (New York: Harper & Row, 1981).

[57]Charles Homer Giblin, S.J., "Confrontations in John 18, 1:27," *Biblica* 65/2 (1984) 210f.

[58]*Ibid.*, 210.

[59]*Ibid.*

[60]*Ibid.*, 211.

[61]Robert C. Tannehill, "The Disciples in Mark: The Function of a Narrative Role," *Journal of Religion* 57 (1977) 386-405.

[62]See Gerhard von Rad, *Old Testament Theology,* 2 Vols. (New York: Harper & Row, 1962, 1965); Oscar Cullmann, *Christ and Time* (Philadelphia: Westminster, 1964); G. Ernest Wright, *God Who Acts* (London: SCM, 1952).

[63]Amos N. Wilder, *The Language of the Gospel: Early Christian Rhetoric* (New York: Harper & Row, 1964) 64.

[64]James Barr, "Story and History in Biblical Theology," *The Journal of Religion* 16 (1976) 1, p. 5.

[65]*Ibid.*, 16.

[66]*Ibid.*

[67]James Wm. McClendon, Jr. *Biography as Theology* (Nashville: Abingdon, 1974).

[68]*Ibid.*, 37.

[69]*Ibid.*, 192.

[70]*Ibid.*, 193-5.

[71]Louis John Cameli, *Stories of Paradise* (New York/Ramsey: Paulist Press, 1978).

[72]*Ibid.*, 71-84.

SELECTED BIBLIOGRAPHY

BOOKS

Buechner, Frederick, *Telling the Truth* (San Francisco: Harper & Row, 1977).

Burrell, David, *Exercises in Religious Understanding* (Notre Dame, Ind.: Notre Dame University Press, 1974).

Cameli, Louis, *Stories of Paradise* (New York: Paulist Press, 1978).

Campbell, Joseph, Ed., *Myths, Dreams, and Religion* (New York: E.P. Dutton, 1970).

Capps, Donald and Walter H. Capps, *The Religious Personality* (Wadsworth, 1970).

Carnell, Corbin Scott, *Bright Shadow of Reality: C.S. Lewis and the Feeling Intellect* (Grand Rapids, Mi.: William B. Eerdmans, 1974).

Cary, Norman R., *Christian Criticism in the Twentieth Century* (Port Washington, N.Y.: Kennikat Press Corp., 1975).

Crossan, Dominic, *The Dark Interval* (Niles: Argus Press, 1976).

Crowe, Frederick E., *Theology of the Christian Word: A Study in History* (New York: Paulist Press, 1978).

Dillistone, F.W., *The Novelist and the Passion Story* (New York: Sheed and Ward, 1960).

Dulles, Avery, *Myth, Biblical Revelation, and Christ* (Washington and Cleveland: Corpus Books, 1968).

Dunne, John S., *A Search for God in Time and Memory* (London: Macmillan, 1967).

____. *The Reasons of the Heart* (New York: Macmillan, 1978).

____. *The Way of All the Earth* (London: Sheldon Press, 1972).

Eliade, Mircea, *The Quest* (Chicago: University of Chicago Press, 1969).

____. *The Myth of the Eternal Return,* tr. by W.R. Trask (Princeton: Princeton University Press, Bollingen Paperback, 1971).

English, John, *Choosing Life* (New York: Paulist Press, 1978).

Fawcett, Thomas, *The Symbolic Language of Religion* (Minneapolis: Augsburg Press, 1971).

Ferlita, Ernest, *The Theatre of Pilgrimage* (New York: Sheed & Ward, 1971)

____. *Film Odyssey* (New York: Paulist Press, 1976).

Greeley, Andrew, *The Jesus Myth* (New York: Doubleday, 1973).

____. *The Mary Myth* (New York: Seabury Press, 1977).

____. *The Sinai Myth* (Garden City, N.Y.: Doubleday, 1975).

Hardy, Barbara, *Tellers and Listeners* (London: Athlone, 1975).

Harper, Ralph, *The Seventh Solitude* (Baltimore: Johns Hopkins Press, 1965).

Hartt, Julian N., *Theological Method and Imagination* (New York: Seabury Press, 1977).

Hauerwas, Stanley, *Character and the Christian Life: A study in theological ethics* (San Antonio, Tx.: Trinity University Press, 1975).

____, with Richard Bondi and David B. Burrell, *Truthfulness and Tragedy* (Notre Dame: University of Notre Dame, 1977).

____. *Vision and Virtue* (Notre Dame: Fides/Claretian, 1974).

Haught, John, *Religion and Self-Acceptance* (New York: Paulist Press, 1976).

Haughton, Rosemary, *The Drama of Salvation* (London: S.P.C.K., 1975).

____. *The World of Fairy Tales and the Spiritual Search* (New York: Seabury Press, 1976).

Holmes, Urban, *Ministry and Imagination* (New York: Seabury Press, 1976).
Jennings, Theodore W. Jr., *Introduction to Theology: An Invitation to Reflection Upon the Christian Myths* (Philadelphia: Fortress Press, 1976).
Keen, Sam, *To a Dancing God* (New York: Harper and Row, 1970).
Kelsey, Morton T., *Myth, History and Faith* (New York: Paulist Press, 1974).
Kermode, Frank, *The Sense of an Ending: Studies in the Theory of Fiction* (New York: Oxford University Press, 1967).
Kort, Wesley A., *Narrative Elements and Religious Meaning* (Philadelphia: Fortress Press, 1975).
Lynch, William F., *Christ and Apollo: The Dimensions of the Literary Imagination* (Notre Dame, Ind.: University of Notre Dame Press Edition, 1974).
____. *Christ and Prometheus: A New Image of the Secular* (Notre Dame, Ind.: University of Notre Dame Press, 1973).
____. *Images of Faith* (Notre Dame: University of Notre Dame Press, 1973).
____. *Images of Hope* (Notre Dame: University of Notre Dame, 1973).
May, John, *Toward a New Earth: Apocalypse in the American Novel* (Notre Dame, Ind.: University of Notre Dame Press, 1972).
McClendon, James, *Biography as Theology* (Nashville, Abingdon, 1974).
McClendon, James and Smith, James, *Understanding Religious Convictions* (Notre Dame, Ind.: University of Notre Dame Press, 1975).
Navone, John, *Everyman's Odyssey* (Rome: Gregorian University Press for Seattle University, 1974).
____. *Communicating Christ* (Slough: St. Paul Publications, 1976).
Novak, Michael, *Ascent of the Mountain, Flight of the Dove* (New York: Harper and Row, 1971).
____. *The Experience of Nothingness* (New York: Harper and Row, 1971).
Olney, James, *Metaphors of Self, the Meaning of Autobiography* (Princeton, N.J.: Princeton University Press, 1972).
Pascal, Roy, *Design and Truth in Autobiography* (Harvard: Harvard University Press, 1960).
Ruland, Vernon, *Horizons of Criticism: An Assessment of Religious-Literary Options* (Chicago: American Library Association, 1975).
Sewell, Elizabeth, *The Human Metaphor* (Notre Dame, Ind.: University of Notre Dame Press, 1964).
Shea, John, *Stories of God* (Chicago: Thomas More Press, 1978).
Simon, Urlich, *Story and Faith* (London: S.P.C.K., 1975).
Tannehill, Robert C., *The Sword of His Mouth* (Philadelphia: Fortress, 1975).
Tennyson, G.B., ed., *Religion and Modern Literature: Essays in Theory and Criticism* (Grand Rapids, Mich.: Eerdmans, 1975).
TeSelle, Sallie, *Speaking in Parables: A Study in Metaphor and Theology* (London: SCM Press, 1975).
Toliver, Harold, *Animate Illustrations: Explorations of Narrative Structures* (Lincoln, Neb.: University of Nebraska Press, 1974).
Tracy, David, *Blessed Rage for Order* (New York: Seabury Press, 1975).
Wicker, Brian, *The Story-Shaped World* (London: Athlone Press, 1975).
Wiggins, James, *Religion as Story* (New York: Harper and Row, 1975).
Wilson, Colin, *The Outsider* (London: Victor Gollancz Ltd., 1956).

ARTICLES

Barr, James, "Story and History in Biblical Theology," *The Journal of Religion,* Vol. 16, No. 1 (January, 1976) 1-17.

Battaglia, Anthony, "Autobiography and Religion," *Horizons,* Vol. 2 (Spring, 1975) 61-74.

Cannon, Dale, W., "Ruminations on the Claim of Inenarrability," *Journal of the American Academy of Religion,* 43, 3 (September, 1975) 560-585.

Cooper, Thomas, "Communicating the Incommunicable: Remarks on the Relation of Theology to Art," *The Clergy Review* (May, 1977) 186-193.

Crites, Steven, "Myth, Story, History," *Parable, Myth and Language,* (Cambridge: Church Society for College Work, 1968) 6.

_____. "The Narrative Quality of Experience," *Journal of the American Academy of Religion,* 39 (September, 1971).

Doran, Robert M., "Aesthetics and the Opposites," *Thought* 52 (June, 1977).

Drury, John, "The Spirit of Storytelling," *Theology,* Vol. LXXIX, No. 668 (March, 1976) 78-83.

Estess, Ted, "The Inerrable Contraption: Reflections on the Metaphor of Story," *Journal of the American Academy of Religion,* XLII (September, 1974) 415-434.

Fox, Matthew, "Hermeneutic and Hagiography," *Spirituality Today* 30, 3 (September, 1978) 263-271.

Gold, Arthur R., "Exodus as Autobiography," *Commentary,* (May, 1976) 46-51.

Hauerwas, Stanley, "Story and Theology," *Religion in Life,* Vol. XLV, No. 3 (Autumn, 1976) 339-350.

Hauerwas, Stanley and David Burrell, "Self-Deception and Autobiography: Theological and Ethical Reflections on Speer's *"Inside the Third Reich,"* *The Journal of Religious Ethics* (Spring, 1974).

Hauerwas, Stanley and Richard Bondi, "Memory, Community and the Reasons for Living: Theological and Ethical Reflections on Suicide and Euthanasia," *Journal of the American Academy of Religion* 44 (September, 1976) 439-452.

Johnson, Luke, ed., "Theology as Biography," *Teaching Religion to Undergraduates: Some Approaches and Ideas from Teachers to Teachers,* (New Haven, Conn.: The Society for Religion in Higher Education).

Jones, Hugh, "The Concept of Story and Theological Discourse," *Scottish Journal of Theology,* 29, No. 5 (1976) 415-433.

Kasin, Alfred, "Autobiography as Narrative," *Michigan Quarterly Review* (Fall, 1964).

Kreig, Bob, "The Theologian as Narrator: Karl Barth on the Perfections of God," (diss. Notre Dame, 1976).

Lerner, L.D., "Puritanism and the Spiritual Autobiography," *Hibbert Journal,* (July, 1957).

Malits, Elena; Burrell, David; Hauerwas, Stanley, "Theology as Biography," *Horizons* 1 (Fall, 1974) 81-87.

McAfee Brown, Robert, "My Story and 'The Story'," *Theology Today* (July, 1975).

McClendon, Jr., James William, "Biography as Theology," *Cross Currents* 21 (1971) 415-431.

Mink, L.O., "History and Fiction as Modes of Comprehension," *New Literary History,* I, 3 (1970) 545.

Navone, John, "Christ, The Beatitude of God," *The Furrow,* 29, 11 (November, 1978) 698-703.

_____. Freedom and Transformation in Christ," *Spiritual Life* 21, 1 (Spring, 1975) 3-7.

_____. "Myth, Man and the Gospel Message," *Doctrine and Life* 25, 12 (December, 1975) 859-868.

_____. "The Divided Self and Its Healing," *Sciences Religieuses/Studies in Religion* 6/6 (Autumn/Fall, 1976-77) 651-63.

_____. "Theologian as Interpreter of Dreams," *Spiritual Life* 22, 2 (Summer, 1976) 115-124.

_____. "The Search for the Self. The Christ-Self and the Christ-figures," *Review for Religious,* 34, 1 (January, 1975) 132-139.

_____. "Symbols for Everyman's Odyssey," *Studies,* 64 (Autumn, 1975) 255, 258-68.

_____. "Write a Gospel," *Review for Religious* 38 (1979) 668-78.

_____. "Beauty Tells a Story," *Doctrine and Life* (1980).

_____. "The Four Gospels: Four Stages in Christian Maturation," *Review for Religious* 39 (July, 1980) 558-67.

_____. "Bipolarities in Conversion," *Review for Religious* 40 (1981) 436-50.

_____. "Conversion Expressed in Dialogue and Story," *Review for Religious* 41/5 (1982) 738-43.

_____. "Conversion and Conflict," *Review for Religious* 42/2 (1983) 192-96.

_____. "Narrative Theology and its Uses," *Irish Theological Quarterly* 52/3 (1986) 212-30.

_____. "The Dynamic of the Question in the Gospel Narrative," *Milltown Studies* 17 (1986) 75-111.

Novak, Michael, *"Story" in Politics* (The Council on Religion and International Affairs), (1970)

Page, Ruth, "The Dramatization of Jesus," *Theology* 81 (May, 1978) 182-88.

Shea, John, "Theology and Autobiography," *Commonweal* 105 (June 16, 1978) 358-362.

Shideler, Mary McDermott, "Philosophies and Fairy-Tales," *Theology Today,* (April, 1973) 14-24.

_____. "The Story-makers and the Story-tellers," *Religion in Life,* Vol. XLV, No. 3 (Autumn, 1976) 351-360.

Stroup, George, "A Bibliographical Critique," *Theology Today,* XXXII, 2 (July, 1975) 133-143.

TeSelle, Sallie, "The Experience of Coming to Belief," *Theology Today,* XXXII, 2 (July, 1975) 159-160.

Weddle, David L., "The Image of the Self in Jonathan Edwards: A Study of Autobiography and Theology," *Journal of the American Academy of Religion,* XLIII (March, 1975) 70-83.

White, Hayden, "The Structure of Historical Narrative," *Clio,* 1, 3 (June, 1972).

Winquist, Charles E., "The Act of Storytelling and the Self's Homecoming," *Journal of the American Academy of Religion,* 42, 1 (March, 1974) 102-113.

Woodward, Kenneth, interview with John Dunne, "The Emergence of a New Theology," *Psychology Today,* (January, 1978) 46-50, 90, 92.

Zuck, John, "Tales of Wonder: Biblical Narrative, Myth, and Fairy Stories," *Journal of the American Academy of Religion,* 44, 2 (June, 1976) 299-308.

The following are among the primary American works in Narrative Theology, presented in chronological order:

1969   Dunne, John, *A Search for God in Time and Memory,* New York, Macmillan.
1970   Keen, Sam, *To a Dancing God.* New York, Harper & Row.
1971   Novak, Michael, *Ascent of the Mountain, Flight of the Dove,* New York, Harper & Row.
1972   Dunne, John S., *The Way of All the Earth,* New York, Macmillan.
1973   Dunne, John S., *Time and Myth,* Garden City, N.Y., Doubleday.
1973   Keen, Sam and Fox, Valley, *Telling Your Story,* New York, Doubleday.
1973   Roth, Robert, *Story and Reality,* Grand Rapids, Eerdmans.
1974   Burrell, David B., *Exercises in Religious Understanding,* Notre Dame, University of Notre Dame Press.
1974   Cox, Harvey, *The Seduction of the Spirit,* New York, Simon & Schuster.
1974   Frei, Hans, *The Eclipse of Biblical Narrative,* New Haven, Yale University Press.
1974   Hauerwas, Stanley, *Vision and Virtue,* Notre Dame, Fides/Claretian.
1974   McClendon, James, *Biography as Theology,* Nashville, Abingdon Press.
1974   Navone, John, *Everyman's Odyssey,* Rome, Gregorian University Press.
1975   Greeley, Andrew, *The Sinai Myth,* New York, Doubleday.
1975   Hauerwas, Stanley, *Character and Christian Life,* San Antonio, Trinity University Press.
1975   Kort, Wesley, *Narrative Elements and Religious Meaning,* Philadelphia, Fortress Press.
1975   McClendon, James, and Smith, James, *Understanding Religious Conviction,* South Bend, Notre Dame University Press.
1975   McFague, Sallie, *Speaking in Parables,* Philadelphia, Fortress Press.
1975   Wiggins, James B. (ed.), *Religion as Story,* New York, Harper & Row.
1976   Crossan, John, *The Dark Interval,* Niles, Ill., Argus.
1976   Haught, John, *Religion and Self-acceptance,* New York, Paulist.
1976   Holmes, Urban, *Ministry and Imagination,* New York, Seabury Press.
1976   Wilder, Amos, *Theopoetic: Theology and Religious Imagination,* Philadelphia, Fortress Press.
1977   Buechner, Frederick, *Telling the Truth,* San Francisco, Harper & Row.
1977   Greeley, Andrew, *The Mary Myth,* New York, Seabury Press.
1977   Hartt, Julian N., *Theological Method and Imagination,* New York, Seabury Press.
1977   Hauerwas, S., Bondi, Richard, and Burrell, D., *Truthfulness and Tragedy.* Notre Dame, University of Notre Dame Press.
1977   Navone, John, *Towards a Theology of Story,* Slough, U.K., St. Paul Publications.
1978   Cameli, Louis, *Stories of Paradise,* New York, Paulist Press.
1978   Dunne, John S., *The Reasons of the Heart,* New York, Macmillan.
1978   Fackre, Gabriel, *The Christian Story,* Grand Rapids, Eerdmans.
1978   Shea, John, *Stories of God,* Chicago, Thomas More Press.
1979   Navone, John, *The Jesus Story: Our Life as Story in Christ,* Collegeville, Minn., The Liturgical Press.
1980   Fowler, James, *Trajectories in Faith,* Nashville, Abingdon.
1980   Groome, Thomas H., *Christian Religious Education,* San Francisco, Harper & Row.
1980   Jensen, Richard, *Telling the Story,* Minneapolis, Augsburg Publishing House.
1980   Shea, John, *Stories of Faith,* Chicago, Thomas More Press.

1981 Goldberg, Michael, *Theology and Narrative,* Nashville, Abingdon.
1981 Harvey, A. E. (ed.), *God Incarnate: Story and Belief,* London, S.P.C.K.
1981 Hauerwas, Stanley, *A Community of Character,* Notre Dame, University of Notre Dame Press.
1981 Navone, John and Cooper, Thomas, *Tellers of the Word,* New York, Le Jacq.
1981 Stroup, George, *The Promise of Narrative Theology,* Atlanta, John Knox Press.
1981 Tracy, David, *The Analogical Imagination,* New York, Crossroad.
1982 Wilder, Amos, *Jesus' Parables and the War of Myths,* Philadelphia, Fortress Press.
1983 Waznak, Robert, *Sunday After Sunday: Preaching the Homily as Story,* New York, Paulist Press.
1984 Navone, John, *Gospel Love: A Narrative Theology,* Wilmington, Michael Glazier, Inc.